The Medieval Household
Daily Living *c.*1150–*c.*1450

To the memory of
Daphne Marian Downing Cleeland
1916–1995

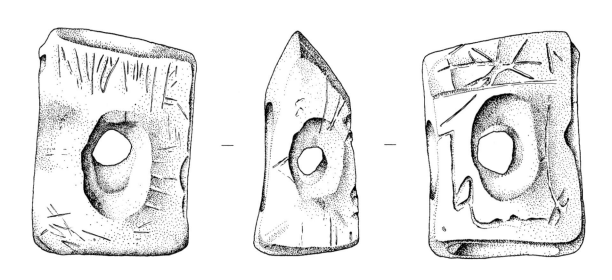

Front cover   Late medieval domestic scene – by Nick Griffiths

Back cover   Enamelled drinking glass OST82 acc nos 129 (top) and 130
(bottom) and detail of latter (middle).

Frontispiece   Miniature gabled house, carved in chalk
(CKL88 site acc no 8, reduced) (see p. 281)

Title page   Woman making a point with a spindle
– redrawn from the Luttrell Psalter

MUSEUM OF LONDON

MEDIEVAL FINDS FROM EXCAVATIONS IN LONDON: 6

The Medieval Household Daily Living *c.*1150–*c.*1450

Geoff Egan

with contributions by
Justine Bayley, Nigel Blades, Jane Brenan, Jackie Keily,
Lynne Keys, Cath Mortimer, Jacqui Pearce and Angela Wardle

Principal illustrators:
Susan Mitford and Nigel Harriss

BOYDELL PRESS
in association with Museum of London

First published 1998
Her Majesty's Stationery Office

New edition 2010
The Boydell Press, Woodbridge

Reprinted 2012

ISBN 978 184383 543 1

A Museum of London Publication
Museum of London, London Wall
London EC2Y 5HN
www.museumoflondon.org.uk

The Boydell Press is an imprint of Boydell & Brewer Ltd
PO Box 9, Woodbridge, Suffolk IP12 3DF, UK
and of Boydell & Brewer Inc.
668 Mt Hope Avenue, Rochester, NY 14620, USA
web site: www.boydellandbrewer.com

A catalogue record for this book is available
from the British Library

This publication is printed on acid-free paper

Printed in Great Britain by
CPI Group (UK) Ltd, Croydon, CR0 4YY

Contents

The colour plates will be found between pages 162 and 163.

List of tables

Acknowledgements

The debt to others for help with a very broad range of matters in a work of this size and scope is enormous. The contributions of the following is gratefully acknowledged: colleagues and former colleagues at the Museum of London – Ian Betts, Lyn Blackmore, John Clark, Julie Edwards, Damian Goodburn, Friederike Hammer, Cath Maloney, Douglas Moir, Alex Moore, Nigel Nayling, Frances Pritchard, Mike Shea, John Shepherd, Brian Spencer, Kay Staniland, Judy Stevenson, Alan Thompson, Alan Vince and Barbara West. Much of the typing was by Wendy Garrett, who also improved the text at several points; the captions were typed by Sheema Ahmed. Conservation of objects for the project was mainly carried out by Gill Barnard and Rose Johnson; much locating and fetching was the work of the late Joan Barker (who also made a substantial contribution to the typing and to checking X-ray plates for coatings), Christine Bedeschi Smith, the late Enid Hill and Joan Merritt, all under the supervision of Penny MacConnoran; Nina Crummy was always ready to locate items transferred from the Department of Urban Archaeology to the Museum of London archaeological archive however many times they were required. In addition to the principal illustrators, drawings were undertaken by Nick Griffiths (whose work includes the front cover illustration), Gill Hale, Sarah Kellaghan, Diane O'Carroll, Jacqui Pearce, Jane Sandoe, Kikar Singh and several students from the Middlesex Polytechnic – Danny Hacker, Dave Johnson and Paul Stroud – under the supervision of Alison Hawkins, Anne Jenner and Tracey Wellman; other drawings are by Miranda Schofield and David Honour, both of the Historic Buildings and Monuments Commission (England) (HBMC(E)), and by Ralph Mills and John Pearson (it proved impossible from existing departmental records to trace the names of all the students and volunteers involved in producing drawings for this volume – sincere apologies are offered, and the contributions of artists unnamed is acknowledged). Photography of items from excavations was the work of Edwin Baker, Maggie Cox and Jan Scrivener; that of items in the Museum's established collections was by Torlah Evans under the supervision of Barry Grey; collation of the figures was by several of the preceding and Jeanette van der Post; Nigel Nayling undertook species identification of most of the wooden items; much liaison and coordination for the project was undertaken by Angela Wardle, working under the supervision of Francis Grew, whose role was taken over in the last stages by John Schofield. Mike Rhodes's key support at a critical time for the project is much appreciated by the author. It is a particular pleasure to have, from outside the Museum (by arrangement with Martin Welch of University College, London) Jane Brenan's contribution on mounts for furnishings in the main catalogue.

Most of the excavations and post-excavation work, including the preparation of this volume, were funded by HBMC(E) and its predecessor organisation within the Department of the Environment; the Swan Lane and Billingsgate watching briefs were mainly supported by the City of London Archaeological Trust Fund and the Museum of London Trust Fund; the Ludgate Hill excavation was supported by the Norwich Union Insurance Group and the latter stages of preparation of some of the script and illustrations was underwritten by the City of London Archaeological Trust.

Special thanks go to the successive presidents of the Society of Thames Mudlarks – Roger Smith, Leigh Hunt and Alan Stewart – as well as to the officers and members of the Society, for sustained and invaluable efforts at the Swan Lane site and the Billingsgate watching brief, which resulted in the retrieval for the Museum of London of over half of the finds included in this volume. Without this contribution several categories of items in the catalogue would have been unrepresented and the entire project would have been much impoverished.

Analysis of copper-alloy items was undertaken by Nigel Blades (based at Royal Holloway and Bedford New College) and analysis of glass was by Cath Mortimer, both working under the supervision of Justine Bayley, who analysed lead/tin items – all under the auspices of HBMC(E). Interpretation of impressions etc. from textiles was by Hero Granger Taylor of the British Museum. Identifications of leather and of wooden items Nos 434, 955, 957–8 and 961 were respectively by Glynis Edwards and Wendy Carruthers, both of HBMC(E). Other valuable help and advice was given by the Anti-Discrimination against Women Group (Cambridge), Marian Archibald, Christopher Bangs, Martin Biddle, Norman Biggs, Michelle Brown, Marian Campbell, John Cherry, R D Connor, Clare Conybeare, David Crook, Philip Crummy (for checking mathematics in an early draft of the section on weights, although any errors remaining are attributable to the main author), Ian and Alison Goodall, John Goodall, Chris Green, Nick Griffiths, Mary Hinton, Edwin Holmes, H Installé, Sian Jones, Ingeborg Krueger, Susan Kruse, A S Law, Jenny Mann, the late Sue Margeson (who made several useful suggestions as external referee, in addition to other contributions), Philippa Marks, Claire Mason, Petter Molaug, Carole Morris, Beverly Nenk, Anthony North, Eddie Potter, the late Alma Ruempol, R W Sanderson, Peter Saunders, Andrea Saccocci, the late Erik Schia, Anne Sutton, Hugh Tait, Dora Thornton, H J E van Beuningen, Stephane Vanderberghe and Oliver Watson.

Copyright of photographs and drawings of all items in the Museum of London collection is held by the Museum's Board of Governors. Copyright for other photographs and drawings included in this volume, for which permission to reproduce is gratefully acknowledged, is as follows: The British Library – Fig 6; Trustees of the British Museum – Fig 45 (top); Bruckmann, Munich – Fig 205; HBMC(E) – Figs 142, 240 (top); Metropolitan Museum, New York – Fig 226 (far right); New York Public Library – Fig 214 (left); Northern Counties Photographers (courtesy of Dr A S Law) – Fig 155 (bottom left); Pierpont Morgan Library, New York – Fig 44; Prado Museum, Madrid – Fig 25; Public Record Office – Fig 45 (bottom); Salisbury and South Wiltshire Museum – Figs 114 (right), 189 (top left); Society of Antiquaries of London – Fig 67; Trustees of the Victoria and Albert Museum – Fig 156 (bottom left); Winchester Research Unit (courtesy of Martin Biddle) – Fig 46; Worshipful Company of Mercers, London – Fig 199 (top right).

Conventions used in the text

Numerical references

For all catalogued items, the first number (the *Catalogue Number*) in a running sequence indicates the position in the category lists in this volume. Then comes the *Site Code* (letter code plus year fieldwork began), followed by the *Accession Number* (unique within each site), the *Context Number* (*layer number*) in brackets, and the *Ceramic Phase Number*: e.g., '**35** BWB83 3175 (286) 11' is item Number 35 in this volume, which is Accession No 3175 from the Billingsgate watching brief, found in layer 286, which has been assigned to Ceramic Phase 11. (For dating assigned to ceramic phases, see below.) Only objects excavated at London sites listed at the end of this section are included in the numbered series.

Abbreviations

Acc No	– accession number (catalogued item)	l	– length
acc no	– accession number (item not in this catalogue)	lead-tin	– lead and tin* (analysed items only)
Add MS	– Added Manuscript (British Library collection)	lead/tin	– lead and/or tin
		MLC	– analysis by Museum of London Conservation Department
AML	– analysis by Ancient Monuments Laboratory, HBMC(E)	MoL	– Museum of London
BM, MLA	– British Museum, Department of Medieval and Later Antiquities	nd	– no date
		PRO	– Public Record Office
c.	– circa	ref no	– reference number
d	– diameter	RHB	– inductively coupled-plasma spectroscopy, by Nigel Blades of Royal Holloway and Bedford New College (University of London)
DUA	– Department of Urban Archaeology (Museum of London)		
EDX	– Energy-dispersive X-ray	SEM	– scanning electron microscope
ER	– Excavations Register (fieldwork by Guildhall Museum)	th	– thickness
		w	– width
estd	– estimated	XRF	– X-ray fluorescence analysis
anhh	– eight	..	– (in inscriptions etc.) one character missing
HBMC(E)	– Historic Buildings and Monuments Commission (England)	...	– (in inscriptions etc.) two or more characters missing
ICPS	– inductively coupled-plasma spectroscopy	//	– marks transition of description from one element of a hinge or a cloth seal to another

*Since the non-quantitative spot tests used by the Museum of London Conservation Department can detect the presence of very small quantities of a metal, some items described as 'lead-tin (MLC)' may contain less lead than others described as 'tin (AML)' – the latter indicates a lead content of *c.*5% or less. In this book 'pewter' is used of items so designated as a result of analysis by Justine Bayley at the Ancient Monuments Laboratory (HBMC(E)).

Site codes

AL74 – 62–64 Aldgate High Street, 1974

BA84 – Long Walk, Bermondsey, site of Bermondsey Abbey, 1984

BC72 – Baynard House, Queen Victoria Street ('Baynard Castle Dock'), 1972

BG76 – 190 Bishopsgate, 1976

BIG82 – Billingsgate lorry park, Lower Thames Street, 1982

BIS82 – 76–80 Bishopsgate Street, 1982

BOY86 – 5–11 Tudor Street, City of London Boys' School, 1986

BUC87 – Bucklersbury, 1987

BUF90 – Bull Wharf, Bull Wharf Lane/16–20 Queenhithe, 1990

BWB83 – Billingsgate lorry park, watching brief, 1983

BYD81 – City of London Boys' School ('Baynard's Castle'), 1981

CKL88 – 9 Cloak Lane, 1988

COL81 – 19–20 College Hill, 1981

CUS73 – Old Custom House, Lower Thames Street, 1973

DUK77 – 2–7 Duke's Place, 1977

ER190A – Watling House, 12–16 Watling Street/31–7 Cannon Street, 1954

ER190C – Watling House, 1954 (items recovered by workmen)

ER1118 – Dyers' Arms, Cannon Street, 1965–6 (Guildhall Museum excavation register)

FIP92 – Finsbury Pavement, 1992

FMO85 – 37–40 Fish Street Hill/16–20 Monument Street, 1985

GAG87 – Guildhall Art Gallery, 1987

GPO75 – General Post Office site, 81 Newgate Street, 1975

GWS89 – Pinners' Hall site, Great Winchester Street, 1989

HTP79 – Holy Trinity Priory site, 10–11 Mitre Street, 1979

LBT86 – Little Britain, 1986

LCT84 – Leadenhall Court, 1984

LH74 – 44–6 Ludgate Hill, 1974

LOV81 – 21–4 Lovat Lane, 1981

LUD82 – 42–6 Ludgate Hill, 1982

MIL72 – 10 Milk Street, 1972

MLK76 – 1–6 Milk Street, 1976

MM74 – ('Mermaid Theatre site'), Baynard House, Queen Victoria Street, 1974

MPY88 – Site of Merton Priory, Surrey, 1988

NEW81 – 36 Clerkenwell Close/Newcastle Row, 1981

NFW74 – New Fresh Wharf, Lower Thames Street, 1974

OPT81 – 2–3 Copthall Avenue, 1981

OST82 – 7–10 Foster Lane, 1982

POM79 – General Post Office site, middle area, 1979

PUB80 – 86 Fenchurch Street, The George public house, 1980

RAG82 – 1–2 Rangoon Street/61–5 Crutched Friars, 1982

SH74 – Seal House, 106–8 Upper Thames Street, 1974

SLH93 – St Leonard's Hospital, Hoxton, 1993

SLO82 – Beaver House, Sugar Loaf Court, 1982

SNS87 – National Car Park, Sans Walk, Clerkenwell, 1987

SUN86 – Sunlight Wharf, Upper Thames Street, 1974

SWA81 – Swan Lane, 95–103 Upper Thames Street, 1981

TEX88 – Thames Exchange, Upper Thames Street, 1988

TL74 – Trig Lane, Upper Thames Street, 1974

TR74 – Triangle, 101–10 Lower Thames Street, 1974

VAL88 – Fleet Valley (extensive area in south-western part of city), 1988

VHA89 – Vintners' Hall, 69 Upper Thames Street, 1989

VRY89 – Vintners' Place, 68 Upper Thames Street, 1989

WAT78 – 41–53 Cannon Street/Watling Court, 1978

WEL79 – Well Court/44 Bow Lane, 1979

All the numbered objects in the catalogue from the sites listed above, together with detailed archive reports and associated information, are stored at the Museum of London, where they can be examined by prior arrangement. Details of comparative items published here from private collections are held by the Early Department of the Museum of London; appropriate enquiries can be answered at the Museum or passed on to the owners.

Reference is made in the section on lighting equipment to the DUA's Ceramic Corpus held at the Museum of London, which consists of individually numbered vessels and sherds selected to represent best the known forms in each fabric.

For detailed location of objects from the BIG82, BWB83, SWA81 and TL74 sites within the sequences, see Dating and context of the finds (Figs 2–5).

Ceramic phase dates

Phase 6	*c*.1150–*c*.1200	Phase 8	*c*.1230–*c*.1270	Phase 11	*c*.1350–*c*.1400
Phase 7	*c*.1200–*c*.1230	Phase 9	*c*.1270–*c*.1350	Phase 12	*c*.1400–*c*.1450
		Phase 10	*c*.1330–*c*.1380		

Foreword to the second edition

GEOFF EGAN

It is a pleasure to contribute this foreword to the second edition of this work. Since the original publication in 1998, apart from some sites from the later 1980s and 1990s which were not included in the syntheses of medieval finds (TEX88, BUF90, UPT90, VRY89 etc.) a couple of further sizeable medieval assemblages from the waterfront in the urban centre have been recovered (UPM05 and RKH06 sites); these are only beginning to be assimilated at the time of writing these words. Finds assemblages which include material pertinent to this volume and are assignable to individual households remain problematic as they continue to be virtually absent in London's archaeological record. The period c1450–c.1500 (particularly the first 30 years) remains elusive not only in London but more broadly across England as a whole in terms of extensive, varied and well preserved non-ceramic finds assemblages like those which are the main subject matter of the present volume (in the capital at least this is in part but not completely explained by the end around the middle of the 15th century of the dramatic reclamation sequence of new land, made up largely of the City's waste material, from the Thames in the City of London (the sequence can be seen as continuing after a delay of about half a century on the south bank of the Thames, where limited assemblages of Tudor-period and later urban material culture have been recovered – Egan 2005). Important series of household finds outside London have continued to be published, notably those from York (Ottaway & Rogers 2002; MacGregor 1999 for items of animal skeletal materials; Morris 2000 and also Wood 2005 for treen) and the remarkable series of finds from Meols (a small fishing village on the coast of the Wirral in the North-West provides several similar items from a rural context about as far in terms of economic and other basic parameters as it is possible to get in medieval England from London (Egan 2007). The new perspective given by finds from across the country recorded by the Portable Antiquities Scheme, largely objects used in rural areas, tends to emphasise that the non-ceramic material culture of the household was fairly uniform by the period dealt with here across the whole of England.

While fresh finds and new studies have left what is presented here largely in need of no correction, inevitably a few points have come to notice that may usefully be noted here. On page 1 the Foreman reference to his 1987 work should be to the 1991 publication on finds from Beverley, edited by Armstrong, Tomlinson and Evans. The important series of late 12th to early 14th-century 'highly decorated' domestic pewterware, a brief but significant fashion (which soon gave way to the familiar plain wares in this metal) represented in this volume by candlestick 134–7 Fig. 102 No. 366 with parallel and spoon parallel 248 Fig. 194, has now been frequently encountered more widely among London finds, and is considered in detail in a separate paper (Egan 2000). The reference to the number of pewterers in 1304 actually refers to Paris not London (thanks to the late Ron Homer for pointing this out). Copper-alloy skimmer 155–7 Fig. 125 No. 437 is likely to be cast (re-examination has revealed a small, rectangular fillet) rather than sheeting as stated in the catalogue. In Fig. 184 the numbering of the drawing of one of the parallels for fragments of white glass (234–6 Nos. 689 & 691–4), acc. no. A17246, is wrongly labelled A17160 (cf. colour pl. 7 A, where it the number is correctly shown; these items have now been separately published – Egan 1998, where the error is replicated – thanks to the late Hugh Tait for pointing this out). Although a broad synthesis of finds of medieval vessel glass found in England has been published (Tyson 2000) no further examples of this particular unusual material has come to light since 1998). The suggestion that the ornate copper-alloy keys 244 Nos. 747–8 were to turn tuning pegs on stringed musical instruments now appears more certain than was the case when the text was originally prepared. Some iron points from London had in fact been identified as a skater's support-stick ends (Guildhall Museum Catalogue 1908, 154 nos. 150–60; cf. present volume 295–5 Nos. 965–6).

While some basic parameters for London's later medieval material culture may have been mapped out, by no means is the full range of what was routinely used by Londoners of those times completely recovered and described, let alone anything like fully understood.

Introduction

GEOFF EGAN

This, the sixth of the volumes dealing with medieval finds from excavations in the City of London between 1972 and 1983, covers a more diverse range of categories than the previous publications in the series: *Knives and Scabbards* (Cowgill et al. 1987), *Shoes and Pattens* (Grew & de Neergaard 1988), *Dress Accessories* (Egan & Pritchard 1991), *Textiles and Clothing* (Crowfoot et al. 1992) and *The Medieval Horse and its Equipment* (Clark 1995). The title of the present volume is not intended to restrict the subject matter so much as to indicate the most obvious focus of everyday life, which, of course, comprised a far wider range of activities and experience than the ones carried on in the dwelling. The objects of the home have been taken to include almost the whole paraphernalia of excavated fixtures, fittings and furnishings of the house, equipment for the preparation and consumption of food, for making heat and light, and for a range of other economic and leisure activities, as well as a few items with superstitious/religious connections. Some objects primarily associated with business and trade (equipment for making and using written records and for weighing) have been included on the grounds that the urban house of the merchant would normally have included office and storage areas for retail and other commercial activities like record-keeping.

The finds that are the main subject matter of this present book are the largest collection of stratified household items from the three centuries represented yet to have been published in Britain. This fittingly reflects the outstanding richness in terms of survival of artefacts of the deposits alongside the Thames in London, where the great majority of the items catalogued below were found. It is difficult to imagine the opportunity arising again to tackle a comparable body of fresh data that illuminates such a wide variety of aspects of the social history of the largest medieval city in the country.

The arrangement and scope of the catalogue

A general setting for the catalogued finds is provided by brief discussions of some excavated structural elements (building materials, roofing, floors etc.) that would have been among the most visually familiar features in medieval London houses. The extensive documentary and graphic evidence for the external and internal appearance of medieval houses in London is reviewed elsewhere (Schofield 1995).

The catalogue of individually numbered finds begins with basic fixtures, such as hinges for doors and other flaps, and continues with other fittings and parts probably from furnishings, like cupboards and large chests (mounts from smaller caskets etc. are also included here). The full range of locks and keys retrieved is also listed. Despite the extensive assemblages recovered, not a single item of furniture even in a fragmentary state has been recognised among the finds from the sites considered, and none of the fixtures (hinges, handles etc.) allows the latter-day researcher to extrapolate the overall form of such universal and prominent features of medieval London houses as doors or windows. A few pieces of wooden medieval furniture – stools etc. – have been excavated at Winchester and Beverley (D Keene in Biddle 1990, 969–72, nos 3438–46; M Foreman in Armstrong et al. 1991, 175–7, nos 962–3, figs 122–3), but at present there seems little immediate prospect from archaeological sources in London of testing the assertion that these finds from provincial towns may represent the full variety available to lesser households at this time, or of adding much to the limited range of survivals in English museums (as exemplified by Eames 1977 and Tracy 1988). A detailed survey of furniture and furnishings from survivals and artistic representations has been undertaken for the Netherlands

(Drijber et al. 1980) but a similar exercise does not appear to be feasible for England.

After the limited discussion that is currently possible about metalwork from furnishings to set the scene, the catalogue considers movable items (the *mobilier*), starting with those that are connected with the essentials of living – articles for heating, lighting, and the storage, preparation and consumption of food and drink (exclusive of ceramic kitchen vessels, which are considered in detail elsewhere, and of stone mortars). Objects used for other daily activities (tools and materials for jobs of maintenance around the house, items relating to the ubiquitous, domestic-scale tasks of spinning and sewing, and also home-based business record-keeping and reading items) are followed by objects for leisure activities (toys, music making and games); items apparently connected with beliefs that do not readily fit into an ecclesiastical context are briefly considered; weighing equipment completes the catalogue.

Some illogicalities may be seen in the categories that are included in and omitted from the present volume, e.g., scissors and needle-cases (already published respectively in Grew & de Neergaard 1988 and Egan & Pritchard 1991) are omitted, as is an item-by-item catalogue of personal seal matrices (those from the appropriate sites have been included in a wider survey of seals found in London – Spencer 1984).

The present major publication programme, financed very largely by HBMC(E), terminated in 1993, and lack of further resources meant not only that such potential duplications had to be avoided, but also that a few categories (generally those widely published elsewhere in Britain, like stone querns and mortars) could not be considered here. For the same reasons, there is slightly more emphasis in this book on photographic illustration at the expense of labour-intensive drawing. Although floor tiles are mentioned (see Fig 22), the large numbers found are felt to warrant a publication in their own right rather than have them form a large part of this one. It is hoped that the very wide variety of the items selected for inclusion here furnish adequate compensation for any perceived omissions of categories among the paraphernalia of the medieval house. Coherent,

broad patterns of development can be discussed for lighting equipment (lamps, candleholders and lanterns) and some of the metal, wood and glass vessels (Tables 1 and 4). Most of the categories included in this book, however, do not readily admit of broad synthesis in the way that, for example, the very large numbers of medieval strap fittings for dress have done (Egan & Pritchard 1991, 18ff). Scientific analyses of some of the metal (copper-alloy and lead/tin) and glass items, carried out with funding and facilities provided by HBMC(E) have considerably enhanced the perspectives on manufacture that the excavated material provides (see Tables 7–9 and 11–13).

The field background

Even though finds from several more sites across the City have been included than in previous volumes in the series, once more the overwhelming emphasis is on objects from waterfront excavations, both from Thames-side reclamation dumps and from riverine deposits, where the remarkable preservation of metalwork and organic materials furnishes outstandingly extensive and diverse assemblages. It had not been fully realised until preparation for this publication was quite advanced that even for categories which do not depend heavily on such conditions for their survival in recognisable form (spindle whorls of stone and elaborate ceramic roof furniture, for example) finds from the waterfront are overwhelmingly predominant, or at least provide by far the best-preserved examples.

By the 1970s, the insertion of cellars and foundations in the City of London over the intervening centuries had left relatively few horizontal deposits – floors, yards, roads etc. – from the 300-year period considered here to be investigated by archaeologists (there seem to be very few post-14th-century ground-accumulation deposits surviving in London anyway, and a similar phenomenon is emerging from several major towns). The assemblages from the surviving pits, wells and other cut features of London's later Middle Ages have markedly failed to match the richness, in terms of both the proliferation and the variety of finds, in the deposits of the Thames-side area. Some further iron candleholders of the commonest cupped forms might perhaps (with considerable effort on the part of the conservation staff) have been added to the catalogue from inland sites investigated up to 1983, but because of their poor state of preservation it seems unlikely that these items would have added significantly to the discussion, since it would have been very difficult to determine reliable cup measurements to set beside those for the well-preserved ones that are included. It is difficult to think of any further categories in the catalogue for which even the numbers of finds would be significantly extended by putting in identified items from inland sites.

Metalwork comprises the majority of the finds discussed in this volume. The single most important factor that made possible the retrieval for the Museum of London of the two largest assemblages included here, those from the Swan Lane site (SWA81) and the Billingsgate watching brief (BWB83), was the skilled use of metal detectors by members of the Society of Thames Mudlarks, who mustered a formidable workforce for a programme of sustained effort and committed involvement as volunteers for the Museum's archaeological department (cf. Egan & Pritchard 1991, x; Egan 1985/6).

Such assemblages are not retrieved without considerable organisation as well as enthusiastic fieldwork. It would be most unfortunate for the future of such studies as the present catalogue if new pressures on archaeology in the capital resulted in the recovery of a smaller proportion of the uniquely informative riverside assemblages that will be removed in the course of redevelopment.

Observations on the finds

The *London Museum Medieval Catalogue* (Ward Perkins 1940) includes some of the categories of household utensils discussed in this present volume (spoons, keys, metal vessels etc.), though a great proportion of the other objects included here, particularly the more mundane fixtures and fittings like Nos 1–138, were omitted. The Guildhall Museum catalogue (1908),

with its greater emphasis on excavated material, listed in addition needles, a single thimble and other humble items. The categories that have been included in both the London Museum catalogue and this present work underline the different approaches to collecting between the comprehensive, unselected retention of finds from the excavations of the 1970s and 1980s and the highly selective acquisition practised by the London Museum, based to a large extent on aesthetic criteria. This is nowhere more evident than in the candleholders, with an overwhelming emphasis in this catalogue on simple iron prickets and cups – an accurate reflection of the proportions in the assemblages considered. The small number of candleholders in copper alloy catalogued below contrasts with their predominance in the 1940 publication. Copper-alloy candlestick No 426 stands out among the finds from the recent fieldwork as virtually the only substantial, complete item of furnishing that was discarded in a usable state. It was almost certainly an import, appropriate to a household that was relatively, but probably not outstandingly, affluent (its having been discarded without serious damage, and other aspects of the particular, extensive assemblage of which it is part from the BC72 site may carry further implications, as discussed in the next chapter). The present volume also includes a highly decorated, but probably quite cheap, lead pricket candlestick, No 366 (Col Pl 2), which represents an important early category that has not previously been adequately published in this country.

The recently excavated keys (Nos 258–73 and 294–332) show relatively little decoration compared with the much more varied and elaborate examples published by Ward Perkins (1940, 133–48). Those catalogued in this present volume are presumably more representative of the generality of keys used in medieval London, though the selective acquisitions by former museum curators admirably illustrate an eye-catching minority. The padlocks (Nos 242–57), a category not covered by Ward Perkins, include the most complicated, composite items in this whole present survey. In some instances, as with the keys, this elaborate complexity was probably in part to suggest to the purchaser a greater security than might have been seen in a simpler but equally adequate version (padlock No 251 has 22 or more parts in the case alone, while No 256 has at least that number, but its complex form appears actually to have diminished its potential robustness). Two of the iron locks, Nos 257 and 281, had been smashed, probably with axes, before they were discarded. Lock No 276 has a fault repaired, the need for this having arisen from poor smithing. A defective part in lock No 280 seems to have been put right by an expert, but the apparent replacement rivets in the mechanism of lock No 277 suggest that here an individual who was not a locksmith, undaunted by the complexity of contemporary precision technology, achieved a workable repair.

The copper-alloy vessels published in 1940 were all complete or nearly so. In contrast, small, flimsy fragments Nos 470–82 from sheet vessels suggest how commonly repairs had to be undertaken (see sheet patches Nos 493–4). The broken legs, rims and handles from cast copper-alloy vessels (Nos 441–64) and the two repair pieces (Nos 465–6, also cast) imply that for this category, too, they were often needed. The patches may represent the tinker level of making good, while the latter would have required some kind of fixed workplace with a furnace. Copper-alloy handle No 487, probably from a vessel, has been repaired with a sheet sleeve, the long-term effectiveness of which is rather doubtful. Lead/tin vessels (unrepresented in the 1940 catalogue) appear in the archaeological record largely in the form of small pieces of rims, some of which were perhaps lost in the process of recycling (presumably on a commercial basis). Repairs to ceramic vessels have been recovered in the form of lead plugs Nos 733–44, which include some very clumsy items, and which generally appear more rough-and-ready than the ones for the vessels of copper alloy (no repairs to the lead/tin tableware are evident, with the possible exception of spoon No 772). The wooden vessels occasionally exhibit repairs to cracks by means of iron staples or 'sewing', presumably with wire.

The earliest evidence for copper-alloy and lead/tin vessels includes a hint that, pre-dating common domestic usage of vessels made entirely of metal, there may have been categor-

ies of composite containers in which the main body was of wood, while other parts (spouts, bases) were of one of these metals, riveted in place (see Nos 441 and 539, both from deposits attributed to the late 12th century).

The complete absence of vessels in wood from the earlier published London catalogues was presumably a reflection of difficulties of conservation, though the category is probably still under-represented in this present volume because of the rarity of survival and the difficulty of recognising small fragments in the field, particularly of coopered vessels (there are no wooden spoons in the catalogue below, though they must surely have been commonplace). The lack of identifiable wooden buckets even from waterlogged deposits in wells of the period *c*.1150–*c*.1450 came initially as a surprise. It seems likely that in London ceramic jugs may regularly have been used for drawing water. Glass vessels were omitted from the *London Museum Medieval Catalogue* (apart from two fragments of a Middle Eastern lamp (pl 84), which came from Westminster Abbey and was therefore hardly a domestic object; No 695 and perhaps No 696 below are of the same general kind of glass – the former being the only item in the present catalogue definitely made outside western Europe). Table 1 gives totals by ceramic phase of vessels (almost all fragmentary), from the six main waterfront sites included in the catalogue below, of wood, copper alloy, lead/tin, glass, leather and stone. The different alloys of the metals, the genera of the wooden items and the various compositions of the glass ones are considered in the detailed discussions under each of these headings. Interpretation of any trends the figures in this Table may suggest is far from obvious because of the wide range of items included (containers for the storage, transportation, preparation and consumption of food and drink etc.), the difficulties raised by differential preservation (as between wood and copper alloys, for example), the potential for recycling in the metals, and the two items mentioned above which are thought to be from composite vessels made substantially of other materials (copper-alloy spout No 441 and lead/tin base No 539). The inclusion of only two identified leather items (Nos 731–2) is presumably an indication of

Table 1: Non-ceramic vessels by material (tableware etc.)
(Assemblages mainly from waterfront sites – BC72, BIG82, BWB83, SH74, SWA81, TL74)

Ceramic phase	6 (c.1150– c.1200)	7 (c.1200– c.1230)	8 (c.1230– c.1270)	9 (c.1270– c.1350)	10 (c.1330– c.1380)	11 (c.1350– c.1400)	12 (c.1400– c.1450)
Wood (72 items) (T=turned, C=coopered)	3T,1C (+ 1 carved)	5T	12T*	16,2C	4T	13T,5C	11T,2C
Copper alloy (36 items) (C=cast, S=sheet)	1C	1S	1C	3C,1S	2C	13C,9S	3C,2S
Lead/tin (33 items)	3	–	–	2	–	18	10
Glass (66 items)	1(?)	2	–	10	5 (+1?)	30	17
Leather (2 items)	–	–	–	–	–	2	–
Stone (1 item)	–	–	–	–	–	–	1**

(Total number of items included 20)

* including 8 vessels from a single pit at the inland MLK76 site
** jet vessel, probably connected with folk beliefs

When a span of more than one ceramic phase is given for an object in the catalogue, the latest phase is counted for the Table.
  (Ceramic vessels are not considered here. Lids, urinals and small fragments of glass (Nos 718–30) are also omitted. There are no iron vessels from any of the sites included in this volume.)

their rarity and perhaps a hint of a late date for their introduction into widespread usage (though the last point may be contradicted by oblique evidence from Winchester – see on these leather vessels, below). The extreme difficulty of identifying leather fragments as parts of vessels could mean that this category is substantially under-represented, and the same is true of copper-alloy sheeting other than the distinctive rim pieces. The numbers for glass, too, may give a biased picture, as, when decayed, this material can be very difficult to see in waterfront dumps. The figures in the Table do, however, provide at least a basic starting point for the discussion of a large body of datable evidence and for comparing it with other excavated assemblages.

Social milieux and different sectors of society

The ideal of retrieving assemblages that accurately reflect individual households has not yet been realised in London and it may prove too elusive ever to be achieved. The waterfront assemblages nevertheless furnish at a general level the best available evidence from which to consider the interrelationships of all the materials, as in Table 1. These finds assemblages, although not demonstrably from contexts of specific use, furnish in some numbers excavated vessels of ceramics, wood, glass and metals (sheet and cast copper alloy, and lead/ tin); the only stone vessel in the Table is a most unusual item with no known parallel (stone mortars are not included in this volume). Glass and metals are likely to have come only from wealthier households and perhaps in some cases from institutions. Wooden vessels in the riverside rubbish dumps and elsewhere tend to be found in groups that presumably reflect particular contexts of use or ownership. Away from the waterfront, even fragments of metal vessels are very unusual; not one of these items in the catalogue is from an inland site. A few excavated London pit assemblages have wood surviving along with fragments of glass (the contrast between relative numbers of finds from waterfront and inland sites seems less marked for the latter than for some other categories), as well as the ubiquitous ceramics (e.g., pit groups from the MIL72 and WAT78 sites). Such assemblages seem to present the best specific evidence currently available for future studies of (?)domestic groups, but the waterfront assemblages with their greater range of survivals are here considered for a wider background picture. The BC72 dumps from the late 14th century (ceramic phase 11) furnish vessels of all materials (including part of a stone mortar, which is not in the catalogue) and are therefore of particular importance in this regard, even if the household that some of these finds may perhaps represent was very wealthy indeed (see Dating and context of the finds). Nowhere, it seems, is leather's contribution to the range of vessels adequately represented from archaeological sources, and there is virtually a complete absence of surviving vessels of that most perishable material, horn (the only items of horn included in the catalogue are lantern panes No 428).

The waterfront finds clearly demonstrate the increasing use of glass and metals through the period considered. There is no indication of any general decline in consumption of glass and metals in the period immediately following the Black Death (cf. ceramic phase 11); arguably the reverse was happening – diversification in manufacture and retail may have been among the responses to the changed situation, and the archaeological pattern at the waterfront is of discarding rather than of acquisition and usage. It is not clear whether the smaller number of items attributed to ceramic phase 12 is entirely due to there being fewer deposits assigned to this period, or whether there was actually a decline in the quality (i.e. as reflected in materials) of goods generally affordable in the early 15th century. The iron cupped candleholders provide a hint at a general level of an increase in the size (thickness) of candles used between *c.*1270 and *c.*1450 (see on Nos 391–420); if this is correct it may mean that there was more money among medieval Londoners for the basics of everyday life and/or that candle materials were becoming cheaper through this period.

The complicated interrelationship of status and borrowed design traits in the vessels catalogued below emerges, at a very modest level, in the presence of what appear to be rim fillets on 13th-century wooden plates Nos 553 and 555, presumably copying this detail from contemporary, more expensive versions of lead/tin

(cf. the later Nos 502 etc.) – though perhaps the metal vessels could equally have borrowed this trait from the wooden ones. It is surprising that all the 32 spoons catalogued are of lead/tin, none made of other materials apparently having been found at the sites in the survey.

Some attempts have been made elsewhere to gauge changes in the materials used for vessels in the Middle Ages. D Keene, considering the wooden and ceramic vessels found in domestic contexts at the Lower Brook Street (Winchester) excavations, suggests that the former were more common than the latter in the 14th century (in Biddle 1990, 961–2). Relationships between ceramic and metal wares have been examined for cooking vessels (Cherry 1987, 145–6, 150–2; Lewis 1978) and for the elaborate ewers known as *aquamanili* (Verhaeghe 1991, 45–9), but they have yet to be considered in detail for mortars of stone, metal and ceramic. The remarkable, early 14th-century assemblage found in Pit 14 at Cuckoo Lane, Southampton (presumably representing some kind of large-scale clearance following enemy action in the town, and including several high-status items that suggest these finds hardly represent the goods of an average urban household) seems so far to be unique among probable domestic urban finds groups in the range of materials represented by the vessels (though even here metal arguably comprises only a single pewter item; Platt 1975, 289–93, with list of finds 356; cf. Platt & Coleman Smith 1975, 38, fig 126).

Activities particular to women in medieval society are represented by a few distinct categories. Spindles (whorls Nos 790–806) were at that time seen as a symbol of the female role. These ubiquitous items remained remarkably plain through the 300-year period considered (in comparison, for example, with the elaboration and diversity seen in men's bladed weapons, which, though not a precise equivalent and outside the normal domestic sphere, can as much as any other category be taken as representing one important aspect of men's role in medieval society). The remarkable jet bowl No 972 is a rare instance of an object that can probably be connected with folk beliefs about one of medieval women's prime roles, the bearing of children. The discovery in the cemetery of the church of St Nicholas Shambles (GPO75 site) of an adult burial with a fully developed, unborn foetus (Wells 1988) is ample evidence of the dangers medieval Londoners might have sought to avoid with such special items. Matilda Islebel's seal matrix (Fig 211) demonstrates that women in London, as elsewhere, were involved in business and commercial transactions. Although many manuscript illustrations depict women as preparers of food in the home, the Luttrell Psalter shows there were male cooks, at least in wealthier households (Fig 123). Sewing (see thimbles, reels and needles, Nos 814–91) was an activity regularly carried out by both sexes, in leather-working as well as in domestic and craft tailoring, and embroidery too, at least in the commercial sphere, was not a purely female preserve at this time (King 1963, 5).

Although only three objects, all of lead/tin, are with varying degrees of confidence identified as children's toys (Nos 930–2, Fig 216), they are likely to be more representative of what was generally available in medieval London (apart from the lack of categories in wood) than the single item suggested by Ward Perkins (1940, 288–9, fig 89, 2, MoL acc no A8874 – part of a miniature sword of copper alloy). Number 931, a bird originally with moving parts, is an indication of how sophisticated mass-produced toys could be at this date. It was repaired with solder after minor breakage, but the independently moving parts were fixed together in this process, so that it was retained with one of the features that was originally most attractive to children no longer in operation – a phenomenon not unfamiliar today.

Manufacture and origins

There is little direct evidence for London manufacture among the catalogued items, apart from cloth seals Nos 807–11 and a piece of turned wood No 642. The latter is the sole, definitely recognised piece of industrial waste in the entire catalogue, though cast copper-alloy (?vessel) fragment No 443 may not have been finished, and a more certain piece of casting waste is analysed in Table 7 (casket/

chest mount No 154 and branched lamp holders Nos 356–7 were probably carelessly finished rather than unfinished). It is possible that needles No 889 were not finished when discarded. Many catalogue items will have been brought to London to supplement those actually made here, though the origin of relatively few can be defined (see on candleholder No 425). Again, cloth seals (Nos 812–13 from Malines and Venice) are very specific indicators, while Near Eastern glass fragment No 695 (?cf. No 696) and ivory writing tablet No 912 (Col Pl 1B) probably have the most remote origins among the present objects, though the latter was carved in France or England. Glass vessel No 652 owes its distinctive form to prototypes from the Islamic world, though at present its place of manufacture seems unlikely to lie outside western Europe. It seems likely that many of the glass items apart from lamps and most urinals are Continental imports; it is possible that soda glass indicates a Continental origin, while potash glass may be of English manufacture, though this may prove too simplistic – see Table 12 (it may be significant in the light of all this that urinal No 778 is of the soda formula). Scale pans Nos 1039, 1044 and 1050 have stamps that relate to French coins, and it seems probable that the balances they were part of were also brought over from France, along with some or perhaps all of the other catalogued items in this category. Jet bowl No 972 is made of a stone likely to be from Yorkshire, but there is no reason for the turned vessels of wood not to have been London products made from timber grown in the hinterland. The stone spindle whorls could be from one or several places outside London – No 800 is of Caen stone, a material that originated in northern France, though this particular item could have been made from an imported building stone abandoned or re-used in London. The textile marks on needles No 889 are probably a rare indication of how these items were packaged in the Middle Ages, whatever their origin. There are several instances in the catalogue of items with close parallels abroad but no indication of the place or places of manufacture (see on lids Nos 537–8, for example, and the highly decorated lead/tin spoons are very widespread across north-west

Europe up into Russia, but, apart from a mould from Winchester (a second in Germany is for a variety so far unrepresented in Britain) there is no clear evidence for the locations of what were probably several production centres).

Signs and literacy, symbols and artistry

A few objects connected with food consumption (wooden bowls Nos 554, 563, 593, 599 and 602, lead/tin vessel fragments Nos 540 and 542, perhaps leather base No 732, and spoons Nos 769 and 773) are marked with simple branded, carved, or scratched devices of identification, presumably to indicate ownership. This suggests that these items may possibly have been used in situations where confusion or dispute could have arisen, such as at communal places of food preparation, consumption or washing up, or while travelling, as well as in the home. Lead weights Nos 990, 997–8 and 1015 bear stylised privy marks, though the reason for these lies in the regulative framework of the more public sphere of daily commerce. The arms, like those probably of the earls of Cornwall on weight No 1032 and the fleurs-de-lis on Nos 1023–4 were presumably intended to imply or to indicate the sanction of some authority, but the specific background is unclear. Scale pans Nos 1039, 1044–5 and 1049–50 have regulatory stamps from dies cut by very accomplished engravers (probably on the Continent, as above). Weights Nos 1007 and 1014 have simple, stamped crown marks which, like cloth seals Nos 807–13, presumably also represent direct official control to maintain honest dealing and good quality. The dots and edge cuts on weights Nos 979, 993, 1000–1 and 1027–8 (Figs 230, 233–4, 239) probably represent weighing systems, though here too precise identification has proved elusive. The adaptation of coin balance No 1059 illustrates the point that attempts were made to deceive, while its subsequent destruction shows that authority (or possibly conscience) prevailed. Copper-alloy tap No 746 (which could be a later, intrusive item – Fig 189) has a maker's mark, as, perhaps, does spoon No 757. Both items are

important, if the prima-facie dating is reliable, in that they appear respectively to be the earliest recorded marked tap, and the earliest pewter spoon known with a producers' mark.

Very few of the household items catalogued feature even as much as an oblique reference to mainstream artistic styles and motifs. Vessel base No 541 (Fig 157) and candlestick fragment No 369 (Fig 102), both of lead/tin, are the only objects in which the angular, Gothic style can be claimed in the metalwork (the complete form of the latter object is by no means certain). The carved crucifixion scene, with its ornamental, architectural-style frame, on ivory writing tablet No 912 (Col Pl 1B), is a conventional and not particularly accomplished piece, despite the exotic origin of the material. There are quatrefoil friezes on high-quality copper-alloy mounts Nos 152–3 (Fig 50), which were probably originally enamelled (compare No 230 for a down-market border or frame made of lead/tin – Fig 60), simple foliate openwork motifs on lantern slide No 427 and the handle of key No 748 (Fig 190), key No 747 (ibid.) has stylised foliage with a more accomplished three-dimensionality, lead weight No 993 has a pattern of fleurs-de-lis (Fig 233), and pewter stand No 971 is decorated with a more naturalistic, but derivative and uninspired, vine scroll (Fig 226). A few of the flat strap mounts also include foliate and heraldic motifs, in which varying degrees of stylisation can be seen (e.g., Nos 158 and 163 of copper alloy, and No 231 of lead – Figs 51, 60). The animal heads on handle No 487 (Fig 143) and book clasp No 920 (Fig 214) come towards the end of a lengthy process of degeneration of this motif on a range of commonplace, cast copper-alloy items used in London from before the time of the Norman Conquest. The heads on the handle have little more than nicks to represent the various features, and, without their more accomplished predecessors, would have been totally unrecognisable as something intended to look animate. Composite tap No 745 (Col Pl 3A), in contrast, has two gaping-mouthed, bulging-eyed animals which stand outside the everyday repertoire of late medieval motifs (its construction is also somewhat curious). Candleholder No 425, in the form of a stag, and also cast in copper alloy, is a bold design, though lacking in sophistication (it is, nevertheless, not quite as far removed from its presumed prototypes and, for that matter from the natural form of the animal, as the stolid parallel in Fig 116 is). Early 13th-century lead candlestick No 366 (Col Pl 2), with its densely packed combination of clumsy linear and naturalistic motifs (closely comparable with the dense decoration on the category of spoons represented by No 756 – Fig 193, and on a range of contemporary, cheap pewter jewellery, e.g., Egan & Pritchard 1991, *passim*) is a useful indicator of popular taste in furnishings at this period. This item too was presumably based, ultimately, on more accomplished prototypes, perhaps of copper alloy. The later toy head No 930 and canine handles Nos 537–8 (probably from salts, Fig 156) exhibit a degree of crude stylisation, and even the enigmatic, three-dimensional lead/tin flower No 545 (Fig 158) from an early 15th-century deposit, owes details of its form to heraldic convention. Toy bird No 931 (Col Pl 4B) from the 14th century perhaps approaches closest to accurately observed naturalism among all the catalogue items.

Iron mount No 169 hints at something of the artistry of the medieval blacksmith (see Ward Perkins 1940, 288, pl 84, for a highly ornate wrought-iron alms box from London, dated to the 15th century), though the other ferrous furnishing mounts, almost all far from complete, offer little more than paired scrolls and isolated, highly stylised foliate and fleur-de-lis motifs (Figs 52–6). There is, nevertheless, a discernible rise in the quality of the finishing of decorative terminals throughout the period represented – compare No 43 from the late 12th century with No 195 from the late 14th century, for example (Figs 31, 55).

Some of the glass fragments hint at former splendour, even luxury – notably the colourful Near Eastern piece No 695 (Col Pl 5C), the decorative drinking vessels (most obviously the enamelled group, which is not in the numbered catalogue, from Foster Lane – Col Pl 8), and perhaps also the remarkable and unusual category of white glass that was previously unrecognised from the medieval period (Nos 689 and 691–4, which include two finely made lids, as well as more familiar forms – see Col Pl 7, Fig 184). Some of the colourless and pale-green

fragments with subtle, mould-blown decoration are extremely delicate (e.g., Nos 669, 671, Figs 181–2). The only recognisably figurative piece of glass, No 703 (Fig 186), in the form of an animal, is not complete enough to assess adequately.

Even the medieval iron padlocks had their own tradition of decoration, using applied wire and strips along with a brazed coating (see No 246, Col Pl 1A), though this had passed its high point with the catalogued examples. A few of the keys combine complexity and precision with a delicate design, like Nos 269–70 and No 272 (Fig 75); they must have been made by master craftsmen.

Fewer than half a dozen of the items published here have inscriptions, which might attest directly to literacy at a popular level in medieval London – see spoon handle No 759 (Fig 196), whistle No 951 (Fig 220) and weights Nos 1011 and 1015 (Figs 235, 237); the first two are everyday items with religious mottos. The writing implements, book clasps and mounts, writing tablet, (?)leather cover and possible library-book chain (Nos 912, 919–29 and 79), together with spectacles No 918, provide some redress to this, though these items could be largely, if not entirely, from institutions, and it could be argued that the main attraction for some of the users of manuscripts may have been the illustrations rather than the text. The spectacles, from a non-religious site, might be cited as evidence for the sophistication of the laity in the capital compared with other parts of the country (frames known from the medieval period outside London are from excavations at the sites of ecclesiastical institutions), though this particular accessory, too, may have been used by a member of the clergy. The various privy marks and other simple signs of identification on some of the vessels and implements included in this volume (noted above) are far more common here than writing. The total absence of any recognised graffiti that include words in this entire published corpus of finds over the three centuries considered is in marked contrast to the fairly large number of runic inscriptions written on finds of several different categories of comparable date (objects of metal as well as of wood and bone) from sites in Scandinavia (e.g., Gosling 1989). Tallysticks Nos 913–17 are a relatively unusual reminder from the soil of London that there was another, widely used system for recording information in the Middle Ages. In contrast, it is doubtful whether more than a handful of people in medieval London (apart perhaps from those privileged to have been on a pilgrimage to the Holy Land, or the élite among veterans of the Crusades) would have been able to recognise the Naskh script on Near Eastern glass No 695 (Fig 185) as writing, let alone actually to read it. The heraldry on weights Nos 1011 and 1015, and on stamped scales Nos 1039, 1044–5 and 1049–50 (like the French legend included on No 1039) would also probably have conveyed their specific meaning to very few individuals, though there would have been wide recognition that they represented quality control – cf. the often poorly stamped legends in abbreviated Latin on regulatory textile seals like Nos 808–13. It is probably at this level that many medieval Londoners would have 'read' signs and symbols, rather than actual writing.

Comparisons with assemblages outside London

The major publication of medieval finds from Winchester (Biddle 1990) became available before the text for this present volume was completed. Comparisons in several categories with this second major body of well-dated finds were thus possible. There are a number of fundamental differences between these two urban assemblages, notably the definable domestic, military and ecclesiastical contexts of many of the Winchester finds, while very few of the London items can be attributed to any more specific milieu than the rubbish heap (see next chapter). Taking the same period of *c*.1150–*c*.1450 for both collections of finds, there are more categories and a larger number of objects from London, while Winchester (the special case of chalices from priests' burials excepted) lacks the large number and variety of lead/tin items that are a remarkable feature of the assemblages in the capital. It is the intention of each of the Winchester and the London publications to provide a base-line against which further urban and other finds groups can be considered. The variations that are already evident from these two major research programmes with quite similar approaches to detailed publication suggest that the emerging picture from large-scale urban excavations of material culture in the high Middle Ages depends as much on differences of preservation and context as on factors that might be considered common to medieval towns in general. Subsequent research could usefully include work on this point as further assemblages are published.

Dating and context of the finds

GEOFF EGAN

As in the earlier volumes of this series, the overwhelming majority of the catalogued finds included were recovered on sites adjacent to the River Thames, both from the dumped fills, mainly of highly organic refuse, deposited for land reclamation, and from the more mixed gravel and silt foreshores that accumulated against the successive medieval revetments. The dumps, which were up to 2m deep, eventually formed almost 100 metres of new land – virtually all of the strip to the south of modern Upper and Lower Thames Streets – as reclamation from the river continued through the three centuries of the later Middle Ages with which this volume is concerned (*c*.1150–*c*.1450). A few other selected finds, including some discarded in the City Ditch near Ludgate, have been included from inland sites (glass items are particularly widespread through the city), but by and large the preservation of metals and leather in soils away from the waterfront is poor. Within most of the present categories (apart from stone building materials) the finds assemblages from inland sites have only very exceptionally approached the diversity and proliferation of those retrieved beside the Thames. Without the waterfront material it would have been quite impossible (even if the finds from the most recent programmes of excavation – those undertaken from 1983 onwards – had also been considered) to produce as extensive a synthesis as that presented here.

Notably absent from recent excavations in the City of London are later medieval assemblages (other than ceramics and glass) from domestic and other more specific contexts. Away from the waterfront, horizontal deposits, such as floors, that could be attributed to the 14th or 15th centuries have virtually all been removed in the City by subsequent activity. The cut features that have survived – foundations, rubbish pits and wells – have generally proved disappointingly unproductive of material in most categories appropriate for inclusion in this and the preceding volumes in the series. It is difficult to pinpoint any assemblage from the sites located away from the waterfront/City Ditch and considered here which could furnish more than two or three non-ceramic categories included in this study. But for the waterfront assemblages, the surviving material culture from everyday life in medieval London – with the exception of ceramics and, less directly, the various structural remains – would give scant indication that this was the most important city of the realm and the thriving market for manufactured goods of all kinds that documentary sources attest.

The freshness of breaks in many pottery sherds found in the organic waterfront dumps, and the unadvanced state of decomposition of some of the plant material there – reeds and moss, for example – suggest that much of the refuse was very recently discarded when deposited. Most of this was presumably domestic rubbish, such as reeds strewn on floors, stable sweepings, and perhaps some pit-clearance material.

There are a few earlier finds among the late medieval deposits – the odd potentially Saxon or Roman object stands out (see spindle whorl No 805). There is always the possibility that a slightly earlier medieval object may have been kept for some time as an heirloom before it was discarded, or that it ended up in a dump with predominantly later material for other reasons (e.g., ceramic curfew fragments Nos 338–9, 342, lead plug No 741 – which may have been over two centuries old when deposited; glass lamp No 355, glass fragments Nos 681 and 717, a fragment of a ceramic vessel re-used as a lantern – Fig 120, and pen No 898 were all found in post-medieval contexts). Instances of this kind can be difficult to pinpoint in the present state of knowledge, particularly with scarcer items, but wider considerations may sometimes indicate where late deposition could have happened (e.g., writing tablet No 912, which is dated by the style of the decoration). Very occasionally an object appears, from all the available information, to be intrusive from a later period (this is perhaps true of tap No 746, and it could also apply to cloth seal No 811; spoon No 757 might possibly fall into this category too, but as there is no closely datable parallel with the same kind of 'mark' as the one it bears it could alternatively be the earliest known example – the 'mark' in question differs from later ones in being integrally cast). Such anomalies may be attributable to a variety of factors – including errors in excavation or subsequent documentation, or an object may be a very early, so far isolated, instance of a category which later became more common. Any special considerations to be taken into account for dating are detailed in the discussion below of each site.

The overwhelming majority of the finds presented here are from well-dated deposits and are thought to have been discarded within a generation or so of manufacture. For further discussion of the context of waterfront finds with particular reference to the Trig Lane site, see Rhodes 1982b, 85–92. For the locations of the sites, see Fig 1.

The waterfront was one of the principal locations for discarding rubbish of all kinds during the medieval period, both on the wharfside at recognised laystalls and, inevitably (despite the attempts of the City authorities to prevent it), in the River Thames and on the foreshore (Sabine 1937, 32, 37–40).

The majority of the extremely varied finds included in this book seem to have been either casually discarded or single losses, though some groups of similar items may have more significance. These include keys Nos 261–2, weights Nos 1024–5 and 1036–7, and some of the assemblages of wooden vessels (see discussion of the latter items in the catalogue).

The finds from two series of mid-14th-century dump deposits at the BC72 site have already been singled out in earlier volumes in the series and elsewhere by virtue of some unusual aspects of the assemblage these layers produced. Some of the shoes, rather than being patched, were discarded when they started to become worn, in contrast with others recovered from London sites (Grew & de Neergaard 1988,

90). The 16 or more used (?)spur straps with varied mounts (Egan & Pritchard 1991, nos 1168–85), the only horseshoes known with stamped marks (Clark 1988, 19, 21, nos 8–9, fig 7 and *idem* 1995, nos 212, 222, 235, 238), an extraordinary spur (Egan & Pritchard 1991, 107, fig 69; B M A Ellis in Clark 1995, 149, fig 108, no 364), silks, including pieces of cloth-of-silver and Chinese damask (Crowfoot et al. 1992, 9, 98–104, 202–8, nos 138–40), with this present volume's pewter lid No 530 (Fig 154), candlestick No 426 (Fig 117 – the last being virtually the only complete, major furnishing item in this catalogue that was found discarded in a usable state), and a peacock's feather (see Col Pl 4A), together further re-enforce the impression that some of the finds in these particular assemblages differ markedly from others along the waterfront. These same dumps nevertheless also produced run-of-the-mill finds, such as bone-bead manufacturing waste (Egan & Pritchard 1991, nos 1572–9) and some everyday textiles (Crowfoot et al. 1992, 9). The social groups that had for disposal such varied and, in several instances, extravagant items as the former ones must have been extremely affluent. It remains to be seen whether any specific connection can be established with the nearby Great Wardrobe. The group of four tallysticks (Nos 914–17, Fig 212) from these same deposits comprises both 'official' and non-standard kinds (the relation of the latter to official record-keeping is obscure, especially when compared with other, possibly selected, survivals that were never lost in the ground).

The dating of the deposits at the waterfront sites depends in the first instance on coins, supplemented where possible by dendrochronology. This has permitted key changes in the ceramic sequence to be assigned approximate dates (principally the work of Alan Vince). The **ceramic phases** thus defined are the essential linchpin of the dating assigned in this volume to each of the groups of deposits that together constituted a reclamation dump or foreshore, and to the other stratigraphic contexts away from the waterfront. A brief summary of the dated sequence proposed for each of the major sites is given below. Post-excavation analysis methods differed from site to site, so that groupings and interpretation may not corre-

Table 2: Ceramic phasing with defining pottery fabrics

Ceramic phase	Date	Pottery fabrics
6	*c.*1150–*c.*1200	Shelly Sandy ware
7	*c.*1200–*c.*1230	London/Rouen wares
8	*c.*1230–*c.*1260/?70	Kingston ware
9	*c.*1270–*c.*1350	Mill Green ware
10	*c.*1330–*c.*1380	Late Medieval Hertfordshire Glazed ware
11	*c.*1350–*c.*1400	Cheam ware
12	*c.*1400–*c.*1450	Coarse Border ware/bifid rims

For further details, see Vince 1985, 25–93.

spond precisely between the proposed sequences.

The slightly simplified site plans for four of the major excavations (Figs 2–5) can be used, in conjunction with the lists of individual contexts and the discussion of each of these sites, to pinpoint the location of a specific find in the sequence. All the contexts – the individual recorded layers – which comprise a single foreshore or a reclamation dump have been assigned a **group number**; and these groups are the key components in the analysis of each site sequence. For example (method for BWB83 and SWA81 sites): the lead weight that is catalogue No 1023 in this volume (SWA81 Acc No 2884) is from context 2106 of dump group 103; group 103 can be located on the Swan Lane site plan (Fig 4). From the plan, it can be seen that the weight was found in a ceramic phase 12 reclamation dump associated with a revetment constructed during the period that is defined as ceramic phase 12 (*c.*1400–*c.*1450) and lying over a foreshore with coins of 1422. Weight No 1024 from layer 2117 at the same site can be traced in the same way and found to be from the same group of dumps (103) – i.e., these two similar weights were probably discarded at the same time. The group 103 dump is likely to have been deposited at some time in the middle of the 50-year period. Where a particular group is part of a sequence within a single ceramic phase and no further dating evidence is available, there is at present no way of telling how early or late within the phase each of the successive pro-

grammes of reclamation and revetment construction took place. As a second example (method for BIG82 and TL74 sites), spectacles No 918 (TL74 Acc No 2216), are from the Trig Lane site, context 274, which is assigned in the list below to a dump from group 15 (i.e., it is associated with structure 15 of ceramic phase 12, *c.*1400– *c.*1450). The site plan (Fig 5) shows that structure 15 is a river wall, dated to 1440+ by dendrochronology. The deposition of the spectacles in the associated land-fill dump can thus be dated to the 1440s, later than some of the other items attributed to ceramic phase 12 at this site. This level of information is not available for all sites, much less for all contexts that produce finds; as assimilation and research progress, further details can be expected to be added and minor alterations made.

The sites

This section provides a brief background to the main City of London sites mentioned in this book. Most finds from inland sites are from rubbish pits or wells (apart from LUD82, which included City Ditch deposits), contemporary horizontal strata in areas away from the waterfront having been almost entirely removed by subsequent activity. Detailed information is given (where it is available) on the sequences at the four sites which were most productive of finds for researchers interested in following up the contexts of specific items; only contexts which produced finds discussed in this book are listed. See Fig 1 for location of the sites.

Fig 1   City of London, location of sites
mentioned in the text

AL74: 62–64 Aldgate High Street (site supervisor,
A Thompson)
Extramural, inland site with material principally of
post-medieval date. An early 18th-century pit produced a residual piece of medieval glass in the
catalogue.

BA84: Bermondsey Abbey site, Long Walk, Bermondsey (south of Thames), (site supervisor,
D Beard)
Inland site, south of the Thames in Southwark (not
in Fig 1), excavated by Department of Greater

London Archaeology for MoL. Provided a parallel for
glass fragments in the catalogue.

BC72: Baynard House, Queen Victoria Street, 'Baynard Castle Dock' (site supervisor, P Marsden)
Two extensive groups of dump deposits, attributed
to ceramic phases 10 and 11, and associated respectively with the construction and infilling of a stone-
walled dock known as the 'East Watergate' (Webster
& Cherry 1973, 162–3; Vince in Cowgill et al. 1987,
2). The finds assemblage from the mid-14th-century
dump group (context 250, ?1330s/1340s) and the
late 14th-century one (contexts 55, 79, 83, 88, 88/1,
89, 150) stand out for the high-class milieux to which
(by implication of internal evidence – see above)
some of the objects relate, though there are also
everyday items from these same deposits.

BG76: 190 Bishopsgate (site supervisor, R Blurton) Inland site; produced a spindle whorl in this volume.

BIG82: Billingsgate lorry park, Lower Thames Street (site supervisor, S Roskams), Fig 2
Finds from a detailed sequence of dumps and foreshores of ceramic phases 6–8 (Youngs et al. 1983, 191–2). Dating is provided by coins, pottery and dendrochronology. Some sieving, and also metal detecting, was undertaken by site staff not previously experienced in the latter method (the Society of Thames Mudlarks was not involved during the controlled excavation here). These efforts at their most intensive covered about a quarter of the volume of material excavated, but they were abandoned in the face of limited resources for completing the excavation. After the formal excavation was completed and further access to the site had been denied to archaeologists, a number of finds were recovered from the spoil heaps by members of the public. Because in some areas water-lain deposits appeared to have accumulated over land-reclamation dumps, and

some deposits defined as foreshores included extensive organic i.e., dump-type material (perhaps rubbish discarded in the river), it is difficult to categorise each context firmly as reclamation dump or foreshore. The group 8 revetments and possibly others may have been replaced at least once, resulting in a complicated structural sequence; interpretation may change as a result of further analysis.

For the subsequent watching brief, covering the remaining five-sixths of the redevelopment site and the later part of the sequence, see BWB83 below.

Note: where there is no structure having exactly the same number as the group, the deposit may relate to any of the structures with a number corresponding to that before the full stop in the group designation. Contexts which do not appear in the following list and which have been phased as part of the relevant groups (see Fig 2) need to have the precise nature of their association with the reclamation sequence clarified by further post-excavation work. For ceramic phasing see individual catalogue entries.

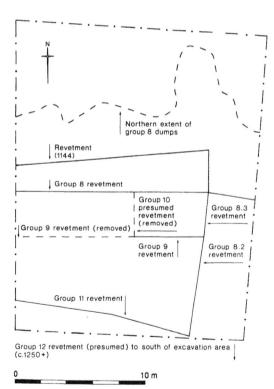

Fig 2 Billingsgate lorry park site (BIG82) – schematic plan

Context	Group	Designation
		f = foreshore; d = dump
1178	13.7	(?)d
2012	12	spit
2053	12	spit
2152	11	spit
2242	12	spit
2246	12	spit
2277	12	spit
2278	12	spit
2424	13.2	(?)d
2591	12	unassigned
2598	12	spit
2913	12	spit
2938	12	spit
3150	11.4	spit
3176	12.3	(?)d
3204	11	unassigned
3562	8.1	d
3620	8.1	d
3682	11.2	spit
3803	8.9	(?)f
3882	11.2	spit
3918	8.1	d
4016	8.1	spit
4030	8.8	spit
4045	11.2	spit
4064	8.1	d
4100	10.1	d
4103	10.1	d
4125	11.2	spit

Context	Group	Designation
		f = foreshore; d = dump
4178	8.1	d
4209	8.9	(?)f
4272	8.9	d
4339	10.1	spit
4342	10.1	spit
4368	(?)7.7	f
4371	10.1	spit
4659	8.8	d
4714	7.10	d
4761	7.7	(?)f
4766	7.13	(?)f
5020	8.2	d
5229	8.1	d
5364	8.2	d
5398	8.2	spit
5400	8.2	d
5511	9.2	d
5560	7.3	d
5992	6.1	(?)d
6279	8.1	(?)d
6759	7.3	(?)f

BIS82: 76–80 Bishopsgate Street (site supervisor, H White)

Inland site; a residual glass fragment in the catalogue was found in a post-medieval pit.

BOY86: City of London Boys' School (old site) (site supervisor, C Spence)

Furnished comparanda for catalogue items: late medieval sequence of dumps continuing into the (?)late 15th century. Metal detecting by Society of Thames Mudlarks.

BUC87: Docklands Light Railway Shaft, Bucklersbury (site supervisor, J Hill)

Inland site; produced a ceramic lamp illustrated in this volume.

BUF90: Bull Wharf Lane/16–20 Queenhithe (site supervisor, J Ayre)

Waterfront site, which produced especially 10th to late 12th-century finds, and some later ones.

BWB83: Billingsgate lorry park, watching brief (site supervisor, G Egan), Fig 3

Extensive finds from ceramic phases 6–12 (mainly 9–12). Access was initially severely constrained by the developers until most of the structural sequence had been removed. Very limited detailed recording of dumps and traces of revetments etc. in at least three adjacent properties provided a sketchy basic sequence in some parts of the site, but the majority of the finds came from foreshores and deeper riverine deposits (some already disturbed when examined) after all structural features had been removed. For these reasons dating must be considered much more rough-and-ready than for other sites. Many of the finds have been assigned to ceramic phase 11 (although individual groups within one broad area of the site appear to be assignable to ceramic phase 10, their locations do not readily combine to produce a coherent overall sequence as on the other waterfront sites). Because of the constraints during recording, major features such as inlets may not have been identified; similarly the division between deposits of ceramic phases 11 and 12 is not clear-cut).

In broad terms the sequence is coherent, and a northern limit for deposits attributed to each ceramic phase is indicated in Fig 3. In this watching brief, the dating for some objects may have been attributed to a later phase than would have been the case had more detailed recording been possible. On the positive side, the very extensive assemblages of finds recovered were the result of metal detecting by the Society of Thames Mudlarks. For the earlier part of the sequence at the site, see BIG82 above. Dating is from numerous coin finds and ceramic phasing.

In the following list, bracketed context numbers indicate deposits that were disturbed before retrieval took place. There is the possibility of contamination by earlier or occasionally later items among finds recovered from the contexts so indicated. For ceramic phasing see catalogue entries.

Context	Group	Designation
		d = dump; f = foreshore;
		m = mixed dump and foreshore
10	20	d
107	7	d
(108)	17	f
(109)	44	f
(110)	28/31/33	m
(111)	28/31/33	m
(113)	31	d
117	31	d
118	50	d
(119)	41	d
(122)	-	recently disturbed
124	50	f
(126)	41	d
(129)	41	d
131	41	?d
(136)	unphased	?d
(137)	unphased	?d
(138)	unphased	?d
142	41	d

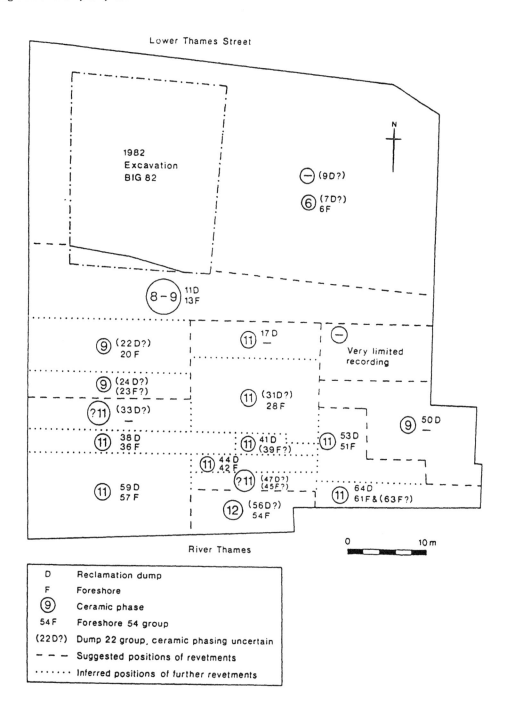

Fig 3 Billingsgate lorry park, watching brief (BWB83) – schematic plan

Context	Group	Designation d = dump; f = foreshore; m = mixed dump and foreshore	Context	Group	Designation d = dump; f = foreshore; m = mixed dump and foreshore
144	42	f	(303)	36	f
146	59	d	(305)	36/38	f
(147)	36/38	m	(306)	28	f
149	36	f	(307)	45/47	m
150	38	d	308	38	f
151	36	f	309	54	f
(152)	57/59	m	(310)	unassigned	
153	57	f	313	54	f
154	57	f	(314)	unassigned	
155	59	d	317	36	f
156	59	d	318	28	f
157	38	d	325	50	d
158	50	f	326	54	f
162	59	d	(328)	61/63/64	m
173	6	f	329	61	f
195	22	d	(330)	61/63/64	m
196	24	d	(331)	61/63/64	m
202	9	f	334	61	f
(204)	57/59	m	(338)	61/63/64	m
(206)	9/11	m	341	61	f
(207)	57/59	m	351	53	d
211	6	f	(352)	61/63/64	m
217	9	f	(354)	57/59	m
(219)	9/11	m	(355)	61/63/64	m
(221)	9/11	m	356	61	f
(222)	9/11	m	357	61	f
256	45	f	(359)	51/53	m
257	39	f	(361)	51/53	m
(260)	9/11	m	362	48	f
(263)	13	f	(367)	48	f
(265)	45/47/57/59	m	(368)	56/59	f
(269)	unassigned		370	51	f
270	24	d	(374)	51/53	m
(274)	unassigned		(376)	61	f
(275)	unassigned		377	61	f
(278)	54/56	m	378	61	f
(279)	36	f	380	33	d
280	38	d	387	61	f
282	36	f	(389)	61/63/64	m
(283)	36	f	391	61	f
(285)	23/33	m	(395)	61/63/64	m
(286)	42/44	m	399	51	f
(287)	57	f	(401)	61/63/64	m
(290)	23/24/36	m			
291	42	f			
(292)	57/59	m			
293	44	d			
297	57	f			
(298)	57/59	m			
(299)	42/44	m			
(300)	unassigned	m			
(301)	42/44	m			

BYD81: City of London Boys' School (new site) (site supervisor, J Burke Easton)
Smallish waterfront site at west end of city, including south side of late medieval Baynard's Castle. Produced wooden vessels in the catalogue.

CKL88: 9 Cloak Lane (site supervisor, J Ayre)
Inland site; produced the miniature house reproduced in the frontispiece of this book.

COL81: 19–20 College Hill (site supervisor, M Barker)
Inland site; internal medieval walls with whitewash surviving were recorded (referred to under Building materials).

CUS73: Old Custom House site, Lower Thames Street (site supervisor, T Tatton Brown)
Published by Tatton Brown (1974, 117–219). Trenches I–VI, XI–XII and XIV–XV included material of appropriate date for this volume. Each trench has a separate series of context numbers. The foreshores and dumps produced a limited number of finds attributable to ceramic phases 9 and 11.

DUK77: 2–7 Duke's Place, St James Passage subway (site supervisor, J Maloney)
Inland site, including part of City Ditch. A residual ceramic vessel used as a lantern was found in a post-medieval context.

ER190 A and C: Watling House, 12–16 Watling Street/31–7 Cannon Street (Guildhall Museum)
The contents of a single pit at an inland site; these include glass items in the catalogue.

ER1118: Dyers' Arms, Cannon Street (Guildhall Museum)
Inland site; produced glass items in the catalogue.

FIP92: Inland site, Finsbury Pavement (site supervisor, G Malcolm)
Inland site just north of city, mainly comprising dumps of material filling a former marsh. Produced tile-making waste referred to in the text.

FMO85: 37–40 Fish Street Hill/16–20 Monument Street (site supervisor, N Bateman)
Inland site; produced part of a ceramic curfew illustrated in this volume.

GAG87: Guildhall Art Gallery (site supervisor, G Porter)
Inland site; produced a ceramic lamp illustrated in this volume.

GPO75: General Post Office site, 81 Newgate Street (site supervisor, A Thompson)
Inland site, with excavation in two areas, including part of the precinct of Greyfriars and the cemetery of the church of St Nicholas Shambles (POM79 comprised the area in the middle of the site).

GWS89: Pinners' Hall, Great Winchester Street (site supervisors, B Watson/C Rosborough)
Inland site; produced a ceramic lamp illustrated in this volume.

HTP79: 10–11 Mitre Street (site supervisor, J Schofield)
Inland site, included location of medieval Holy Trinity Priory.

LBT86: 5–24 Little Britain/200 Aldersgate Street (site supervisors, M Nally et al.)
Inland, extramural site; a pit produced several glass items paralleling ones in the catalogue (some of them illustrated as comparanda in this volume) and part of a ceramic curfew.

LCT84: Leadenhall Court/1–6 Leadenhall Street (site supervisor, G Milne)
Inland site, including the medieval municipal corn-store building, the Leadenhall (mentioned under discussion on Building materials).

LH74: 44–6 Ludgate Hill (site supervisor, C Hill)
Inland site; produced a wooden vessel fragment in the catalogue.

LOV81: 21–4 Lovat Lane (site supervisor, D Gadd)
Inland site, with remains of a late medieval undercroft illustrated in this volume.

LUD82: 42–6 Ludgate Hill (site supervisor, P Rowsome)
Inland site including the City Ditch. The main ditch fills have been dated, by a coin of 1302–10 and documentary evidence of development over the former ditch area by 1340, to the middle part of ceramic phase 9; earlier fills in another area seem to date to the mid-13th century (ceramic phase 8). See Vince in Cowgill et al. (1987, 4) and Youngs et al. (1983, 194). Finds include wooden bowls from the early 14th-century ditch fills.

MIL72: 10 Milk Street (site supervisor, N Farrant)
Inland site (see Schofield et al. 1990); produced several wooden and glass vessel fragments in the catalogue.

MLK76: 1–6 Milk Street (site supervisors S Roskams, J Schofield)
Inland site (see Schofield et al. 1990); several medieval pits, which produced wooden bowls etc. in the catalogue.

MM74: Baynard House, Queen Victoria Street (adjacent to Mermaid Theatre) (site supervisor, P Herbert)
Waterfront site with limited reclamation sequence; produced a couple of fragments of wooden vessels in the catalogue.

MPY88: Site of Merton Priory, Surrey (site supervisor, S McCracken)

Monastic rural site (not shown in Fig 1), which produced a parallel for bone spectacles in the catalogue.

NEW81: 36 Clerkenwell Close/Newcastle Row, Clerkenwell (site supervisor, P Mills)
Site to the north of the city, excavated by Department of Greater London Archaeology, in area formerly occupied by the nunnery of St Mary Clerkenwell; a 16th-century deposit produced a fragment of glass cited as a parallel for a catalogue item (site not shown in Fig 1).

NFW74: New Fresh Wharf, Lower Thames Street (site supervisor, G Clewley)
Waterfront site with reclamation sequence; produced a spindle whorl included in this volume.

OPT81: 2–3 Copthall Avenue (site supervisor, C Maloney)
Inland site; produced a key in the catalogue.

OST82: 7–10 Foster Lane (site supervisor, I Blair)
Inland site, in goldsmiths' area of medieval London. A pit produced an important assemblage of high-quality medieval glass illustrated in this volume, as well as a fragment of a glass lamp in the catalogue.

POM79: General Post Office site, 81 Newgate Street (site supervisors, P Allen et al.)
Inland site comprising part of precinct of the Greyfriars (middle area between the two parts of the GPO75 site). Produced a glass fragment and part of a curfew in the catalogue.

PUB80: 86 Fenchurch Street (site supervisor, A Upson)
Inland site; produced parallels for catalogue items.

RAG82: 1–2 Rangoon Street/61–5 Crutched Friars (site supervisor, D Bowler)
Extramural, inland site at north of the city; produced some glass items in the catalogue (from documentary evidence probably the site of an affluent household – see Nos 352–4).

SH74: Seal House, 106–8 Upper Thames Street (site supervisor, J Schofield)
Waterfront site with sequence of dumps and foreshores (ceramic phases 6–8). The four successive wharves can be dated to 1133+, 1163–92+, and 1193+ by dendrochronology, and to *c.*1250 by pottery.

SLH93: St Leonard's Hospital, Hoxton Street, N1 (site supervisor, N Elsdon)
Extramural site to north of City (not shown in Fig 1); provided a parallel for a key in the catalogue.

SLO82: Beaver House, Sugar Loaf Court (site supervisor, M Barker)
Inland site where an undercroft mentioned in the text was uncovered; evidence for whitewashing of external walls in the medieval period was found.

SNS87: National Car Park, Sans Walk, Clerkenwell (site supervisor, A Thompson)
Inland site to north of City (not shown in Fig 1); produced a parallel for a spigot tap in this catalogue.

SUN86: Sunlight Wharf, Upper Thames Street (site supervisor, R Bluer)
For comparanda: sequence of reclamation dumps and foreshores (ceramic phases 6–12 and later). Metal detecting by Society of Thames Mudlarks.

SWA81: Swan Lane, 95–103 Upper Thames Street (site supervisor, G Egan), Fig 4
Small, controlled excavation and subsequent extensive watching brief comprising reclamation dumps and foreshores with up to ten successive revetments in three adjacent properties (ceramic phases 6–12). Despite watching brief conditions, the helpful contractors (Sir Robert MacAlpine and Sons) permitted prolonged access to the fullest reclamation sequence recorded among the main sites included in this volume. Metal detecting by the Society of Thames Mudlarks produced extensive and varied finds assemblages that can be dated closely (Egan 1985/6, 42–50), though recording of the earliest (ceramic phase 6) and some of the later (ceramic phase 11) parts of this sequence is limited. Dating is from numerous coin finds and ceramic phasing, and there is one indication from dendrochronology. The late 13th-century and early 15th-century deposits were especially productive (ceramic phases 9 and 12). The latest two successive dumps date to 1394+ by dendrochronology and to 1422+ from coin evidence, and the foreshore associated with the former and underlying the latter can be dated to *c.*1400–30 (the absence of coins of the reign of Henry VI is taken to be inconsistent with deposition as late as the 1430s – Vince in Cowgill et al. 1987, 6).

For ceramic phasing see individual catalogue entries; for foreshore/dump designations see Fig 4.

Context	Group	Context	Group
888	70	1595	26
966	93	2000	70
994	100	2006	104/106/107
1031	93	2008	redeposited
1354	33	2018	74
1581	61	2020	74

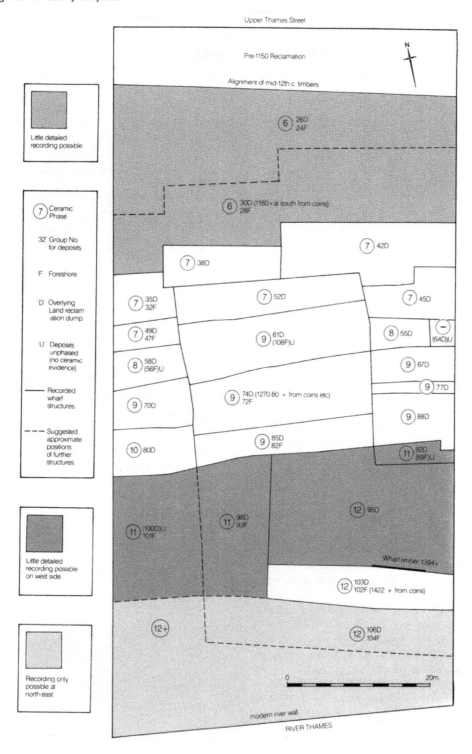

Fig 4   Swan Lane site and watching brief (SWA81) – schematic plan

Context	Group	Context	Group
2022	74	2115	102
2025	(?)74	2117	103
2030	74	2130	49
2031	74	2133	67
2032	100	2134	74
2033	74	2136	61
2040	74	2137	74
2050	74	2139	61
2051	74	2140	61
2055	85	2141	74
2057	74	2142	61
2061	74	2144	74
2062	74	2145	61
2063	74	2147	61
2065	85	2149	74
2069	100	2157	26
2070	74	2176	24
2072	74	2185	24
2078	74	2187	24
2081	74	2188	24
2082	103	2198	24
2084	103	2209	24
2085	102	2211	28–30
2097	103	2252	38
2098	95	2254	38
2100	103	2256	61
2101	102	2262	42
2103	103	2257	(?)38
2105	95	2266	42
2106	103	2267	45–6
2107	102	2270	61
2108	103	2277	52
2109	102	2278	42
2112	103	2279	42
2113	103	3015	26
2114	103		

TEX88: Thames Exchange, Upper Thames Street (site co-ordinator, G Milne, supervisors, C Milne and K Tyler)

Produced comparanda for catalogue items, cited in the text. Extensive waterfront site with controlled excavation areas and wider watching brief (ceramic phases 6–11, possibly 12). Metal detecting by the Society of Thames Mudlarks; very large finds assemblages (Gaimster et al. 1990, 179–80, site 63). Details of coin and dendrochronological dating for the very full sequence have not been fully completed at the time of writing.

TL74: Trig Lane, Upper Thames Street (site supervisor, G Milne), Fig 5

Well-dated sequence of reclamation dumps and foreshores from c.1250 to c.1440 (ceramic phases 8–12). Dating of the 17 revetments/repairs and foreshore structures for three adjacent properties is from dendrochronology, coins and pottery. The field records do not permit specific identification of all contexts as either foreshore or reclamation-dump deposits. Extensive finds from ceramic phases 10–12. The structural evidence has been published (Milne & Milne 1982). Because all the recorded deposits associated with each major structure (i.e., the earlier foreshore contexts immediately adjacent and underlying, as well as the later ones accumulating to the south against each revetment, and the reclamation dumps immediately to the north of the structure) have been put together under one group number, some of the foreshore deposits at this site have in post-excavation analysis been divided between an earlier structural group to the north and a later one to the south. This way of grouping contexts may thus place finds from the same foreshore strata recorded at slightly different points under different group numbers.

In the following list d = dump; f = foreshore; accumulated foreshore = post-dating each structure; underlying foreshore = pre-dating each structure. For ceramic phasing see individual catalogue entries.

Context	Group (i.e., relates to revetment no)	Designation
10	?	d
99	7	?
225	15	d
274	15	d
275	15	d
291	(?)11	d
306	11	d
309	7	?
353	7	?
364	15	d
368	15	d
378	15	?
414	(?)7/11	d
415	11	d
416	10/11/13/15	underlying/accumulated f
429	9/11	d/f
453	11/15	d/accumulated f
1264	12	d
1388	(?)15	underlying f
1456	12	d
1457	12	unassigned

Context	Group (i.e., relates to revetment no)	Designation
1588	2	d
1628	12	?
1634	7	d
1644	10	?
1740	7	d
1743	7	d
1783	7	f
1877	3	d
1955	13	f
1956	10/13	accumulated f
1992	13	f
2230	14	?

Context	Group (i.e., relates to revetment no)	Designation
2299	12	d
2332	10	d
2416	2	d
2443	3	d
2467	2	?d
2472	2	?d
2532	2	d
2608	13	f
2666	10	d
2731	12	?
2808	10	f
2840	10	f

Fig 5   Trig Lane site (TL74) – schematic plan

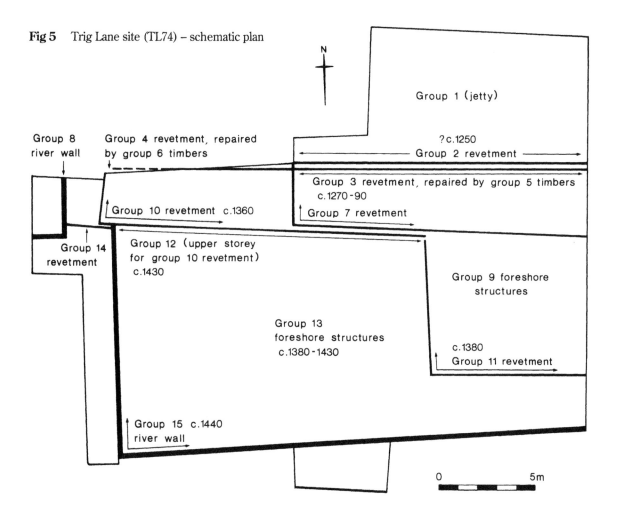

TR74: Triangle, 101–10 Lower Thames Street (site supervisor, D Jones)
Inland site.

VAL88: Comprised several excavations in large inland area between Blackfriars and Holborn Viaduct at the west of the city (site supervisor, W McCann)
Produced finds cited as comparanda for catalogue items.

VHA89: Vintners' Hall, 69 Upper Thames Street (site supervisor, R Malt)
Cofferdam excavation and spoil from VRY89, which produced comparanda for items in the catalogue.

VRY89: Vintners' Place, 68 Upper Thames Street (site supervisor, R Malt)
Waterfront site with extensive reclamation sequence; produced comparanda for catalogue items. Metal detecting by members of the Society of Thames Mudlarks. Large, varied assemblages through entire period considered in this volume, including extensive late 12th-century groups (Nenk et al. 1992, 230 site 125).

WAT78: 41–53 Cannon Street/Watling Court (site supervisor, D Perring)
Inland site (see Schofield et al. 1990) with several medieval pits and wells, which produced glass items (lamp fragments etc.) in the catalogue.

WEL79: Well Court/44 Bow Lane (site supervisors, P Allen / D Perring)
Inland site (see Schofield et al. 1990); produced early roof tiles referred to in the text.

General observations

Overall, the finds attributed to ceramic phases 9–12 are far more numerous than those considered to be earlier than *c*.1270. This may in part be because fewer finds in the categories relevant to the present series of publications were discarded in either the dumps or the foreshores during the earlier part of the sequences. However, none of the waterfront sites for which the records have been fully analysed has so far employed standard methods of retrieval using the same equipment for all the deposits excavated. The Thames Exchange (TEX88) site may in due course provide a clearer perspective on this point. At some sites, relatively few deposits with finds have been assigned to ceramic phase 10, probably because of the chronological overlap with other phases (see, e.g., Tables 1, 4, 7, 8 which show materials used for various categories of goods). The absence of finds of the 1260s in the original ceramic dating scheme (between phases 8 and 9) is a minor anomaly that needs resolution; it would probably be appropriate to regard the end date of ceramic phase 8 as *c*.1270.

The relative size of the assemblages recovered can be taken to reflect a general increase in affluence in terms of material culture in the categories considered through the later medieval period. This accords quite well with the major trend of economic growth at this time, especially during the 13th century, though there is no clear indication from the finds of recession following the Black Death. For the future, it may well be possible to define the extent and nature of change in further categories of objects more closely in the light of these and other datable finds. Varied emphases from site to site in assemblages attributed to the same ceramic phase may prove to be subtle indicators of more precise dating than is yet definable. The objects discarded in any particular waterfront dump or foreshore may reflect changing fashions in goods available to Londoners for only a short part of a particular decade (cf. discussion in Egan & Pritchard 1991, 12, 271). The catalogued skimmers (Nos 437–9, 507) were recovered only at the TL74 site, even though these must have been very widespread items of kitchen equipment, and deposits of the same ceramic phases are well represented at several other sites included in this volume. The only catalogued leather-vessel pieces (Nos 731–2) are from the BC72 site, but these too must have been more common throughout the period considered than the two recognised items alone suggest. These and other unresolved points must await the retrieval of further assemblages for fresh perspectives.

The fabric of the medieval London house

JACKIE KEILY

The evidence for medieval houses, as for other secular and religious buildings in London, comes from five main sources: surviving standing buildings, archaeological excavation, contemporary documentary evidence, contemporaneous plans, and later illustrations such as panoramas, engravings, watercolours and early photographs. From these varied sources a picture of medieval London can be built up which is as detailed as that of any other European city (e.g., Keene & Harding 1987; Dyer 1989, 189; Schofield 1984, 1995, *idem* et al. 1990). To give a single London documentary example, a contract from 1405 for the construction of a building in Bucklersbury provides particularly detailed information (Salzman 1952, 478–82).

Excavation in the capital, particularly on the waterfront, is continually unearthing fragments of medieval timber buildings re-used in the riverside revetments which supported the dumps containing many of the artefacts reported below and elsewhere in this series; a number of these structural fragments are published (Milne 1991; Brigham 1992). The forms and histories of individual properties and houses at the waterfront are also being pre-

pared for publication (Schofield & Dyson in preparation).

In the light of these studies, a restricted objective has been chosen here: to outline some of the archaeologically perceptible textures of the medieval house, in brick, tile and stone, as a background and introduction to the material which follows.

Survival of medieval buildings above contemporary ground level is a rarity in London. Undercrofts (cellars) have proved an especially useful source of information and are briefly considered below. Despite the lack of survival and the problems of decay and destruction, the study of vernacular architecture in the medieval capital has been neither slow nor insignificant (a more detailed review of the construction of medieval London buildings is given in Schofield 1991).

Roof furniture

The form of roofing most commonly found during London excavations is ceramic tile. There is also a small quantity of stone, and very

Fig 6 A major English town ('Constantinople' seen through 14th-century English eyes) – the Luttrell Psalter (British Library)

Fig 7 A mill, a half-timbered vernacular building – redrawn from the Luttrell Psalter

occasionally fragments of wooden shingles are identified. No excavated evidence has been recognised for the thatch that must have been a common form of roofing, at least before the introduction of anti-fire measures following several serious conflagrations during the 12th and early 13th centuries, when a number of building regulations were introduced. By 1212 the use of reeds, straw and rushes for roofing was banned and the use of ceramic tiles, shingles (*sclats* in contemporary sources), or boards was enforced (Schofield 1984, 76). In 1245 it was decreed that houses in principal thoroughfares should be roofed with tiles or shingles (Bell 1938, 4; Schofield 1984, 76). There are few other documentary references to stone roofing in London (Schofield 1995, 97) but there are a great many to ceramic tiles from the 13th century onwards. Recent work on the building materials from a number of sites in the Cheapside area confirms that prior to the mid-12th century there was no stone or ceramic roofing, and that timber, thatch and straw must have been used (I Betts in Schofield et al. 1990, 221–5). Cheapside was one of the more wealthy parts of the city and may have been one of the first areas to use stone and ceramic roofing tiles.

It is likely that stone roofing was quite expensive due to the absence of locally available raw material. Slates, moreover, were supplied untrimmed and unpierced (Lewis 1987b, 5). Ceramic tiles, by contrast, which were supplied to London by local tile makers, could be made to a uniform size and were already provided with nail holes (Salzman 1952, 234). All the tile fabrics mentioned below are believed to be made from clays available in the immediate vicinity of the city.

The use of wooden shingles is well documented in England from at least the mid-12th to the 15th centuries (Lewis 1987b, 4). Due to a shortage of timber during the 14th century, there was a general rise in the price of wooden goods. A thousand shingles brought from Croydon to Westminster in 1329 cost 9 shillings and 4 pence, and by 1386 the price had risen to 13 shillings and 4 pence. Compared to this, ceramic tiles were much cheaper. In 1350, when the effects of the Black Death were also causing price rises in London, the city authorities fixed the maximum cost of a thousand ceramic roof tiles at 5 shillings. During the second half of the century the usual price of a thousand tiles varied between 4 shillings and 5 shillings and 6 pence (Salzman 1952, 228–9).

A *ceramic fabric number* is given to each building material and pottery vessel fabric identified from London excavations. A sample of each fabric is stored in the MoL reference collection and can be examined by prior arrangement.

Dimensions of complete roof tiles, bricks and floor tiles marked * are given in Table 3.

CERAMIC TILES

Ceramic roofing tiles begin to appear regularly on sites in London just before the mid-12th century. Deposits from *c.*1100–*c.*1150 (ceramic phase 5), particularly at the WAT78 site, have produced a large quantity of roofing tile. The earliest documentary evidence refers to the

---

Table 3: Dimensions of ceramic tiles and bricks (in mm)

Flanged tiles (ceramic fabric 2273)

Length	Breadth	Thickness	Nail hole diameter
357	255–97	32 (excluding flange)	10

Curved tiles (fabric 2273)

Length	Breadth	Thickness	Nail hole diameter
343	137 (bottom)	16–25	11
	177 (top)		
–	140 (bottom)	14–23	10
	180 (top)		
–	170 (bottom)	8–12	13
	190 (top)		

Shouldered peg tiles (fabric 2273)

Length	Breadth	Thickness	Nail hole diameter
313	201 (bottom)	16–22	9
	143 (top)		

Plain peg tiles

Fabric	Length	Breadth	Thickness
2271	260–69	140–70	9–18
2587	256	149	13

Slate tile (POM79 acc no 381)
225×150×10

Hearth tiles (SWA81, acc nos 99 and 194–5)

Fabric	Length	Breadth	Thickness
	250	210	22–34

Bricks

Fabric	Length	Breadth	Thickness
3031 (dated *c.*1350–*c.*1380)	–	–	47
3031 (dated *c.*1350–*c.*1450)	226	108	59
3033 (dated *c.*1380–*c.*1400)	250	120	58

Penn floor tiles

Length/breadth	Thickness
105–15	19–26
119–31	22–7
131–6	22–6

'Westminster' floor tiles

Length/breadth	Thickness
101–3	25–7
110–20	25–30
126–37	22–7

roofs of stone buildings being covered with 'thick tile' following a fire in 1135 (Bell 1938, 4), which coincides with the first appearance of medieval ceramic roof tile in large quantities in the archaeological record (I Betts in Schofield et al. 1990, 221). The earliest forms of 12th-century roof tiles are flanged and curved, shouldered peg and decorated ridge forms. All these are in the same distinctive sandy fabric (known as ceramic fabric 2273) and were undoubtedly manufactured at the same tilery. These were gradually replaced by plain peg and undecorated ridge tiles during the late 12th to 13th centuries. Such tiles occur in a variety of fabric types indicating more than one source of supply. A few peg tiles occur in fabric 2273, but the tilery making them no longer dominated the London market.

All roof tiles were made in sanded moulds. A considerable amount of hand finishing was needed on flanged and curved tiles, but peg tiles required little finishing. The early forms have a quite uniform coating of glaze on their upper surface, whereas later peg tiles are normally only splash-glazed (Pritchard 1982, 10).

Flanged, curved, and shouldered peg tiles are all relatively heavy, whereas plain peg tiles are thinner and lighter. Armitage et al. (1981) estimate the weight of each form of tile and approximately how many would be needed to cover a square metre of roof as follows:

	Flanged	Curved	Shouldered peg	Plain peg
Weight per tile	3.3kg	1.6kg	2.0kg	1.3kg
Tiles per sq metre	11	11	47	36

Peg tiles were, therefore, not only cheaper and easier to make, but were also a lighter form of roofing.

None of the kilns supplying roofing tile or brick to London has yet been located, but documentary evidence indicates that they lay very close to the outskirts of the city (the FIP92 site just to the north produced some probable wasters from the end of the medieval period/16th century – Ian Betts pers comm). In 1259 tiles were being supplied from a tiler in Smithfield, and in 1275–6 clay excavated from the moat for the Tower of London was sold to local tilers (Schofield 1984, 63). Between 1404 and 1421 brick and tile were supplied to London Bridge from works at Deptford (ibid. 126).

Flanged* and curved* tiles were used together in the same way as the Roman roofing tiles on which they must have been modelled – that is, the curved tile overlapped the flanges of the flat tile, and each row overlapped the one below it (Fig 8). Both forms tapered to facilitate this overlap. Medieval flanged and curved tiles are, however, much smaller than the majority of their Roman counterparts. It seems likely that this form of tiling would have been used on roofs of low pitch, similar to those still used in southern France and Italy. Most flanged and curved roofing tiles recovered are too fragmentary to provide original measurements. Only one complete flanged tile is known from London (Fig 8, MoL acc no A25232). At the SWA81 site, two sizes of curved tiles have been noted (Pritchard 1982). A nearly complete tile, 343mm long, which corresponds to the smaller size group, came from the MLK76 site (Betts 1985).

Shouldered peg tiles* are tapered mid-way down each side, forming a characteristic bat shape. These too date from the mid-12th century (ceramic phase 5 at WAT78) to the late 12th/early 13th century. A nearly complete example comes from the SWA81 site (Fig 9; ceramic corpus no 21534).

Small quantities of **plain peg tiles*** begin to be found in London from the late 12th century, and they appear in large quantities from the 13th century onwards (Fig 10). They occur in a number of different fabrics. Evidence from several sites points to their being made in a variety of sizes.

Ridge tiles are curved for setting along the crest of a roof. They differ from the curved tiles mentioned above in having parallel sides. Ridge tiles used in London are normally plain, but a few have been found with decoration along the crest (Fig 11). Three fragments of crested ridge tile were recovered from the WAT78 site, all in fabric 2273, and they probably date from the mid-12th to early 13th century. Ridge tiles continued to be used throughout the medieval period. They are found in the same fabrics as peg tiles and were presumably manufactured at the same tileries.

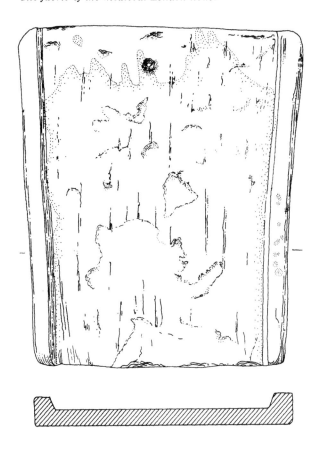

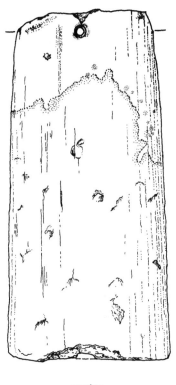

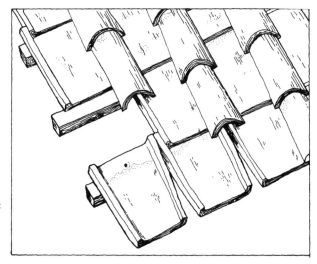

Fig 8   Flanged tile (MoL acc no A25232) and curved tile (ceramic corpus 2153; both 1:4) with reconstruction of roof form

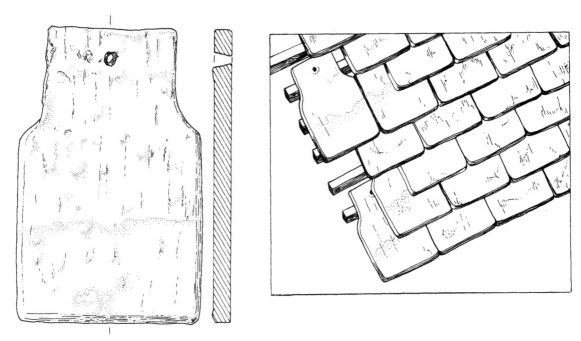

Fig 9   Shouldered peg tile (SWA81 site; 1:4) with reconstruction of roof form

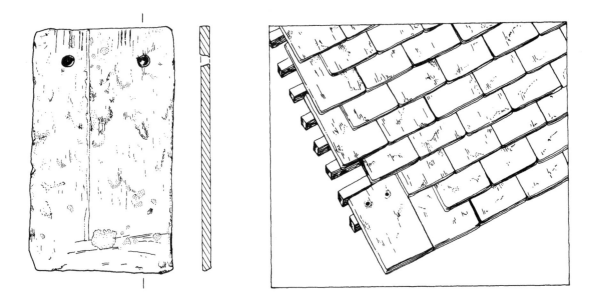

Fig 10   Plain peg tile (MIL72 site from context 149; 1:4) with reconstruction of roof form

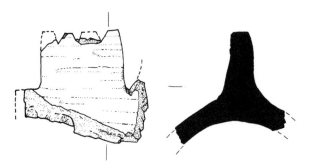

Fig 11 Decorated ridge tile from roof (WAT78 acc no 1349; 1:4)

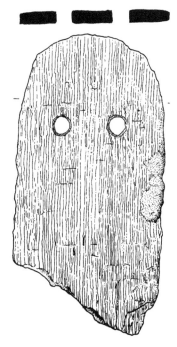

Fig 12 Shingle of oak (TEX88 acc no 903; 1:4)

WOODEN SHINGLES

Although wooden roof tiles have been found on excavations elsewhere, few examples of any date have been found in London and no definite late medieval examples have been identified from the extensive anaerobic deposits at the sites considered in this volume (see Fig 12 for an example from the TEX88 site, acc no 903, from a 12th-century context; and an incomplete oak shingle with a wooden peg, dated to the 10th century, came from the MLK76 site – Pritchard 1991, 243–4, 277, no 379). Wood had a ready use as fuel, and this may have been the fate of most shingles. They can, however, be difficult to identify from small fragments unless some diagnostic features such as the nail holes remain.

Oak shingles excavated at Winchester range in date from the 10th to the 13th century (D Keene in Biddle 1990, 320–7, nos 441–68); only two of these are dated to the period corresponding to that of this present study – no 467 from (?)the mid-12th to early 13th century and no 468 dating to the mid- to late 13th century; the majority are from the 11th/early 12th century.

STONE TILES

Many medieval London sites have produced fragments of slate that were almost certainly used for roofing. At the SWA81 site, 11 fragments were recovered, but no indication of the original size can be obtained. One fragment has part of a circular perforation (8mm in diameter). At the WAT78 site, roofing slate first occurs in the second half of the 12th century and small quantities were recovered in most later phases. The limited amount retrieved from excavations suggests that slate roofs were always unusual compared with tiled ones. The nearest sources for slate are in Devon and Cornwall (see Jope & Dunning 1954, 209 for the extensive trade by sea of Cornish slate). Seven of the pieces found at the SWA81 site, all provisionally dated between the late 12th and the 15th century, are dark blackish-grey phyllitic slate, comparable with specimens from the Devonian strata of south Devon and Cornwall. Another fragment from the same excavation is a dull-grey, fissile calcareous mudstone of uncertain source and provisionally dated to the mid-12th century or earlier. Identifications are by Professor R W Sanderson (Institute of Geological Sciences).

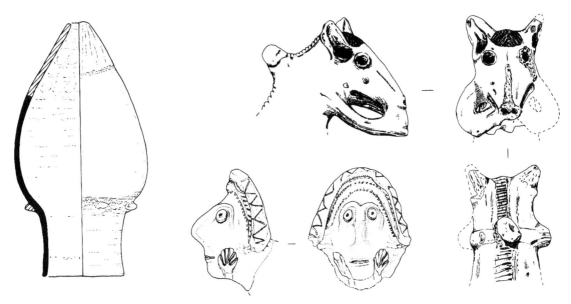

Fig 13   Roof finial (MoL acc no A13848) and decorative finial fragments (after Pearce et al. 1985, fig 79; 1:4)

METHODS OF ATTACHING
ROOF TILES

Flanged, plain and shouldered peg tiles were all hung on wooden laths by means of wooden pegs or iron nails driven into the holes near the top of the tile, and each row of tiles overlapped the one below (Salzman 1952, 233), as in Figs 8–10. It is possible that pegs and nails may have been used on the same roof. At Faccombe Netherton in Hampshire, wooden pegs were the main method of attachment, although some iron nails were also found still attached to tiles. The nails may sometimes have been used on parts of the roof where it was impossible to use pegs, such as over the rafters (Fairbrother et al. 1990, 214). At Winchester, right-angled iron nails (cf. Fig 36, top left) may have been used to secure tiles (I H Goodall in Biddle 1990, 234–5). Two tile fragments from the WAT78 site (contexts 3562 and 4079, dated to *c*.1200–*c*.1230 and *c*.1270–*c*.1350 respectively) still have iron nails in their holes (I Betts in Schofield et al. 1990, 223). Wooden pegs appear from documentary evidence usually to have been of oak (Salzman 1952, 234). A peg tile from the BWB83 site was found with its oak peg still *in situ* (acc no 2576; identified as

Quercus by I Tyers). Tiles were sometimes bedded on moss to stop wind and rain from penetrating (Salzman 1952, 233), and the lowest layers particularly were pointed with mortar, as surviving pads of this material show (Armitage et al. 1981, 362).

FINIALS AND LOUVERS

Roof finials are decorative, usually ceramic, fixtures having a roughly globular body on a tubular stem. They were placed at the gable ends of buildings. Several fragments of tile with human and animal heads almost certainly come from decorated finials (Fig 13, cf. Pearce et al. 1985, fig 79, nos 443–5). Dunning divides ceramic finials into two classes: those with a closed stem and those with an open one (1976, 52). Some of the latter may have functioned as ventilators (although none of the finials found in London has any signs of the sooting or smoke staining consistent with this). Only one complete London-type ware finial has been found (Fig 13). A large number of fragments were recovered from the TL74 site from dumps dated to *c*.1270, *c*.1340 and *c*.1360 (Pearce et al. 1985, 16, 47–51).

Louvers are large roof ventilators with a number of apertures. The majority of these items from excavations are in very small fragments. All are in known London pottery fabric types, most in a London-type ware fabric slightly different from that of ordinary roof tiles, and they were made by a separate group of artisans (ibid. 47–51). Several of the London-type ware louvers have closed stems. The most complete example came from the TL74 site and dates to *c.*1360 (Fig 14; also in Pearce et al. 1985, 50, 121, fig 80). Some fragments have sooting on the inside from smoke; however most found in London do not, and they were therefore probably used as ventilators. A louver fragment in Coarse Border-ware fabric was recovered at the TL74 site (Pearce & Vince 1988, 68) and a fragment in Kingston-type ware is wheelthrown, whereas most London-type ware louvers were handmade (MoL, no acc no; ibid. 52, fig 104).

GUTTERING

A single, small fragment of what is thought to be a ceramic roof gutter was found in a late medieval foundation at the SWA81 site. The fabric is London-type ware (Fig 15, ceramic corpus no 21913).

Regulations from 1477 mention 'gutter tiles' (Salzman 1952, 230–1). The scarcity of recognised tiles of this kind suggests that gutters were normally made of other materials, such as lead.

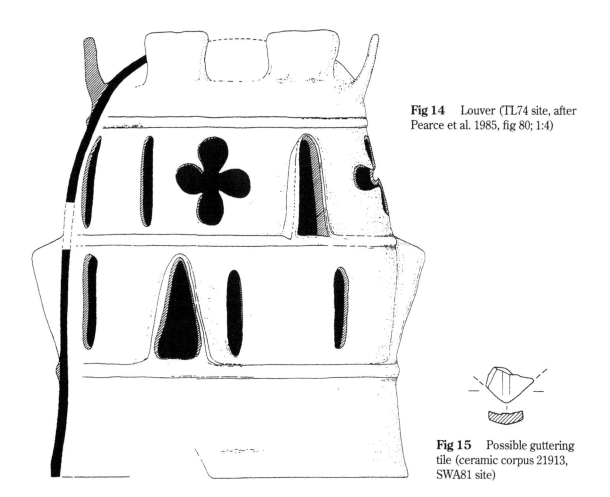

Fig 14   Louver (TL74 site, after Pearce et al. 1985, fig 80; 1:4)

Fig 15   Possible guttering tile (ceramic corpus 21913, SWA81 site)

CHIMNEYS

Ceramic chimney pots appear to have been a regional speciality in southern and south-eastern England from the 13th century onwards (Cherry 1991c, 196). Although no fragment of chimney pot has as yet been identified from excavations in London, there is documentary evidence for their use. Ralph de Crockerlane was selling clay chimney pots south of Fleet Street at Whitefriars in 1278 (Schofield 1984, 95). It is possible that small fragments of pottery chimneys may have previously been misclassified as vessels.

Building materials

During the early post-Conquest period most domestic buildings in London appear to have been built largely of timber and of daub. By the 13th century there was an increasing use of stone. In 1215 the wealthy Jews of of the capital already had stone houses (Kingsford 1971, i, 9). By the 14th century buildings were mainly of timber and stone, but many continued to be built of clay and timber (Salzman 1952, 187). There is documentary evidence for the use of bricks in London from the late 13th century onwards, but excavated evidence confirms that they were not widely used until the mid-15th century.

TIMBER

Wood, one of the key materials used in construction, is relatively poorly represented *in situ* in excavated medieval buildings in London (see Fig 16 for a wattle-and-timber rubbish pit).

Fig 16   Wattle-lined rubbish pit with collapsed timber frame, 13th century (MLK76 site)

Fig 17 Entrance to undercroft built of ragstone; with impression from removed steps down from street (a door at the threshhold was hinged at the left, shown by the worn floor to the right); late 13th/early 14th century (SWA81 site)

Brigham (1992) discusses timbers found re-used in wharves (and possibly originally from domestic structures) in a survey of the excavated evidence for vernacular buildings in medieval London.

STONE

The following kinds of stone are regularly excavated in the fabric of buildings from medieval London:

Kentish ragstone This very hard, grey or blue-grey, sandy limestone from around Maidstone in Kent is the most commonly used building stone from medieval London. Ragstone was readily shipped to the capital along the Medway and Thames rivers (Salzman 1952, 128). It was mainly used as roughly hewn blocks or rubble for external walls, wall facings (Fig 17) and foundations. It was also occasionally used as paving in kitchens, as in the Grocers' Hall in 1469–70 (Schofield 1995, 208–9, gazetteer no 149).

Chalk This hard to moderately soft white limestone occurs very widely in southern England. It was extensively used in internal walling and foundations throughout the period considered. Walls of the later medieval period increasingly included chalk on their internal faces, and from the 14th century onwards the walls of most undercrofts were built mainly of chalk (Fig 18). Its most familiar use in the ordinary dwelling house, particularly during the 14th and 15th centuries, would have been for lining rubbish pits (Fig 19) and walls. Chalk was sometimes used together with dark flint to create a strikingly decorative chequerwork pattern (Fig 20).

Reigate stone This greenish-grey sandstone (or malmstone) was often used for decorative mouldings since it is soft and easy to work

Fig 18 Chalk-built wall of undercroft (re-used in later brick structure; indication of spiral stair upwards survives at right, (?)14th century (LOV81 site)

Fig 19 Chalk-lined rubbish pit, late medieval (WAT78 site)

when freshly quarried but hardens on exposure to the air. London used the Surrey quarries in the neighbourhood of Reigate and Merstham (Salzman 1952, 129–30). Fragments of Reigate mouldings from the 15th-century garner at Leadenhall were found on the LCT84 site (Samuel 1989, 141). Reigate stone was also used in London Bridge from 1179 and in Westminster Abbey and Palace in the middle of the 13th century (Colvin 1971, *passim*).

Laminated sandstone A range of moderately hard, yellowish, reddish or brownish grey sandstones are frequently found on sites in the city. Some fragments may have been used for paving, while thinner pieces could be parts of roofing tiles.

Caen stone This moderately hard, dense, cream-coloured, fine-grained limestone was imported from Normandy in northern France and used in prestigious residences for moulded door jambs, window embrasures and loopholes (Salzman 1952, 137). There are documentary references to its use in London Bridge in 1429 and at Westminster Abbey in 1252 and 1290 (ibid. 135). Caen stone quoins were found at the site of Holy Trinity Priory (founded in 1108; HTP79 site, e.g., acc no 94) and in the 15th-

century garner at Leadenhall (Samuel 1989, 142). Part of a Caen stone spindle whorl is catalogued below as No 800).

Flint The extremely hard, very dark blue, grey or brown varieties of chert, found as nodules in the chalk, were widely used in London. A house in London is referred to in 1399 as *le Flynt Hall*, presumably from the material of its walls (Cal Wills 1890, 2, 346). During the 14th and 15th centuries some secular interiors in London (and also churches) had chequerwork walls, usually with chalk for the contrasting lighter colour (Fig 20; see on chalk above).

Brick The earliest bricks used in London appear to be of Flemish origin. Yellow Flemish brick is known to have been used in building construction at the Tower of London as early as 1278 (Salzman 1952, 140). Bricks in a yellow fabric (ceramic fabric 3031) found at the BIG82 site, and dating to *c.*1350–*c.*1380, may be Flemish imports (I Betts in Schofield et al. 1990). Small yellow bricks have also been found elsewhere in the London area from the second half of the 14th century (cf. Schofield 1995, 124). The earliest documentary reference to manufacture in the London area is from 1404, when bricks were being made in Deptford to the east for use in London Bridge (Salzman 1952, 142). Locally produced red brick (ceramic fabric 3033) first appears in walls on the BIG82 site dated *c.*1380–*c.*1400 (Betts 1991). According to archaeological and documentary evidence both yellow and locally produced red brick were not widely used in London until the mid-15th century.

Internal details

FLOORING MATERIALS

Local brickearth was the most common flooring material used in buildings in the early part of the period considered (Fig 21). These clay floors were normally around 30–40mm thick and were frequently replaced. Later, more sophisticated and expensive materials (mortar, timber, stone) were adopted; stone-slab floors,

Fig 20 Chequerwork walls of building in contrasting colours – black flint and white chalk – late medieval (NFW74 site)

Fig 21   Floor of brickearth – a standard material in medieval London homes – with part of timber wall (BIG82 site)

for example, have been found in a few excavated medieval houses in London (Schofield 1995, 111).

Floors were often strewn with rushes, which helped to protect the surface from wear and could be discarded once they became dirty (this practice may account, at least in part, for the large quantities of rushes often excavated in waterfront dumps and foreshore deposits). There is documentary evidence that rushes were used even on tiled floors, for example at the Bakers' Hall (Thrupp 1933, 164).

Ceramic floor tiles, both decorated and plain, eventually became quite widely used in medieval London. Floor tiles had been in use from the second quarter of the 13th century in a few institutional establishments, but they probably came into widespread domestic use only during the 14th century. There is no evidence from recent excavations for the precise location of medieval kilns in London, but one was found in

the 1860s below Farringdon Street in the city; floor tiles found around the structure included some that appear to have been wasters (Eames 1980, 26–8; none of this material can now be traced).

Most of the decorated floor tiles found in London belong to two groups, both in a number of fabrics. These fabrics represent variations in each of the main clay sources. **'Westminster' tiles** were first recognised in the Muniment Room at Westminster Abbey. They were originally dated to the late 13th/early 14th centuries, but the recent discovery of similar tiles in a pavement in Lambeth Palace Chapel places them slightly earlier, as documentary evidence suggests that the floor was laid in the second quarter of the 13th century (Degnan & Seeley 1988, 18). No kiln site has been found, but the concentration of these tiles in the London area suggests that they may have originated near the city. 'Westminster' tiles occur in three distinct size groups (Crowley 1992). **Penn tiles** were produced at Penn in Buckinghamshire (Eames 1980, 221–5) from c.1350s–c.1390s. They, too, were apparently made in three sizes (Betts 1991; Crowley 1992).

Decorated tile floors *in situ* have proved to be very unusual discoveries in secular buildings in London. The majority of tiles from recent excavations were found in dumped deposits and cannot be related to any particular structure. The SH74 site, however, included a medieval house with a damaged tile floor laid in mortar, in what was probably the main hall (Fig 22). Both plain and decorated tiles were used, all in 'Westminster' fabrics. Their haphazard location in the floor meant the tiles did not form a unified decorative scheme. This may have been because some of them had been re-laid to repair damaged areas; alternatively they could all have been bought as a job lot (Betts 1986, 16–17).

Plain, glazed floor tiles are also found in both Penn and 'Westminster' fabrics. During the 14th century Flemish plain glazed floor tiles began to be imported. It can be difficult to differentiate between Flemish and English tiles, but there are a few distinguishing features (I Betts in Schofield et al. 1990, 226). English tiles (which were fired only once) usually occur in different fabrics from those of the Flemish

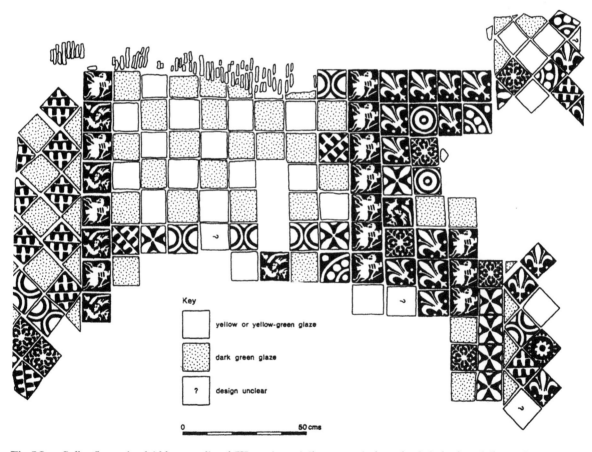

Fig 22 Cellar floor of re-laid late medieval 'Westminster' tiles; part of a hearth of pitched roof tile survives at top left

imports. Flemish tiles were fired twice and can normally be identified by holes in the corners of the upper surface. The holes were made by nails which held a template block in place on the clay while the tiler cut around it with a knife.

HEARTHS

In the early medieval period open hearths were situated in the middle of the room, with no surround or chimney, but during the 14th century they began to be placed against a side wall. In London this development can be seen, at least in part, as a response to pressure on living space (which also encouraged the subdivision of large halls into a number of smaller rooms; Schofield 1995, 115).

Hearths made with pitched ceramic roof tiles are common on medieval sites, and floor tiles are occasionally found used in the same way. At the SH74 site, a 14th-century open hearth bordered by the decorated floor tiles men-

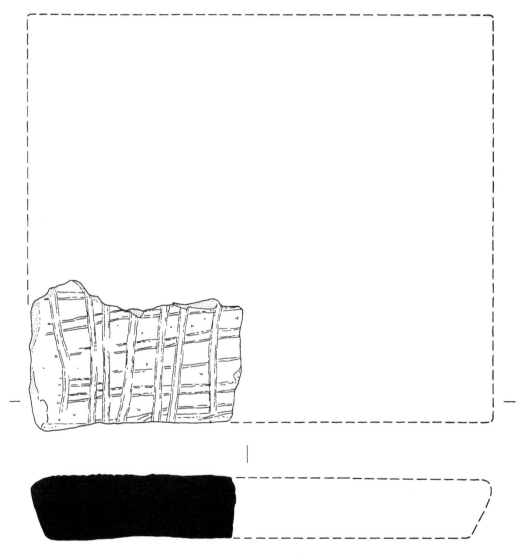

Fig 23   Hearth tile with keying (re-used as found), late 12th/early 13th century (SWA81 acc no 195)

tioned above probably lay in the main hall of a tenement (see Fig 22).

Fragments of what seem to be specially made **hearth tiles** came from the SWA81 site, all but one being re-used in industrial hearths (Fig 23). Three examples have scoring on one face, possibly to act as keying. No other sites in London have produced this form of tile, and they seem to have been a short-lived development that failed to catch on (cf. Pritchard 1982, 12).

INTERNAL WALL DECORATION

There is no evidence from excavations in London for medieval painted wall plaster in non-ecclesiastical buildings. Archaelogical evidence has, however, been found for whitewash painted directly onto internal stone walls at the COL81 site.

A contract from 1317 records the use of plaster of Paris to finish off walls and flues in the London hall of the Earl of Richmond (Salzman 1952, 425–6). The principal surviving wall paintings from prestigious buildings in London, investigated while they were still standing, are those discovered last century on the walls of the royal Palace of Westminster (Binski 1986).

Undercrofts

The remains of several undercrofts have been excavated in London, and a number dating from the late 13th century onwards continued in use into the 19th century, providing a very useful source of structural information. Vaulted undercrofts in London date back to the 12th century, with brick vaulting appearing in the mid-15th, though by this time they were becoming quite rare. The size and design of undercrofts varied, and a number of different styles are known (Schofield 1995, 74–81).

Access was commonly by steps down from the street, and there was often a second, external stair to the main part of the building above. At the north end of an undercroft found at the SWA81 site, imprints of removed steps that would have led up towards medieval Thames Street were uncovered (see Fig 17). A well-preserved undercroft at the LOV81 site survived to street level at one end and even higher at the other (see Fig 18). An internal stair at the rear survived with the door jamb of the entrance into the stair; a recess had been cut into the wall to house the door when it was fully opened (door recesses are known in other buildings of 13th-century date). Some undercrofts were lit by small windows high in the wall, close to street level, as in a well-preserved 15th-century example at the BIG82 site. An undercroft beneath the Saint Peter and Saint Paul tavern in Paternoster Row was provided with windows at street level and fireplaces in 1342 (Salzman 1952, 432–4).

Undercrofts in mercantile houses were used for storage, for displaying goods for sale and perhaps even for residence (one in Southampton dating to *c.*1320 has a hooded fireplace; Wood 1965, 81–9). Undercrofts in the Vintry and Dowgate wards of London were used in connection with the wine trade, and an undercroft by the church of St Mary le Bow served as a tavern in the early 14th century (Schofield 1995, 174, gazetteer no 51).

Fixtures and fittings

GEOFF EGAN

Fixtures Nos 1–90 are all of *iron*, except window cames Nos 49–53 and decorative mounts 89–90, which are of lead/tin. Fittings Nos 91–138 are movable items, of iron and copper alloy. Furnishings (Nos 139–241) are generally less robust than the items categorised here as fixtures; they comprise several kinds of copper-alloy and iron mounts, many of which are likely to be from chests or caskets. The fixtures listed here are in the main quite straightforward items that would probably have been taken for granted in the course of everyday living, unless repair became necessary. Many of them may be compared with the extensive range published from Winchester (I H Goodall et al. in Biddle 1990, 328–49).

Most of the categories represented exhibit little variation through, and in some cases for some time either side of, the period considered, and so it would be very difficult to assign a date to an unstratified example. Two apparent developments do emerge from these and other assemblages: stubs seem to be characteristic of some forms of fixed hook from the late 14th century onwards but not of those from earlier (see on Nos 54ff), and around the end of the 13th century (dated from evidence at Winchester); there seems to have been a move away from wide-looped strap hinges like No 43 to the kind familiar today that pivot on a rod, like Nos 33–42 (see on Nos 43–4). There is also a hint in the more neatly finished appearance of No 44 compared with No 43 of what seems to have been a general enhancement through the period considered of the skill brought to bear by the blacksmiths who manufactured these standard items, resulting by the late Middle Ages in more accomplished products that looked to be of better quality.

Some of the iron fixtures included below could equally well have come from a gate, well cover, stable, or cart, as from a house or other domestic building. Nails and simple clamps ('dogs' etc.) have been omitted as their poten-

tial for almost universal usage makes it difficult to discuss the London riverside finds from a primarily domestic standpoint (a few of the catalogued hinges etc. retain nails – see for example Nos 33ff, 43 and also No 789).

Salzman discusses contemporary documentary references to structural iron work (1952, 286–319), though only a few of the terms used can be identified certainly with excavated objects listed below. He notes the use of pitch to protect structural ironwork from rust in the late 14th century, as well as tinning (ibid.

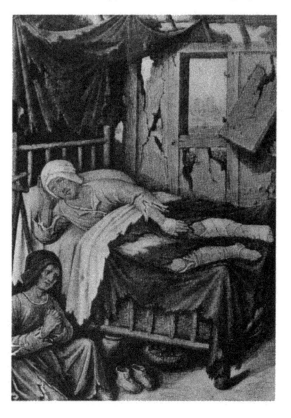

Fig 24   Fallen on bad times: a timber-framed building that has seen better days, *c*.1500 (from Salzman 1926)

294–5). Spain, in addition to Gloucestershire and the Sussex Weald, seems to have been a major source for the iron used in England for fixtures etc. from at least the 13th century (*ibid.* 286–7).

Fig 25 A genteel interior – *Saint Barbara* by Robert Campin, early 15th century (Prado Museum, Madrid)

Hinges

The most substantial of these, together with pintles Nos 5–30 and probably No 42, would have been suitable for major openings in buildings, like doors.

Salzman discusses contemporary documentary sources that mention hinges (1952, 295–9) and cites a reference from 1365 to tin 'for whitening hinges'. No coating has been noted on the following hinge pintles, but it has survived on several of the strap hinges.

PINTLES

These hinge pivots – on which a swivelling door, window, hatch etc. hung (and from which they might in appropriate circumstances readily have been lifted off) – are far more common among excavated items than the rather less substantial, looped part of the hinge (No 43 could perhaps be one of the corresponding fittings). A similar pattern is evident among the finds from Winchester, which include over 100 pintles (I H Goodall in Biddle 1990, 330, 338–43, nos 557–651). Pintles like Nos 5–30 have close parallels in the Roman period and also in the post-medieval period (Manning 1985, 127, pl 59, no R12 – this one has an additional flange; see Stone 1974, 223–5, fig 135 J–N for 18th-century examples). Salzman gives the contemporary medieval name as 'hook' or 'crook', or 'stone hinge' when set in masonry (1952, 295–6; some are recorded as being set in lead for both windows and doors at Corfe in Dorset in 1285). Goodall suggests that those for setting in masonry have spikes which are deeper than they are wide in cross-section (see Nos 1–4). Two pintles apparently like Nos 5–30 are shown set in a wooden frame for a window shutter in Fig 24. Nos 26 and 27 retain mortar or stone on lead settings, and No 28 retains mortar on the spike, showing these ones were definitely set in masonry. Several incomplete examples have been omitted. See also Nos 71–3.

Listing is in order of length of spike, within ceramic phases.

Round-section pivots with flat spikes for attachment

1 SH74 Acc No 278 (Context 536) Ceramic Phase 6
Fig 26
Spike l 54mm; pivot l 73mm.
2 SWA81 3510 (2211) 6
Spike l 55mm; pivot l 26mm.

3 SH74 267 (484) 7 Fig 26
Spike l 70mm; pivot l 56mm.
4 SWA81 2251 (2266) 7 Fig 26
Spike l 83mm; pivot l 31mm+ is broken off.

Fig 26   Hinge pintles (1:1); dimensions for pintles
lower right

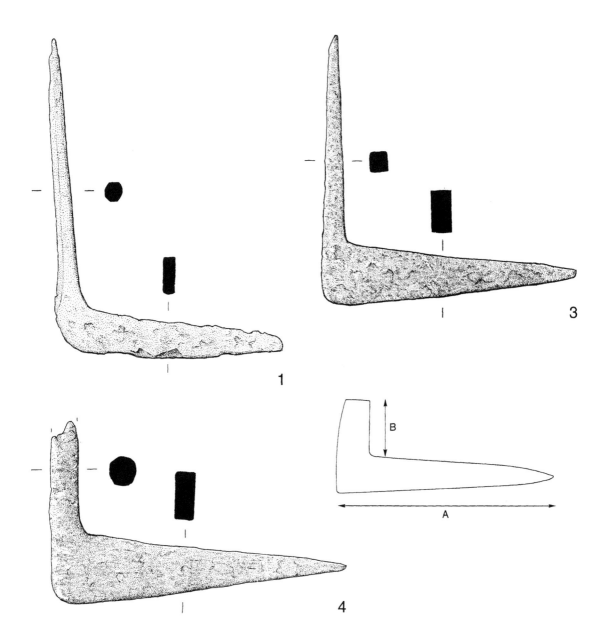

Round-section pivots with rectangular or square-section spikes for attachment

5 BIG82 Acc No 3735 (Context 5020) Ceramic Phase 6
Spike l 73mm, pivot l 17mm.
6 BIG82 3720 (4125) 7
Spike l 75mm; pivot l 34mm.
7 SH74 165 (394) 7
Spike l 103mm; pivot l 35mm.
8 SWA81 2536 (2267) 7
Spike broken off; pivot broken off, l 44mm.
9 BIG82 3734 (2913) 8
Spike l 79mm; pivot l 20mm.

Fig 27   Hinge pintles (1:1)

10 SWA81 1129 (2144) 9 Fig 27
Spike l 89mm; pivot l 20mm is at acute angle; worn in angle (arrowed in Fig).
11 BWB83 3293 (367) 9
Corroded; spike l 55mm+; pivot l 21mm.
12 CUS73 1205 (I,12) 9
Spike l 60mm; pivot l 22mm.
13 SWA81 1957 (2061) 9
Spike l 63mm; pivot l 22mm.
14 CUS73 86 (I,12) 9
Spike l 75mm; pivot l 23mm.
15 BWB83 3064 (158) 9
Spike incomplete, l 73mm+; pivot l 27mm.
16 BWB83 4393 (108) 10
Spike l 90mm; pivot l 21mm.
17 BWB83 2809 (147) 11
Spike l 62mm; pivot l 19mm is bent over.

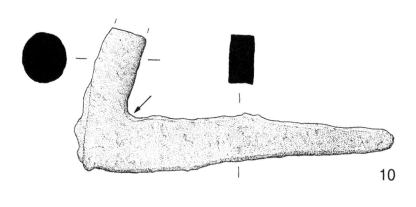

10

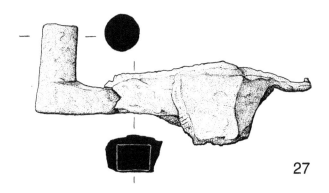

27

18 BWB83 4352 (110) 11
Spike broken off; pivot l 20mm.

19 CUS73 185 (IV,14) 11
Spike l 54mm; pivot l 20mm.

20 BWB83 4242 (307) 11
Spike l 67mm; pivot l 26mm.

21 BWB83 2861 (292) 11
Spike broken off; pivot l 27mm.

22 SWA81 3887 (2018) 9
Spike l 107mm; pivot l 35mm.

23 BWB83 3080 (283) 11
Spike l 90mm; pivot l 28mm.

24 BWB83 164 (153) 11
Spike broken off; pivot l 29mm.

25 BWB83 2998 (110) 11
Spike l 74mm; pivot l 30mm.

26 BWB83 3354 (359) 11
Spike embedded in lead setting; pivot l *c.*30mm; traces of mortar on the setting.

27 BC72 4443 (150) 11 Fig 27
Spike embedded in lead setting pivot l 48mm; the imprint of chisel marks and traces of Kentish rag-stone (identification by Ian Betts) on the setting show this pintle was fixed in masonry.

28 TL74 1271 (1456) 12
Spike l 105mm; pivot l 27mm; mortar attached to spike.

29 TL74 1129 (275) 12
Spike l 66mm; pivot l 30mm.

30 TL74 77 (225) 12
Spike l 100mm; pivot l 42mm.

Pintles with strapping attached

31 BC72 Acc No 2610 (Context 79) Ceramic Phase 11 Fig 28
Pivot l 160mm, attached to U-shaped fold of incomplete strapping, w 31mm, l of surviving arm 225mm, the other broken off; three holes in surviving arm, two of which have nails surviving.

Probably from a wooden window shutter or a chest lid etc. rather than a door. Compare the earlier No 43.

32 BWB83 4837 (326) 12 Fig 28
Square-section pivot l 150mm, attached to a single piece of strapping w 35mm, l 120mm with three holes (one retaining part of a nail).

PLAIN, ROD-PIVOTED STRAP HINGES

All are of the form 1 // 2 loops and have rectangular straps, unless otherwise stated. The strap with the single loop is described before that with two where both straps survive. This form may replace those with wide, U-shaped loops like No 43.

33 TL74 Acc No 2524 (Context 1740) Ceramic Phase 10
Corroded; strap with single loop; l 85mm (possibly broken off); w 35mm; four holes, two with surviving nails l 17mm.

34 BWB83 No 577 (111) 11
Incomplete; l 18mm+; w 13mm; broken off at hole // l 52mm; w 13mm; two holes.

35 BWB83 3175 (286) 11
Distorted; l 55mm+; w 14mm; two holes // l 18mm; broken off at hole; tin coating.

36 BWB83 3807 (137) 11
Slightly tapering strap with two loops around pivot rod; l 62mm; max w 25mm; broken off at end; two off-central holes.

37 BWB83 3436 (293) 11
Strap with two loops; l 77mm, w 23mm, three holes, two of which retain bent nails; tin coating.

38 BC72 4222 (150) 11
Incomplete and corroded; l 97mm+; w 42mm, broken off at other end from pivot that consists of entire width bent over; corroded areas may conceal one or more original nail holes; tin coating.

39 BC72 4290 (150) 11 Fig 29
Expanding strap with single loop; l 92mm; max w 44mm; three holes; tin coating.

40 TL74 2143 (2731) 12 Fig 29
Incomplete and very corroded; l 47mm+; w 13mm; two holes with nails up to 16mm // l 33mm+; w 15mm+; hole survives; tin coating.

41 BWB83 3113 (275) 12 Fig 29
Incomplete; l 47mm+; w 22m; two nail holes // l 46+mm; w 21mm; retains nail l 30mm in surviving hole; tin coating.

(See also iron Furnishing mounts Nos 164, etc., some of which are hinged)

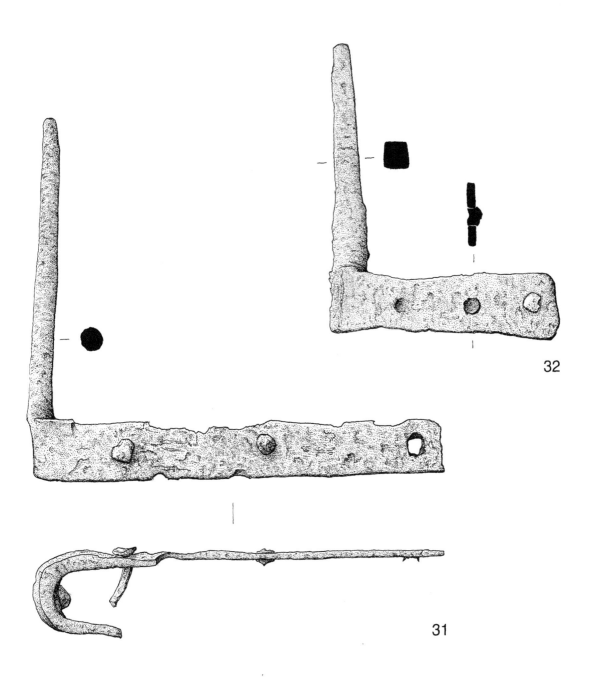

Fig 28 Hinge pintles with strapping (1:2)

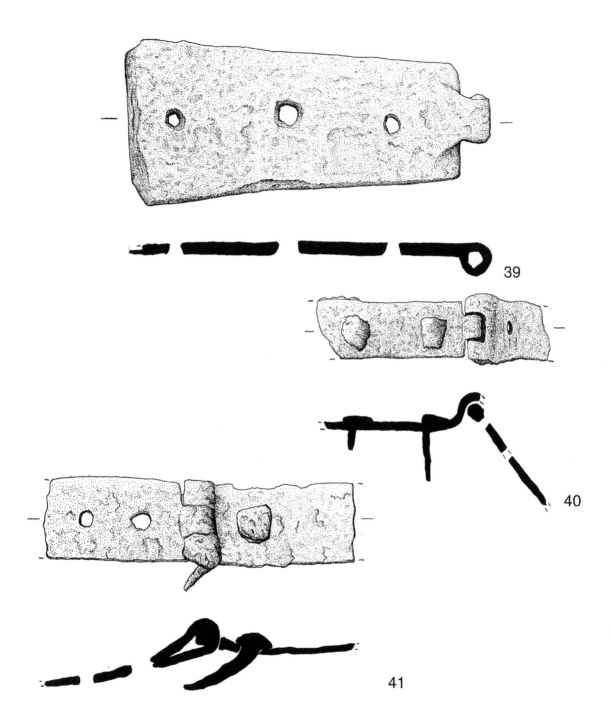

Fig 29   Rod-pivoted hinges (1:1)

Fig 30   Strap, probably from a hinge (1:2)

42

PROBABLE HINGE STRAP

42 BWB83 Acc No 350 (Context 147) Ceramic Phase 11 Fig 30
Incomplete; tapers somewhat irregularly towards circular terminal with point; 1 207+; w 31mm; max th 5mm; three nail holes.

This robust mount would have been strong enough to hold a substantial door etc.

Compare I H Goodall in Biddle 1990, 344–5, no 653, for an earlier, also fragmentary, example found with what may be its loop.

U-LOOPED HINGES OR OTHER PIVOTING FITTINGS

(For use with a ringed attachment, or possibly with a pintle)

The two following items are listed as fixtures/ fittings, though No 43 in particular could equally be from a chest (see Furnishing mounts Nos 212–26). U-looped pivots appear, from recent finds at the VRY89 site and at Winchester (I H Goodall in Biddle 1990, 977–9, nos 3495–505, fig 304), to be standard for lock hasps on casket lids in the 12th century and earlier (cf. Fig 57, top), after which the loops are bent right round nearly in a circle and pivot on rods (as in Nos 33–42; see also Nos 31–2). Similar fittings attributed to the Roman period have been published as parts of drop hinges (Manning 1985, 126–7, pl 58, nos R8–9).

43 SH74 Acc No 329 (Context 553) Ceramic Phase 6 Fig 31

L 150mm; crudely made; bifurcated, recurved terminal; narrowed at U-shaped bend; pointed terminal on other side; holes for attachment (one on each side); retains nail with end bent over; for attachment to wood c.20mm thick.

44 TL74 2653 (368) 12 Fig 31
Incomplete bar with terminal loop (broken off at other end) and four holes for attachment, surviving l 110mm; strap w 12mm; tin coating; fragment of a more robust loop broken off from attached item.

PIVOTING STAPLES

Pairs of joined, looped staples were set into wooden objects, then bent outwards at right angles and back inwards to be hammered back into the wood. Pairs were presumably to join two boards, one fixed, and the other the lid of a simple box, a hinged shutter or shelf, etc. (cf. Stone 1974, 193, 195, fig 112B for a pair from the 18th century; single examples from the same site and period with rod-like hooks attached are regarded as being for doors, gates or shutters – 235, 240, fig 145). For single examples, spanning the whole period considered in this present volume, cf. I H Goodall in Biddle (1990, 334–5, nos 523–6, fig 78); one with an iron ring (?cf. No 82 below) is interpreted as a furniture handle (ibid. 978–9, no 3517, fig 304). The form is also known from the Roman period (e.g., Crummy 1983, 119–20, nos 4059–69; Manning 1985, 130, pl 61, nos R34–8 implies that they tended to be used with iron rings at that time, again perhaps like No 82 below). Single, copper-alloy staples of this kind

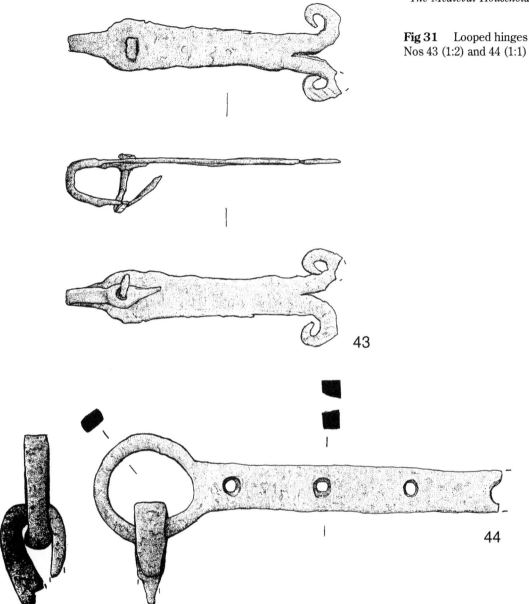

Fig 31   Looped hinges
Nos 43 (1:2) and 44 (1:1)

43

44

hold each end of the handle on a casket lid found at Winchester (see Fig 46).

45 BC72 Acc No 4476 (Context 150) Ceramic Phase 11 Fig 32
Pair of staples, one retains enough of the original shape to suggest that it was for an object *c*.25mm thick.

46 BWB83 4370 (117) 11
Pair of staples, for objects *c*.30mm thick.

47 BWB83 456 (282) 11
Pair of staples, both for objects *c*.30mm thick.

48 BWB83 2965 (136) 11 Fig 32
Single staple with both ends bent right back.

(This could not have been used in the present configuration in the same way as the preceding examples.)

Fig 32 Pivoting, looped
staples (1:1)

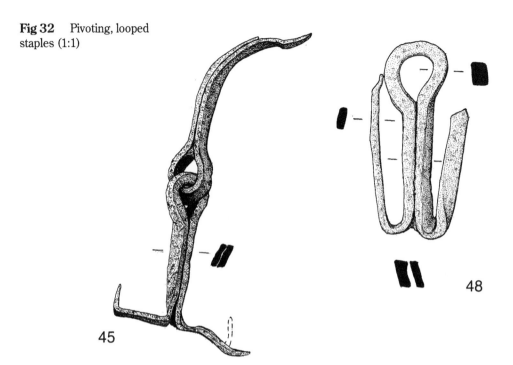

45

48

Lead window cames

Cast, relatively thick, cames with lozenge-section flanges (unless trimmed or otherwise adapted) are characteristic of the medieval period (see B Knight in Hare 1985, 154–5, fig 48, 2, and *idem* in James & Robinson 1988, 224–5, fig 84). A large number of lengths of cames have been excavated on several London sites. In this category (as in many others) the waterfront sites produce the most extensive assemblages. While it is not possible to identify the specific buildings from which these cames were discarded, it is highly likely that dwellings of the wealthy as well as ecclesiastical buildings are represented in this way.

The apparent absence of domestic window lead from excavated deposits from the period before ceramic phase 9 (*c*.1270–*c*.1350) from the recent excavations in the City (church sites have not been considered here) seems to reinforce the view expressed by Harden (1961, 56–7) that window glass first began to be used in palaces and better-class houses in the 13th century, becoming relatively common by the end of the medieval period (cf. Salzman 1952,

173ff). Window glass is known, however, from apparently secular Saxo-Norman contexts in London (Pritchard 1991, 173–5, 260, nos 192–7; leads are also known from ecclesiastical buildings elsewhere from the Saxon period onwards, e.g., Cramp 1970, 329–30, and Harden 1961, 52–4 – though those from Old Windsor illustrated in his fig 3.5 are apparently reeded and therefore of much later date).

A glazier living in Aldgate in the 14th century may have had a workshop there, though he worked at Westminster and Windsor Castle for the king from 1349 to at least 1383. A private house in Paternoster Row is known to have had 87 windows in 1389/90 (Veale 1969, 148–9).

A stone mould for casting cames was recovered among medieval objects, mainly of 14th-century date, from spoil removed from the Billingsgate site (MoL acc no 84.199/7; cf. Deneux 1929, who describes part of another stone mould dated to the 13th century found at Rheims in France). Milling through a hand-turned vice, which gave the reeding along the web (heart), a characteristic of virtually all later lighter window leads seems, on present evidence, to have become widespread in the

16th century (Egan et al. 1986), though there is now a growing number of plain, light-weight leads from the late medieval period which may be the earliest milled products (e.g., Knight in Hare 1985, 156, where a plain, light-weight lead is attributed to the early 15th century – see also on the following, much earlier, item).

49 SWA81 Acc No 1873 (Context 2142) Ceramic Phase 9 Fig 33
Three fragments of apparently unused cames 9×4mm (longest l 235mm); found folded and bent together.

The markedly sub-lozenge-shaped profile of the two flanges, evident in a number of single lengths of excavated medieval window leads (but not in articulated or soldered, ie., demonstrably used pieces) would probably have presented considerable difficulty when it came to securing glass in place without some kind of cement or putty – a watertight seal would otherwise appear particularly difficult to achieve for this shape without such provision. All the medieval leads with glass still attached that have been seen by the writer have a much more readily malleable H-shaped profile, and this suggests that adaptation by a finishing process (perhaps trimming as suggested by Knight, but possibly using some kind of primitive mill) was regularly carried out, at least by the end of the 13th century.

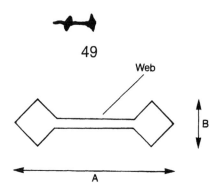

Fig 33   Window-came section (1:1) and dimensions specified as measured

Four of the largest fragments of multiple cames excavated in London, which give some indication of the form of the lights of which they are parts, are illustrated in Figs 34, 35. These items were each found bent into a relatively small compass, as if in preparation for the melting pot, which the absence of glass (apart from one quarry in No 50) tends to confirm. Approximate dimensions of the section of the came are given in the order A×B in brackets (see Fig 33), following the overall dimensions for the surviving piece.

50 SWA81 Acc No 2244 (Context 2030) Ceramic Phase 9 Fig 34
*c.*150×*c.*150mm   (7×3.5mm);   square,   retaining quarter circle of blue; grozed glass in one corner.
51 BWB83 5457 (204) 11 Fig 34
Main piece *c.*430×355mm (6×4mm); the prominent curve, emphasised by doubling the cames at this point, could perhaps be from a human figure, or from the edge of a shield of arms (?held by supporters) etc.; the protruding cames to the sides preclude its having been simply the edge of a round-arched light (see R Marks in Alexander & Binski 1987, 407, nos 477–8 for medieval window leading which provides a clear indication from its outlines of the broad nature of the subject matter painted on the glass).
52 BWB83 4522 (287) 11 Fig 35
*c.*150×*c.*100mm (6×4mm).
53 TL74 2200 (368) 12 Fig 35
Main piece *c.*160×*c.*135mm (4×5mm).
    Another fragment was found in the same deposit (acc no 2199).

Fixed hooks of iron

Stubs, which would have facilitated hammering during fixture, appear from the items catalogued below to be characteristic of hooks from the late 14th century onwards – see Nos 54, 56, 58 for earlier examples lacking stubs. (Although the change to stubs seems to be regarded as taking place in the 13th century at Winchester, a 13th-century hook excavated there, and listed among items similar to the form that is seen in London later, is incomplete and may not necessarily belong with them – I H Goodall in Biddle 1990, 328, 333, no 492.) Like other fixtures, some hooks may have remained in place for generations before the building concerned was demolished.

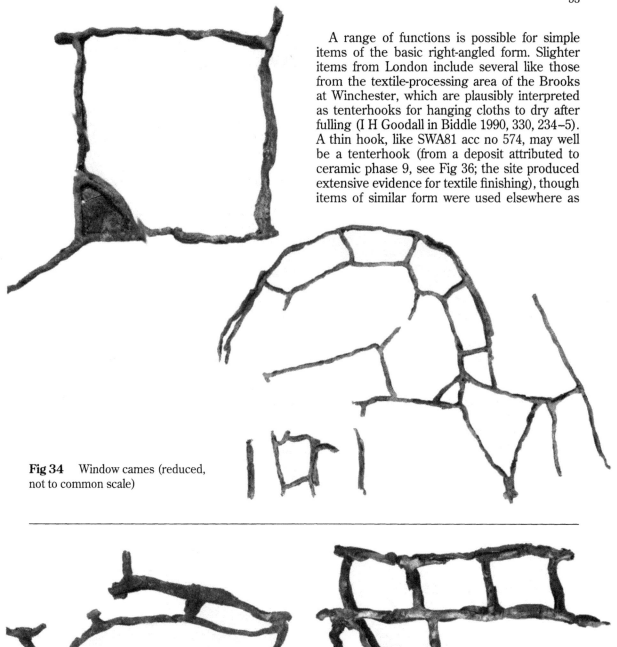

A range of functions is possible for simple items of the basic right-angled form. Slighter items from London include several like those from the textile-processing area of the Brooks at Winchester, which are plausibly interpreted as tenterhooks for hanging cloths to dry after fulling (I H Goodall in Biddle 1990, 330, 234–5). A thin hook, like SWA81 acc no 574, may well be a tenterhook (from a deposit attributed to ceramic phase 9, see Fig 36; the site produced extensive evidence for textile finishing), though items of similar form were used elsewhere as

Fig 34 Window cames (reduced, not to common scale)

52

Fig 35 Window cames (reduced)

53

nails for roof tiles (ibid., 234–5). Finds from sites where textile finishing appears unlikely may help in future to define alternative functions. The unspecific context of many of the London finds is not helpful in this respect. Longer examples of such objects with slender spikes in one dimension might be a simple form of pricket candleholder (Michaelis 1978, 25; cf. Nos 385–90 below, which are defined by their scrolls) and others might perhaps be hinge pintles (usually defined by a round-section pivot, though see No 32).

RECTANGULAR OR SQUARE SECTIONS IN BOTH PARTS, SLENDER ARMS

54 CUS73 Acc No 90 (Context I,12) Ceramic Phase 9
Spike l 57mm+; arm l 55mm; (no stub).

55 SWA81 3407 (2082) 12 Fig 36
Arms and spike at slightly less than a right angle to each other; spike l 54mm has possible traces of wood adhering; with stub; arm l 47mm.

HOOKS WITH CURVED ARMS

There is a stub unless otherwise stated; those lacking this feature are from before (?)c.1380 (cf. a somewhat similar chronological pattern at Winchester – I H Goodall in Biddle 1990, 331–3). The curve means that these could have been fixed with the arms set vertically or horizontally.

56 SWA81 Acc No 568 (Context 2055) Ceramic Phase 9 Fig 36
Spike l 75mm; l of arm 27mm; (no stub).

57 TL74 244 (99) 10 Fig 36
Spike l 64mm; l of arm 24mm.

58 TL74 920 (429) 10–11
Spike l 94mm; l of arm 46mm; (no stub).

59 TL74 803 (414) 11
Spike l 60mm, possibly incomplete; l of arm 33mm.

60 BWB83 3051 (142) 11
Distorted; spike l c.68mm; l of arm c.55mm.

61 BWB83 2786 (318) 11 Fig 36
Spike l 82mm; l of arm 24mm.

62 BC72 4112 (88) 11
Spike l 112mm; l of arm 30mm.

63 TL74 1222 (368) 12
Spike l 102mm; arm incomplete.

ROBUST HOOKS WITH DEEP, ANGLED ARMS

Two similar items (presumably of iron, as their colour implies, rather than of wood) are shown set high in a ceiling beam in an early 15th-century Flemish painting (Fig 25), and one is fixed in the central frame of a window in the *Arnolfini Marriage* by Van Eyck, as if for holding a bar when the window was shut. Although medieval items of this form have been published as latch rests (see, e.g., I H Goodall in Biddle 1990, 347–8, fig 86, no 694 for a 13th/14th-century example), such an identification is made uncertain by the absence of convincing items of associated ironwork in similar numbers (i.e., latch raisers with their handles, latch bolts or slotted latch plates – though Goodall (336, no 536) and similar items could perhaps account for the last) from most excavated medieval assemblages that include hooks of this kind. A similar lack is evident among the present finds groups from London. There may have been some alternative system for lifting a latch; wooden latches and other parts are a possibility, which Salzman appears to favour in discussing some medieval documentary references (1952, 299–300). Detailed contemporary illustrations of the working parts of latches seem to be lacking (Fig 7 shows a door with a ring handle of the form often associated today with lifting latches, though this one could represent a simple handle). Salzman, however, takes 'six rings with latches and catches' recorded in 1363 at Hadleigh Castle, and 'six pairs of latches and hagondays' (*haggadays* – the word is still used in Northern dialect for a thumb latch) which cost three shillings at Westminster in 1353 to be latches of the liftable kind (1952, 299–300). Stone believes 18th-century parallels for the items listed below to be for door latches (1974, 235, 242, fig 147F, etc.), which is probably correct for ones that late in date. The precise function of the following excavated items remains unresolved.

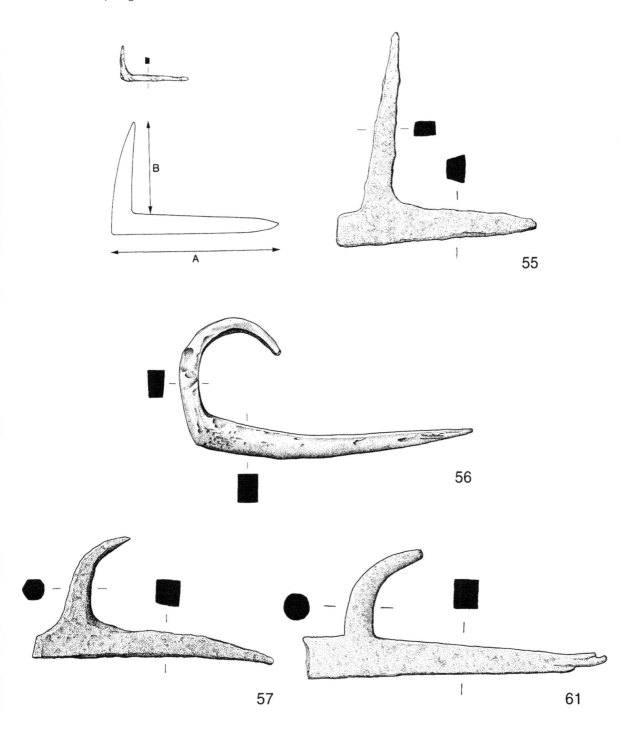

Fig 36 Fixed hooks and dimensions for hooks; top left is unnumbered (?)tenterhook or nail (SWA81 acc no 574 – not in catalogue) (all 1:1)

Fig 37   Fixed hooks (1:1) and
dimensions for hooks

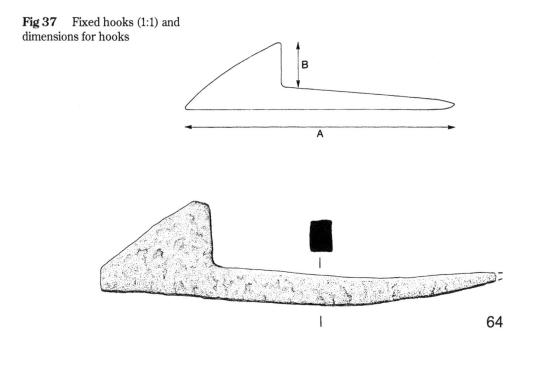

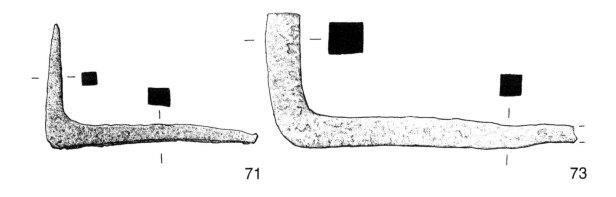

64 SWA81 Acc No 1936 (Context 2134) Ceramic
Phase 9 Fig 37
Spike l 108mm; h of hook 12mm.

65 BWB83 3414 (308) 11
Incomplete spike l 69mm+; h of hook 14mm.

66 BWB83 5250 (334) 11
Incomplete; surviving l of spike 74mm; h of flat-
section hook 15mm.

67 BWB83 4742 (256) 11
Incomplete; distorted spike l 94mm+; h of hook
20mm.

68 BWB83 5183 (308) 11
Distorted; spike l 108mm; h of hook 16mm.

69 BWB83 551 (310) 12
Spike l 92mm; h of hook 14mm.

70 BWB83 3938 (310) 12
Distorted spike l *c.*118mm; h of hook 18mm.

RIGHT-ANGLED HOOKS

(Rectangular or square sections in both parts)

These could perhaps be pintles; cf. No 32.

71 BWB83 Acc No 3173 (Context 286) Ceramic
Phase 11 Fig 37
Spike l 59mm; arm l 34mm.
72 BWB83 3449 (298) 11
Spike l 62mm; arm l 34mm.
73 BWB83 4849 (317) 11 Fig 37
Spike l 82mm; arm l 25mm.
Of comparable robustness to pintles (possibly an
unfinished example).

SWIVELLING HOOK

74 BWB83 Acc No 4371 (Context 117) Ceramic
Phase 11 Fig 38
Nearly right-angled hook, l 70mm; l of arm with
recurved point 52mm; loop at other end; presumably
to hold open a window, hinged shutter or chest lid
etc.

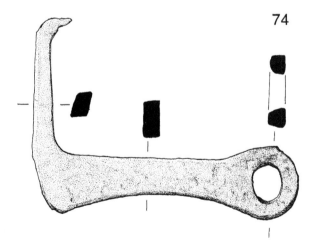

74

Fig 38   Swivelling hook (1:1)

LOOP HASPS

Loops bent inwards so that the opposite sides
almost touch at the centre, and bent in the
other plane nearly to a right angle.

These were probably used in connection with
padlocks or simple bolts to secure doors, shutters, gates etc. A hasp of a similar kind with a
bent-back, looped end tab survives on a chest
of about 1500 in the Victoria and Albert
Museum (Tracy 1988, 183–4, pl 112, no 312)
and another excavated in Hull was found associated with two U-shaped iron staples by which
it is thought to have been attached and, with
the help of a padlock, secured (I H Goodall in
Armstrong & Ayers 1987, 199–200, fig 113, no
121).

75 BIG82 Acc No 4992 (Context 5992) Ceramic
Phase 6 Fig 39
L 76mm.
76 SWA81 2206 (2065) 9
L 94mm; bent-back, looped tab at end.
77 SWA81 3889 (2018) 9
L 116mm; bent-back, looped tab at end.
78 BWB83 2966 (146) 11 Fig 39
L 120mm; bent-back, looped tab at end.

CHAINS OF IRON

For securing doors, windows etc. and for suspending cooking vessels, as well as for a range
of other possible purposes (see No 499 for an
item similar to No 80 but branching into two,
which probably indicates the specific function
of holding a cooking vessel over a fire). There
can be confusion between chains for library
books (see No 79), for horses' harnesses, and
for tethering dogs and other animals (see No
970), etc.

79 SWA81 Acc No 569 (Context 2055) Ceramic
Phase 9 Fig 40
Three D-section oval links with the opposite sides
bent inwards, each l *c.*50–*c.*55mm; riveted loop at
one end; hook with flattened loop at the other; total
l 193mm; tin coating; possibly for a book cover from
a chained library (see on probable book mounts Nos
926–8), though other uses are possible.

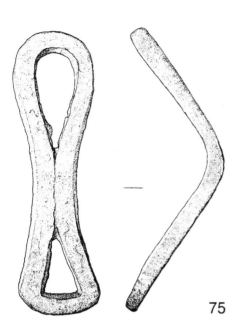

75

Fig 39   Loop hasps (1:1)

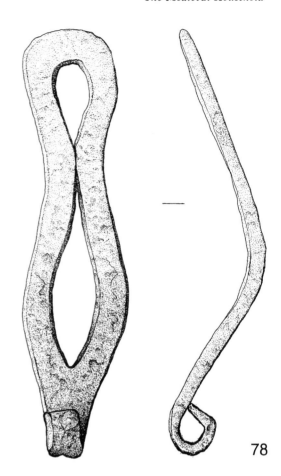

78

80 BC72 4176 (250) 10 Fig 40
Three D-section oval links with the opposite sides
bent inwards, each l 57mm (one link distorted – this
is omitted from the Fig); oval loop, w 30mm, with
transverse hole for swivelling; total l 172mm.

81 BC72 1756 (55) 11 Fig 40
Seven links as for preceding item but flatter in
section, each l *c*.60mm and with unjoined collar bent
around waisted centre; total l 360mm.

PENDENT IRON RING

This would have been suitable for suspending
a hook or acting as a tie, e.g., for pets' leads,
etc. See discussion of staples Nos 45–8 for
possible parallels from the Roman period.

82 BWB83 Acc No 4313 (Context 157) Ceramic
Phase 11 Fig 41
D 32mm; on (?) split pin l 45mm.
   Also published in Egan & Pritchard (1991, 60, 62,
fig 38, no 114).

OTHER HOOKS

Fittings, all of iron
A variety of functions are possible, including
securing doors, windows and hatches shut or
open, holding items in storage and suspending
cooking vessels over the fire.
   (See also possible drape rings with hooks
Nos 131–8.)

Bent bars with a loop at the top

(These are a relatively weak form.)

83 SH74 Acc No 231 (Context 484) Ceramic Phase
7 Fig 41
L 79mm.

84 TL74 713 (415) 11 Fig 41
L 144mm.

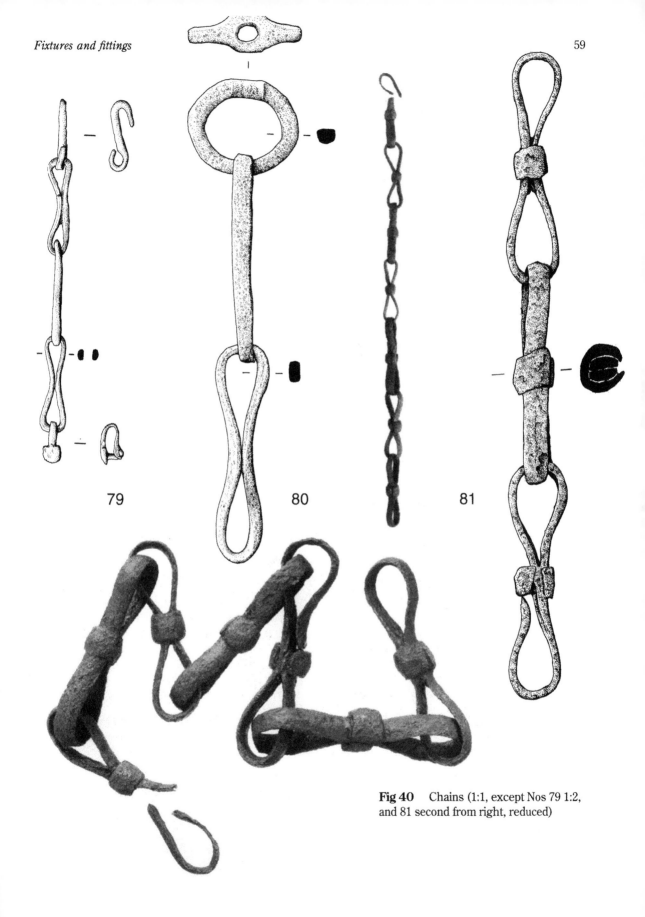

79   80   81

Fig 40   Chains (1:1, except Nos 79 1:2, and 81 second from right, reduced)

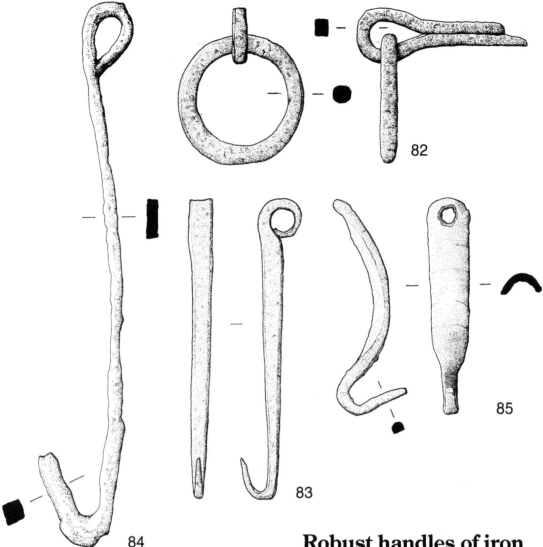

Fig 41   Pendent ring and hooks (1:1)

Curved hook with a hole at the top and an arched section

(This is a much stronger form than the preceding one.)

85 BC72 Acc No 2461 (Context 79) Ceramic Phase 11 Fig 41
L 110mm.

Robust handles of iron

The following right-angled handles have a distinctive curved profile. It is not known what they were attached to, but the (?)nail holes are very roughly pierced. The curvature would suggest rounded, presumably wooden, objects with a diameter of somewhat over 0.40m if they were fully circular. Two such handles, one on each side of a lid or cover, might be appropriate, perhaps for a privy, vat, oven or well.

86 SH74 Acc No 343 (Context 394) Ceramic Phase 7 Fig 42
L 212mm; h 48mm; two holes on each side, two of which retain incomplete nails.

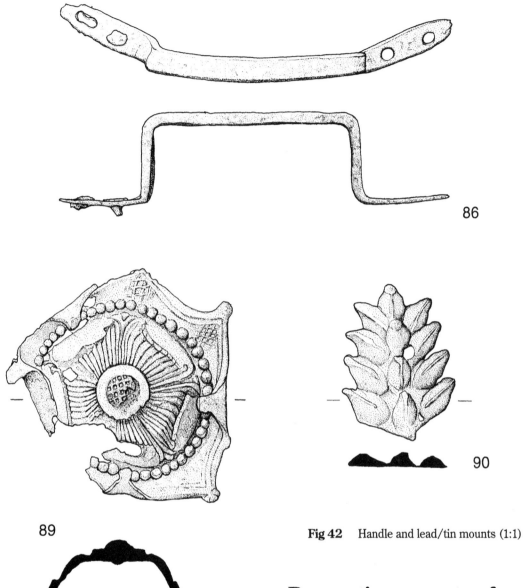

Fig 42   Handle and lead/tin mounts (1:1)

89

86

90

87 SWA81 3926 (2030) 9
Broken off at both ends, surviving l 163mm; h 50mm;
single hole survives on each side.

88 BWB83 2549 (207) 11
Incomplete; right-angled handle made from bent bar;
broken off at holes for attachment; surviving
l 129mm; w 17mm.

Decorative mounts of lead/tin

89 SWA81 Acc No 2208 (Context 2084) Ceramic
Phase 12 Fig 42
Corroded; pewter (MLC); d *c*.70mm; central boss in
form of five-petalled rose with relief detail, flat surround with beading and cross-hatching in eight-
pointed tressure with bead at each point; mark in
centre of reverse from missing rivet etc. for attachment; from a three-part mould.

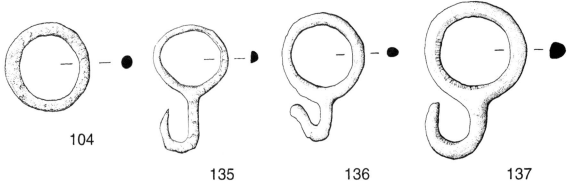

104

135   136   137

Fig 43   (?) Drape rings (1:1)

Perhaps a ceiling ornament. Another, better preserved, example is in the MoL's established collection (acc no 85.95).

90 SWA81 1958 (2117) 12 Fig 42
Incomplete ear of corn; 42×30mm; trace of gilding survives; crudely pierced off-centrally, from front.

The piercing may be from a secondary usage.

This accomplished casting is probably to be compared with the gilded lead stars and other motifs sometimes found on upper-class dwelling sites, including royal palaces, and interpreted as decorative fixtures for ceilings etc. inside the building (e.g., MoL acc nos 8662, 79.183, 87.77/3; others have been published from Clarendon Palace, Wiltshire; James & Robinson 1988, 226–8, nos 2–8, figs 85–6, pl 59C).

An ear of wheat, sometimes crowned, was the badge of the dukes of Exeter (the Holland family) from at least the mid-1440s to *c*.1475. Several late 15th-century livery badges of this form found in London and Salisbury have been identified with the family (Spencer 1990, 106, no 288, 127, fig 247). The present mount may be a purely decorative motif with no specific significance.

Possible drape rings

PLAIN RINGS

These plain rings are characterised by an irregular, often slightly flattened or sub-hexagonal section and coarse filing marks from the finishing. The identification of No 130 of iron is uncertain, but the form is the same as those of copper alloy.

No	Site	Acc No	Context	Ceramic phase	Fig	Diameter (mm)
Copper alloy						
91	BWB83	4192	401	11		18
92	BWB83	1164	361	11		19
93	BWB83	5194	306	11		19
94	BWB83	3731	338	11		19
95	BWB83	2225	151	11		20
96	BWB83	3748	338	11		20
97	BWB83	3491	162	11		20
98	BWB83	2131	307	11		21
99	SWA81	3087	2069	11		21
100	BWB83	1479	136	11		22
101	BWB83	5821	287	11		22
102	BWB83	2179	131	11		23
103	BWB83	4446	256	11		23
104	BWB83	5822	298	11	43	23
105	TL74	432	415	11		23
106	BC72	2727	79	11		23
107	BWB83	1438	119	11		24
108	BWB83	1478	136	11		24
109	BWB83	4183	401	11		24
110	BWB83	4442	256	11		24
111	BWB83	1266	109	11		25
112	BWB83	1234	110	11		27
113	BWB83	1537	256	11		27
114	BWB83	3545	354	11		27
115	BWB83	4958	376	11		29
116	SWA81	4650	2107	12		20
117	SWA81	2580	2117	12		20
118	SWA81	3412	2082	12		21
119	SWA81	809	2097	12		21

Fig 44   Curtains held by rings – David and Bathsheba (Maciejowski Old Testament, Pierpont Morgan Library, New York)

No	Site	Acc No	Context	Ceramic phase	Diameter (mm)
Copper alloy					
120	SWA81	876	2112	12	21
121	BWB83	5819	310	12	21
122	BWB83	5931	310	12	21
123	SWA81	2989	2101	12	22
124	SWA81	3027	2103	12	23
125	SWA81	2949	2109	12	23
126	SWA81	3362	2112	12	23
127	SWA81	3411	2082	12	24
128	BWB83	5934	310	12	25
129	BWB83	5933	310	12	26

No	Site	Acc No	Context	Ceramic phase	Diameter (mm)
Iron					
130	BWB83	475	150 area	?11	29

Some undivided rows of four copper-alloy rings of this kind, conjoined as cast but of uncertain date, have been found in London (MoL acc nos 8004, A22736; see MacGregor 1982, 87–8, no 416 for a similar iron item and discussion of examples of much earlier date than the present late-medieval rings). The possible drape rings could perhaps have been imported in this form or else cast in workshops in the city.

RINGS WITH HOOKS

No	Site	Acc No	Context	Ceramic phase	Fig	Diameter (mm)	Comment
Copper alloy							
131	BWB83	1917	290	9		19	
132	BWB83	1257	108	10		24	
133	BWB83	2691	330	11		19	Hook broken off
134	BWB83	5916	291	11		19	
135	BWB83	5913	298	11	43	20	Worn opposite hook
136	BWB83	2126	307	11	43	22	Tip of hook recurved
137	BWB83	1336	138	11	43	27	
138	BWB83	5914	314	12		18	

Compare Biddle 1990, 1122, 1150, no 4310A for a ring with a hook from a domestic context; see also Fig 44, curtain at lower left.

No definitive explanation of the function of the rings has been provided by archaeological finds. Although similar to a category of buckle frames (e.g., Egan & Pritchard 1991, nos 30, 32), some or all of the plain rings may well have been for drapes such as wall hangings, curtains etc. They may have been suspended from hooks along a wall or there could have been other arrangements (curtains that could be drawn, held by rings on iron bars, are known in Italy from at the least the 14th century – Peter Thornton pers comm; cf. the 'iron rods for curtains' in a London inventory of 1373 – see under Equipment for food preparation and consumption, below); no medieval curtain rod has yet been identified among archaeological material. The plain rings could have been sewn directly onto the textile (see Margeson 1993,

82, fig 47, no 524 for a later example which retains thread wound tightly round parts of it). The hooked version, which appears on the above evidence to begin earlier than the plain ones, may have been attached to plain rings or to loops of some other kind. A length of wire chain was discovered attached to a plain ring of this kind excavated at Kirkstall Abbey, West Yorkshire (Duncan & Moorhouse 1987, 134–5, fig 70, no 193), though this single find gives no indication of how common such an arrangement was. Although the plain rings continued into the post-medieval period, none of the kind with a hook has been found from a context of that date.

The import of rings for curtains was officially restricted in 1464, just subsequent to the period considered here (C Blair & J Blair 1991, 98). 'Curten rings' are among the categories of imports listed for taxation in 16th-century books of customs rates (e.g., Willan 1962, 21).

Furnishings

JANE BRENAN

Mounts for chests, caskets (coffers), etc.

Chests were made by wood workers while caskets (generally somewhat smaller) were made by leather workers (see Cherry 1991b, 314). It is seldom possible to separate excavated mounts, apart from very large and very small ones, definitively into these two categories. None of the leather covers nor the wood from these objects has been identified in London assemblages (there are not even any traces of the former adhering to the catalogued mounts) and it seems possible that something in their preparatory treatment may have made them particularly vulnerable to decay in the ground compared with other leathers.

There are 25 copper mounts, in the main of fairly plain strapping although some have knops and other ornamentation. They were found in deposits attributed to ceramic phases 6–12, over half coming from ceramic phase 11 contexts. They are, on the whole, smaller and finer, and not as readily categorised as the iron examples. There are 48 iron mounts listed (not counting those with lock hasps), almost two-thirds of them coming from the BWB83 site. The ferrous mounts can broadly be divided into five main groups – plain strapping, strapping with circles, those terminating in foliate shapes, those terminating in opposed scrolls, and those terminating in variations of a fleur-de-lis. The majority come from deposits attributed to ceramic phases 9–12 (*c*.1270–*c*.1450) and none is from a context thought to be earlier than *c*.1230. Two of the copper-alloy mounts and at least 20 (about a third) of the iron ones show traces of having been tin-coated. Three of the copper ones were gilded (Nos 140, 145, 147) and two were probably enamelled (Nos 152–3; these are likely to have been part of the same original item). Tin coating does not appear to be restricted to any particular form of mount, but it occurs only on those from deposits attributed to ceramic phase 9 onwards, whereas gilding seems to be characteristic of some of the copper-alloy mounts from the earlier part of the period. Elaborate engraved scroll/foliate designs appear on three sheet mounts (Nos 158, 162–3; in the case of No 162 this is combined with relief stamping.

The range of quality in the catalogue items is wide, particularly in the copper-alloy mounts, from the very rough (No 149) to the highly elaborate (Nos 152–3). The copper mounts are probably from caskets and other small boxes, the iron examples from more substantial boxes and chests. It is of course possible that mounts were also used on other items; some of the copper-alloy ones may have been for books, or were possibly used as textile or leather-strap fittings or attached to other items of dress. Similarly, some of the iron mounts may have been used on window shutters or cupboard doors etc. Plain iron strapping may, exceptionally, have been employed in the construction of coffins.

Eames has shown that the chest was probably the mostly widely used piece of furniture in the medieval period (1977, 108; cf. D'Allemagne 1968, pls 391–5 and Jenning 1974, nos I–II and IV–VI) and that most medieval furniture was designed to be either fixed and unmovable, as in the case of beds and built-in cupboards (*armoires*), or easily portable as in the case of chests. These two categories of furniture were responses to the custom of wealthy households to move around during the year from one dwelling to another in various locations. Built-in furniture was not likely to be stolen while the owners were away and its solid appearance could easily be disguised by being draped with textiles when the house was occupied. Chests were useful for storing textiles and other items and also for transporting them (Eames 1977, 76) and they also provided

Fig 45   Top, the Talbot Casket (British Museum); bottom, wooden chest (Public Record Office) (reduced, not to common scale)

security for a range of household possessions, a primary concern during this period (ibid. 108).

The majority of the iron mounts are likely to have been strapping on household chests, often to give an appearance of robust strength rather than for any specific function. A chest at Winchester College (Hampshire) is completely covered in iron bands so that practically none of the wood shows on the outside (ibid. 165),

the intention being to give the impression that the chest was made entirely of iron.

It seems likely that copper-alloy strapping was used in a similar way. Strapping with nail-hole surrounds in the form of flowers is set at regular intervals along the top of the casket from the Burgess Bequest (BM, MLA acc no 1881, 8–2, 13). The British Museum also has a number of small wooden caskets with similar strapping, including the Talbot Casket (Cherry 1982a),

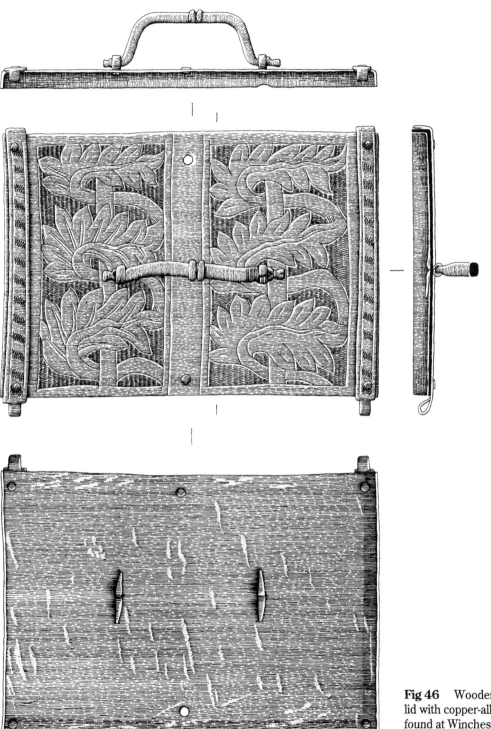

Fig 46 Wooden casket lid with copper-alloy fittings, found at Winchester (from Biddle 1990; 1:1)

which is covered with decorative leather, and a hexagonal wooden box which contained the Royal Gold Cup, an extremely valuable drinking vessel of enamelled gold (MLA acc no 1892, 5–1, 2). The range of small boxes in the same collection shows that copper-alloy mounts could be used in a number of ways. Strapping could give the box an appearance of robustness and at the same time secure a leather covering. Although the boxes in the British Museum were prestigious objects (a number of them having domed or gabled lids – cf. mount No 147 in the catalogue below), they are all very simply made; the individual pieces of wood are butt-jointed and held together with nails. In some examples, pieces of decorative sheet metal have been used to cover unsightly joints (perhaps the function of Nos 157 etc. below). A box from London, formerly in the Roach-Smith Collection (MLA acc no 56, 7–1, 1664A) and that from the Burgess Bequest have strips of decorative metal running along and covering the joins between the pieces of wood. Other copper-alloy mounts may have been used in a purely decorative way, such as the stars set between the strapping on the lid of the Burgess Bequest box.

Fig 47   Lid of decorated leather on wood, with iron fittings – SUN86 acc no 1562 (reduced)

Similar copper-alloy fittings have been found widely in archaeological contexts. They are often found on castle sites, e.g., Ascot Doilly Castle (Oxford), Bramber Castle (Sussex), Lydford Castle (Devon), Castle Acre (Norfolk), and also at the manor house, Goltho in Lincoln (Jope and Threlfall 1959, 267–8, fig 21, with references to others elsewhere; Goodall 1977, 58, 60, nos 26–8, fig 18, with several further references; A R Goodall in Saunders 1980, 164–5, nos 1, 2, fig 16; 1982, 235; 1987, 173–6, nos 18–64 – some of these are slightly earlier than the ones considered below). They have also been found on urban sites, for example at Exeter (*idem* in Allan 1984, 344–5, no 194, fig 193) and there is a small fragment from Taunton (Leach 1984, 132–3, no 5, fig 48) as well as several from Meols in Cheshire (Hume 1863, 192–7).

In contrast to the copper mounts it is difficult to find close excavated parallels for those of iron, but several existing boxes and cupboard doors having similar strapping with leaf-shaped or fleur-de-lis terminals are illustrated by Eames (1977). Wide iron straps with scrolled terminals, which held together the wooden planking of a well cover found at Lydford Castle (J Geddes in Saunders 1980, 165–6, no 1, fig 7) and other pieces used in the construction of shutters and various fixtures found on different castle sites are much larger than any of the objects discussed here.

In most instances caskets were probably for use in the home, while chests might have had a wider institutional and commercial role (Keene 1990, 36 notes their use in 14th- and 15th-century shops in London). The Winchester finds report categorises some mounts, earlier than those described below, as coming from reliquaries, based on their discovery at the site of the Minster, but the majority of the Winchester finds of comparable form and date to those listed below are from domestic contexts – D Hinton in Biddle 1990, 762ff).

Figure 45 shows a surviving chest and an upper-class casket; the latter and the cheaper casket lid excavated at Winchester (Fig 46) are particularly informative about the precise positioning of different mounts in the following catalogue. See Fig 47 for two iron mounts (held by iron nails) on a late-medieval, circular, leather-covered wooden lid, d 175mm, from the SUN86 site (acc no 1562, unstratified); the leather is decorated with a shield with a chevron in an ornate border, all against a field of stamped beading.

Strap-type mounts

Among strap-type mounts Nos 139–226, the copper-alloy items are of sheeting unless otherwise stated, and the iron ones are all wrought. None of the iron mounts has the three-dimensional quality of the finest wrought ironwork from the period considered (e.g., J Geddes in Alexander & Binski 1987, 174–5, *idem* 1991, figs 82–5). Almost all the catalogued items are basically of bar-like or rectangular strap form, and the holes are for nails or rivets, the surviving examples of which are of the same metal as the mount, again unless indicated otherwise.

Catalogue order is according to surviving length, within ceramic phases, for each metal. The order in each description is as follows: length; width (given for the main part, i.e. the strap rather than any knops etc.); the cross-section of non-sheet items is specified if it is not rectangular; the presence of holes is noted; whether either end of the mount has been broken off is indicated; a description of decoration follows, noting any coating or other finish. Of the following mounts Nos 139, 144, 146–7, 149, 155–7, (?)172, 176 and 196 are complete. Numbers 227–39 are of more varied categories; they comprise both more robust and also much flimsier items, different in character from the strap-type mounts.

For iron lock hasps, some still attached to strap mounts, see Nos 212–26, and for copper-alloy lock escutcheons, probably from caskets, see Nos 333–4 under Security equipment.

Copper alloy
(Cast unless otherwise stated)

139 BIG82 Acc No 2842 (Context 4064) Ceramic Phase 6 Fig 48
L 37mm; w 6mm; strap with D-shaped section; circular terminal with hole at both ends (trace of

Fig 48   Casket/chest mounts (1:1)

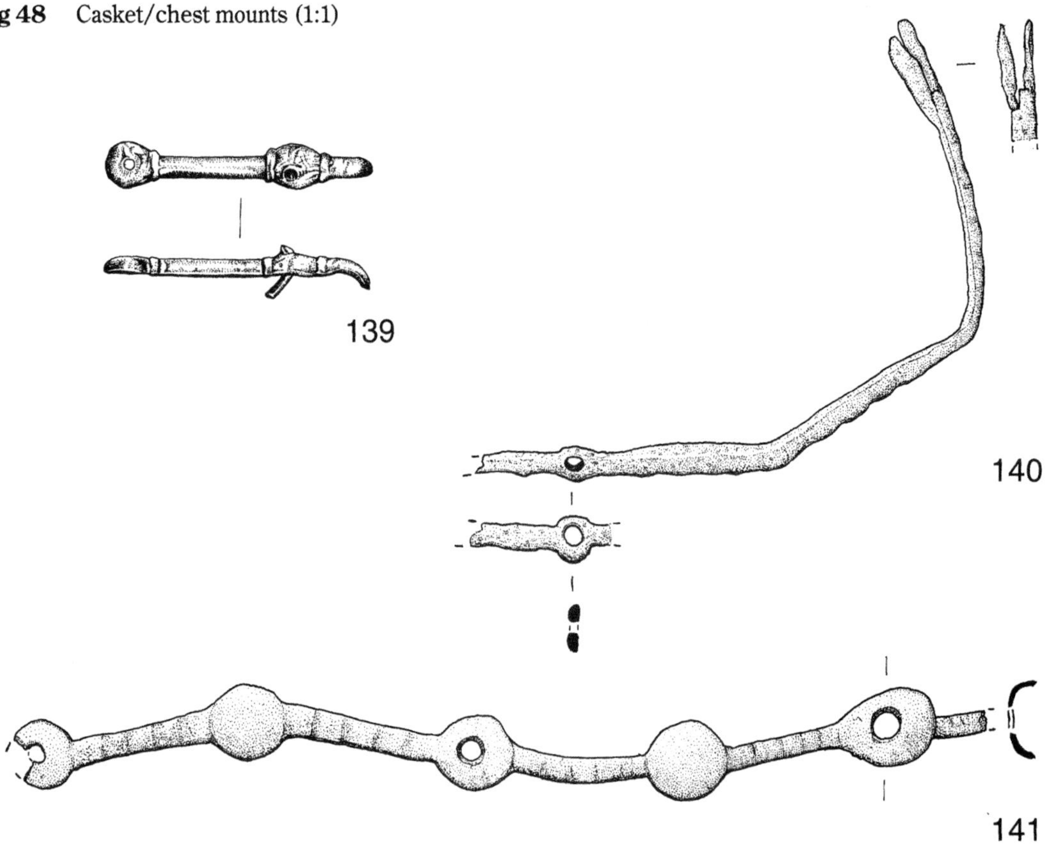

139

140

141

decoration on one), ridge to each side; retains one brass and one copper rivet (AML); one terminal extends into a (?)hinge or loop, now broken off.

Also published as a possible dress mount in Egan & Pritchard 1991, 214–15, fig 134, no 1166.

140 BIG82 2886 (4714) 6 Fig 48
L 110mm; w 4mm; D-shaped section; close to one end is a circle with a hole; the other end has been (?)accidentally split; slight transverse ridging; trace of gilding; both ends broken off.

Compare No 143.

141 SH74 253 (536) 6 Fig 48
L 129mm; w 3mm; D-shaped section; slight transverse ridging; interspaced with five knops, the alternate ones having a hole; both ends broken off.

142 BIG82 2926 (4103) 7 Fig 49
L 47mm; w 4.5mm; D-shaped section; one end terminates in (?)hinge or loop, now broken off; holes next to hinge and at other end; distorted on each side by knocking. Also published as a possible dress

mount in Egan & Pritchard 1991, 214–15, fig 134, no 1167.

143 SWA81 2352 (2266) 7 Fig 49
L 65mm; w 4mm; tapers to break at one end; the other terminates in a circle with a hole and two opposed, curving extensions; slight transverse ridging.

Transverse ridging seems to be characteristic of several copper-alloy mounts from the early part of the period considered in this volume. Compare Nos 140–1, 150, MoL acc no 4539, and an example found at Saffron Walden (Drury 1982, with references to several others of 12th/13th-century date); see also Hume 1863, pl 20, nos 1, 12 and Oakley 1979, 254–5, no 54, fig 10.

144 BIG82 2804 (4100) 7 Fig 49
Distorted; total l 137mm; w 10mm; sheet strap consisting of two lengths, with single hinge loop at

Fig 49   Casket/chest mounts (1:1)

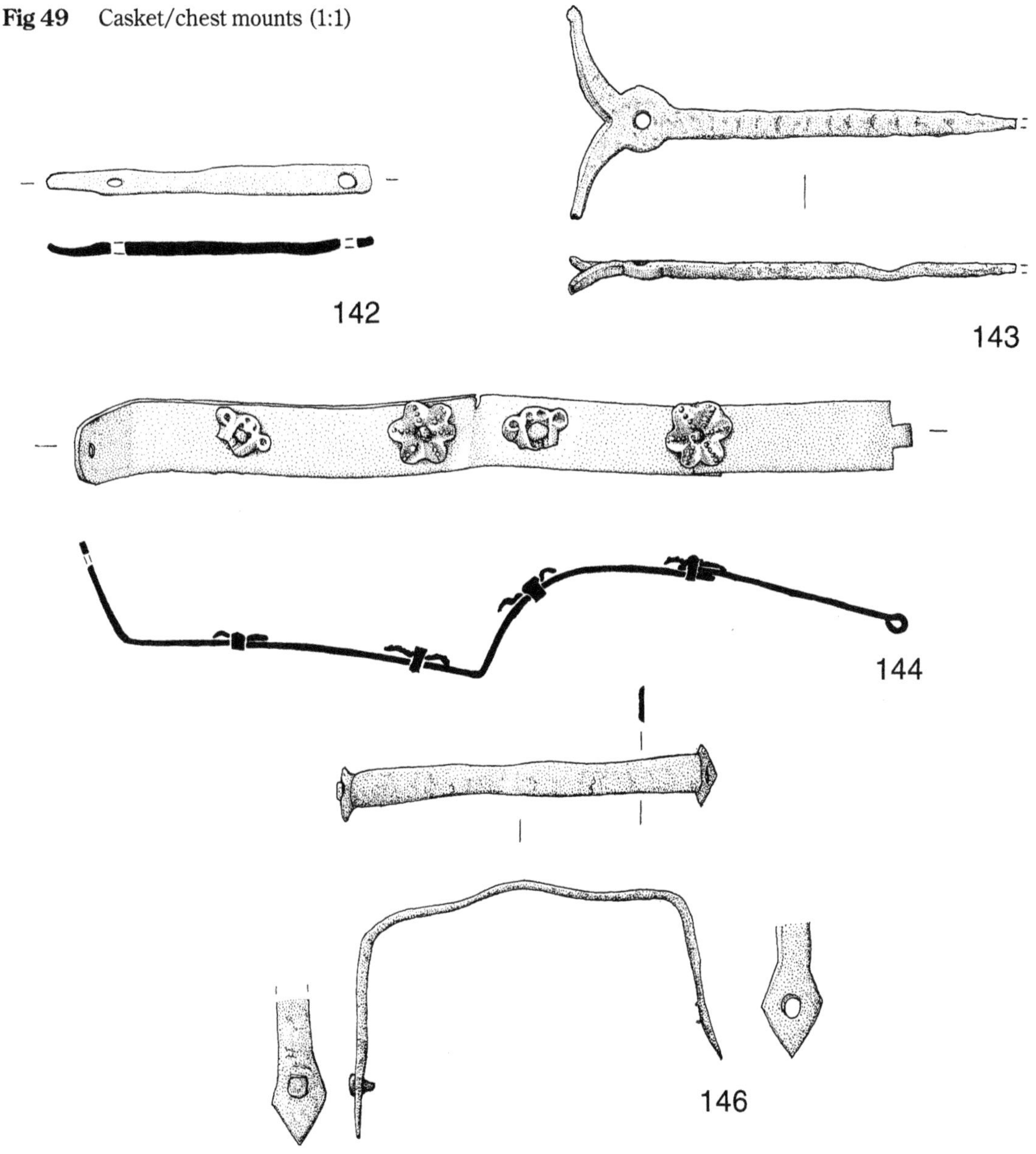

142

143

144

146

one end; tin-coated on both sides; decorated with two sexfoil mounts with three dots along the centre of each lobe and two incomplete (?)fleur-de-lis mounts, from which trilobed ends survive, all riveted; other end is rounded and pierced.

Presumably from the lid of a casket. Also pub-lished as a possible dress mount in Egan & Pritchard 1991, 242–3, fig 155, no 1295.

145 SH74 33 (291) 8

L 91mm; w 12mm; curved profile (probably an original feature), with D-shaped section; one end broken off, the other has a circle defined by a transverse ridge and with a pointed terminal; circle has a hole; gilded.

Presumably originally part of the same object as No 147 from the same deposit; perhaps from a curved lid.

146 SH74 237 (468) 8 Fig 49
D-shaped section; bent, with two right angles and slightly raised arc at centre; total l 99mm; w 4mm; lozenge-shaped terminals, each with a hole, one retaining an incomplete iron nail; trace of tin coating.

147 SH74 32 (291) 8 Fig 50
L 114mm; w 12mm; curved profile; D-shaped section; each end has a circle defined by a transverse ridge and with a pointed terminal; the circles each have holes; gilded.

Presuming the profile is an original feature, this may come from a casket etc. *c.*45mm wide.

Compare No 145 above from the same deposit and Hume 1863, pl 20, no 11 (which is straight).

148 BWB83 1178 (270) 9
Sheeting; l 39mm; w 5mm; arched in section; (?)both ends broken off; hole at each end; a relatively flimsy mount.

149 BWB83 1523 (222) 9 Fig 50
Distorted; roughly cut sheeting; l 120mm; max w 25mm; overall lozenge shape; one end terminates in an oval, other broken off; three holes; tin coating.

This crude, relatively flimsy mount cannot have been the product of a craft worker in copper alloy.

150 POM79 406 (1578) 7–9 Fig 50
L 110mm; w 4mm; D-shaped section; slight transverse ridging; broken off at both ends; bifurcated at one end, roundel with eight large, decorative holes around central, convex knop and having alternate curves and angles around edge at other end; main length has three convex knops, the one at the bifurcation having a hole.

Probably from the earlier part of the period indicated, in view of the parallels – see on No 143.

The large roundel may be compared with a stylised flower. A similar mount was found in spoil from the VRY89 site (reference no V87); cf A R Goodall 1987, 173–4, no 18, fig 154.

151 BWB83 1331 (108) 10
Distorted; l 135mm; w 5mm; triangular/D-shaped section; both ends broken off at holes.

152 BWB83 2194 (146) 11
L 20mm; w 9mm; contiguous, reserved quatrefoils in a central band defined by lines along each side; beaded edges; broken off at both ends.

Perhaps originally enamelled, and possibly from a reliquary; likely to be of Continental manufacture.

153 BWB83 1396 (150) 11 Fig 50
L 20mm; w 9mm; broken off at one, possibly both ends; similar to preceding item (presumably part of the same original object).

154 BWB83 5244 (306) 11
L 29mm; w 7mm; broken off at one end; circular terminal with hole, expansion at incomplete end; file-marked (its roughness is due not so much to being unfinished after casting as being carelessly/quickly smartened up, presumably as part of a batch).

Compare the shape of No 156.

155 BWB83 4466 (256) 11 Fig 50
L 30mm; w 4mm; D-shaped section; rectangular mount with holes at both ends retaining integral rivets; three panels of cross-hatching.

Also published as a possible dress mount in Egan & Pritchard 1991 (212–13, fig 133, no 1143).

156 BWB83 1168 (361) 11
Sheeting; l 54mm; max w 9mm; central expansion, and circular terminals, each with a hole; finished by filing.

Possibly a dress mount.

157 BC72 1759 (55) 11 Fig 50
Sheeting; l 65mm; w 19mm; central ridge lengthways; individually stamped beading along sides; four holes.

Although the mount's size seems suitable for a leather strap, the flimsiness of the sheeting suggests it may have been primarily a covering, from a robust object.

Compare Addyman & Priestley 1977, 141, 145, no 83, fig 11, found in York.

158 BC72 2883 (150) 11 Fig 51
Sheeting; l 73mm; w 9mm; curved strip; broken off at one end; two rough holes; engraved decoration of recurved leaves springing from alternate sides of a stiff, angled stem that passes from one side to the other and is bent back at the end, against a field of closely set, engraved zigzags, all within a plain perimeter band.

Compare No 163 and the cover on the lid in Fig 46.

159 BWB83 1196 (113) 11
Distorted; l 102mm; w 3mm; D-shaped section, apart from at the two slightly expanded terminals, each with holes; broken-off at one terminal, the other is filed to give a rudimentary foliate motif.

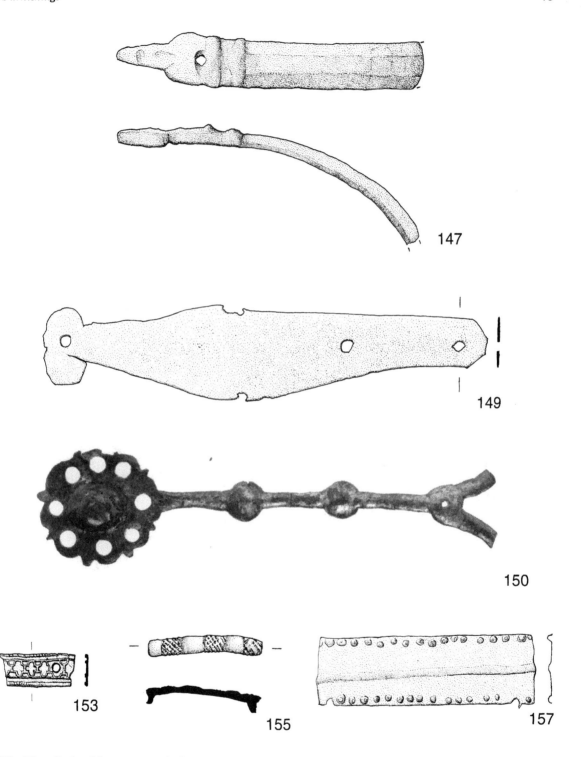

Fig 50 Casket/chest mounts (1:1)

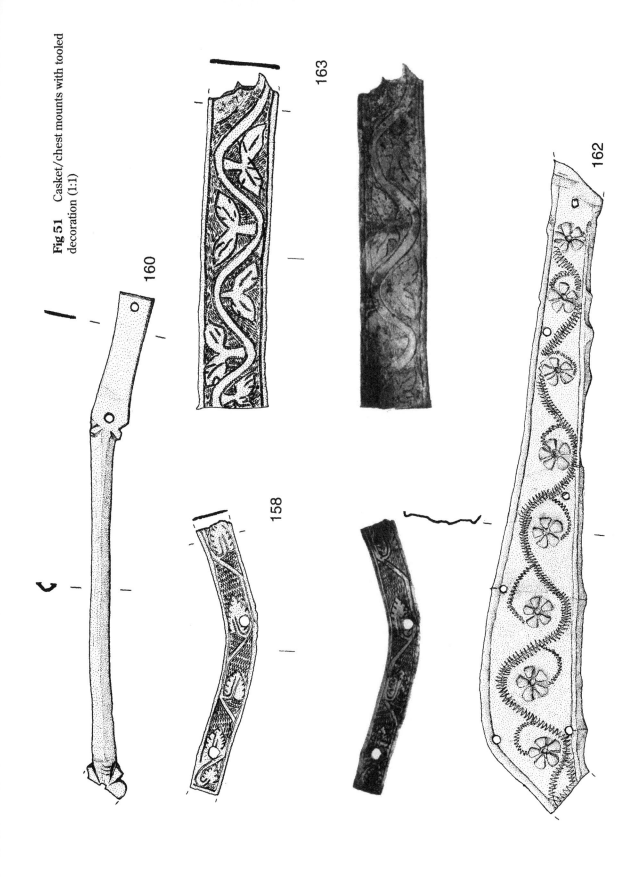

Fig 51 Casket/chest mounts with tooled decoration (1:1)

160

163

162

158

160 BC72 2765 (83) 11 Fig 51
Sheeting; l 102mm; w 5mm; narrow, central strap with V-shaped section between expanded ends; three holes; one end has a foliate motif that is partly broken off at a hole, the other terminates in a rectangle with a foliate motif at the junction.

161 BWB83 1320 (122 area) (?)11
L 109mm; w 4mm; half-hexagon section; broken off at one of the two holes.

162 BC72 2708 (79) 11 Fig 51
L 176mm; max w 29mm; asymmetrical, flimsy sheeting, showing some signs of having been folded; straight along one side, curved on the other; widens towards one end and then narrows sharply to terminal; both ends broken off; eight stamped cinquefoils, sprouting from engraved zigzags out of a sinuous, scrolling stem of wider engraved zigzags; ridge around perimeter; six holes.

Possibly some kind of framing piece; it is difficult to envisage what kind of object this carefully shaped mount would have come from. See on Nos 227ff.

163 BWB83 5924 (310) 12 Fig 51
Sheeting; l 91mm; w 19mm; one end broken off at a hole, roughly cut off at the other; central band defined by lines along edges and with engraved, sinuous stem running the length, from which stemmed, double lanceolate leaves sprout, all on a field of engraved zigzags.

Compare No 158 for foliate decoration.

Iron

164 SH74 Acc No 143 (Context 386) Ceramic Phase 8
Incomplete, l 140mm; max w 22mm; tapers towards opposed terminal scrolls, only one of which survives; broken off at other end at possible hole.

Compare No 204.

165 SWA81 1822 (2018) 9
L 38mm; w 3mm; D-shaped section; broken off at both ends; expansion at one end, with hole, with small protrusions on each side; tin coating.

166 SWA81 4997 (2057) 9
L 38mm; w 22mm; two opposed scrolls at one end, broken off at the other.

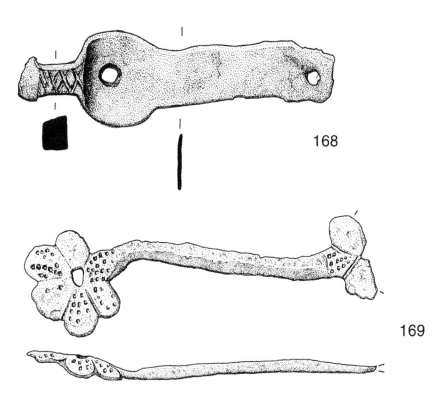

Fig 52 Casket/chest mounts (1:1)

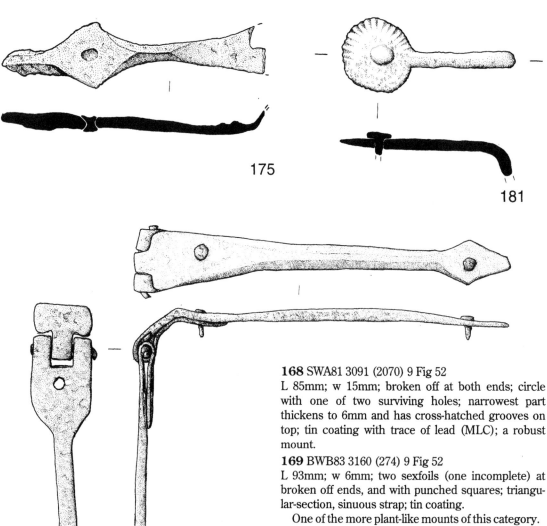

175

181

185

Fig 53   Casket/chest mounts (1:1)

167 SWA81 579 (2055) 9
L 73mm; w 9mm; two opposed scrolls branching from central stem at one end (stem and one scroll broken off); the other end is broken off at a circle with the remains of a nail.

168 SWA81 3091 (2070) 9 Fig 52
L 85mm; w 15mm; broken off at both ends; circle with one of two surviving holes; narrowest part thickens to 6mm and has cross-hatched grooves on top; tin coating with trace of lead (MLC); a robust mount.

169 BWB83 3160 (274) 9 Fig 52
L 93mm; w 6mm; two sexfoils (one incomplete) at broken off ends, and with punched squares; triangular-section, sinuous strap; tin coating.
   One of the more plant-like mounts of this category.

170 SWA81 726 (2070) 9
L 95mm; w 6mm; broken off at circle with nail hole at one end; expands to folded, two-loop hinge pivot, also with hole, at other end.

171 SWA81 1882 (2134) 9
L 110mm; robust, fleur-de-lis-like terminal; scroll survives on one side; broken off at other end.

172 SWA81 2904 (2065) 9
Corroded and bent (described from X-ray plate); l *c*.130mm; w 22mm; narrows towards one end; retains two nails in holes.

173 BC72 4662 (250) 10
L 50mm; w 5mm; D-shaped section; lozenge-shaped terminal with incomplete nail; broken off at expansion at other end; tin coating.

174 BC72 4658 (250) 10
L 59mm; max w 5mm; terminates at one end in an oval with a nail and expands towards the other end, which is broken off near a second nail; tin coating.

175 BWB83 4653 (108) 10 Fig 53
L 73mm; w 5mm; one lozenge, and possibly a second on D-section strap; tin coating; both ends broken off, one at a hole.

176 BWB83 4408 (108) 10
Distorted; l 97mm; max w 12mm; slightly tapering; hole at each end, one retaining a nail.

177 BC72 4698 (250) 10
L 103mm; w 10mm; right-angled bend; rounded end retains nail, other is broken off at triangular terminal.

178 BWB83 466 (110) 11
L 42mm; w 11mm; broken off at expansion, with hole at one end and at one of two opposed terminal scrolls at the other.

179 BWB83 4743 (331) 11
L 42mm; w 11mm; pointed, foliate-oval terminal at one end; broken off at the other.

Possibly from a fleur-de-lis or other decorative terminal, as there is no hole for attachment.

180 BWB83 5252 (352) 11
L 46mm; w 20mm; broken off at one end; opposed bifurcation (cf. incipient scrolls) at the other; a robust mount.

Compare No 184.

181 BWB83 2967 (146) 11 Fig 53
L 47mm; w 4mm; D-shaped section; circle at end (possibly broken off) with punched, radiating grooves around edge, and hole retaining incomplete nail; broken off at other end at right-angled bend (probably an original feature).

Compare Nos 183, 190, 196.

182 TL74 785 (415) 11
L 55mm; w 4mm; broken off at one end; other terminates in foliate oval with hole.

183 BWB83 364 (147) 11
Distorted; l 56mm; w 5mm; D-shaped section; broken off at one end; at the other a circle with punched, radiating grooves around the edge has a hole retaining an incomplete nail; tin coating.

Compare No 181.

184 BWB83 2899 (306) 11
L 65mm; w 30mm; broken off at one end; opposed bifurcations (cf. incipient scrolls) at the other; tin coating; a robust mount.

Compare No 180.

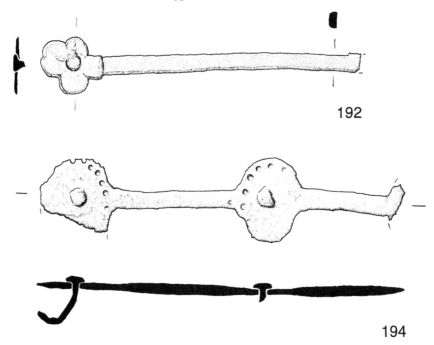

192

194

Fig 54   Casket/chest mounts (1:1)

185 BC72 4286 (150) 11 Fig 53

Two triangular-section straps hinged together (pivot loops 2 // 1); one l 69×5mm, with expansions at each end, broken off at one, the hinge being folded and having a nail hole; the other strap is similar and complete, but l 107×7mm, with a lozenge-shaped terminal, and retains a nail l 6mm at each end.

The complete strap is presumably from the lid of a casket, while the other is probably from its side.

186 BWB83 5627 (204) 11

L 72mm; w 14mm; broken off at expansion at one end, other terminates in foliate oval with a hole.

187 TL74 533 (416) 11

Distorted and corroded; l 75mm; w 5mm; central (?)circle retains incomplete nail; broken off at expansions at both ends.

188 BWB83 4181 (300) (?)11

L 76mm; w 4mm; D-shaped section; both ends broken off, one terminates at an expansion, the other at a hole in a circle.

189 BC72 2625 (79) 11

L 82mm; w 4mm; two circles with holes, each retaining a nail (one bent over for attachment to an object 8mm thick), cusps at the joins with the strap; tin coating; broken off at right-angled bend (probably an original feature).

190 BC72 2626 (79) 11

In two pieces (described from X-ray plate) l 83mm; w *c*.5mm; broken off at both ends at expansions with holes; central circle has punched, radiating grooves and hole; tin coating.

Compare No 181.

191 BWB83 3132 (280) 11

Distorted; l 86mm; w 12mm; hole near one end, which also has series of grooves lengthways; broken off at other end.

192 BWB83 408 (357) 11 Fig 54

L 87mm; w 4mm; D-shaped section, broken off at one end; trefoil terminal defined by transverse ridge at the other end, which retains incomplete nail.

193 BC72 4279 (150) 11

L 94mm; w 5mm; D-shaped section; broken off at elongated expansions at both ends, one at a possible nail-hole, the other at two loops for a hinge, this end retaining an incomplete nail.

194 TL74 753 (414) 11 Fig 54

L 99mm; w 5mm; two ovals and the remains of a possible third, decorated with rings of punched dots, each having a hole with a nail; tin coating.

195 BC72 1734 (55) 11 Fig 55

L 99mm; w 15mm; one end has a pointed, foliate terminal with a pair of opposed scrolls and a hole; other end broken off; strap is bent upwards (?)to accommodate a transverse mount beneath.

(?)Fleur-de-lis-type terminal.

196 BC72 2280 (83) 11

L 109mm; w 5mm; D-shaped section; central circle with punched, radiating grooves and hole; small, paired side projections at each end.

Compare No 181.

197 BC72 2455 (79) 11

L 109mm; w 6mm; triangular section; expands at each end, both with a hole; one end is spatulate, the other broken off.

198 BC72 4438 (150) 11

L 114mm; w 5mm; D-shaped section; central circle, and parts of others at each end, both ends being broken off; hole in central circle and trace of another at one end.

199 TL74 917 (415) 11 Fig 55

L 118mm; w 25mm+; arched section; broken off at one end; expands towards broken off, folded two-loop hinge pivot at the other; retains nail l 10mm; tin coating.

200 BWB83 5011 (300) (?)11 Fig 56

L 159mm; w 6mm; D-shaped section; circle with hole towards one end and having a nail; other end broken-off at expansion (?broken-off hinge) with nail head or rivet surviving at hole.

201 BC72 2650 (79) 11 Fig 56

Distorted (straightened in illustration); l *c*.175mm; w 6mm; triangular section; broken off at one end at expansion; two further octagonal expansions with holes, and triangular terminal also with a hole; tin coating.

202 BWB83 4175 (300) (?)11

L 93mm; w 5mm; expands towards broken off ends, one of which retains an incomplete nail.

203 BWB83 3964 (310) 12 Fig 56

L 36mm; w 33mm; two opposed scrolls (one broken off) with triangular element between, broken off at expansion.

(?)Fleur-de-lis-type terminal.

204 BWB83 4794 (309) 12

Corroded; l 59mm; w 21mm; two opposed (?)scrolls at one end; broken off at the other end at expansion.

205 SWA81 3867 (2008) 12

Folded; l 60mm; w 25mm; tapers towards bifurcated,

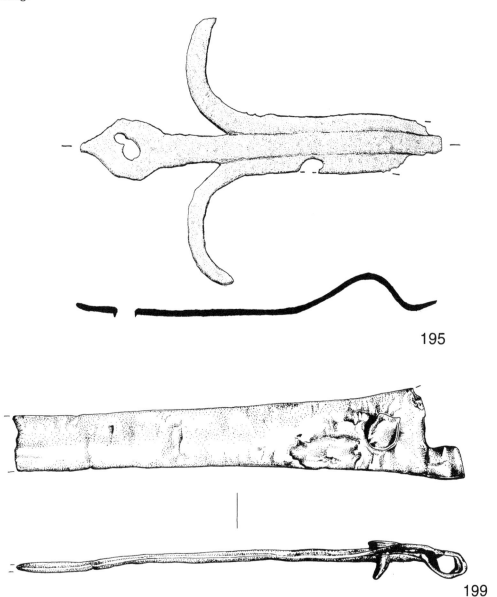

Fig 55 Casket/chest mounts (1:1)

opposed spiralled terminal; broken off at other end; two holes survive, one retaining a broken-off nail.

206 TL74 1113 (274) 12
L 64mm; w (?)22mm; two broken-off, opposed scrolls with continuing grooves lengthways; broken off at expansion with hole.

207 BWB83 553 (310) 12
L 65mm; w 8mm; two circles, one incomplete, and both with holes.

208 SWA81 1864 (2113) 12
L 80mm; w 8mm; expands at one end, broken off at both; three holes, one broken off at one end.

209 BWB83 3406 (309) 12
L 82mm; w 6mm; circle near one end retaining nail in hole, broken off at expansion at the other; tin coating.

210 TL74 2167 (2299) 12
L 84mm; w (?)23mm; one end broken off; at the

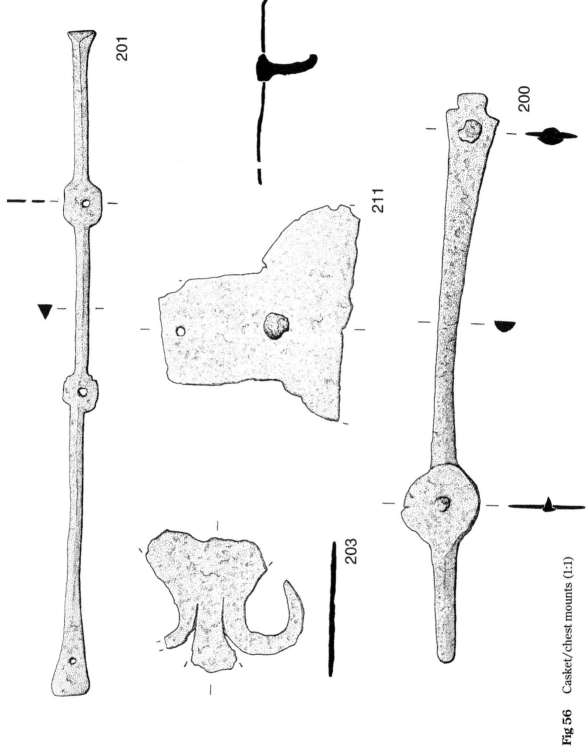

Fig 56 Casket/chest mounts (1:1)

other is a terminal of two opposed scrolls with looped ends.

211 BWB83 4755 (Unstratified) Fig 56
L 50mm; w 29mm; broken off at both ends, with incomplete circle at one; two holes, one with nail at join of circle and strap; tin coating.

Strap mounts with hinged lock hasps

Iron

These mounts come from chests, caskets and perhaps other kinds of furnishings. The bolt loops are riveted in place. All the hasps are hinged with a single-loop pivot.

Earlier examples than the complete ones listed have a much wider loop (?universal joint) at the end instead of a hinge (see Fig 57 top, from the VHA89 site, and compare Nos 43–4 listed under Fixtures and fittings).

See also mounted locks Nos 278 and 285, which retain hasps secured in place.

212 SWA81 Acc No 1183 (Context 2157) Ceramic Phase 6
L 61mm; elongated oval; one end has bulbous tab, the hinge loop is broken off at the other; hasp loop 8×2mm.

213 SWA81 2088 (2031) 9
Incomplete and corroded; l 64mm+; w 12mm; hasp loop 11×3mm; attached by hinge to D-section strap mount l 89mm; w 3mm, expanding and with hole at hinge; tin coating (MLC).

214 SWA81 657 (2061) 9
L 78mm; w 10mm; bevelled edges; bent-back terminal at end; hasp loop 9×3mm; tin coating (MLC).

215 SWA81 656 (2061) 9 Fig 57
Elongated oval; l 87mm; w 12mm; bevelled sides and flanges at bent-back terminal grip, hasp loop 10×2mm; attached by hinge to D-section strap; surviving l 66mm; w 4.5mm; pair of cusps at expanded end, which is bent over for hinge and secured with two rivets.

216 SWA81 2481 (2133) 9
Corroded; l 144mm; w 19mm; robust; tapers slightly towards hinge; corners rounded at the other end; hasp loop *c.*12×*c.*3mm; tin coating.

217 BC72 4673 (250) 10
L 74mm; w 12mm; expands towards centre, narrows towards bent-back end grip; hasp loop 10×2.5mm.

218 BWB83 173 (153) 11 Fig 58
Lozenge-shaped, with bevelled sides; l 57mm; w 11mm; bent-back end grip; hasp loop 9×2.5mm.

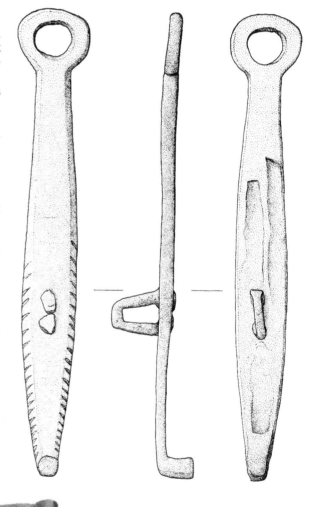

Fig 57   Casket chest
lock hasps (top 1:1 from VHA89 site; bottom reduced)

215

Fig 58   Casket/chest lock hasps (1:1)

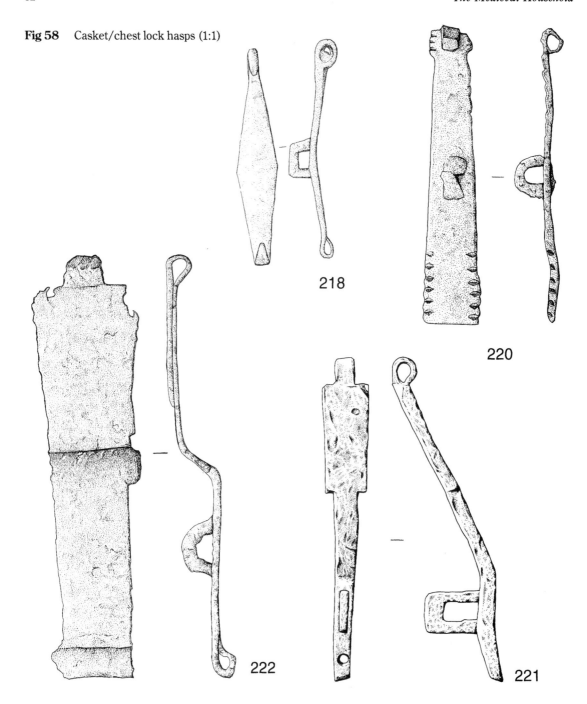

218

220

222

221

219 BWB83 4782 (305) 11
Incomplete and corroded; expands in centre; surviving l 73mm; w 18mm; bent (?)tab at end for grip; hasp loop 22×(?)3mm; tin coating.

220 BWB83 608 (150) 11 Fig 58
Expands towards end; l 77mm; w 16mm; transversely grooved flanges at hinge and transverse side grooves near other end; hasp loop 10×2.5mm.

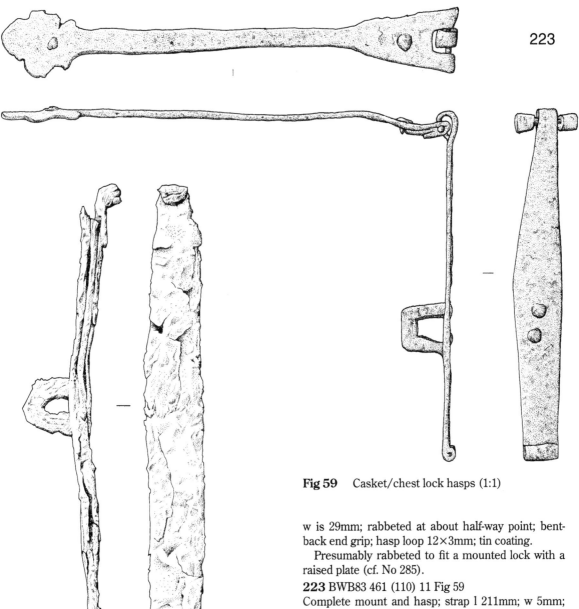

Fig 59   Casket/chest lock hasps (1:1)

w is 29mm; rabbeted at about half-way point; bent-back end grip; hasp loop 12×3mm; tin coating.

Presumably rabbeted to fit a mounted lock with a raised plate (cf. No 285).

223 BWB83 461 (110) 11 Fig 59
Complete mount and hasp; strap l 211mm; w 5mm; (?)foliate terminal with part of nail; other end widens, terminating in two-loop hinge pivot with single rivet; elongated, sub-lozenge-shaped hasp (l 92mm; w 13mm) has bent-back end tab and hasp loop 12×3mm.

224 BWB83 4848 (326) 12
Mount and hasp (described from X-ray plate); corroded; l 71mm; w 18mm; hasp loop 13×3mm; attached by hinge to incomplete strap (surviving l 25mm; w 32mm) with a surviving nail.

221 BWB83 2926 (318) 11 Fig 58
Bent; l 89mm; max w 12mm near hinge; narrows towards pierced end; hasp loop 9×2mm.

222 BWB83 3307 (380) 11 Fig 58
Corroded; l 113mm; expands towards hinge, where

225 BWB83 3120 (278) 12
Elongated oval; l 80mm; w 16mm; bent-back end tab; hasp loop 17×3mm.

226 TL74 1571 (1628) 12 Fig 59
Corroded; surviving l 122mm; w 15mm; narrower towards ends; bent-back at one end (?for hinge or tab); hasp loop 14×3mm.

See also No 336 listed under Security equipment for a copper-alloy lock hasp, probably from a satchel or similar container of leather.

Other mounts
Geoff Egan

A variety of sheet coverings, more substantial openwork friezes, lengths of framing, and cut-out motifs of foil were for attachment to flat surfaces with tacks, or perhaps glue in the case of some of the flimsier items. Only with some of the more complete of these mounts is it possible to suggest a specific category of object for which they may have been intended (e.g., No 229). Caskets, furniture, devotional panels and even the walls etc. of the house are among the possibilities, while some of the smaller motifs could have come from articles of dress (e.g., No 239; see Egan & Pritchard 1991, 238–9, nos 1284, 1287).

Bone mounts for caskets etc. (MacGregor 1985a, 197–200) seem to be entirely absent from the appropriate period at the recent sites considered for this volume. Their main vogue was certainly slightly earlier (see Pritchard 1991, 210, 267, nos 264–8).

ROBUST FORMS

Copper alloy

227 BWB83 Acc No 131 (Context 263) Ceramic Phase 9 Fig 60
Hammered, square sheet mount, 50×50mm; slightly convex; holes in one corner and at one of the opposite edges; engraved zigzags around perimeter; cross potent at centre; gilded.

228 BWB83 4490 (285) 9 Fig 60
L 159mm; w 17mm, with flange bent at a right angle 6mm deep; rounded corners; three torn holes for attachment; a slight extension almost at a right angle has a fourth hole for attachment at one end.

Perhaps an edge cover from one corner of the base of a casket etc.

229 BC72 2707 (79) 11 Fig 60
Incomplete sheet rectangle, 90×47mm, with rounded corners and central cut-out slot; a raised band has stamped beading along both sides (only on the outside in the case of the incomplete edge) around the perimeter; another band with beading along one side surrounding the slot; stamped dots in groups of three forming crude flower motifs; hole for attachment at each corner; the asymmetrical decoration has been clumsily applied, the beading having pierced the sheet in the majority of cases.

Perhaps from the top of a casket, the slot being to accommodate a handle.

See also No 162.

Lead/tin

230 BIG82 Acc No 3086 (Context 5364) Ceramic Phase 6 Fig 60
Cast edging mount or cresting; one straight D-section side, the other with transversely hatched, interlaced arcs with stemmed beads in the interstices; w 8mm; surviving l 23mm (broken off at both ends).

Perhaps from a casket, or a religious panel, etc.

231 SWA81 3309 (Unstratified) Fig 60
Cast lead sheet (AML); rectangular, 26×12mm; lion passant, plant motif to side and possibly another below; beaded border.

Also published as no 1287 in Egan & Pritchard 1991 (238–9, fig 152).

FOIL

(Very thin sheeting)

These very flimsy, both plain and decorative, items are made from sheeting *c.*0.75mm thick or less, presumably to be stuck on to flat, robust surfaces, perhaps on furniture or walls and ceilings. They may originally have been strikingly shiny. All were found folded. They seem too slight to have been appropriate for fixing to textiles for dress, though some have edge holes for attachment, possibly by sewing. The larger, plainer items (Nos 232, 234) could be parts of

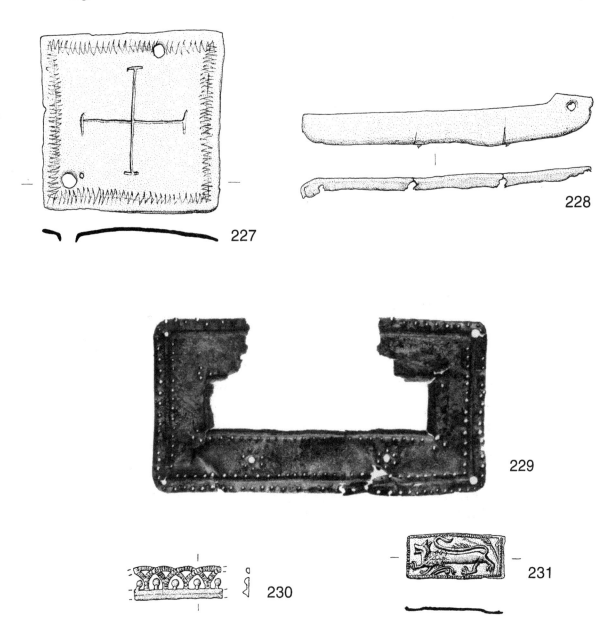

Fig 60   (?)Casket/chest mounts (1:1)

external or internal coverings from caskets etc. A number of pieces of foil which have no obvious regular shape have been omitted.

See M Foreman (in Armstrong et al. 1991, 158) for fragments of lead/tin foil excavated in Beverley, Yorkshire; an 11th- or 12th-century casket with openwork bone mounts has a surviving backing of lead/tin foil (MacGregor 1985a, 198–9).

Measurements for thickness are approximate, as the sheeting varies slightly from point to point.

Copper alloy

232 BWB83 Acc No 1520 (Context 222) Ceramic Phase 9 Fig 61

Incomplete; (?)rectangle, cut away irregularly along one side, 62×41+mm; th 0.35mm; ridge near longest surviving edge.

Lead/tin

233 SWA81 Acc No 1395 (Context 2185) Ceramic Phase 6 Fig 61

Rectangular strip; 10×45mm; th 0.15mm; angled cuts at one end, broken off at the other; paired holes (of different sizes) at sides.

234 BWB83 5456 (206) 9 Fig 61

Strip; w 33mm; with ridges lengthways; torn off at both ends; surviving l 80mm; th 0.65mm.

232

233

234

236

237

239

238

Fig 61   Foil mounts (1:1)

Fig 62   Handles (?)for caskets/chests (1:1)

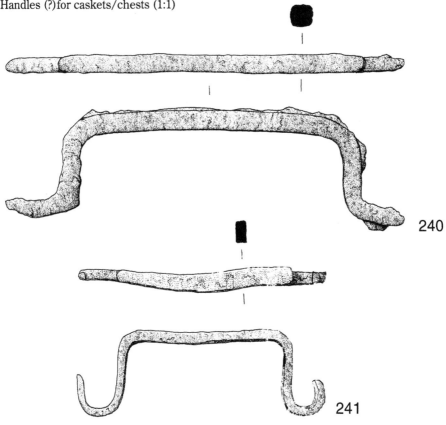

240

241

235 SWA81 730 (2070) 9 Fig 61
Crudely cut sexfoil; d 36mm; th 0.75mm.

236 SWA81 2729 (2062) 9 Fig 61
Crude rectangle; 40×28mm; th 0.65mm; torn tack or pin-holes around perimeter.

237 SWA81 604 (2065) 9 Fig 61
Crudely cut sexfoil; d 42mm; th 0.20mm.

238 SWA81 2087 (2031) 9 Fig 61
Incomplete, crude, five-armed star; radius *c*.43mm; th 0.70mm.

239 SWA81 2122 (2112) 12 Fig 61
Irregular petal-like shape with two small holes near edge; 29×16mm; th 0.15mm.

Drop handles
Geoff Egan

These probably come from casket lids – cf. Fig 46; see also copper-alloy handle No 487, listed under Copper-alloy vessels (Fig 143).

Iron

240 SWA81 Acc No 2956 (Context 2050) Ceramic Phase 9 Fig 62
Right-angled rod; l 109mm; h 30mm.

241 BC72 4110 (88) 11 Fig 62
Right-angled strip with recurved ends; l 67mm; h 23mm; tin coating.

Security equipment

GEOFF EGAN

Ancient and medieval locks and keys have been the subject of general studies by Cuming (1856), Pitt Rivers (1883), Musty (nd), Vaudour (1980) and Mandel (1992), and excavated examples have been analysed in detail by I H Goodall in Biddle (1990) and Crabbe (1971). A large number of keys from London were published in the Guildhall Museum Catalogue (1908, 341–7) and by Ward Perkins (1940, 133–50). The former also included some locks and padlocks (354–6), while the latter omitted illustrations of these items but made an innovatory contribution by defining nine 'types' of rotary keys (slide keys were treated separately). The types were based on the form of the bit (except VIII, which seems to have been defined by its heart-shaped bow) with type VII further divided according to differences in the wards into sub-group A (clefts generally simple and at a right angle to shank), and sub-group B (clefts of more complex form, generally at the middle of the bit) (Ward Perkins 1940, 141–2). Some of the incomplete keys listed below cannot be assigned by this system. The form of bit also determines the order of items within the following listing (with subdivisions according to shape of bow where appropriate), with the exception of a series of small, crude, simple keys of both copper alloy and iron (Nos 294–304), which stand out as a definable group by their overall similarity to each other, despite variations in some traits.

Comparison of the keys listed below from the recent excavations with those from London published in 1940 (very few of those described in the Guildhall Museum Catalogue were actually illustrated) immediately reveals a basic difference of emphasis between the range of very decorative forms in the old collection and the relative plainness of the great majority of those found at the sites considered in this volume. The elaborate keys in the London Museum collection must have been acquired very selectively. The same is likely to be true of the large collections of medieval keys in the British Museum and the Salisbury and South Wiltshire Museum (Dalton 1924, 159–60, fig 107 and Shortt 1973, 58 illustrates a small selection).

The basic requirements of a key were, as today, firstly that it had to fit into the lock, catering with channels (bullets) for any barriers on the case (like the tabs on locks Nos 276, 285) and with clefts, or with holes in some sliding keys, for any internal baffles (wards). (The aperture in the bit of rotary key No 312 can have had no practical function.) The key thus had to be compatible with the lock in two dimensions. Secondly, it had to turn or slide so as to move the mechanism, with which it also had to be compatible in shape, sometimes very precisely, in order to open or close the lock. The lock, for its part, was designed, with varying degrees of elaborateness, to accept and allow only a corresponding key to operate the mechanism. None of the mounted rotary locks listed below retains the complex, riveted wards that survive in an early 12th-century example excavated in Winchester (I H Goodall in Biddle 1990, 1017–19, no 3687). The presence of these details on other locks would have given a more accurate idea of the form of the appropriate key bit, but among the London finds only lock No 280 has a rivet hole that suggests it may originally have had this kind of internal feature (unless the hole results from a repair). This particular lock appears in that respect to have been unusually complicated, judging from the others listed below (Nos 274–5 and 282 are too fragmentary to tell, while Nos 276–7, 279 and 283 certainly did not have internal wards, nor did the only complete case with a separate back, No 285).

There are no wooden keys from the recent excavations, but two bone items from the TEX88 site may hint at a category that appears not to have been recognised elsewhere in Britain (acc nos 1337 (unstratified) and 5460 from

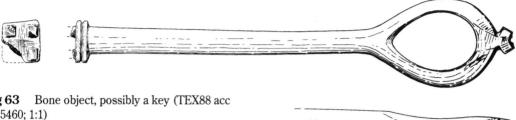

Fig 63 Bone object, possibly a key (TEX88 acc
no 5460; 1:1)

a ?late 12th-century context; see Fig 63). No
keys are noted in MacGregor's survey of
worked bone objects (1985a), though items in
Hungary attributed to the Roman period
include an unstratified, near-parallel from Brigetio for the former TEX88 find – Bíró 1987,
166, fig 7, 34; reference kindly supplied by
Arthur MacGregor). The two London finds
share a number of characteristics: a terminal
loop that may be compared to the bow of a key
(this and the shank are considerably worn) and
a complex terminal at the other end, which is
in both instances partly broken off. The stubs
of four broken-off projections on the illustrated
example may be compared with the bits of
padlock slide keys like No 273, which have
these set at a right angle to the shank. The
date of these apparently not very satisfactory
bone items must await further finds before it
can be considered to be established beyond
doubt; at present it remains a possibility that
they are from the very beginning of the period
considered in this volume, though they could
date from the Roman era.

Judging from the locks recovered at the sites
considered in this survey, the rotary keys listed
below would all have been intended for
mounted locks or for the cased padlocks that
developed from them towards the end of the
period considered (see Nos 285–6), while all
the slide keys were for padlocks which operated with double-spring strips ('leaf springs').
Rotary keys with symmetrical wards could have
been inserted and operated from either side of
a lock, e.g., on a door (archaeological confir-
mation for this in practice in the period considered seems to be lacking). Asymmetrical
keys of this kind would presumably have
worked only from one side of the lock, unless
the mechanism was actually very much simpler

than the key's bit implies. Some of the later
locks and padlocks are among the most complicated composite medieval items recovered
from the sites included in this survey. Locks
were probably the only mechanical objects
ordinary Londoners would regularly have
owned. Padlock No 251 has 22 or more separate
components in the case alone; No 256 has at
least this number in the case and mechanism
together; and No 257 has 21 or more components, not counting the mechanism (the
undated padlock in Fig 67 appears to have at
least 35 parts). Some of the keys and cases
were probably intended by the makers to
appear far more complicated than was mechan-
ically necessary in order to suggest a greater
degree of security to the customer (e.g., key
No 312 and the substantial, intricate case of
padlock No 256, which was in fact made more
vulnerable by its robust-looking external bolt
sheath). The bit of No 268, and perhaps of
other padlock keys, suggests that the corresponding lock mechanism could have had four
spring strips. Although none of the listed padlocks certainly had more than three strips,
medieval examples with four are known from
London (see Fig 67; Anon 1928 – this item is
now MoL acc no 11973) and key No 267 below
might perhaps have catered for a lock with five.
The best of the locks and keys are high-
precision objects, presumably produced by
skilled blacksmiths or specialist locksmiths.
Salzman lists some prices for both (?)mounted
locks ('platelocks' etc.) and padlocks in the
medieval period, for example, a 'springlock' for
a door cost 16 pence in 1366 and two padlocks
together cost the same in 1438, while 16 large
platelocks with fittings cost 6 shillings and

8 pence each in 1364, and a new platelock with keys for a church door cost 2 shillings in 1389 (1952, 301–3).

All the copper-alloy padlocks and padlock slide keys listed below are from deposits dated to the early 14th century or before. It seems likely that some if not all of these items were imported from the Continent. Copper-alloy rotary key No 313, with its extremely complex bit, asymmetrical in both main planes, implies a high degree of skill among some copper-smiths as well as workers in iron, though, from the evidence of the finds considered here, iron locksmiths would seem to have cornered the London market by at least 1350. Many of the iron cases for slide-mechanism padlocks from the whole period considered have applied strips of iron (or sometimes in later ones of copper alloy, e.g., Nos 253, 255–6) and most have been finished by being coated (in part) by brazing, arguably so as to look as if they were made of copper alloy (see Col Pl 1A). This embellishment would have helped keep rust at bay, but the brazing does not seem to have been applied as an overall coating, so it may have had some other primary purpose, such as simply looking more attractive or more technologically highly wrought. Although several of the keys and rotary locks are tin-coated, this appears to be largely absent from the padlocks with slide mechanisms (see No 253 for one that may have a tin coating). While padlock keys of copper alloy and of iron seem likely to go with locks of the same respective metals, there is no copper-alloy lock of any kind to correspond with rotary keys Nos 294–8 of this metal (in fact there is no mounted lock of copper alloy at all from the assemblages included here); it would be particularly useful to know details of the lock for which elaborate key No 313 was intended.

These preferential uses of different metals through the period considered presumably reflect broader organisational developments in the precision-metal crafts of London, or perhaps changes in this particular aspect of international trade. The rarity of mounted locks from the assemblages prior to the end of the 13th century is notable.

Some of the well-made iron keys have preserved a series of shallow grooves on one or both faces of the bits (see Nos 269, 270, 317,

322, 326, 328). These features (which appear to have been noticed elsewhere only at Winchester – I H Goodall in Biddle 1990, 1032, 1034, fig 329, no 3826) may be purely decorative, like the grooves on the shanks of Nos 309, 315, 317 etc., or they might possibly be guidelines of some kind, perhaps to help in the precision cutting of functional clefts and channels. In themselves, they have no practical function, unlike the deeper grooves on the shanks of padlock keys Nos 264 and 273, which were presumably to help orientation (?in the dark) of these otherwise virtually symmetrical items.

With some elaborate items, it may eventually become possible to recognise traits that point to specific workshops or even to individual smiths. There is, for example, a striking difference between keys excavated at Winchester and the London finds listed below; none of the London finds has fully – i.e., centrally placed – cruciform clefts (see Nos 322–3, 326 for the nearest to this), while almost one in five of the rotary keys of similar date from Winchester have them (Goodall, ibid. 1025–35, types 3–9; cf. the cruciform ward in Winchester lock no 3687 mentioned above). This trait is, however, present in other, less well-dated finds of keys from the capital in the MoL's established collection (especially in ones of Ward Perkins's type VIIB – almost by definition of that category). The general lack of closely comparable wards among the more complicated of the recently excavated keys from London when set beside those from Winchester may point towards different regional traditions, at least for part of the later Middle Ages. Further, more closely dated examples with cruciform clefts are needed from London before it can be established whether the present possible hint of regional differences is really valid. The circular wards that survive in the rotary locks listed below are of relatively simple forms – see Nos 276, 280, 283–4.

There are two instances of pairs of very closely comparable keys from the same sites (Nos 261–2, 322–3 – Figs 74, 90), the former two coming from the same deposit. Each pair might possibly have been for the same lock.

Two of the larger locks listed, padlock No 257 and mounted lock No 281, bear marks consistent with their having been deliberately and forcibly broken, probably with axes (Figs

72, 81). While the immediate reasons for such actions must remain obscure, the apparent means of effecting them are as much a testament to the robustness of the locks as to the determination of the perpetrators of the damage. Other kinds of damage that appear to go beyond accidental mishaps are shown by padlock case No 246 and key No 331 (Figs 68, 92).

Iron lock-escutcheon plate No 334 was probably for a door or chest and copper-alloy escutcheon plate No 333 is probably from a small casket; in both instances the locks were presumably mounted on the inside.

Padlocks

The following padlocks are unmounted, completely metal-cased, spring-strip locks, all worked by sliding keys, with the exception of Nos 284–6, which have rotary mechanisms.

The smaller examples were probably for caskets and cupboards, while larger, more robust examples seem more appropriate for chests and doors, and the largest (No 256) may have been appropriate for a warehouse. No detailed contemporary depiction of a medieval padlock in place has been traced. A 15th-century finger ring found in London has an engraved signet with a padlock on a chain (Murdoch et al. 1991, 94, no 116), suggesting that some publications of excavated examples have illustrated them upside down, as the late medieval term 'hanging lock' (Salzman 1952, 303) also implies (see Fig 67, which has been inverted here from its original drawn orientation, and Crabbe 1971, 191–6).

The variety of slide-key padlocks recently excavated at the London sites included in the catalogue below is impressive, and there are no certain repeats within this series.

I H Goodall suggested four basic categories for the padlocks found at Winchester, which include some earlier than those discussed here (in Biddle 1990, 1001–3). Since only two of these categories appear to be represented below and some of the listed items cannot be attributed to either, that classification has not been used. All the locks listed under the present heading are variations on a basic cylindrical

shape for the cases. The common use of the term 'barrel' by modern writers to describe this shape does not seem particularly appropriate (apart perhaps from No 245, which seems to have no known parallel). The medieval term *turette* used of some padlocks (including ones at Westminster in 1275 'for fastening falcons on their perches' – Salzman 1952, 303) may refer to their cylindrical shape. The range in sizes of padlock available can be seen by comparing Nos 249 and 256. Some forms are widely paralleled elsewhere, others appear to be the first examples published. This diversity probably implies that locksmiths tended not to share details of their own or their family's/workshop's traditions of manufacture (as might be hoped and expected with security devices) and also that the variety in use was by no means confined to the range so far recovered. An 11th-century padlock found at Winchester retains its slide key (I H Goodall in Biddle 1990, 1004, 1012, 1014, no 3674, figs 310, 315), giving a useful indication that, while it may be possible to infer, from the appropriate key's bit, the number of spring strips in a lock, this does not provide a certain guide to their orientation – one strip in this lock being at 90 degrees to the position expected from examining the key. The spring-strip/slide-key form of mechanism remained in common use up to quite recently in parts of the Arab world and the Far East. Padlocks worked by rotary keys may be represented only by two items in the assemblages from the later part of the period considered, Nos 285–6, both apparently with rectangular iron cases (the earlier No 284 is not certainly a padlock).

Cylindrical padlock cases of iron are the only category of object of this metal among the medieval assemblages from the sites considered which were regularly coated (in part at least) by brazing (Col Pl 1A). This has been recognised on half of the iron examples listed below (and at least four of the others listed have applied copper-alloy case parts).

Specialist padlocks ('fetterlocks') were sometimes used in the medieval period to secure animal and human limbs as well as to fasten doors and chests. I H Goodall suggests that a relatively plain form with a hinged shackle may have been designed to avoid chafing on limbs

Fig 64   Padlock slide-key mechanism and terminology

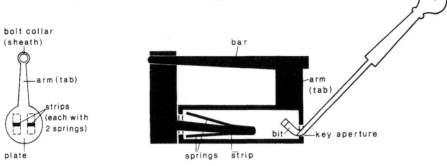

Locked

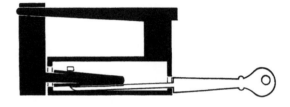

Springs pushed in against strip

end view of key bit for
two spring strips as above

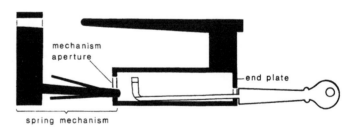

Mechanism withdrawn

(published, for example, among Norwich finds in Margeson 1993, 155–6, fig 115, no 1231, and represented among the present London assemblages only by a 'manacle' with an attached chain (BWB83 acc no 202, which is unstratified, but likely to be from the period 1150–1450; see Pritchard 1991, 253, fig 3.22, no 78 for an earlier, less complete example). Different forms

may have been for a variety of uses in practice (cf. the 'horse locks' used for garden gates, recorded in 1500 – Salzman 1952, 303).

Copper-alloy cases

Copper alloy seems to have been used only for small padlocks, probably in the main intended for caskets. None of those listed is from later than the 13th century. Some copper-alloy locks from the VRY89 site, probably from the 12th century, have copper-alloy springs, but Nos 242–3 have more satisfactory iron mechanisms (it was not possible to examine No 244 internally to determine the metal used there).

242 BIG82 Acc No 3071 (Context 5398) Ceramic Phase 6 Fig 65
Incomplete cylindrical case of sheeting, d 21mm, with a lengthwise upstanding (?)seam, and a strip around most of the surviving end plate, which has a sub-rectangular bolt aperture 10×8mm; a strip of iron held in the aperture by corrosion products is probably part of the mechanism; discarded locked.

243 SWA81 3563 (2277) 7 Fig 65
Mechanism only; two strips, each with riveted iron springs, l 22mm, and both riveted onto a cast, copper-alloy circular plate, d 8mm, with an arm l 13mm having a projecting rounded tab and a collar to house the fixed bolt on the missing case; filing marks on the plate from the finishing.

The bolt aperture on the lock would have had to be at least 5×4mm.

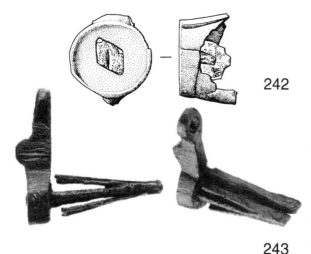

242

243

Fig 65 Padlocks (1:1)

244 BIG82 2472 (2277) 8 Fig 66
Cast, octagonal-section case, l 40×9mm, with fixed bolt l 43mm on rectangular arm; three of the faces of the case have sinuous double lines of opposed, punched triangles; spring mechanism has circular end plate with a strip holding a bifacially bevelled

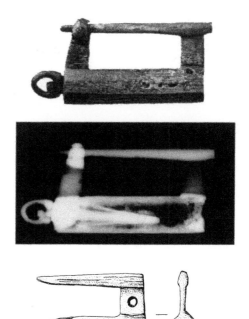

245

Fig 66 Padlocks and X-ray to show mechanism (1:1)

collar for the bolt; the mechanism's end plate has a riveted sub-circular loop, presumably for attachment of a chain to avoid loss; there is damage (possibly corrosion) on the case, and as most of its end plate is missing the shape of the key aperture does not survive; the X-ray plate shows there were two spring strips. Discarded locked.

Similar padlocks have been excavated in Oxford and Winchester (A R Goodall 1989, 223, 226, fig 62, nos 103–4, and I H Goodall in Biddle 1990, 1010, 1012, fig 313, no 3666, with a perforation in the arm and two spring strips) and also at Århus in Denmark (Crabbe 1971, 191, nos BSH and JP). Compare also iron padlock No 250.

245 BWB83 2491 (11) Unphased Fig 66
Cast, cylindrical case l 27mm; max d 10mm, with fixed bolt l 29mm on rectangular, pierced arm, and ridges around sides defining central swelling (top and base are flat); T-shaped key aperture (main part 5×3mm) in end, continuing into side; an internal vertical saeptum at other end indicates a mechanism with two spring strips; case has extensive finishing marks from filing.

Iron cases

All cases of definable forms are included, but some small fragments have been omitted. The highly intricate applied decorative wires on slightly earlier padlock cases (e.g., Hall 1984, 110) have a plainer counterpart in No 246, and the use of applied strips and rods (see Fig 67) up to the end of the period considered can be seen as a continuation of this decorative tradition.

246 SWA81 Acc No 1819 (Context 2130) Ceramic Phase 7 Fig 68 and Col Pl 1A

Flattened sheet casing, originally (?)cylindrical, l 78 × estd d *c*.32mm, with applied strips lengthways and around one end, some with rivets (two of these have ?decorative heads); one strip extends at a right angle at the side of the probable key aperture; two bands of opposed, slightly asymmetrical decoration (incomplete) of circles joined by angled lines, all made of strips set sideways-on; there is a sheet triangle at the original join of the edges of the case; only fragments of the end plate with the key aperture survive; all or most of the outer and part of the inner surfaces are brazed.

Flattening this casing (th approx 0.5–0.75mm) must have taken some effort; the motive remains obscure.

247 SH74 234 (484) 7 Fig 69

Mechanism only; incomplete, slightly oval plate 37×34mm, with remains of three spring strips l 60mm+; applied circular strip on the end forms a well protecting the terminals of the spring strips – one is bent over a transversely applied strip, and there is also a robust, looped handle; all the external parts are extensively brazed; there are two small, sub-rectangular holes or depressions on the end strip (?blocked from the brazing).

The looped handle may originally have been held on a chain.

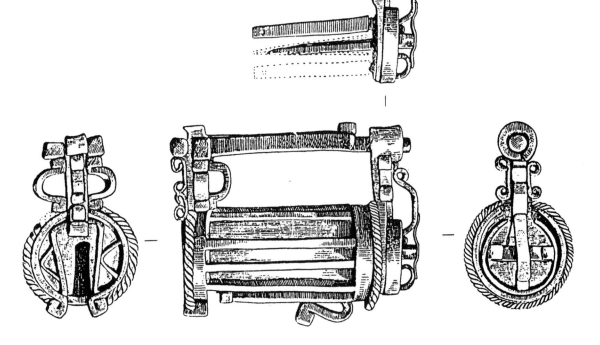

Fig 67   Padlock (from Anon 1928, courtesy Society of Antiquaries of London; MoL acc no 11973, approx 1:2)

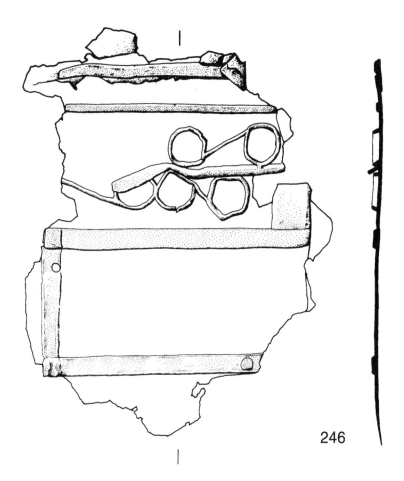

246

Fig 68   Flattened padlock case (1:1)

248 SWA81 2406 (2279) 7 Fig 69
Fragment of cylindrical case, d 36mm, with applied strips lengthways and an arm consisting of three pieces of sheeting set around the shorter part of an L-shaped, tapering bolt, l 55mm (the two side sheets extend around the main casing and splay outwards at the top, and the third has a terminal spike here, which is bent over to hold the bolt); the incomplete end plate has a distorted key aperture *c*.20×6mm; traces of brazing survive.

249 SWA81 1762 (2057) 9 Fig 69
Cylindrical case; l 23mm, d 12mm, with three applied-strip ribs and flanges around the ends; the bolt sheath is connected by a tab running the full length of the case; rectangular, diametrical key aperture, 9×3mm, at one end; central, pierced, tab at base; (mechanism is missing).

250 SWA81 2104 (2061) 9 Fig 69
Cylindrical case; l 41mm, d 13mm; damaged at end for insertion of key; bolt l 45mm on rectangular, pierced, arm; key aperture is a transverse slot extending at a right angle almost across the end plate; spring mechanism has a circular end plate with an applied strip holding a collar for the bolt, and a cylindrical (?copper-alloy) housing sleeved into the case; single spring strip (or possibly two).

Very similar to copper-alloy case No 244.

A similar lock was excavated at Winchester in a 15th–(?)16th-century deposit (I H Goodall in Biddle 1990, 1010, 1012, no 3667, fig 313).

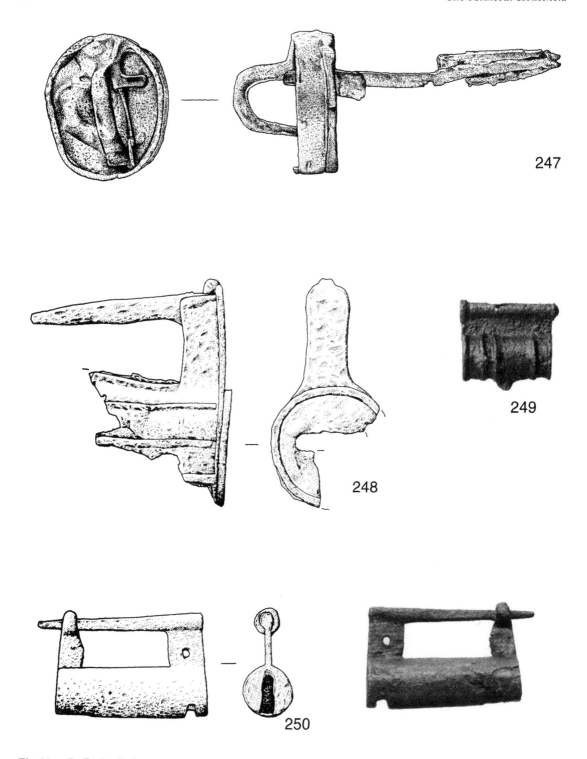

247

249

248

250

Fig 69   Padlocks (1:1)

251 LUD82 252 (1042) 9 Fig 70
Corroded; (?)slightly oval, cylindrical case, *c.*48×*c.*53mm, l 90mm, consisting of at least 22 components; applied strips lengthways and around the ends on the upper half; on the lower half there are four applied oblique (?)rods on each side (opposed to give a herringbone pattern when seen from below) between lengthways strips and others around the ends; incomplete end plate has damaged (?rectangular) key aperture, which extends into a transverse slot (estd *c.*25mm wide) on the base; the other end plate has three apertures for the spring strips of the missing bolt and has a bent-back strip extension at the top; a U-shaped sheet at the opposite end, with curved tabs attaching it to the case, has applied strips along its edges, and a further (?)bent

strip reduces the aperture for the bolt; the surface is extensively brazed. The bent-back strip was presumably for attaching the bolt to the case by a chain.

252 BWB83 4316 (355) 11 Fig 70
Fragmentary cylindrical case; l 53mm, d 25mm; applied rods lengthways and strips around ends; key slot 16×6mm in side continues at a right angle from end plate; two of the rods have D-shaped (?pierced) tabs near the other end (mechanism missing).

253 BWB83 4470 (256) 11
Cylindrical case; l *c.*55mm; d 25mm; copper-alloy applied strips around end and laterally; (?)tin coating.

254 BC72 4109 (88) 11
Distorted, cylindrical case of relatively robust sheeting (th *c.*1.5mm); l 100mm; original d estd approx

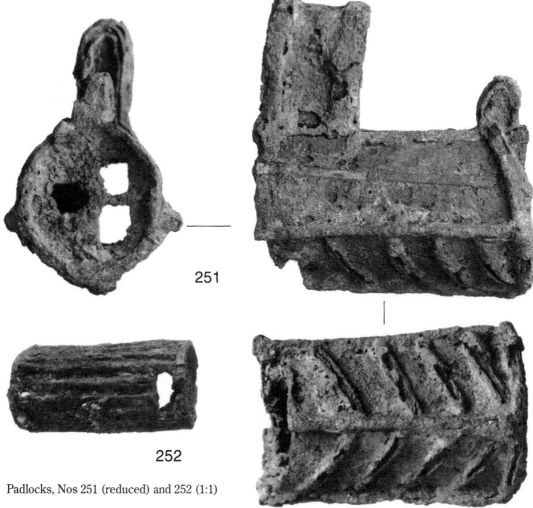

251

252

Fig 70   Padlocks, Nos 251 (reduced) and 252 (1:1)

Fig 71   Padlock (reduced;
X-ray not to scale)

256

  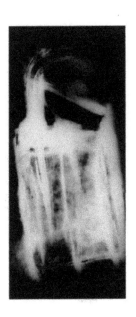

50mm; applied strips around each end and two (extending only half way) around middle part; distorted aperture *c*.22×9mm for key near one end; brazing on all parts.

255 SWA81 1851 (2097) 12
Fragmentary, very corroded case in form of cylinder with sub-rectangular top (sheath) to accommodate missing bolt; l (?)*c*.36mm; d 19mm; h 35mm; surviving portion consists largely of applied, copper-alloy binding strips around ends and base; trace of lengthways ribbing; holes for three spring strips in end plate; (?)tin coating or brazing.

256 SWA81 732 (2098) 12 Fig 71
Cylindrical case, l 56mm; d 89mm, with overlapping end plates, and applied strips around the middle and defining the key aperture and bolt plate; a tapering sheath for the bolt is set on a diametrically applied strip on one end plate, and the other has diametrical and slightly narrower transverse strips, with a copper-alloy strip defining the top of the key aperture of *c*.20×*c*.8mm, which continues along the base; much of the surface is coated with brazing; part of the sheeting around the bolt aperture has been pulled up out of place. The internal mechanism consists of two spring strips at a right angle to each other; the U-shaped bolt, l *c*.110mm, with a sub-rectangular plate, has a decorative, applied copper-alloy strip along the outside of the curve, and tapered, flanking additions next to the plate, together with an incomplete oval chain link (l 58mm+); tin coating.

The key probably had the bit at a right angle to a centrally attached shank (cf. No 273).

Compare an unstratified smaller lock (l 55mm;

d 30mm) found at the BC72 site (acc no 870) for a similar form of case.

257 SWA81 1867 (Unstratified) Fig 72
Cylindrical case, l 56mm, d 35mm; applied strips lengthways and around ends; full-length tab holding the bolt sheath has applied copper-alloy strips near each end, with triangular sheet-iron plates on ends; the incomplete key aperture (6×*c*.7mm+) is defined by a transversely applied strip on the bottom of the case, and continues into the end plate; there is a small, applied right-angled sheet tab above the aperture here; the other end retains the circular bolt plate with the stub of the expanded bolt; tin coating; two scrolled sheet strips flanking broken-off (U-shaped) bolt; the case has been knocked flat in the middle with a bladed tool (?axe) which has cut into the applied strips at one end (but was not definitely responsible for breaking the bolt); discarded locked.

Compare mounted lock No 281 for the damage.

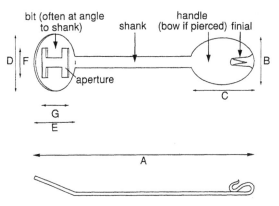

Fig 73 Slide key terminology – overall length A, handle B×C, bit D×E (aperture F×G) – B is diameter for round bits, F and G are dimensions for simple apertures; other measurements for more complicated forms are specified in the text

Padlock slide keys
SHANKS NARROWING TO STRIPS

Copper alloy

258 BIG82 Acc No 2701 (Context 3562) Ceramic Phase 6 Fig 74
Slightly distorted; l 54mm; sub-round bow (d 7mm), with collar and off-centred hole; 25mm of shank is in

257

Fig 72 Damaged padlock (1:1)

form of expanding strip; bit (7×6×2mm) is set to one side of shank.

Compare MoL acc no 84.268/1.

259 SWA81 1878 (2139) 9 Fig 74
L 45mm; bow d 6mm; pair of D-shaped flanges at right angle to shank on each side, each 3×4mm; total width at end 5mm.

Despite the differing forms of the ends, which were for differently shaped apertures, both the preceding keys would have been appropriate for similar lock mechanisms with two spring strips (cf. padlocks Nos 243–5). Compare also keys found in Exeter dated to the late 16th century (A R Goodall in Allan 1984, 344–5, no 183) and in Norwich dated to the 15th/16th century (I H Goodall in Margeson 1993, 162–3, fig 120, no 1312).

ANGLED BITS

(Cf. Ward Perkins 1940, 147, fig 44, and I H Goodall in Biddle 1990, type A)

Iron

All of the following have a circular bit. Listing is in order of overall length, within ceramic phases.

Several of the following keys are broken or otherwise incomplete. This suggests that the quality may sometimes not have been particularly good.

A kind of 18th-century hasp which is superficially similar in form might, if unstratified, be confused with medieval keys of this kind (see Stone 1974, 199–201, figs 115–16 K–Q).

260 BIG82 Acc No 2756 (Context 4016) Ceramic Phase 6
Overall l 92mm; damaged finial (cf. following item) at right angle to flat, arrow-shaped handle 12×19mm; bit d 14mm (simple aperture 9×5mm); (?)for lock with one spring strip.

261 BIG82 3429 (6759) 6
L 95mm; arrow-shaped handle, 12×21mm, having circular finial, d 11mm, at right angle and with central hole; bit 13×15mm (aperture 10×5mm and as in preceding item).

262 BIG82 3431 (6759) 6 Fig 74
As preceding item (from the same deposit);

l 111mm; handle 13×28mm, finial d 10mm; bit 11×15mm (9×5mm).

263 SH74 265 (536) 6
Most of bit broken off; surviving l 128mm (?originally *c*.140mm); expanded handle similar in form to that of many modern spoons 16×*c*.45mm, with finial having large loop and small bent tip.

264 SWA81 2408 (2279) 7 Fig 74
L 148mm; oval handle 12×21mm; sub-round bit 18×21mm (21×17mm); shank has transverse grooves on one face near finial, which is as in the preceding item; aperture with cleft, probably for two spring strips at a right angle to each other.

265 BIG82 2697 (4371) 7
Bit broken off; oval handle 16×24mm with finial folded into S-shape; surviving l 157mm.

266 BWB83 149 (110) 11 Fig 74
Bit at right angle; irregular, lozenge-shaped handle with large loop and small bent tip; l 115mm; handle 15×27mm; bit d 21mm; H-shaped, asymmetrical aperture, with additional cleft 15×12mm.

BITS IN SAME PLANE AS SHANK

Compare Ward Perkins' type IX (1940, 143 – there called casket keys). The form with shield-shaped, symmetrical bits like Nos 269–72 is attributed to the Roman as well as to the medieval period by Ward Perkins (following Wheeler 1946, 74, pl 30B, nos 9–12) but an absence of reliably dated Roman examples from excavations now calls this into question.

Compare I H Goodall in Biddle 1990, 1005–6, 1024, fig 324, type C) for bits of other shapes. The three relatively complete examples with shield-shaped bits are the most neatly (and perhaps also the most accurately) finished of all the lock items included in this study; they appear to be very high-precision keys. The only padlock of corresponding form (i.e., with an aperture at one end and a slot running almost the length of the case) among those listed above is No 252 (Goodall ibid. cites an example from Winchester – see Cunliffe 1964, 189, fig 66, no 8, and the 1990 Winchester finds volume includes five keys of this kind, but there is

Fig 74   Slide keys (1:1)

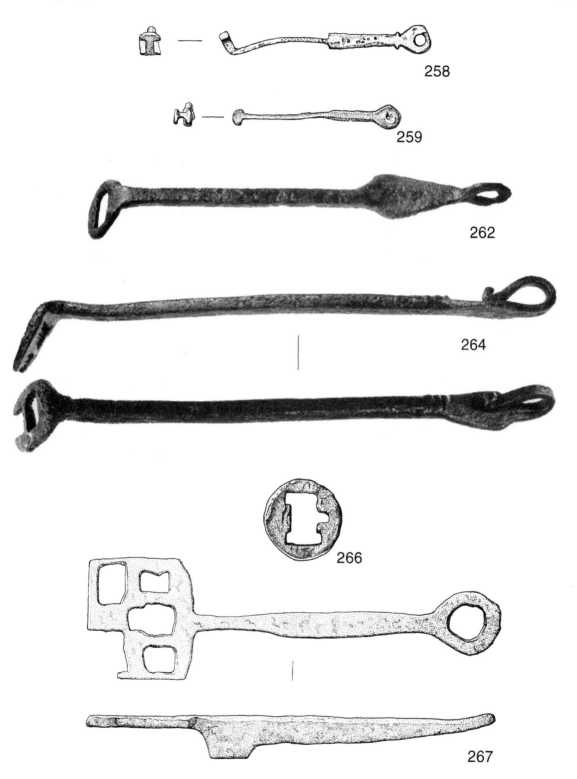

258

259

262

264

266

267

apparently no matching lock among those published from the same assemblages). This seeming widespread under-representation of corresponding locks is enigmatic.

Iron

RECTANGULAR BIT

267 SWA81 Acc No 1381 (Context 1595) Ceramic Phase 6 Fig 74

L 112mm; bow d 17mm; bit 32×27mm (extent of apertures 29×21mm); circular handle on square-section shank swelling towards the middle and an upstanding tab at the end; the rectangular bit has a curving top and a symmetrical arrangement of five rectangular apertures (two are slightly narrowed, perhaps unevenly worn from use) and is broken off on one side; tin coating.

The two side apertures (at the right in Fig 74) may have been for guard pins inside the lock, leaving the three larger apertures each for a spring strip, or there may perhaps have been five strips.

ROUND BIT

268 BWB83 4340 (107) 6–9 Fig 75

Incomplete; fragment of round-section, hollow shank, with round bit d 19mm, having cruciform aperture (11×12mm) for three or four spring strips; tin coating.

SHIELD-SHAPED BITS AND RELATED FRAGMENTS

(These keys are all notably well made.)

From the dating assigned to the London finds, this category may have replaced the somewhat more roughly made varieties above (Nos 267–8) around the middle of the 14th century. Monk describes much later, 19th-century examples of this form as 'latch keys' (1974, 43).

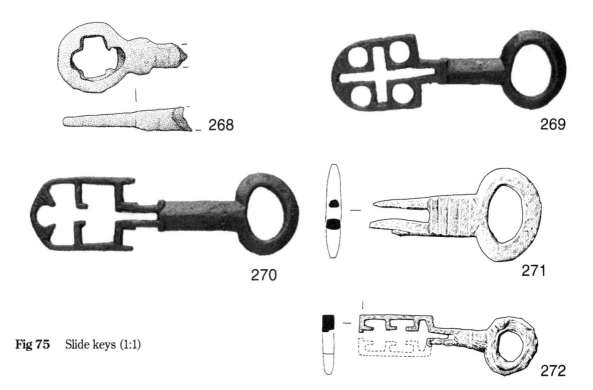

268

269

270

271

272

Fig 75   Slide keys (1:1)

Fig 76 Slide key (1:1)

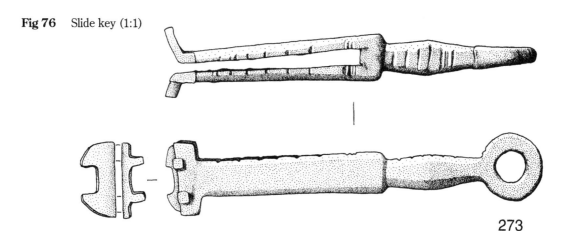

273

269 BC72 Acc No 2239 (Context 79) Ceramic Phase 11 Fig 75

L 63mm; oval bow 21×17mm; lozenge-section shank; shield-shaped bit 19×29mm (15×26mm) with cruciform aperture having pierced circles between the arms, and grooves (obliquely at the base) on both faces.

The circles here may possibly have been to admit guard pins within the lock.

270 BC72 2862 (150) 11 Fig 75

Similar in basic form to preceding item; 74mm; 22×17mm; 19×29mm (16×22mm); with wider, simpler aperture and radiating grooves on both faces.

271 BWB83 2907 (286) 11 Fig 75

Incomplete; bit broken off; l 46mm+; oval bow 25×18mm; rectangular shank has transverse grooves on both faces.

272 SWA81 1114 (2105) 12 Fig 75

Corroded; wards incomplete; bit (possibly rectangular) 48mm; bow d 15mm; ?10×20mm (?18×?8mm).

BIT AT RIGHT ANGLE TO CENTRALLY ATTACHED SHANK

(Cf. bone item in Fig 63, and I H Goodall in Biddle 1990, 1005–6, type B)

273 SWA81 480 (2030) 9 Fig 76

L 103mm; bow d 17mm; square-section shank is bevelled at corners, expands towards middle, and has widened, bifurcated end, with complex and asymmetrical, bipartite 'bit' 19×*c*.16mm; transverse grooves filed along the shank on one side, presumably to help orientate the key correctly.

A well-made, quite complicated key. Compare the elaborate lock in Fig 67 and the conjectural key figured in its original publication (Anon 1928).

Rectangular iron locks

(Mechanisms worked with rotary keys)

Wooden cases for this kind of lock, like a rare survival excavated in York (MacGregor 1982, 80, 82–3, no 430), seem to be of an earlier date than the period considered here, though they may account for the current absence – apart from the enigmatic fragment No 284 from an early 12th-century context – of excavated examples prior to the late 13th century in London to go with early keys like Nos 294–6 and 305. Mounted metal locks, not all of which are necessarily the original ones, survive on a number of large medieval chests (e.g., Fig 45 bottom; Clifford Smith 1923, pl 37, nos 287–8; Jenning 1974, no V; J Geddes in Zarnecki et al. 1984, 297, no 327 – a 12th-century chest) and caskets (e.g., Fig 45 top). At least two, possibly three, of the locks listed below are cased, with separate back plates (Nos 285–6, both from the late 14th century, and perhaps the earlier No 284 as well; backs have possibly been lost from some of the other locks listed below). Nos 285–6 are padlocks from the early stages of a tradition of manufacture that continues today.

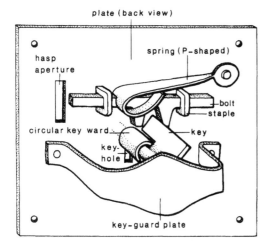

Fig 77   Rotary lock terminology

All the lock plates listed below appear to be roughly rectangular. P-shaped springs occur in locks with simple plates found in contexts attributed to ceramic phases 9–11, and also in one of the locks (?)with a separate back plate and attributed to phase 7, while S-shaped springs are in listed locks of this kind attributed to phases 9–12 (the former, which may have been less liable to stress breakage as the metal had been bent in only one direction rather than two, was also used in post-medieval locks). The bars are each held by two riveted, U-shaped staples, unless stated otherwise. The tops of keyholes are all rounded for the shanks of the keys, apart from in Nos 275 and 277. The first dimensions given are those of the lower parts of the holes (the part to accommodate the bit – i.e., they omit the rounded top part for the key shank, in order to allow more direct comparison with the dimensions given for keys); the total lengths of the holes are given afterwards in brackets. This information provides the basis for assessment of the compatibility of individual keys and locks.

LOCKS WITH SIMPLE PLATES

(?Mounted locks)

274 SWA81 Acc No 1923 (Context 2136) Ceramic Phase 9 Fig 78
Fragmentary plate, surviving dimensions 26×27mm; P-shaped spring and bolt, l 28mm, survive.

275 SWA81 1154 (2145) 9
Incomplete, corroded plate, surviving dimensions 47×38mm, with one surviving hole for attachment; damaged, rectangular/tapered keyhole 12×5mm; bolt l 29mm; P-shaped spring, and distorted key-guard plate.

276 BWB83 215 (285) 9 Fig 78
Concave-sided plate *c*.132×112mm with one corner broken off and another bent back; two of the four corner holes retain flat iron nails, l *c*.35mm; keyhole 13×4mm (20mm) has central tab at bottom (implying the key had a central groove or channel in the outside edge of the bit – see No 311 for the only example with this feature among the listed keys); hasp aperture 18×6mm; bolt l 59mm; distorted S-shaped spring, and circular key ward survive; a crude rivet holds the plate together where it had split into two layers because of poor smithing (there are signs of a similar fault to the right of the top of the keyhole); two further rivets suggest there was originally a key-guard plate; tin coating.

277 BC72 3839 (119) 10–11
Plate 47×31mm; rectangular keyhole 11×3.5mm; hasp aperture 9×4mm; bolt l 29mm is held at one end by the usual looped staple and at the other between two rivets (possibly replacements); another rivet and the distorted key-guard plate survive.

278 TL74 1504 (2608) 11
Very fragmentary and distorted plate 55+×40+mm; one corner hole for attachment survives; key-guard plate and bolt l *c*.35mm+; hasp l 63×15mm, with looped terminal and expanded at presumed hinge, is attached in locked position.

279 BWB83 172 (279) 11 Fig 79
Slightly bevelled plate, 72×49mm, with one corner broken off; one of the four corner holes retains part of an iron nail; keyhole 9×4mm (13mm); two hasp apertures each 10×4mm; bolt l 60mm has U-shaped end for second hasp; P-shaped spring; distorted key-guard plate survives; file marks on lower part of front; tin coating.

280 BWB83 747 (303) 11 Fig 80
Incomplete, (?)rectangular plate, 71+×79mm;

Fig 78   Mounted locks (1:1)

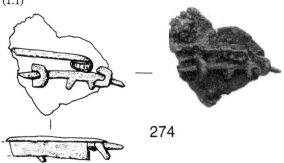

274

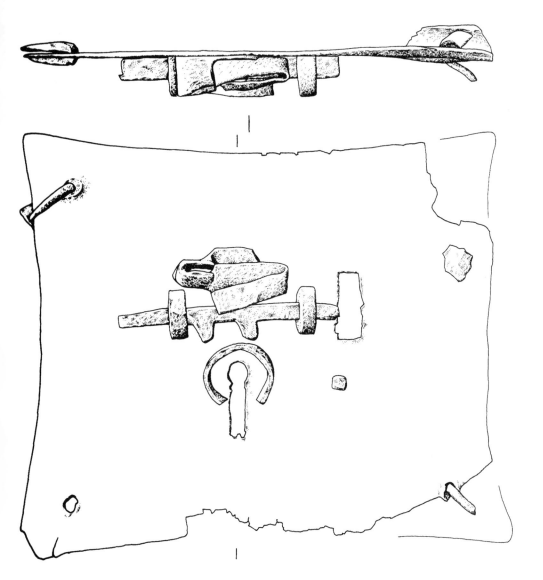

276

Fig 79 Mounted lock (1:1)

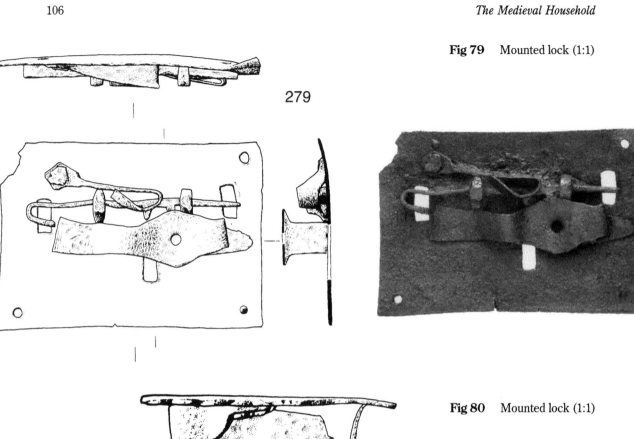

279

Fig 80 Mounted lock (1:1)

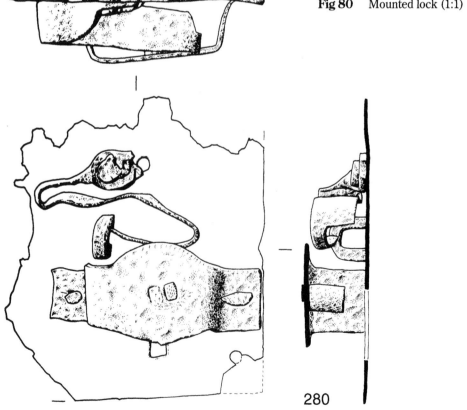

280

Fig 81 Damaged mounted lock (approx 1:1 at top)

281

(?)corner holes for attachment; keyhole 14×4mm (18mm); one of original two staples for missing bolt, S-shaped spring and riveted key-guard plate with riveted, circular key ward survive; a second hole near the rivet for the spring may mean that parts of the mechanism have been replaced, while one near the guard plate could be for another, missing key ward.

281 BWB83 5643 (308) 11 Fig 81
Corroded, incomplete and distorted plate (bent almost in half) 127×96mm; (?)concave sided; two corner holes for attachment and S-shaped spring

survive; hasp aperture 17×6mm; tin coating; the keyhole is distorted.

The considerable force, apparently exerted from the front, needed to bend the plate into its present shape along a slightly curved plane across the centre, appears consistent with a blow from an axe blade.

Compare padlock No 257 for the damage.

282 SWA81 1208 (2100) 12
Incomplete and corroded, concave-sided plate, 75×41+mm; bolt 1 39mm+ and part of spring survive; hasp aperture 5×15+mm; tin coating.

283 TL74 1103 (368) 12 Fig 82
Corroded, slightly concave-sided plate, *c.*130×
65mm; two corner holes for attachment survive, one
with round head of a nail or rivet; round-topped
keyhole 12×3.5mm (17mm) and two hasp apertures
14×6mm; S-shaped spring, key-guard plate with
circular key ward, and bolt l 80mm (with U-shaped
end for a second hasp) survive; tin coating.

283

284

Fig 82   Mounted locks (1:1)

RECTANGULAR MOUNTED LOCKS/PADLOCKS WITH RAISED FRONT AND SEPARATE BACK PLATES

(Cased locks)

Number 284 is probably a mounted lock, perhaps originally with a back plate (though not certainly), while Nos 285–6 are late medieval padlocks of similar form to the preceding mounted locks (see Fig 83 for a complete example with a case 66×60mm, possibly of slightly later date, found in London (MoL acc no A27876; Tracy 1988, 125, fig 49 shows a padlock of this form on a 15th-century alms box, though this particular lock is not necessarily of the same date as the box). See Treue et al. for a German maker of rectangular padlocks of *c*.1425 (1965, fig 48).

All of the following have angled sides (cf. I H Goodall 1981, 58, 60, fig 57, no 7). Some of the more fragmentary items listed in the preceding category may originally have had back plates.

284 SWA81 Acc No 2254 (Context 2266) Ceramic Phase 7 Fig 82
119×88mm, th 16mm; small fragment survives, perhaps of a back plate held by an iron rivet (its original position is suggested by a record sketch; otherwise it would have been taken for part of the warding/mechanism arrangement – it is not shown in the illustration); keyhole with expanded base 19×5mm (28mm); two hasp apertures 13 and 14×5mm; four (?of original five) nail/rivet holes survive along diameter; P-shaped spring; bar, l 68mm, has U-shaped end for a second hasp; tabs from broken-off keyguard plate survive; two concentric, circular key wards (inner one not shown in illustration).

Presumably a mounted lock in view of its size and the provision for two hasps, despite the possible piece of back plate. A more complete example from this date is needed before the existence of mounted iron locks which are enclosed at the back can be demonstrated this early.

285 BWB83 5607 (308) 11 Fig 83
63×59mm, th 14mm; back survives intact; keyhole *c*.15×5mm, with side tab (for key with channel); hasp aperture 15×5mm; tin coating; the X-ray plate shows that the S-shaped spring has been displaced relative to the bar; key-guard plate; bar l 39mm; hasp, l 57×13mm, tapering to upswept end tab, survives in locked position.

Perhaps discarded because of the misaligned spring, which may have jammed the mechanism.

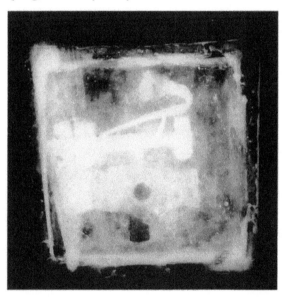

285

Fig 83　Rectangular, rotary padlocks: (X-ray (1:1); bottom, MoL acc no A27876 (1:2)

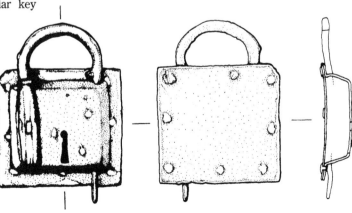

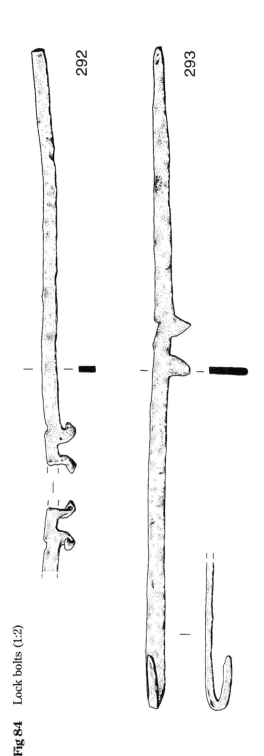

Fig 84   Lock bolts (1:2)

286 BWB83 2512 (256) 11

Fragment of case; surviving dimensions 50×47mm; th 11mm; a rivet joins the front and back; incomplete bolt, surviving l 29mm; S-shaped spring; tin coating.

(?)Originally similar to preceding item.

BOLTS FROM ROTARY LOCKS

(Minor fragments are omitted.)

Numbers 287–91 have a slight ridge or tab on the upper side, while the later Nos 292–3 have a notch here, serving as a catch against the spring to prevent the bolt being forced open without the proper key (see MacGregor 1982, 81–2, nos 430–2; cf. I H Goodall in Biddle 1990, 1017, 1020, no 3692, fig 321).

Iron

287 SWA81 Acc No 2109 (Context 2051) Ceramic Phase 8

L 130mm.

288 BWB83 3092 (285) 8

Broken off at both ends; surviving l 40mm.

289 BWB83 3815 (196) 9

Surviving l 125mm (originally *c.*160mm if symmetrical).

290 BWB83 2990 (257) 11

L 53mm.

291 BC72 1771 (55) 11

(?)Incomplete, relatively thin bolt (thicker at key tabs); surviving l 228mm (originally *c.*275mm if symmetrical).

292 SWA81 1147 (2105) 12 Fig 84

(?)Incomplete; surviving l 220mm (originally *c.*440mm if symmetrical); key tabs hammered into spirals.

Probably from a large chest.

293 BWB83 5431 (310) 12 Fig 84

L 353mm; one end is U-shaped.

The bent end suggests that this is from a lock catering for two hasps (cf. Nos 283 etc.).

Rotary keys

Shanks (stems) are solid, and copper-alloy keys are cast, unless otherwise stated. For terminology see Fig 85.

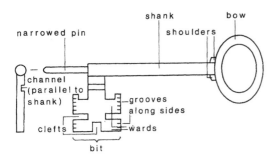

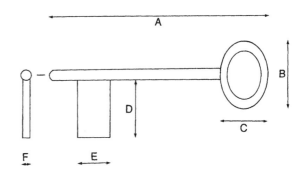

Fig 85 Rotary key terminology – overall length A, bow b×C (bit D×E×F)

Ward Perkins (1940) considered that a hollow shank (or pipe) up to 1½ inches (*c*.40mm) long was usually indicative of a casket or chest key (cf. Nos 294–8), while a solid shank ('pin' in his terminology) was more appropriate for a door key. While this may be generally true, it cannot be considered an absolute criterion.

Keys with hollow shank ends might have a corresponding pin set in the lock to help align them for the bolt, but no such feature has been recognised among the excavated locks listed above (there is one on the wooden casing of an earlier mounted lock found in York; Mac-Gregor 1982, 80, 82–3, no 430).

SMALL, CRUDE KEYS WITH CIRCULAR BOWS AND MAINLY VERY SIMPLE BITS

The dating evidence suggests that this was a long-lasting form, from at least the late 12th to the late 14th century. The absence from the excavated assemblages (and apparently elsewhere at the appropriate date) of copper-alloy locks with mechanisms worked by rotary keys raises the unsolved question as to what kinds of locks keys Nos 294–8 were for. Possibly copper alloy was used, in some instances at least, for duplicate or replacement keys of iron originals.

The keys assigned to this category are between 30 and 45mm in length (the upper limit is based purely on the main range from the recent excavations). Several of the bits are extremely simple. Copper-alloy key No 298 (and possibly No 297 too) seems not to have been finished by filing, and the plain bits of Nos 299 and 304 also appear somewhat rough-and-ready, though some of the other iron keys, like No 300, are more neatly finished. These sometimes almost rudimentary keys may have been for locks on caskets. See Egan (forthcoming a) for a group of at least 33 iron and copper-alloy keys of this kind found together in a bunch at the site of a medieval hospital in London, perhaps used for individual lockers for the patients.

Copper alloy
(All have hollow shank ends)

294 BIG82 Acc No 3083 (Context 5364) Ceramic Phase 6 Fig 86
L 35mm; bow d 11mm (bit 7×9×1.5mm); symmetrical rounded clefts.
295 SWA81 2503 (2257) 7
Similar to preceding item; l 35mm; bow d 10.5mm (bit 6×9×2mm).
296 BIG82 3406 (3204) 7
L 37mm; bow d 13mm (bit 7×8×1.5mm); symmetrical rectangular clefts; worn.
297 SWA81 1750 (2000) 9
Part of bit broken off; l 34mm, bow d 13mm (bit ?×8×2mm); inside edge of bow is uneven (unfinished by filing).
298 BWB83 3664 (359) 11 Fig 86
L 37mm; shouldered bow d 13mm (bit 8×6×3mm); asymmetrical clefts with offset, opposed channels; apparently untrimmed after casting.

Fig 86   Rotary keys (1:1)

294

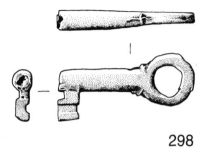

298

300

301

305

307

Iron
(Hollow shanks unless indicated otherwise)

299 BWB83 Acc No 3863 (Context 290) Ceramic Phase 9
Incomplete bow; l 27mm+ (plain bit 8×11×2.5mm).

300 SWA81 3273 (2141) 9 Fig 86
L 30mm; bow d 13mm (bit 7×4×4mm); collar below bow; solid shank; asymmetrical clefts with offset, opposed channels; tin coating.
   Similar form of bit to the larger one on No 302.

301 SWA81 3068 (2070) 9 Fig 86
L 38mm; bow d 16mm (bit 7×7×3mm); shouldered bow; asymmetrical clefts and channels; tin coating (MLC).

302 SWA81 3942 (2040) 9
L 42mm; bow d 16mm (bit 10×9×2.5mm), asymmetrical clefts and offset, opposed channels; tin coating.
   Compare the bit on No 300.

303 BWB83 634 (151) 11
Bit and end of shank broken off; l 38mm+; bow d 12mm; tin coating.

304 SWA81 3854 (Unstratified)
Sub-pentagonal bow with round hole; l 44mm; bow d 13mm (plain bit 6×10×1.5mm); found with fibres around both sides of bow (possibly from string).

SOLID SHANKS AND BITS

Iron

Circular bows

305 BIG82 Acc No 2715 (Context 3882) Ceramic Phase 7 Fig 86
Corroded; l 34mm; bow d 13mm (bit 5×6×1mm); asymmetrical bit (possibly incomplete) with single cleft.

306 BC72 4187 (118) 10–11
L 50mm; bow d 21mm (bit mainly broken off but one channel survives); collared knop below shouldered bow.

307 BWB83 3780 (149) 11 Fig 86
L 40mm; oval bow 18×20mm (bit 10×6×3mm); asymmetrical clefts, with channels on one face; tin coating (MLC).

308 BC72 2646 (79) 11 Fig 87
Corroded (drawn partly from X-ray plate); upper part of shank has rectangular section at a right angle to the bow, with trace of engraved saltire cross in rectangle; lower part is narrower, with (?)round section; l 60mm; bow d 24mm (bit ?14×15×?4mm); asymmetrical clefts.

309 BWB83 3386 (314) 12 Fig 87
Wards missing; circular bow; l 59mm; bow d 22mm; moulded shank has faint oblique grooves.

Kidney-shaped bow

310 TL74 Acc No 2155 (Context 1743) Ceramic Phase 10 Fig 87
L 65mm; bow 32×26mm (bit 18×22×5mm); asymmetrical clefts with opposed channels.

Lozenge-shaped bow

Compare Ward Perkins' type V (1940; also 138–9, where bows of this shape are said to be relatively common in the 13th/14th centuries).

311 SWA81 Acc No 2271 (Unstratified) Fig 87
L 73mm; bow 36×36mm (bit 21×19×4mm); asymmetrical clefts with channel; X-ray plate appears to show coating, though tin was not detected (MLC).

Shape of bow uncertain

312 BWB83 Acc No 4248 (Context 307) Ceramic Phase 11 Fig 87
Asymmetrical clefts and end of shank only; (bit 17×24×4.5mm); the enclosed aperture in the bit adds to the appearance of complexity, but can have served no practical purpose in a rotary mechanism at this date (there is no evidence among medieval locks for much later technological developments which do use such features for the mechanism – the author is grateful to Alan MacCormick for discussion of this point).

ELABORATE BIT ON HOLLOW, DRILLED SHANK

Copper alloy

313 SWA81 Acc No 2096 (Context 2033) Ceramic Phase 9 Fig 88
Bow broken off at collared knop; l 66mm+; octagonal shank; asymmetrical bit 13×25×9mm, with asymmetrical channels, including one along outside edge.

This is much the most complicated bit among the keys listed here. It seems most unlikely that all the features would have had corresponding ones in the lock. The closest parallels in the MoL established collection of keys have round and lozenge-shaped bows. It is possible that keys with such elaborate channelling would have been matched by lock apertures (or escutcheon plates) with corresponding outlines, though since none has been identified from the appropriate period, this too seems improbable.

FOLDED BITS AND HOLLOW SHANKS

(Ward Perkins 1940, type II)

Copper-alloy sheeting

314 SWA81 Acc No 418 (Context 2018) Ceramic Phase 9 Fig 89
L 28mm; oval bow 9×11mm, with two rounded protrusions at top and two at the base (bit 10×10×3mm); symmetrical clefts.

Presumably for a casket lock.

This is the only listed copper-alloy key that was not cast. The method of manufacture is paralleled by

Fig 87   Rotary keys (1:1)

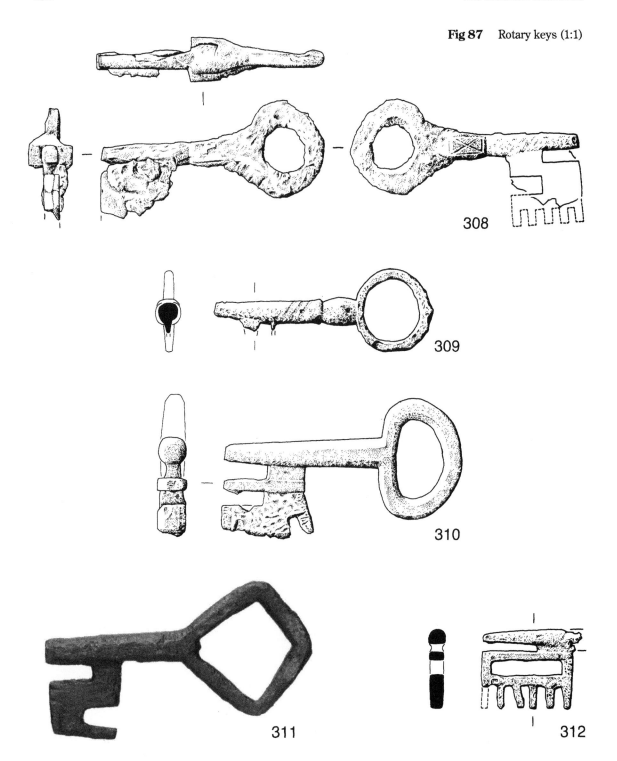

308

309

310

311

312

Fig 88   Incomplete rotary key (1:1)

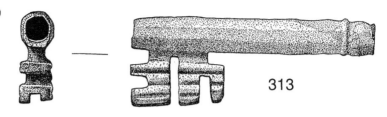

313

keys published by Hume (1863, pl 19). The locks cannot have been particularly robust to have been operated by such flimsy keys.

Iron

Oval bows

315 BWB83 Acc No 2521 (Context 367) Ceramic Phase 9 Fig 89
Corroded; l 87mm; bow d 31mm (bit 19×20×3mm); oblique lines on shank and pair of circumferential grooves at end; asymmetrical clefts.

316 BWB83 2985 (142) 11
Very corroded; l 76mm; bow 30×20mm (bit 16× *c.*15×?4mm); asymmetrical clefts.

Kidney-shaped bow

317 BWB83 Acc No 4745 (Context 303) Ceramic Phase 11 Fig 89
L 164mm; bow 53×30mm (bit 25×35×4mm); pair of circumferential grooves at end of shank; symmetrical clefts with grooves along sides; one pair of clefts is rounded.

Circular bows

318 OPT81 Acc No 147 (Context 58) Ceramic Phase 6 Fig 89
Corroded; l 60mm; bow d 21mm (bit 15×15× *c.*3mm); clefts incomplete, possibly originally asymmetrical.

319 BWB83 4238 (331) 11 Fig 90
L 113mm, bow d 33mm (bit 20×26×2mm); bow has hint of shoulders; asymmetrical clefts.

320 BWB83 406 (359) 11
L 134mm; bow d 36mm (bit broken off).

Shape of bow uncertain

321 TL74 Acc No 1501 (Context 1956) Ceramic Phase 11
Very corroded; only asymmetrical clefts and part of shank survive; bit 25×30mm; tin coating.

NARROWED PINS – SOLID SHANKS AND BITS

(Ward Perkins 1940, type VII)

Iron

Kidney-shaped bows

322 BC72 Acc No 3059 (Context 250) Ceramic Phase 10 Fig 90
L 126mm, bow 32×21mm (bit 22×30×2mm); symmetrical clefts with grooves along sides on one face.
   Size and form of warding closely similar to those of next item.

323 BC72 4306 (150) 11 Fig 90
L 119mm; ovoid bow 35×22mm (bit 20×29×3mm); symmetrical clefts.
   Size and form of bit closely similar to those in No 322.

324 BWB83 2785 (318) 11
Corroded; l 130mm; bow 43×23mm (bit 18×30×*c.*6mm); clefts incomplete, perhaps originally asymmetrical.

325 BWB83 4825 (330) 11 Fig 90
Corroded and distorted, clefts incomplete; l *c.*130mm; bow *c.*35×27mm (bit 17×20+×?4mm).

326 BC72 4140 (88) 11 Fig 90
L 132mm; bow 45×23mm (bit 18×28×3.5mm); flattened-oval section shank, with two transverse grooves at end; narrowed pin is further narrowed at tip; bit has symmetrical clefts and grooves along sides on both faces.

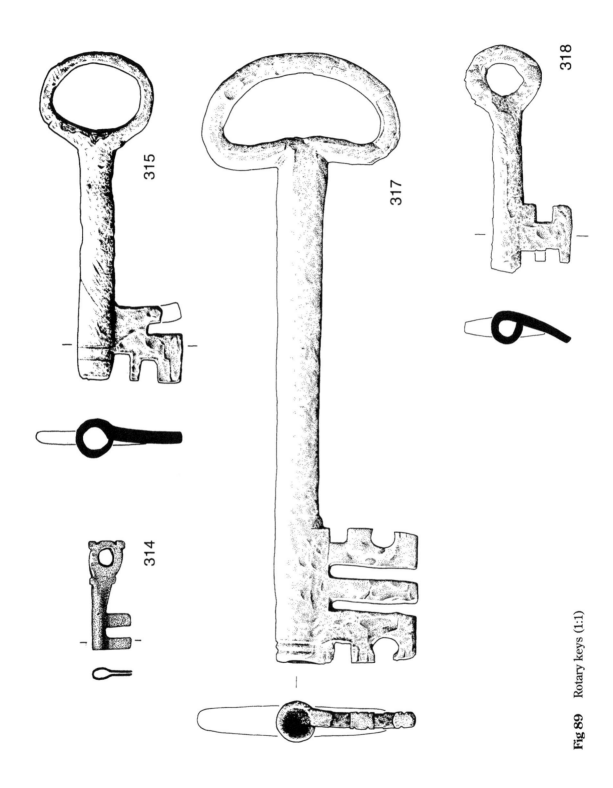

Fig 89   Rotary keys (1:1)

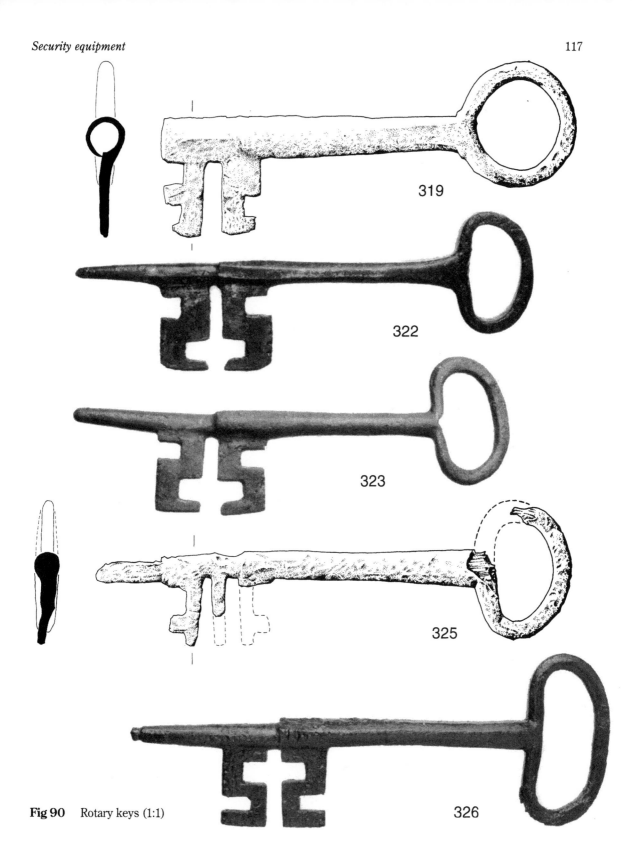

319

322

323

325

Fig 90 Rotary keys (1:1)

326

327 BC72 2611 (79) 11 Fig 91
L 149mm; bow 39×27mm (bit 22×36×2.5mm); flattened-oval section shank; symmetrical clefts.

328 BC72 2434 (79) 11 Fig 91
L 159mm; bow 43×34mm (bit 24×38×3mm); shank has transverse grooves at end of thicker part and pin is narrowed further at tip; bit has symmetrical clefts and grooves along sides on both faces.

329 TL74 1102 (368) 12 Fig 91
Corroded; l 134mm; bow 37×27mm (bit 20×31×2.5mm), flattened-oval section shank; symmetrical clefts.

See also No 331.

Shape of bows uncertain

330 BWB83 Acc No 3358 (Context 374) Ceramic Phase 11
Corroded, bow missing; l 112mm+ (bit 27×32×2mm); incomplete bit; clefts perhaps originally symmetrical.

331 BWB83 468 (110) 11 Fig 92
Bow distorted, probably originally kidney shape; wards broken off by bending; l c.120mm, bow max (?)37mm (bit l 28mm); tip of shank burred from wear or striking.

The damage to this key may represent a deliberate attempt to render it useless.

Fig 91   Rotary keys (1:1)

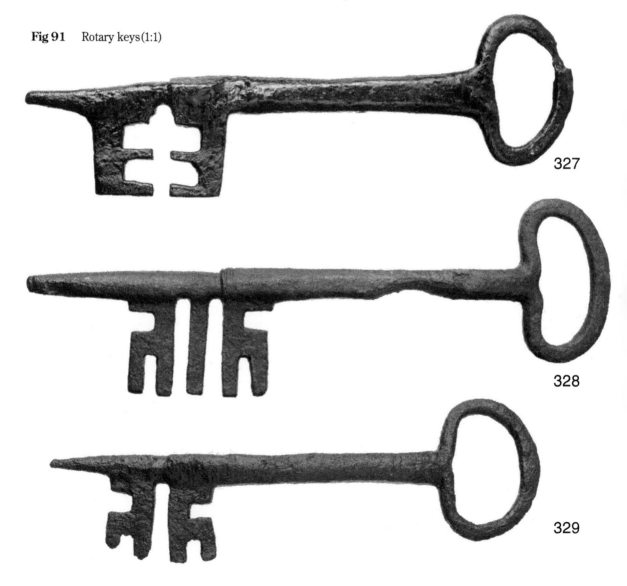

327

328

329

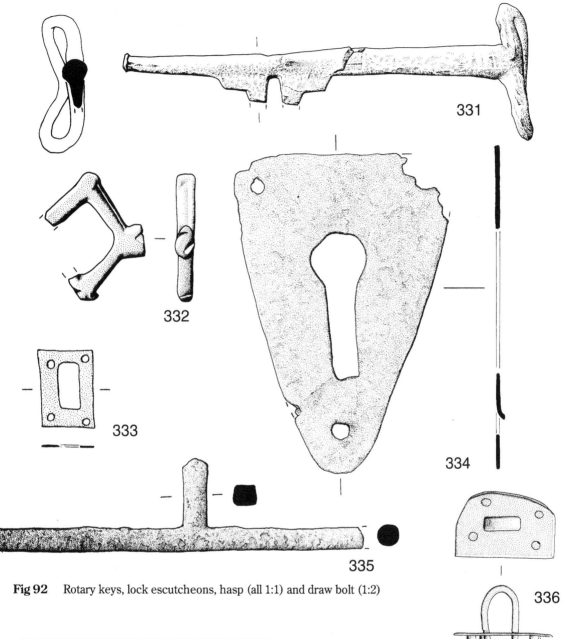

Fig 92   Rotary keys, lock escutcheons, hasp (all 1:1) and draw bolt (1:2)

BOW FROM INCOMPLETE KEY

(Unattributable to any of the preceding categories with certainty)

Copper-alloy

332 BWB83 Acc No 5112 (Context 325) Ceramic Phase 9 Fig 92
Fragment of lozenge-shaped bow 34×28+mm, with irregular knops at corners; broken off at a hollow on one side (possibly a fault from the casting).

Keys with lozenge-shaped bows are relatively more common among those found at Winchester, and their warding is often very elaborate. See on No 313.

Lock escutcheon plates

Copper-alloy sheeting

333 SWA81 Acc No 436 (Context 2018) Ceramic
Phase 9 Fig 92

Rectangular; 21×15mm; hole for attachment at each
corner.

   Probably from a casket.

Iron

334 BWB83 Acc No 3011 (Context 152) Ceramic
Phase 11 Fig 92

Shield-shaped; 86×*c*.60mm; three holes for attachment, one corner broken off at this point; keyhole
39×7mm, with rounded top; tin coating.

   Probably from a door (see Fig 7).

Draw bolt

Iron

335 BWB83 Acc No 3966 (Context 307) Ceramic
Phase 11 Fig 92

Round section; l 200mm; square-section handle.

   Very few medieval draw bolts have been recognised among excavated assemblages. An earlier
example from Lund in Sweden (T Nilsson in Mårtensson 1976, 405–6, fig 363 and parallel in fig 364)
includes a hasp for a mounted lock on the handle; as

does one from a 12th-century context excavated in
Winchester (I H Goodall in Biddle 1990, 978–9, no
3513). Several others survive on medieval furniture
illustrated by Eames (1977, pls 2A, 10, 11 on French
armoires of *c*.1176, and pls 14, 15A, 15B, 18B on 15th-
century *armoires* in the Low Countries; pls 32B, 32C
show a late 15th-century simple form close to the
present example, also in the Low Countries. Some of
the elements of these bolts may be replacements).
The contemporary term seems to have been 'slot' or
'shutle' (Salzman 1952, 300–1).

Lock hasp

(Probably from a satchel or saddlebag, etc.)

Copper alloy

336 BWB83 Acc No 2135 (Context 290) Ceramic
Phase 9 Fig 92

Two sub-rectangular sheet plates with two rounded
corners, *c*.7×*c*.27mm, held together by four rivets;
loop 10.5×3.5mm.

   Presumably originally attached to leather.

For iron lock hasps attached by hinges to strap
mounts probably from caskets, chests and perhaps cupboards etc., see Nos 212–26 under
Mounts for chests, caskets, etc.

Heating equipment

GEOFF EGAN

Despite the vital role of heating in the comfort of the home and in the preparation of cooked food, relatively few traces in terms of objects connected with the processes of making and extinguishing fire have been recognised among the assemblages considered (for hearth tiles see The fabric of the medieval London house, internal details and Fig 23). Ceramic material from the MoL established collections and from post-1983 fieldwork has been used to provide satisfactory illustrations for curfews.

Fire steel

(Strike-a-light)

For striking with a flint in order to produce a spark to kindle a fire. None of the flints used in this way in medieval London has been identified.

Iron

337 SWA81 Acc No 1897 (Context 2137) Ceramic Phase 9 Fig 93
The slightly tapered striking plate, 83+ ×18mm, is broken off at one end; recurving handle; the plate shows considerable wear from being struck.

The metal has been analysed by Douglas Moir, who writes:

> The steel was sectioned in two places, on opposing edges, in order to determine whether the structure was the same throughout the object. The sections show a very clean metal with only a few slag inclusions (both stringer and spheroidal). The structure is one of massive ferrite with a high phosphorous content, as can clearly be seen in a 'ghosting' effect within the grains. There has been no working (carbonisation or piling) of the object save for its forging. The strike-a-light is not of a high standard of workmanship, and is only of the hardness of a low-carbon steel, i.e., around 200HV (Vickers diamond pyramid hardness test), but

harder in areas of high phosphorous content (280HV). It nevertheless would have been more than adequate in providing a spark when struck, but would have been susceptible to wear through use, as can be seen by the grooves on one face. The hardness tests were conducted using a 100gm load for 30 seconds.

These objects might have been expected to be more common in medieval London than this single find from the sites considered suggests. There is one from the SNS87 site (acc no 78) in Clerkenwell. Fire steels are difficult to identify, particularly if the characteristic handle, the most vulnerable part, has been broken off.

Compare I H Goodall in Biddle 1990 (982–3, nos 3538–9, fig 306); both these examples from Winchester are of slightly earlier date and have a hole (implying some kind of hinged case) at

337

Fig 93   Fire steel (1:1)

the opposite end from the handle. Further medieval examples excavated in Lund in Sweden are of different forms (T Nilsson in Mårtensson 1976, 240, fig 194). Despite the large variety of later strike-a-lights illustrated in Christy (1926, 26–40, 195–205, nos 200–516), none has a hole to help explain the function of those in the Winchester examples. Also from London and of a different form is another (Guildhall Museum Catalogue 1908, 317, no 85 and pl 46, no 6), probably of a much later date.

Ceramic curfews
Jacqui Pearce

Fragments of five different curfews from recent excavations are listed below. All are made in fabrics local to the London area, current from the second half of the 12th century to the first half of the 14th century. None is complete, but all exhibit diagnostic features which enable them to be classed as curfews or fire covers (from the French *couvre-feu*), with the possible exception of No 340.

Curfews were an important feature of the medieval household from at least the 10th century onwards and are relatively common 13th–14th-century finds from archaeological excavations throughout the country. Made in the form of a large lid, their purpose was to cover overnight the gathered embers of an open central fire or a hearth by a wall. They had the twofold function of keeping the fire alive while unattended by allowing air and smoke to circulate through vents in the body, and of preventing sparks from setting the house on fire while the occupants slept. (Vessels of similar form with a central chimney have recently been recognised as fish-smokers – McCarthy & Brooks 1988, 117 – but these have yet to be recognised in London.)

Firepans, used to carry hot embers, are described in various medieval inventories (Moorhouse 1978, 13). They are recognised in the archaeological record as vessels of cooking-pot form, but with internal rather than external sooting. It has not been possible for the purposes of the present volume to conduct the thorough search necessary to identify all such forms in excavated pottery from London.

All but one of the London curfews discussed here appear to conform with the most widely recognised form, first identified at Laverstock in Wiltshire (Musty et al. 1969, 138, fig 23, no 195), although it is difficult to be certain since most are represented only by small sherds. Curfews are, of necessity, thick-walled and heavy, made as large, wide bowls to be used inverted. Consequently, a substantial handle is required. In most complete examples this takes the form of a wide, thick strap across the top. Air vents are commonly provided at each end of the handle, as in the Laverstock example. Another very common feature, found in many parts of the country, is the application of thumb-impressed strips of clay in various patterns, some quite complex, around the top and sides of the vessel. Internal blackening and sooting are good indicators of function, and are particularly useful in identifying small sherds.

Only one, incomplete, curfew handle is known from London (FMO85 site, context 190, ceramic corpus no 24526 – see Fig 95). It is made in Shelly Sandy ware, a wheel-thrown coarseware probably produced in the London area during the second half of the 12th century (Vince 1985, 43). It is a broad, heavy strap, turned up and thumbed along each edge. At the one surviving end two large, circular holes were made through both the handle and the body of the curfew, which is very heavily sooted inside. In form, this handle is comparable with the Laverstock example (see above). Sherds from two more curfews (Nos 338 and 339), also in Shelly Sandy ware, are too small for the complete forms to be reconstructed.

Fragments of two curfews are recorded in South Hertfordshire Grey ware, No 342 below (Fig 95) and one from the LBT86 site (context 220). Both come from large, wheel-thrown, bowl-shaped vessels with thick, substantial walls and heavy internal sooting. The latter sherd comes from the top of a curfew and has two circular vent holes (neither of which is associated with the end of a handle). It is likely that there were originally several similar holes in the top in addition to any larger ones which may have been made at the junction of the handle with the body. South Hertfordshire Grey ware was used in London from c.1150 and through the 13th century.

Two curfew fragments from London in Surrey Whiteware fabrics are published elsewhere (Pearce & Vince 1988, fig 101, no 395 and fig 119, no 526). The latter, in Coarse Border ware, comes from a rim and has several rows of small, closely spaced holes in the body, which have closed up noticeably in firing. The other sherd comes from the body of a curfew made in Kingston-type ware and was found in a context dated to *c*.1320 (ibid., fig 101, no 395). A row of finger-tip impressions made directly on to the body of the vessel gives a decorative effect.

Another example of a curfew with thumb-impressed decoration, No 341 (Fig 95), is made in Mill Green coarseware from the kilns at Ingatestone, Essex (Pearce et al. 1982, 289–92). This fabric is dated in London to *c*.1270–*c*.1400, and the sherd comes from a context dated to the mid-to-late-14th century. As with the Kingston-type ware curfew described above, the thumbed impressions were made in the thicker clay at the change of angle in the profile, in the manner of a heavily and continuously thumbed jug base (e.g., ibid., figs 10–11). However, the orientation of the impressions is different from that generally applied to jugs, and it more closely resembles the thumbed strips common on curfews from other parts of the country, typified by the Laverstock example referred to above. There are no air vents or holes in the London sherd, nor any remains of a handle. Part of a large, heavy strap handle in Mill Green ware probably also comes from a curfew (ibid., fig 15, no 43). It has a white slip, clear glaze and is deeply stabbed in three rows along its length. The edges are thumbed, as in the Shelly Sandy ware example described above.

Fragments of a very unusual vessel from London are included here with the curfews, on the grounds of general similarity to the form and the presence of certain diagnostic features (No 340, Fig 94). The three sherds are in London-type ware, the major glazed pottery used in London from the 12th to the mid-13th century and which continued to be made into the 14th century (Pearce et al. 1985). No other forms similar to the present example have yet been recognised in this fabric. The original vessel may have been roughly sub-rectangular in plan. It is suggested that, for the sake of

balance, there may originally have been more than two handles, perhaps four. On at least one side, the rim is cut away in a shallow arc, an extremely unusual feature for a curfew. Patches of sooting internally and at least one hole or air vent cut in the top suggest a use similar to that of a curfew. A vessel like this one in certain respects was found at Southampton (Platt & Coleman Smith 1975, fig 151, no 456 – although incomplete, at least four slots of different shape and height had been cut out from the rim, and the internal surfaces were blackened). G Dunning (ibid., 47–8) suggested that it had been used inverted for 'some process involving smoke-laden air', and tentatively termed it an 'aberrant form of fire-cover'. In the absence of firm evidence to the contrary, the London vessel may, with caution, be described as an unusual form of curfew.

338 BIG82 (no Acc No) (Context 2246) Ceramic Phase 8
Sherd from top and side of bowl-shaped, Shelly Sandy ware curfew; thick-walled; the large diameter cannot be accurately calculated; burnt internally; date of fabric *c*.1100–*c*.1200.
Presumably residual in this context.

339 BIG82 (no Acc No) (2246) 8
Sherd from body or top of wheel-thrown, Shelly Sandy ware curfew, with part of circular air vent; heavily burnt and sooted internally; date of fabric *c*.1100–*c*.1200.
Presumably residual in this context.

340 POM79 Ceramic Corpus No 25643 (160 and 231) 7–9 Fig 94
Three sherds from an unusual, probably sub-rectangular vessel; possibly a London-type ware curfew; wheel-thrown, then altered in shape; externally thickened rim; heavily knife-trimmed and smoothed internally and externally; rim cut away in shallow arc (at one end at least); two horizontal loop handles of sub-rectangular section survive, one with a deep, knife-cut notch at the junction with the body; part of a large, circular hole or air vent on the top of the vessel; patches of blackening and sooting internally.

341 BWB83 Ceramic Corpus No 25641 (401) 11 Fig 95
Sherd from a very large, thick-walled, wheel-thrown Mill Green coarseware curfew; horizontal rows of thumbing around change of angle between sides and

Fig 94   Fragments of probable curfew (1:4)

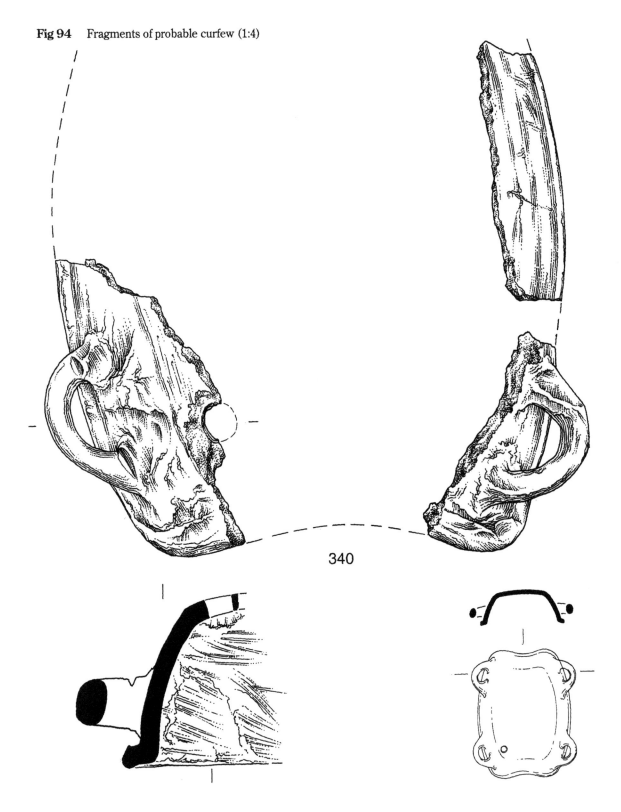

340

top; spots of clear glaze externally (probably accidental); patches of blackening and soot internally; date
of fabric *c*.1330–*c*.1380.

342 TL74 Ceramic Corpus No 25640 (378) 12 Fig 95
Rim sherd from a large, bowl-shaped, wheel-thrown

South Hertfordshire Grey ware curfew; rim externally thickened and rounded; d over 460mm; burnt
internally; date of fabric *c*.1150–*c*.1300.

Presumably residual in this context.

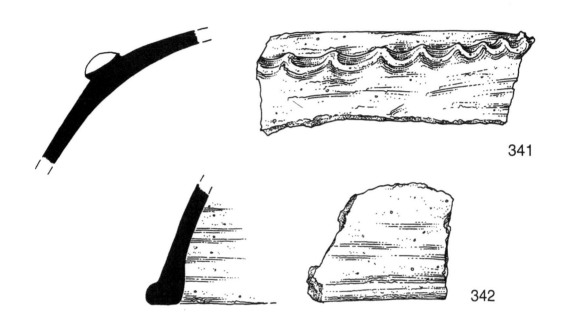

341

342

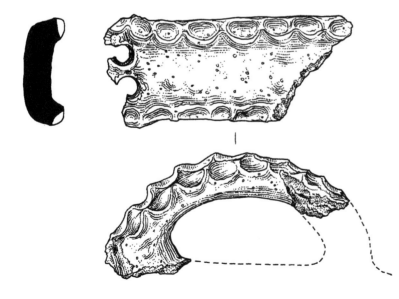

Fig 95 Curfew fragments:
rim and wall, handle at bottom,
FM085 site (all 1:4)

Lighting equipment

GEOFF EGAN

The large body of lighting equipment recovered during the recent excavations permits some major changes to be defined (see Table 4). The demise of hanging ceramic oil lamps in the 13th/14th century probably matches the rise of versions in glass, which was a more satisfactory material because of its translucency. Iron is strongly represented among light holders in all phases (comprising some 75% of the metals), continuing in use despite major changes in form, along with pewter or lead. From the late 13th/14th century onwards, copper alloy forms a small proportion of the range represented (including part of a lantern). The non-ferrous metal holders include what were, presumably, the more expensive items. A single rushlight holder from the late 13th/early 14th century is a rare survival from the medieval period.

A prestigious 12th-century multiple lamp of copper alloy, with an openwork tower and six spouts (found in St Martins le Grand in London – N Stratford in Zarnecki et al. 1984, 253, no 258, with references) has no counterpart among recently excavated finds.

The survey of lighting equipment excavated at Winchester (M Biddle & D Hinton in Biddle 1990, 990–1) has suggested that there was a marked increase in the use of candles over oil lamps around 1300. The late 12th- and 13th-century London candlesticks of iron listed below, and to a lesser extent those of lead/tin, seem to attest a transition somewhat earlier in the capital. The discussion of the Winchester finds includes a diagram (based as much on historical inference as on the archaeological data) setting out the suggested overall trends in the development of domestic lighting there (ibid., fig 307). The introduction of metal candlesticks around the 13th century, later than in London, is seen as being associated with a rise in popularity of, particularly, tallow candles (coming somewhat later than a suggested increase in the use of the more expensive ones of wax).

The stone lamps and lamp holders discussed by Ward Perkins in an earlier catalogue on London finds (1940, 174–6, fig 54, nos 1–4 – these include a Coventry example attributed to the late 12th/early 13th century) probably mainly belong to the very beginning of the period considered in this present volume, at the latest. His conclusion, that in England stone lamps were exceptional, is reinforced by their seeming complete absence from the recently excavated London assemblages (see Pritchard 1991, 160–1, 259, fig 3.44, nos 148–9 for London ones of a slightly earlier date). In contrast, the

Table 4: Lighting equipment
(P=pricket, C=cup)

Ceramic phase	6	7	8	9	10	11	12
Iron candleholders	2P	1P	2P	7P, 9C, 2C&P	IC, IC&P	1P, 8C, 5C&P	2C
Lead/tin candleholders	1?P	1P	–	?1C	–	3?C, 3?P	1?C
Copper-alloy candleholders	–	–	–	?1C	–	1C	–
Ceramic hanging lamps	1	–	–	–	–	–	–
Glass hanging lamps	–	–	–	1	2	4	3
Lantern (copper alloy)	–	–	–	–	(horn leaves)	1	–
Iron rushlight holder	–	–	–	1	–	–	–

Only items attributed to a single ceramic phase are included. (There are no stone lamps, which are known in London from deposits attributed to slightly earlier dates than the period considered in this volume.)

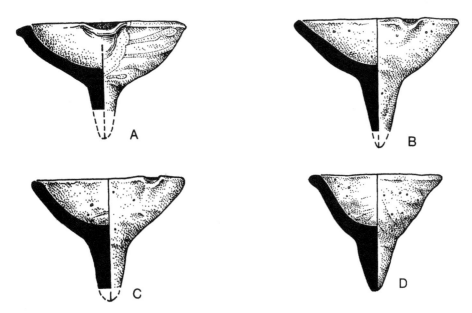

Fig 96 Ceramic lamps (1:2): A) MoL acc no A25740 (London type ware); B) GAG87 acc no 564 (Local Grey ware); C) GWS89 acc no 160 (Local/South Hertfordshire Grey ware); D) BUC87 acc no 7 (Local Grey ware)

finds from Winchester imply that stone lighting equipment continued there right through to the post-medieval period (Biddle 1990, 985, 991–4, nos 3541–52). Stone lamps may have been used particularly in ecclesiastical buildings (cf. Robins 1939, 37), which are not well represented among the sites considered for this present volume.

Hanging lamps
Lynne Keys, Jacqui Pearce

(For metal holders, probably to suspend this kind of ceramic or glass lamp, see Nos 356–64; cf. Fig 101.)

Ceramic (Jacqui Pearce)

Only five ceramic lamps which can be dated with reasonable confidence to the late 12th century or later have been identified from recent DUA excavations. All are cresset or hanging lamps made in South Hertfordshire Grey ware, a fabric dated between *c*.1150 and

c.1300 in London. All come from excavations carried out after 1983, from contexts given approximately this same late 12th/13th-century date range. There are two comparable lamps in the same fabric (MoL acc nos A27986 and 68.11/9) as well as a complete hanging lamp in London-type ware (Fig 96(A), MoL acc no A25740), a fabric which is dated from the 12th to the late 14th centuries. The former two lamps are partially glazed outside. One lamp is also known in Coarse London-type ware, No 343, dated to the late 12th century (see also Pearce et al. 1985, fig 77, no 428). At least twice as many lamps of similar form and mostly made in Local Grey ware come from contexts dated to the late 11th/early 12th century. Although hanging lamps are the only form identified in South Hertfordshire Grey ware and Local Grey ware (and particularly those dated later than 1150), a variety of free-standing and double-shelled forms are found in these fabrics. The relative scarcity of ceramic lamps in London from the late 12th century onwards bears comparison with other parts of the country, where lamps are quite well known from Saxo-Norman deposits but are rare in later material (McCarthy & Brooks 1988, 116–17).

South Hertfordshire Grey ware (Vince 1991, 267) is a wheel-thrown, unglazed, hard, sandy fabric, fired in a reducing atmosphere, which gives it its characteristic grey or brownish-grey colour. On the basis of fabric and form, it can be suggested that the late-11th-to-14th-century Grey ware lamps from London came from the same ceramic tradition, probably centred on Hertfordshire and Middlesex. Lamps, which formed only a minor element in production, did not change noticeably in form over almost 250 years.

All the South Hertfordshire and Local Grey ware lamps under consideration here are of the form variously described as cresset, suspension, hanging or spike lamps. The London-type ware and Coarse London-type ware lamps (see above on No 343 etc.) are of the same form, and examples are known also in the various Saxo-Norman fabrics. The form consists of a small bowl surmounting a blunt spike, all made as one piece by hand. Rim diameters are consequently rather uneven, but range from 40–110mm, with the majority approximately 80mm. Overall height ranges from 40–70mm, although in many cases the tip of the spike is missing. The average length of the spike is about half the total height, so that the capacity of the bowl for holding oil is generally quite small. Rims are most commonly simply rounded and unthickened (e.g., Fig 96(B), ceramic corpus no 26536, acc no 564, from a context at the GAG87 site attributed to ceramic phases 8–9), although a few are also slightly everted (e.g., Fig 96(D), ceramic corpus No 26535 acc no 7 from a context at the BUC87 site attributed to phases 6–8) or beaded. Four of the lamps in South Hertfordshire Grey ware, including two in the Museum of London's established collection, have a slightly pinched and pulled pouring lip. A number of the more complete Local Grey ware lamps also have portions of their rims missing, so whether or not a lip was originally present cannot be determined. However, no complete examples have been found which definitely had no lip.

A few Local Grey ware lamps and one South Hertfordshire Grey ware vessel (MoL acc no 68.11/9) have a slight ridge emphasising the transition in profile from bowl to spike. This may have been helpful in suspending or otherwise standing the lamp upright. The majority of lamp bowls meet the spike in a fairly gentle curve.

All the ceramic hanging lamps are blackened and sooted to some extent, some very heavily (e.g., Fig 96(C), ceramic corpus no 26539, GWS89 acc no 160, from a context attributed to ceramic phase 6). A few are burnt and blackened completely, but the usual pattern of partial burning clearly demonstrates their usage. Lamps were used as containers for oil in which a burning wick floated, so signs of heating are typically found inside or just over the rim and around the lip, where the wick generally settled. Moreover, the bottom of the lamp bowl inside is, in all but the most heavily blackened examples, less burnt and sooted than the rim, if at all. This marks the level at which the oil was generally maintained, blackening and sooting occurring above the oil. In most cases, this level is between a quarter and a half the internal depth of the lamp bowl, showing that the oil was not allowed to burn too low before it was renewed.

The form of hanging lamp found in London is well known in other parts of the country, in ceramic dating back to at least the early 10th century (McCarthy & Brooks 1988, fig 77, no 128; fig 82, nos 175–6; Platt & Coleman Smith 1975, fig 140, no 175; fig 177, no 919). Imported glazed lamps were also found at Bramber and Pevensey Castles in Sussex, but none have yet been recognised in London. Other forms of lamp known elsewhere in the country, such as pedestal, double-shelled, ovoid or bowl-shaped with a flat base, are not found in London from contexts dated later than *c*.1150. There are bowl-shaped and double-shelled lamps in Early Medieval Sandy ware and Late Saxon Shelly ware (e.g., MoL acc nos 29.94/28, 10613, A5201), but these have rarely been found in formal excavations. The London lamps show nothing of the variety of form found in other parts of the country and even in some cases at the same kilns, such as Laverstock (Wiltshire), from the 12th century onwards (Musty et al. 1969, 136–7, fig 24, nos 184–8).

One disadvantage of earthenware lamps was their porosity and this may have weighed against their use once other materials were available. Apart from London-type and Coarse London-type ware lamps which are glazed externally, none of the Grey ware lamps from London are glazed, which would have reduced the problem. However, documentary evidence shows that earthenware pots were recommended for the storage of lamp oil (Moorhouse 1978, 7), which is frequently mentioned in accounts. There are also references to the use of earthenware for lamps or *kressettes* (ibid., 8). Other references recommend the use of glass for lamps (see Nos 344–55 below, which are generally later than the excavated ceramic lamps) because of the tendency of oil to soak into the ceramic fabric (*idem* 1981, 115).

343 BIG82 (no Acc No) (Context 3620) Ceramic Phase 6
Coarse London-type ware; d 68mm; h 32mm; clear glaze on exterior. Also published in Pearce et al. 1985 (46, fig 77, no 428).

Glass (Lynne Keys)
Hanging lamps of glass, like those of ceramic (which are generally earlier in date – see above), take the form of a saucer-shaped top and a long, finger-shaped spike, which in the present material is hollow (see Fig 97; cf. Charleston 1991, 258–9, fig 116, and *idem* in Biddle 1990, 935 for what is claimed to be the only reconstructable example known in Britain; see also Baumgartner & Krueger 1988, 436–9). This form remained unchanged throughout the period represented. The lamp was filled with oil and suspended from the ceiling, singly or grouped (see Nos 352–4; the pit in which these three were found may be from a hall associated with an inn belonging to the Earl of March and his heir; the latter died in 1426 and the inn passed to the Earl of Northumberland – Schofield 1995, 181, gazetteer no 71).

The lamps listed below are all dated to later than *c*.1270 and up to *c*.1450; none is complete. Bases are the only parts which have been identified in London as coming from lamps (fragments of upper parts are extremely thin and fragile and can only be identified when found in association with a base). Owing to the fragmentary nature of the listed items, measurements are not obtainable.

344 WAT78 Acc No 900 (Context 3665) Ceramic Phase 9
Three fragments; decayed; green.

345 Watling House 37 (ER190C) 10
Decayed; green.

346 OST82 118 (190) 10
Decayed; green.

347 WAT78 506 (3677) 8–11
Decayed.
(Not counted in Table 4 because of uncertain dating.)

348 BC72 4359 (88) 11
Dark green.

349 BC72 4362 (88) 11
Decayed; green.

350 BC72 4373 (88) 11 Fig 97
Decayed.

351 MIL72 142 (502) 11
Decayed; originally green.

352 RAG82 703 (1205) 12 Fig 97
Fragments of base and part of rim; green.

353 RAG82 704 (1205) 12 Fig 97
Fragments of base and part of rim; green; (illustration restores complete form).

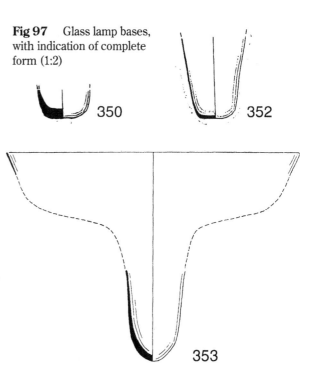

Fig 97 Glass lamp bases, with indication of complete form (1:2)

350

352

353

354 RAG82 909 (1205) 12
Dark green.

355 BC72 2935 (113) ?Residual in post-medieval
context
Decayed.

Possible holders for hanging lamps

The hanging lamps of ceramic and glass (see
above) would normally have been suspended
from the ceiling. Although there are a number
of contemporary illustrations, generally little
detail is provided of the means of suspension
beyond showing some kind of thin, circular
frame held by multiple strands branching from
a central point at the top, presumably made of
wire or slender chains rather than of string
(Fig 101 provides an exceptionally clear indication of the arrangement; cf. R Charleston in
Biddle 1990, 935–6 and Foy & Sennequier
1989, 353–5); precisely this kind of suspension
is still widely used for ecclesiastical oil lamps in
the Russian Orthodox Church. (The method of
holding a lamp by hand shown in Fig 98, left,
appears rather awkward and may have been
expedient only for moving a light from one
location to another.)

A category of branched fitting, usually of cast
copper alloy and with three lower arms having
holes, with further holes at the top and at the
centre of the base, seem the most likely excavated items to have served as lamp holders.
The function of the basal hole is unclear – no
contemporary illustration of lids for these holders has been traced. These objects occasionally
retain lengths of chain, like one which has iron
links (VRY89 site, ref no V1349; closely comparable to No 356). Some of the chains published
elsewhere could be from this kind of holder
(Egan & Pritchard 1991, 319–20, nos 1593–7).
There are also some complicated, relatively
flimsy iron-wire chains (e.g., No 360), which
branch from what seem to be twisted iron-wire
versions of the copper-alloy holders, and there
are also copper-alloy chains of comparable
form. One holder is known in lead/tin, with
four arms retaining parts of all the chains, also
in lead/tin (see Fig 99 right, SUN86 acc no 331,
from a context ascribed to ceramic phase 8).

The three chains branching from a top element in medieval ecclesiastical censers are
essentially similar to, but usually more robust
than, the London finds discussed here, though
a similar example to No 357, found at a church
site in Norfolk, could be from a censer or a
lamp (Williams 1987, 73, no 2; Sue Margeson
pers comm; Theophilus's term for a censer's
elaborate suspender, *lily*, seems inappropriate
for Nos 356–7 and for comparable holders –
Dodwell 1986, 112). Number 356 is a markedly
rough item, incompatible with the quality of
workmanship normally associated with items
intended for churches, and several of the parallels mentioned below also lack neat finishing;
perhaps as they would have been high up, out
of sight, this would not have mattered.

Fig 98   Lamps held in the hand: left, from
psalter/book of hours from South Netherlands/
Liège (13th century) and right, missal from Amiens
in France (1323)

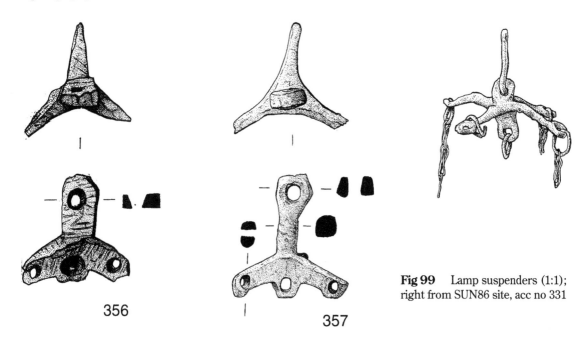

Fig 99 Lamp suspenders (1:1); right from SUN86 site, acc no 331

356

357

A copper-alloy chain with spiralled links (BWB83 acc no 5852, from a deposit attributed to ceramic phase 11) is identical to that surviving on a north-German censer in the British Museum (acc no 1873, 7–15,1; Oddy et al. 1986, 12, pl 1, no 15); it is likely that there was quite an overlap in the forms of suspenders for domestic lamps and ecclesiastical censers, but at present this cannot be demonstrated (the SUN86 holder with its lead chains could not have been used as a censer, as the chains are unlikely to have supported the swinging of a heavy metal container for very long).

The suggestion that the late 14th- and early 15th-century items listed below are parts of pendent lamp holders (presumably of glass to judge from the available dating) requires examples which are more complete before it can be considered certain.

BRANCHED HOLDERS

Copper alloy

356 BWB83 Acc No 5965 (Context 298) Ceramic Phase 11 Fig 99
Three arms, each l 14mm, branching from central stem h 16mm; somewhat crude and asymmetrical,
with roughly drilled holes and prominent file-finishing marks.

357 BWB83 4486 (Unstratified) Fig 99
Three arms, each l 16mm, from central stem, h 31mm; the holes are drilled (or at least finished by this process).

Similar to an example excavated in a domestic context in Coventry (just possibly a local production site for these items; Wright 1987, 92–3, no 37, fig 51).

Comparable finds from London include VHA89 site acc nos 110, 1675 and 2014 (the first is untrimmed from the mould, though this need not mean it had not been used).

WIRE CHAINS

(The main links each consist of a straight length with end loops, usually bent in opposite directions.)

Copper alloy

358 BWB83 Acc No 6021 (Context 291) Ceramic Phase 11 Fig 100
Link l 84mm, joined by one of its loops to two others, each l 30mm.

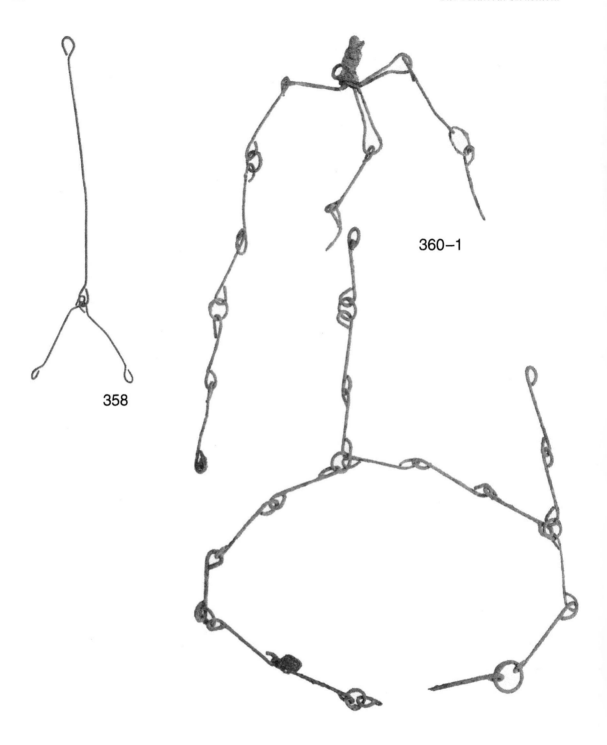

Fig 100   (?)Lamp suspension chains, Nos 360–1 in conjectural configuration (1:1)

Fig 101   Hanging lamp, after Bodleian Library MS Laud misc 409 fol 3v (St Albans, late 12th century)

An iron-wire chain of precisely similar form (complete) was seen on modern ('folk tradition') hanging candle lamps on sale in Helsinki in 1992.

359 BWB83 4931 (278) 12
Single link; l 27mm.

Iron

The lengths of chain consist of groups of three or two, or single links, as above, each joined to the next group by a circular link (d 6–10mm), which is usually riveted in the manner of chain mail; all parts are tin-coated. The main parts of Nos 360 and 361 have been put together in Fig 100 to illustrate one possible way of suspending a lamp; they are unlikely to have gone together originally, and other configurations for No 361 are equally plausible.

360 BWB83 Acc No 3369 (Context 308) Ceramic Phase 11 Fig 100
Top piece with twisted central stem and three elongated loops, each having a widened lower end; parts of the three chains survive, the longest totalling 160mm; l of each main link *c.*28mm (found with a further smaller length of similar form).

361 BWB83 2947 (291) 11 Fig 100
Complicated major piece, with two three-way branches comprising paired and three main links; l of main links each 23–30mm (found together with two further, smaller pieces of similar form).

The original configuration of the major piece is uncertain, but three sets of three main links etc. could have formed a circular holder of suitable size, with paired main links forming the vertical strands (as per illustration).

362 BWB83 1463 and 3068 (110) 11
Several fragments: up to three main links survive together; l of main links each *c.*40mm.

363 BWB83 3097 (297) 11
Single main link; l 43mm.

364 BWB83 3182 (279) 11
Single, incomplete main link; l 51mm+.

Candleholders

Some tables referred to in this catalogue section appear in later chapters: Table 7 in Analysis of copper-alloy vessels and candleholders; Tables 8 and 9 in Analysis of lead/tin alloy objects.

There are two basic means of holding a candle, both having many variations in form. Prickets, generally the earlier category among the excavated, presumably domestic, items, continued in use in churches at least into the 16th century, while cupped (socketed) holders appear in London assemblages from the late 13th century onwards. A cupped holder found at Winchester and dated to the late 11th/12th century (no 3531 in Biddle & Hinton in Biddle 1990, 983–4) seems to be the earliest English example of this form, which apparently originated in the Islamic world. The dating below (confirming the broad picture of development given by Ward Perkins 1940, 177) shows there was some overlap in London of prickets with cupped holders in the late 13th/early 14th centuries. Several of the later iron holders combine cups with spikes. It has been suggested that when they appear together the two

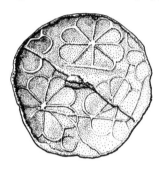

Fig 102   Decorative candlesticks: No 366 (1:1); opposite far right, private collection (reduced)

different forms may have been for different qualities of candles – prickets for the more expensive wax, and cups for the cheaper tallow (ibid. cf. Michaelis 1978, 14). Wax made into candles etc. was said in a Statute of 1433 (11 Henry VI c12) to be worth no more than 6d. per pound weight, while tallow candles might have cost as little as a penny per pound in 1468. Some of the iron cupped sticks and probably lead/tin stick No 369 were to hold two candles, but no double pricket has been excavated in London (see Biddle & Hinton in Biddle 1990, 983–4, no 3530, fig 306 for an early 13th-century iron example, and Guildhall Museum Catalogue 1908, 313, no 15 and pl 85, no 9 for a triple pricket attributed to the 16th century). Tripod feet are an early feature of candleholders (Ward Perkins 1940, 180), probably continuing in the copper-alloy ones listed below into the 14th century.

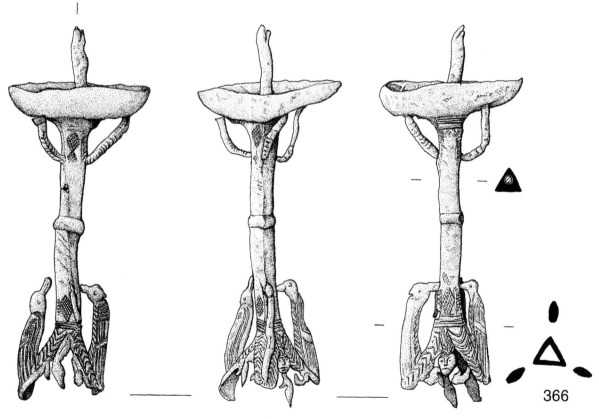

366

Iron rushlight holder No 421, from a late 13th/early 14th-century context (it seems most unlikely to have been for some kind of very small tallow or wax candle) is an important indicator that this form of lighting was used in the medieval period (cf. Michaelis 1978, 15–16, where rushlights are alleged to have been absent from the Roman period until the middle of the 18th century).

See on Nos 391ff for a hint of a slight, but consistent, increase in the *average* size of candles between *c.*1270 and *c.*1450, as attested by the internal diameters of the generally parallel-sided, iron-cupped holders (the only category among the listed items where this dimension can directly be attributed some significance, because most of the other cups taper or are distorted).

Lead/tin

The non-ferrous white-metal candleholders include both highly decorated and relatively plain sticks. The number of, particularly, later fragments listed below supports the observation by Hatcher & Barker that pewter candleholders were not uncommon in the medieval period (1974, 60).

365 SWA81 Acc No 1576 (Context 2187) Ceramic Phase 6 Fig 103
Fragment; incomplete, shallow dish, with slightly raised rim; d 47mm; turning marks internally; rough circle apparently cut away at centre and portion cut away from one side. Probably a drip tray from a pricket candlestick. This appears to be a notably early piece of turned 'pewter', presuming the dating is correct.

366 SWA81 1121 (2130) 7 Fig 102 and Col Pl 2
Lead (AML, Table 8); found flattened, shape restored after retrieval; h *c.*95mm; d of dish *c.*39mm; the iron spike is split in two at the top and protrudes from the stem on one side below; the dish has a field of octofoils and is supported by three transversely hatched branches from the triangular-section stem,

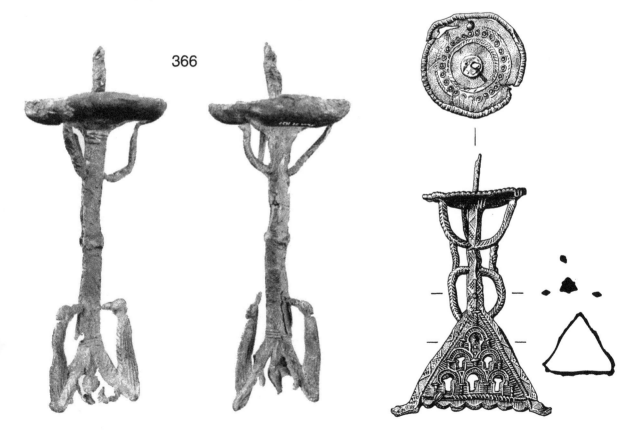

366

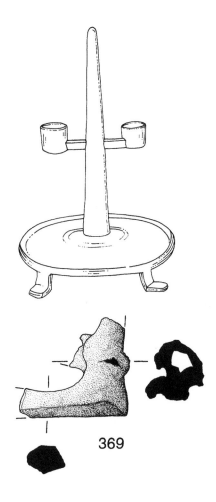

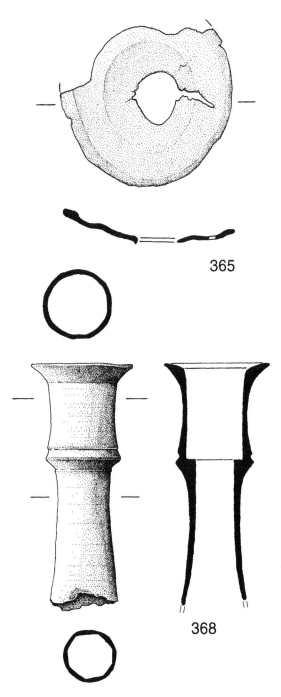

365

368

369

Fig 103   Candleholders (1:1) and top right possible form of No 369 (reduced)

which has a central collar and cross-hatched lozenges between two bands with (?)herringbone hatching on each face; a bird with wings addorsed perches on each of three herringbone-hatched feet and pecks at the main stem; a human face surviving between two of the feet has a blob of metal below for the body, and is flanked by transversely hatched, bent arms – the metal did not flow properly here, and the design is substantially incomplete on two of the sides; the dish has crudely scratched lines making a lozenge around the spike, and the stem has been roughly abraded on all sides, removing some of the linear decoration (cf. No 951, Fig 220).

The feet do not provide an even base in their present state; this may be due to removal of a lower portion rather than to distortion – if, as seems likely, the former suggestion is correct, the human figures could originally have been full length. A six-part mould would have been needed to produce this object.

This particular ornate, crowded design is not paralleled, but some broadly similar lead/tin tripod candlesticks are known, found in London (Fig 102, private collection), Kent (Weaver 1909, 219–20, fig 372 – a remarkable, largely naturalistic design featuring oak leaves and acorns), Dublin (apparently identical to the London find in private hands – National Museum of Ireland 1973, 43, no 182, from a deposit dated to the early 14th century – the author is grateful to Andy Halpin and Bernard Guinan for allowing him to see this item) and the Low Countries (Vandenberghe discusses some items from this group – 1988, 179–81, fig 161). The split-ended iron spike, which also strengthens the stem, is a feature of several, if not all, of the other candlesticks of this distinctive series. Their place or places of origin have still to be established. Small fragments from the ornate decoration on these items may prove difficult to identify. A plainer tripod version was found in Lincoln (WW89 site acc no 293 – Jenny Mann kindly gave access to this object).

367 BWB83 7063 (290) 9
Distorted, incomplete tubular fragment, d *c.*19mm, surviving l 50mm, irregularly cut off at one end.

Presumably the stem of a candleholder (rather than some kind of spout etc.).

368 BWB83 1183 (307) 11 Fig 103
Pewter (AML, Table 8); fragment: slightly waisted cup with angled rim and internal d of 18mm at top, and part of hollow stem; an angled collar is defined by grooves at the junction of the cup and stem; external turning marks; the octagonal internal section of the stem suggests that the lathe-chuck used in turning was of this shape; scratches from removal of wax inside cup.

Lead/tin chalices excavated at Winchester from priests' graves of the late 14th to early 16th centuries have octagonal internal stem sections (M Biddle & B Kjølbye Biddle in Biddle 1990, 791–9, nos 2461ff, figs 232–3; this Winchester series was abruptly ended by the Reformation).

369 BWB83 2230 (131) 11 Fig 103
Pewter (AML, Table 9; cf. Table 8); fragment; lozenge-section (i.e. 'square' in contemporary terminol-

ogy) horizontal branch l 28mm, with damaged (partly melted) cup h *c.*20mm with horizontal ridge; the branch may have broken off at an original soldered joint.

Probably from a two-branched stick; cf. two examples of copper alloy with a central spike (Michaelis 1978, 32, figs 11, 12) as in Fig 103.

370 BWB83 4702 (291) 11 Fig 104
Fragment; flattened cup with bead rim and rabbet at base, and part of stem; original d of cup estd *c.*22mm at top (original shape restored in illustration).

371 TL74 521 (414) 11 Fig 104
Fragment; disc d 81mm, with slight rabbet near edge and around central hole; turning marks on both faces.

Probably a flattened drip tray.

372 BWB83 6064 (308) 11 Fig 104
Pewter (AML, Table 8); edge fragment of tray with 'full-skirted' flange, d *c.*55mm.

Compare Michaelis 1978, 41, figs 25, 26, and 46, figs 50, 41.

373 BWB83 1184 (307) 11
As preceding item; d *c.*110mm; turning marks internally.

The previous two items could perhaps be from flagons with similar bases to this category of candlestick, but the flagons seem from the available evidence to have had less angular corners with different profiles at this point (cf. Figs 105 bottom right and 155 left; lid No 530 in Fig 154 has a more vertical rim with a rabbet).

Numbers 372–3 are not counted in Table 4.

374 BWB83 7058 (301) 12
Fragment of basal tray with angled lip surrounding central hole for stem of cup; surviving d *c.*34mm.

375 SWA81 2156 (Unstratified – from a part of the site where 14th-century finds predominated) Fig 105
Slightly distorted; cup with internal d *c.*12mm, on ?dish-shaped tray d 47mm with three triple-ridged feet; crude decoration of nine bosses surrounded by beading and a single, leaf-like motif, all within a beaded border; the base of the cup has been broken off – possibly in the removal of wax.

Several varieties of broadly similar squat, relief-decorated late medieval tripod candlesticks of lead/tin have been found in London in recent years (e.g., Hornsby et al. 1989, 55, no 20; Bangs 1995, 175, 375, no 170); for two further examples found in Bruges,

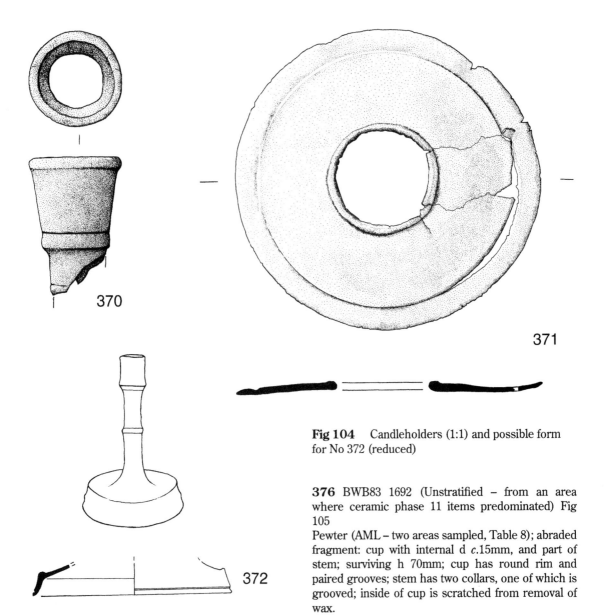

370

371

Fig 104   Candleholders (1:1) and possible form for No 372 (reduced)

372

376 BWB83 1692 (Unstratified – from an area where ceramic phase 11 items predominated) Fig 105
Pewter (AML – two areas sampled, Table 8); abraded fragment: cup with internal d *c.*15mm, and part of stem; surviving h 70mm; cup has round rim and paired grooves; stem has two collars, one of which is grooved; inside of cup is scratched from removal of wax.

see Vandenberghe (1988, 180, 182, fig 162), and for another from Nieuwlande in the Netherlands see G Groeneweg in Bos et al. 1987, 73–4, no 603. An inscription in dialect French on another London find of late 13th-century date suggests that it may well have come from Amiens, probably brought back by a pilgrim visiting the local shrine of St John (Spencer forthcoming, pl 3). There is as yet no precise parallel for No 375.

No close parallel of comparable date is known for broken-off cup No 368 (including among copper-alloy candlesticks). This cup is somewhat similar to those of some post-medieval candleholders, most published cups of medieval date being plainer. The nearest published medieval examples traced for comparison with Nos 368 and 376 are on candlesticks with dish-shaped trays having 'full-skirted' flanges

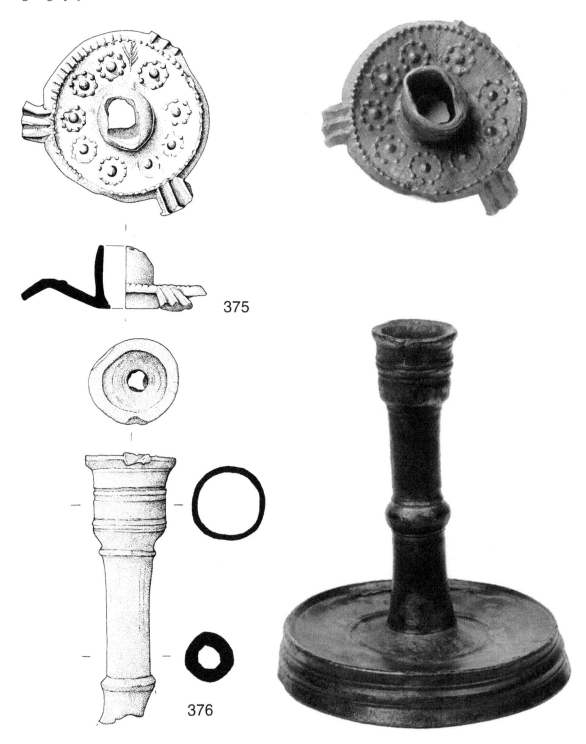

375

376

Fig 105 Candleholders (1:1) and MoL collection parallel, acc no 78.238/1 (reduced)

(Michaelis 1978, 41, figs 25–6; 46, figs 40–1; Hornsby et al. 1989, 54, no 18; see Fig 105 lower right, MoL acc no 78.238/1, h 108mm – this one is of pewter, analysis details are given in Homer 1991, 78, fig 42).

Iron

These comprise by far the largest group among the candleholders listed here, as was anticipated by Ward Perkins writing at a time when there were apparently no well-dated iron examples from the Middle Ages in Britain (1940, 177; an earlier survey by Curle in 1927 took little account of iron holders from the medieval period). This material presumably furnished the cheapest versions available.

PRICKETS

In each of the following, an upper, central spike is flanked on two sides by thinner, outward-curved scrolls (see Nos 54–5 for similar items lacking scrolls and listed as hooks). Fixing the basal spike into woodwork could not have been easy with such little obvious means of purchase, unless it was inserted into a crack.

The simplest form (Nos 377ff) seems to be the earliest, with the right-angled version apparently overlapping in time with cupped holders, which eventually came to supersede prickets.

A pricket stick with two paired, folding feet, excavated at the TEX88 site, is the only free-standing iron example found recently in London; see Fig 106 (acc no 1978, h 310mm; cf. MoL acc no 8378).

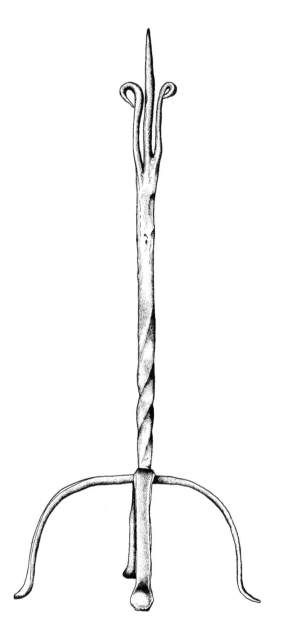

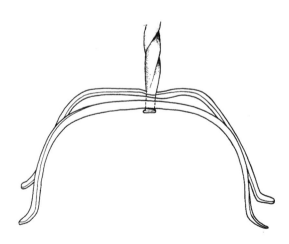

Fig 106   Freestanding iron candleholder with folding feet, TEX88 acc no 1978 (1:2)

'Spike' in the following catalogue descriptions refers to the basal one by which the holder was fixed in place.

Simple, straight stems

(The form is known possibly a century earlier from Winchester; Biddle 1990, 983, no 3531.)

377 SH74 Acc No 271 (Context 536) Ceramic Phase 6
H 175mm.
378 BIG82 3694 (4272) 6
Incomplete at both ends; surviving h 51mm.
379 SH74 266 (483) 6–7
Pricket spike missing; surviving h 78mm.
   (Not included in Table 4 because of uncertain dating.)
380 SWA81 2456 (2262) 7
H 110mm.
381 SH74 364 (386) 8
One scroll missing; h 98mm.
382 SWA81 1387 (2137) 9 Fig 107
H 127mm.
383 CUS73 677 (XII,3) 9
H 135mm.
   Previously published by Henig (1974, 191–2, fig 38, no 69).
384 CUS73 704 (XIV,5) 9 Fig 107
H 140mm.
   Previously published by Henig (1974, 191–2, fig 38, no 70).

Right-angled stems

385 SH74 Acc No 150 (Context 386) Ceramic Phase 8
H 70mm; spike l 70mm; scrolls in same plane as spike.
386 CUS73 486 (IV,55) 9
H 68mm; spike l 49mm; scrolls in same plane as spike.
   Previously published by Henig (1974, 191–2, fig 38, no 71).
387 SWA81 2112 (2061) 9
Corroded; h 87mm; spike l 53mm+; scrolls (ends of both missing) at right angle to spike.
388 SWA81 2543 (1581) 9 Fig 107
H 125mm; spike l 54mm; scrolls (one missing) at right angle to spike.

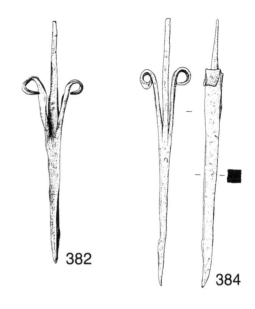

382   384

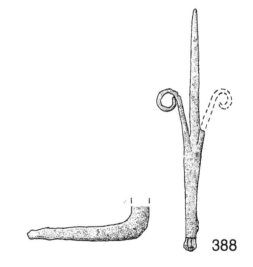

388

Fig 107   Pricket candleholders (1:2)

389 BC72 2961 (118) 10–11
L 114mm; scrolls (one missing) in same plane as spike.
   (Not included in Table 4 because of uncertain dating.)
390 BWB83 5264 (355) 11
H 133mm; incomplete spike l 24mm+; scrolls at right angle to spike.

CUPPED STICKS

Diameters given for the cups, which usually have parallel sides, are *internal*, though distortion may mean these measurements are in some cases unreliable (see No 420). All survive between 10 and 20mm (see No 421 for a rushlight cup, d 5mm). A slight, but consistent, increase in the average diameter of candles through the *c*.180-year period indicated is suggested from these measurements, even though ceramic phases 10 and 12 are not particularly well represented; in each of phases 9 and 11 there is a wide variation of 9mm (cups in phase-9 sticks average d *c*.14mm; phase-10 ones, 15mm; phase-11 ones, *c*.16.5mm and phase-12 ones, 17.5mm).

See flesh hook No 436 (Fig 124) for a similar arrangement to the candleholder cups, there for holding the hook onto its wooden handle; cf. on No 423 (see Fig 114 right). Two cups broken from sticks have been omitted from the listing because of the potential for misidentification.

Single cups

SIMPLE, STRAIGHT STEMS

Some holders of this form that have never been lost and which are attributed to the 18th century retain small turned wooden bases, which means they were readily movable rather than fixtures (Caspall 1987, 150–1, figs 324–7).

391 SWA81 Acc No 3507 (Context 2141) Ceramic Phase 9
Flattish stem broken off; surviving h 44mm; cup distorted, d *c*.15mm (gap between flanges).

392 SWA81 3267 (2141) 9 Fig 108
H 54mm; cup d *c*.12mm (flanges overlap).

393 SWA81 2110 (2063) 9
Stem broken off; surviving h 69mm; d *c*.15mm (flanges overlap).
　Perhaps originally a more elaborate form.

394 BWB83 3094 (274) 9 Fig 108
H 85mm; cup d 16mm (flanges contiguous).

395 BWB83 3159 (274) 9 Fig 108
H 120mm; cup d 18mm (flanges overlap).

396 SWA81 3928 (2030) 9
Corroded; h 122mm; robust, square-section stem.

397 BWB83 574 (111) 11
Incomplete; flattened cup on flat-section stem
w 6mm, which continues above and below (?broken off at both ends); surviving h 58mm.
　(?Compare No 413.)

398 BWB83 479 (156) 11
H 63mm; cup distorted, d *c*.14mm (flanges overlap).

399 BWB83 3814 (137) 11
H 67mm; cup distorted, d *c*.12mm (flanges overlap).

400 TL74 772 (291) 11
Almost complete; surviving h 92mm; cup d 17mm.

392

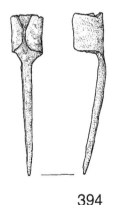

394

395

Fig 108　Cupped candleholders (1:2)

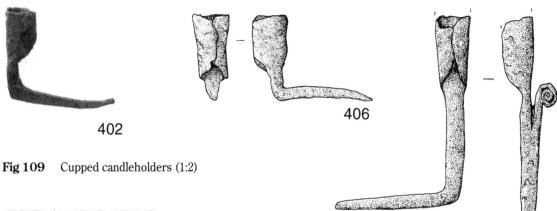

Fig 109   Cupped candleholders (1:2)

RIGHT-ANGLED STEMS

In four of these, the cup is on the inside of the right angle, e.g., No 402, but on four others it is on the outside, e.g., No 406, and in No 408 it is at 90 degrees to it (see Fig 109). No clear pattern emerges beyond the very even representation of the two main varieties. It is possible that individual smiths would have produced only one version. There is also considerable variation in the thickness of the spikes, e.g., Nos 392 and 394 (straight stems, above) are rather slender, whereas No 408 is much more robust.

401 TL74 Acc No 2375 (Context 2443) Ceramic Phase 9
H 35mm+; flat-section spike l 49mm; cup incomplete, d *c*.10mm, inside angle.

402 SWA81 2137 (2081) 9 Fig 109
H 49mm; spike l 60mm; cup d *c*.15mm (flanges overlap) inside angle.

403 SWA81 2231 (2061) 9
H 59mm; spike l 59mm; cup distorted, d *c*.15mm outside angle.

404 BC72 4120 (250) 10
H 64mm; spike l 71mm; cup incomplete, d 15mm outside angle.

405 BWB83 3425 (307) 11
H 41mm; flattish stem l 20mm, is probably incomplete; cup d 18mm (flanges overlap) inside angle.

406 BWB83 4334 (110) 11 Fig 109
H 44mm; spike l 48mm; cup d 16mm (flanges overlap) outside angle.

407 BWB83 628 (151) 11
H 57mm; spike l 22mm; cup incomplete, d *c*.18mm inside angle.

408 CUS73 643 (VIII,10) 11 Fig 109
H 97mm; single scroll at right angle to spike, l 67mm; cup d 17mm (flanges contiguous) facing away from scroll.
Previously published by Henig (1974, 192–3, fig 39, no 72).

409 BWB83 3957 (313) 12
(Described from X-ray plate) h 74mm; spike l 87mm; cup d *c*.18mm outside angle.

CANDLEHOLDER WITH WAX TRAY

410 BWB83 Acc No 3460 (Context 300) Ceramic Phase (?)11 Fig 110
Flattish, horizontal spike l 125mm, with branched stem h 57mm having riveted cup d 16mm (gap between flanges); an approximately square sheet tray, 70×68mm, with upward-folded sides is set on the spike; a plug of carbonised wood fills the cup as found.
Compare I H Goodall 1981 (59–60, fig 58, no 7) for an example from Grenstein, Norfolk.

OTHER FORMS

411 BWB83 Acc No 160 (Context 110) Ceramic Phase 11
H 48mm; cup d 17mm (flanges overlap); stem has constriction near end and hammered terminal (cf. rivet).
Presumably originally attached to a metal base; compare with preceding item.

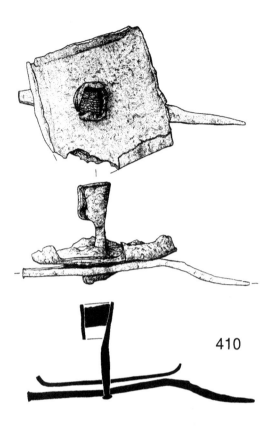

Fig 110   Cupped candleholder with drip tray (1:2)

412 BWB83 2923 (265) 12
H 50mm; tapered cup with straight edges which
overlap (no flanges) max d 17mm; stem bent in U
shape, with tip hooked outwards; possibly distorted.

It is difficult to see how the stem in its present
shape could have been hammered into a wooden
support; presumably there was some other arrangement (see parallel for No 422, Fig 114).

CUP(S) AND
PRICKET TOGETHER

It is uncertain whether the 'prickets' in these
sticks were purely decorative or whether they
might occasionally have been used as alterna-
tives to the cups to hold candles of a different
material (??wax rather than tallow) from those
that the cups were for.

Single cup

413 BWB83 Acc No 3299 (Context 362) Ceramic
Phase 9 Fig 111
H 97mm; cup incomplete d 14mm (gap between
flanges); spike at acute angle l 30mm+; 90-degree
twist between cup and stem; scrolls (one broken off)
to sides of cup.

414 BC72 4634 (250) 10
H (?)45mm; spike at right angle l 56mm; cup
d 15mm (flanges contiguous); pricket (?)bent at
angle.

415 BWB83 175 (110) 11
H 129mm; spike at right angle l 73mm; cup d 20mm
(flanges contiguous).

Two cups

416 SWA81 Acc No 2201 (Context 2070) Ceramic
Phase 9 Fig 111
Central pricket h 80mm; inward-facing cups d 14 and
15mm, respectively, with overlapping and contiguous flanges on right-angled branches; l 47mm.

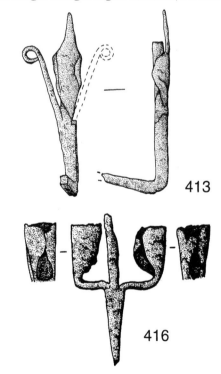

Fig 111   Candleholders (1:2)

Fig 112   Candleholder (1:2)

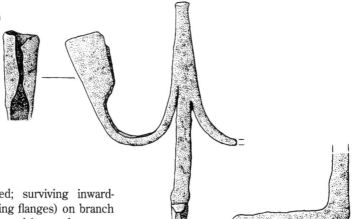

419

417 TL74 142 (291) 11
As preceding form; corroded; surviving inward-facing cup d 16mm (overlapping flanges) on branch l 40mm; other branch broken and incomplete; central pricket h 73mm; spike pierced near base (hole too narrow for nail).

418 TL74 2345 (2332) 11
Central spike with pricket h 96mm; one inward-facing cup survives d *c.*19mm (overlapping flanges) on right-angled branches of estd original w 120mm; traces of wood at top of spike.

419 BC72 2245 (83) 11 Fig 112
Central spike with upper end blunted (?) by hammering; h 116mm; inward-facing cups, only one of which survives, d ?19mm (distorted) on U-shaped branches, estd original w approx 120mm; pricket l 63mm at right angle.

420 BWB83 405 (359) 11 Fig 113
Crude and slightly distorted; horizontal arm w *c.*95mm; outward-facing cups d 16mm and 13mm (gaps between flanges) on right-angled stems h 34mm; central hole for missing, separate support etc.

Rushlight holder

421 SWA81 Acc No 3910 (Context 2018) Ceramic Phase 9 Fig 113
Cup d 5mm (overlapping flanges) on flat-section stem, l 141mm, with hooked top end.

No parallel with a cup of this small size seems to be known from a certain medieval context, but compare Fig 114 (middle), for the form.

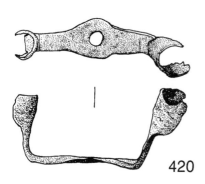

420

Fig 113   Candleholder and rushlight (1:2)

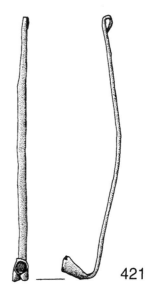

421

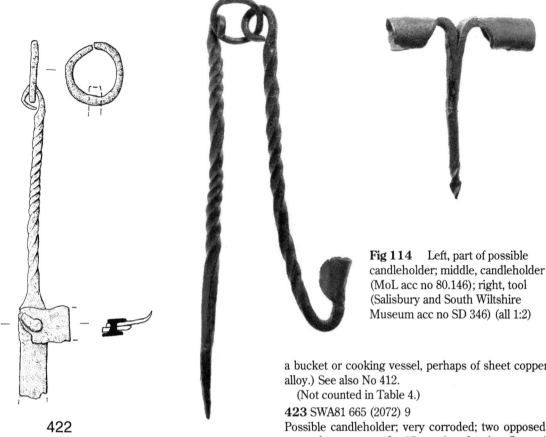

422

Fig 114   Left, part of possible candleholder; middle, candleholder (MoL acc no 80.146); right, tool (Salisbury and South Wiltshire Museum acc no SD 346) (all 1:2)

a bucket or cooking vessel, perhaps of sheet copper alloy.) See also No 412.

(Not counted in Table 4.)

423 SWA81 665 (2072) 9
Possible candleholder; very corroded; two opposed, tapered cups, max d *c*.15mm (overlapping flanges) at each end of robust stem l 141mm.

(Not counted in Table 4.)

See Ward Perkins (1940, 179, fig 56, no 2) for a candleholder with three cups, all set in different directions (meaning that only one could be used at any one time).

An item in the Salisbury and South Wiltshire Museum, somewhat similar in that it has two 'cups', is from a gimlet (a rotary tool), which would have had a wooden handle held in the cups (Fig 114 right; acc no SD 346). The present object lacks the central stem at a right angle to the 'cups' in the Salisbury implement.

Possible parts of candleholders

422 SWA81 Acc No 504 (Context 2018) Ceramic Phase 9 Fig 114
Strip 14mm wide, possibly broken off at one end, changing to twisted bar with hooked end, total l 161mm; hook holds an irregular, unjoined ring, d 30mm; the main strip is riveted to two further fragmentary strips, one w 18mm, set at a right angle to the first.

It is uncertain what this item was part of, but a general similarity to decorative elements on a complex cupped candleholder (MoL acc no 80.146, see Fig 114 middle) and to some much later iron lighting equipment (Caspall 1987, 213, figs 490–1; 215, fig 496, all late 17th- or 18th-century lamps) may point to a comparable medieval form (?elaborate chandelier of some kind) that has not survived complete. (No 422 may alternatively be part of the handle of

Copper alloy

No sheet copper-alloy candleholders have been recognised among the items from the recently excavated sites, though medieval cup sticks made from sheeting are known in London, including an ingenious, adjustable version allowing for three different positions, fixed by a folding tab; see Fig 115 left (MoL acc no 84.163

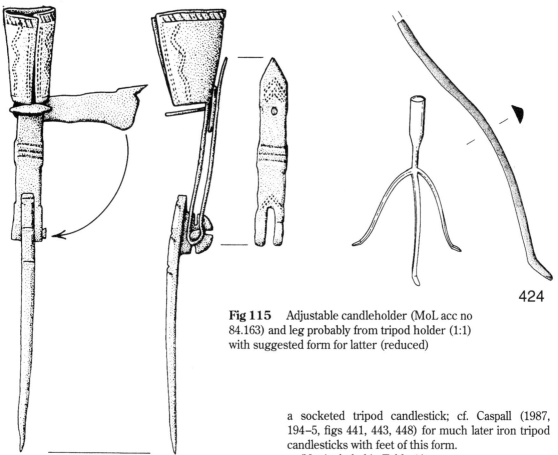

424

Fig 115 Adjustable candleholder (MoL acc no 84.163) and leg probably from tripod holder (1:1) with suggested form for latter (reduced)

– cf. A R Goodall in Armstrong & Ayers 1987, 206, fig 117, no 214, from Hull). See Ward Perkins (1940, 179, fig 56, no 1) and Baker (1981) for much more elaborate, foldable travelling sticks of cast copper alloy found in London and Bedfordshire. Also entirely absent from the recently excavated assemblages are copper-alloy holders with octagonal cups (e.g., Ward Perkins 1940, 181), though compare the collar on No 426. The alloys of Nos 424 and 425 are very similar (see Analysis of copper-alloy vessels and candleholders).

424 BWB83 Acc No 4055 (Context 362) Ceramic Phase 9 Fig 115
Fragment; gunmetal (RHB, Table 7); cast, D-section curving foot with angle near base. Probably from

a socketed tripod candlestick; cf. Caspall (1987, 194–5, figs 441, 443, 448) for much later iron tripod candlesticks with feet of this form.
(Not included in Table 4.)

425 SH74 18 (207) 9 Fig 116
(Object mislaid – described from photographic and other records; a tiny remaining fragment was analysed.)
Cast stag, with splayed feet; gunmetal (RHB, Table 7); h approx 110mm; l approx 125mm. There is little accurate anatomical detail, but a circular mark in the middle of the back shows that this is the base of an 'animalier' candleholder of a kind that was in vogue in the late medieval period (Fig 116, bottom left, shows the probable original form).
A similar example was found at Aldgate (MoL acc no C703, Fig 116 right). Other, somewhat different examples dated to the 14th century have been found in France (Ward Perkins 1940, pl 39, bottom left; Caspall 1987, 74–5, fig 125, left, here attributed to Dinant in Belgium), in Denmark (Liebgott 1973, 14) and in Göttingen, Germany (Grupe 1984, 6). The two excavated in London seem to be relatively cheap

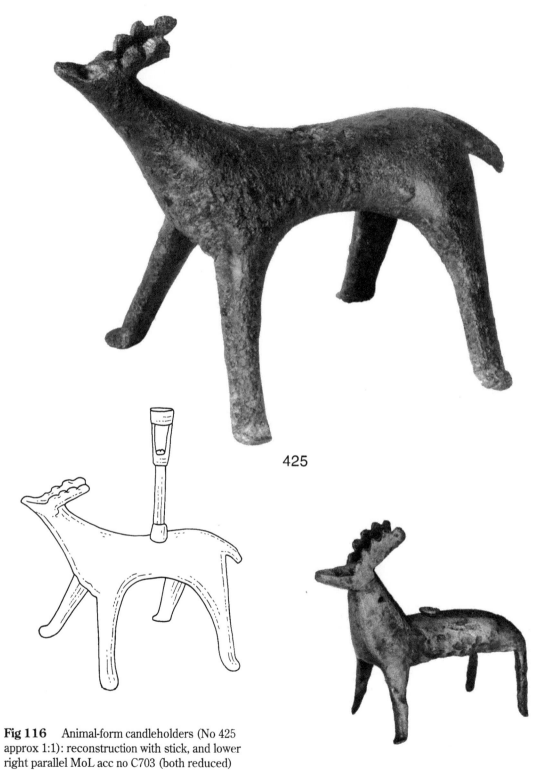

425

Fig 116   Animal-form candleholders (No 425
approx 1:1): reconstruction with stick, and lower
right parallel MoL acc no C703 (both reduced)

versions, essentially a U-shaped panel for the body and the legs, with only the head and neck fully in the round, while the others elsewhere, which have cylindrical bodies and use much more metal, were presumably more expensive. It would be useful to know where the respective categories were made (perhaps Continental originals, and cheaper English ones copying the fashion? – cf. Bangs 1995, 47 for a more elaborate version, possibly of English origin).

426 BC72 2276 (83) 11 Fig 117
Socketed, cast tripod candlestick; leaded gunmetal (RHB, Table 7); h 136mm; turned, broad saucer base, d 76mm, with two pairs of concentric grooves

and a raised edge; on three step-like feet, each having a ridge in the angle and trifid ends; the stem tapers towards an octagonal collar with alternating long and short sides, which supports the two flat sides of an open socket that is surmounted by a tapering collar (internal d 17–13mm); one of originally two bifurcated projections ('wings'/'flanges') from the socket survives; h of stem and socket 113mm; internal d of latter 17mm; central chuck hole in base from turning; prominent filing marks from finishing at several points, notably on the feet and socket; stem appears worn from handling over a period of time, and the bottoms of the feet are worn flat at the points of contact with the surface on which it stood.

This stick was presumably imported from the Continent. Two candlesticks of similar form from French hoards dated to the 14th century were published by Ward Perkins (1940, 180, pl 39 – cf. his type 1; see also Ruempol & Van Dongen 1991, 59, 61; Caspall 1987, 74–5, fig 126; Bangs 1995, 50–1, 197, no 6 – for which a French origin is also mooted, though the possibility of English manufacture is also raised; Michaelis 1978, 40, fig 24, which has a more elaborate stem). Michaelis (ibid., 42) suggested that the side projections would have enabled this kind of stick to be hung, presumably for storage, on a 'bracket with a U-shaped opening' set in a wall (unless this means some form of staple, no such bracket has been identified; there is no obvious candidate for one among the assemblages excavated at the sites covered in this survey). The candlestick's feet were clearly intended to be the normal means

426

Fig 117   Candleholder (1:1, base reduced)

of support during use, but inversion of the stick could have provided a simple means of storage on a forked wall hook, if that was appropriate. There is, furthermore, no hint of wear on the underside of the surviving projection, which would have been consistent with Michaelis's suggestion. Instead, the projections could have been used to clean whatever tool was employed either to clear wax from the socket when the candle needed replacing or to attend to the wick (even in the mid-19th century candle wicks required constant attention – Harrison 1928, 37 – reference kindly supplied by Chris Green). There is a tiny dent on one side of the socket, which might have come from cleaning off wax, though there is no clear indication of wear inside the fork of the projection.

Lanterns

(These would presumably have held candles.)

Copper alloy
427 TL74 Acc No 2354 (Context 2808) Ceramic Phase 11 Fig 118
Rectangular sliding aperture cover h 140mm, w 52mm; slightly arched in section; series of trefoil and

427

Fig 118 Lantern-aperture slide (1:1), and lantern (MoL acc no A1366, reduced)

multifoil apertures; side strips each w 7mm and held with four rivets (partly missing on one side); strips w 3mm at top and bottom superimposed on the former and sharing their rivets; apertures have rough edges on both faces and may have been enlarged by filing or gouging outwards from initial smaller piercings.

Compare two lanterns, complete except for their aperture covers, tentatively attributed to the 14th century (Ward Perkins 1940, 182–5, fig 58; one of these, MoL acc no A1366, h 285mm, appears in Fig 118 right).

A rectangular frame, 90×56mm, made of paired sheet copper-alloy strips (like the single ones on No 427) may be from another lantern (BWB83 acc no 1238, from a deposit attributed to ceramic phase 11).

A highly decorative 12th-century lantern, like other surviving examples, has the top pierced to allow heat and smoke to escape (MacGregor 1983, 267–70, no 209, fig 99).

See No 483 (Fig 140) for a possible lantern top.

Horn leaves

428 BC72 (no Acc No) (Context 250) Ceramic Phase 10 Fig 119
Two incomplete, slightly curved leaves with both faces smoothed and polished and presumably originally cut to rectangular shape, probably from lanterns, or possibly windows (cf. MacGregor 1989, 120; horn books seem unlikely at this early date). Previously published by Armitage (1982, 102, fig 45).

These are rare survivals because of the great susceptibility of horn to decay in the ground.

Ceramic

Adapted or re-used ceramic vessels were also used as lamps. Jacqui Pearce writes:

> Three examples have been identified among excavated material from London. A small dish or saucer in Cheam Whiteware, dated to the late 14th to early 15th century, is sooted inside and around the rim outside and could well have been used as a lamp (Fig 120 top; also published in Pearce et al. 1988, 77, fig 125, no 580). The form is well suited to this function and could have been free-standing rather than suspended. The form was also well known in the 13th/14th centuries in Kingston-type ware (ibid., fig 98) and London-type ware (Pearce et al. 1985, fig 72, nos 392–7), although so far only one example with internal sooting has been recognised. More unexpected are two jugs adapted for use as lanterns. Both are made in London-type ware. One is an undecorated pear-shaped vessel with five circular holes around the body and blackened inside (Fig 120 bottom; also published – ibid. 95, fig 53, no 195). The other is a baluster-shaped drinking jug of late 14th-century form, with a simple triangular opening cut in the lower half of the body from the base to approximately half way up the vessel (DUK77, context 501, which is assigned a 16th-century date; this may be an old vessel re-used around that time, or it may have been adapted as much as a century or more before it was discarded).

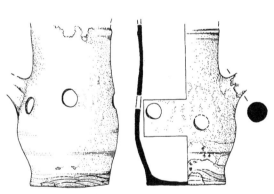

Fig 120　Ceramic dish, possibly used as a lamp, and fragmentary ceramic jug pierced for probable re-use as a lantern (after Pearce & Vince 1988, fig 170 and Pearce et al. 1985, fig 53; 1:4)

428

Fig 119　Horn lantern pane (1:1)

Miscellaneous household equipment: kitchen and tableware, storage and other vessels, urinals

GEOFF EGAN

Two late 14th-century inventories of kitchen contents from well-to-do London households are reproduced here (Tables 5 and 6), with minor emendations, for comparison with the excavated items listed in the catalogue below (cf. ceramic phase 11; the inventories appear in Thomas 1929; they have also been reproduced by S Moorhouse in Moorhouse 1987, vii–viii).

Notable absences from, or so far unrecog-nised among, the excavated assemblages considered in this volume are iron vessels, spits and spit wheels (as well as iron curtain rods), and any wooden sieve – other specific wooden items could be present, though definitive identification is difficult. (The archaeological equivalents of mortars etc. of stone listed in the inventories are not discussed in this present volume.)

Table 5: Inventory of kitchen contents (1368)
Listed in a case of proof of ownership awarded to Thomas Kyneball, rector of St Martin Pomeroy, London (Thomas 1929, 92)

Copper alloy	Iron	Lead/tin	Wood	Stone
6 brass pots	3 brandreths	1 pewter pot for vinegar	4 large pails	3 mortars of marble
1 posset	2 griddles		1 small pail	2 stones for mustard [?pestles]
4 cauldrons	5 hooks		2 wooden pestles	
2 collanders	1 iron frying pan		2 tables for the dresser	
	2 iron slices		3 large vats	
	1 flesh hook		3 tubs	
	1 skimmer		1 cask	
	1 iron ladle		1 trough	
	4 spit wheels			
	1 hoist			

Table 6: Inventory of kitchen contents (1373)
In the eight-roomed house of Thomas Mocking, a London fishmonger (Thomas 1929, 156)

Copper alloy	Iron	Wood	?Stone
5 pitchers	5 large spits	2 vats	2 mortars
7 pots	6 tripods	1 water tankard	
7 pans	2 gridirons	5 tabs [?taps]	
2 cauldrons	1 frying pan	1 sieve (hairsieve)	
	1 hook		
	1 firepan		
	4 iron rods for curtains		

Trivet

Iron

429 BWB83 Acc No 5673 (Context 292) Ceramic
Phase 11 Fig 121
Corroded and distorted tripod (distortion due at least
in part to its recovery by machine from foreshore
deposits – shape restored in drawing); flat, circular
top retaining part of two of the presumed original
three internal radial supports (precise arrangement
at the centre uncertain) and three external strap
feet, each placed as if continuing the radial bars but
set at right angles to them, apparently through holes
in the horizontal top elements; original height approx
140mm; estd max d 350mm.

The trivet's purpose was to support vessels during
cooking over a fire. Prolonged use would have taken
its toll on wrought iron exposed to the direct heat of
a fire. No other substantially complete trivet is
known from this period (cf. G E Oakley 1979, 273–4,
no 85, fig 120 and I H Goodall 1981, 59–60, fig 58,
no 5 for a simpler, incomplete tripod from Northampton, and *idem* in Biddle 1990, 820, 822, fig 242, no
2545 is part of a 15th-century pentapod from Winchester; see Seymour Lindsay 1970, fig 109 for an
early illustration and Feild 1984, 72, fig 52 for later
surviving examples).

429

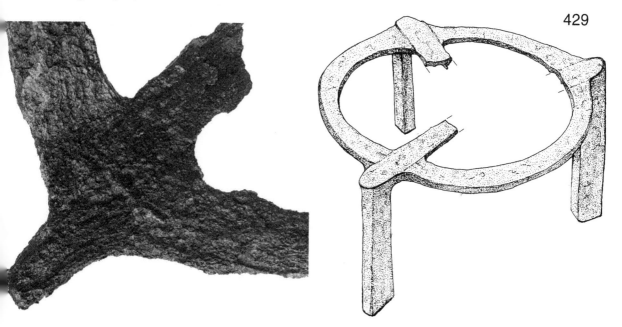

Fig 121   Trivet with restoration of original form (reduced) and detail (1:1), left, showing join of wrought parts

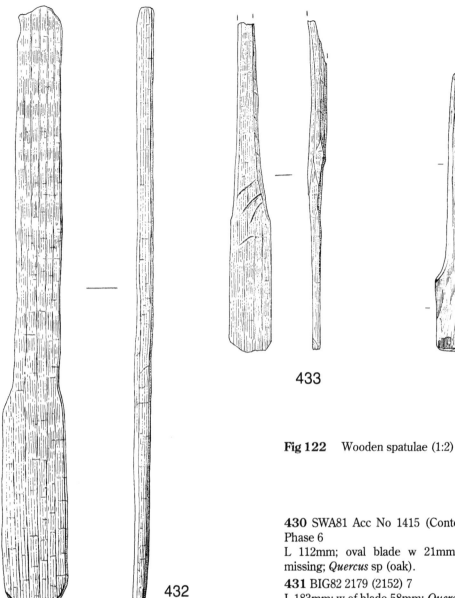

433   434

Fig 122   Wooden spatulae (1:2)

Wooden spatulate implements
Lynne Keys

All are roughly carved. They were presumably used to stir food during cooking and perhaps also to serve it.

430 SWA81 Acc No 1415 (Context 2187) Ceramic Phase 6
L 112mm; oval blade w 21mm; most of handle missing; *Quercus* sp (oak).

431 BIG82 2179 (2152) 7
L 183mm; w of blade 58mm; *Quercus* sp (oak).

432 SWA81 1731 (2050) 9 Fig 122
L 312mm; w of blade 36mm; *Quercus* sp (oak); handle burnt at one end.
   Possibly incomplete.

433 TL74 492 (364) 12 Fig 122
L 173mm; part of handle missing; *Taxus baccata* (yew).

434 BC72 3626 (150) 11 Fig 122
L 149mm; rectangular blade w 19mm; *Taxus baccata* (yew).

432

Flesh hooks

Iron

Flesh hooks were used for picking pieces of meat etc. from the stewpot (Fig 123). Compare Ward Perkins 1940, 125, pl 24 and I H Goodall in Biddle 1990, 820, 822, nos 2549–53, fig 242 for a variety of forms from the 13th to 15th centuries.

A fragmentary flesh hook from the TL74 site (from a deposit attributed to ceramic phase 11 – M Rhodes in Milne & Milne 1982, 89) had deteriorated further when examined for this current publication and is omitted.

435 SWA81 Acc No 2105 (Context 2057) Ceramic Phase 9 Fig 124
L 107mm; shank divides into three curved prongs; handle missing.

436 BC72 2652 (79) 11 Fig 124
Distorted (original shape restored in illustration); l 172mm; three curved prongs; socket (possibly incomplete, as there is no obvious nail hole, even on the X-ray plate) internal d *c*.15mm, for missing handle.

Skimmers

Copper-alloy sheeting

Skimmers were used for removing items from stew pots. These seem to have superseded flesh hooks (see above) at the end of the medieval period, though Fig 123 shows that skimmers were used together with flesh hooks in the 14th century. Figure 126 (right) illustrates a more complete example of the former (MoL acc no 90.45; d 172mm; this one is probably of early post-medieval date as it has rivets made from rolled sheeting – which seem to be from later than the mid-15th century). Another example that has been attributed to the Roman period (Guildhall Museum Catalogue 1908, 40, no 147, pl 30, no 1) may well be of later date.

437 TL74 Acc No 1083 (Context 368) Ceramic Phase 12 Fig 125
Slightly distorted fragment of relatively thick (*c*.1mm) sheeting (?or possibly cast); d 180mm; seven compass-engraved concentric circles on one side have been used for setting out the holes, which

Fig 123 Skimmer and flesh hook used with cauldrons (redrawn from the Luttrell Psalter)

Fig 124   Flesh hooks (1:1)

435

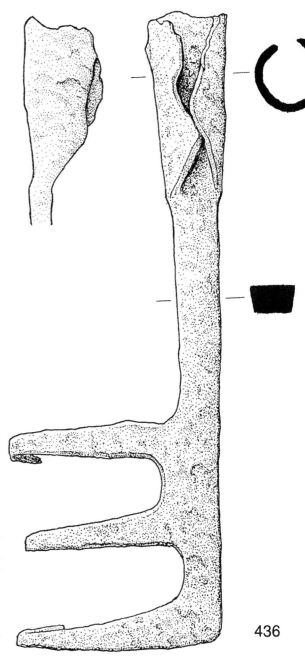

436

appear to have been finished from the other side; three enigmatic small pieces of (?)sheeting set neatly through the main disc may be from the fixture of a handle – their present flush finish may indicate re-use of the disc as a drainage grille etc.

438 TL74 2391 (1388) 12 Fig 125
Fragment with thickened rim; d *c*.360mm; neat, decorative pattern of small holes; turning marks on both faces.

Compare a complete bowl (with a similar arrangement of holes but no handle) from the Netherlands and dated to *c*.1400 (Gaimster & Verhaeghe 1992, 315, fig 8, left).

439 TL74 1207 (368) 12 Fig 126
Two arrow-shaped plates 102×84mm; turning (?or possibly scouring) marks on one face; riveted

together; for securing (missing) wooden handle to circular strainer, a fragment of which survives, with part of one hole; estd original d of strainer approx 350mm.

See also lead/tin fragment No 507.

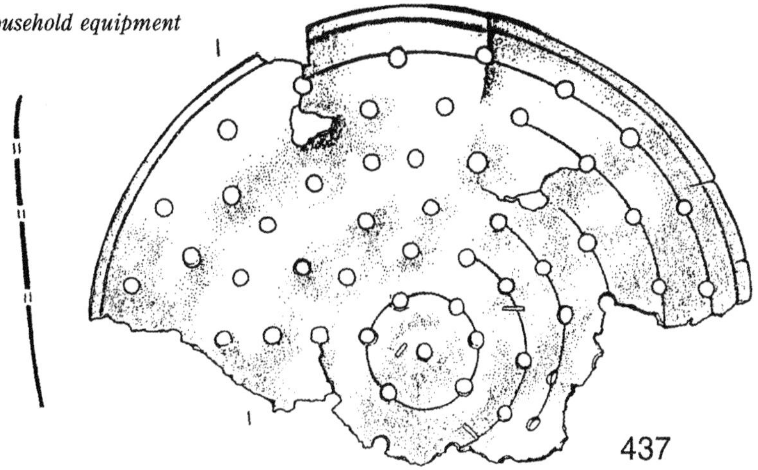

Fig 125   Skimmers (1:2)

437

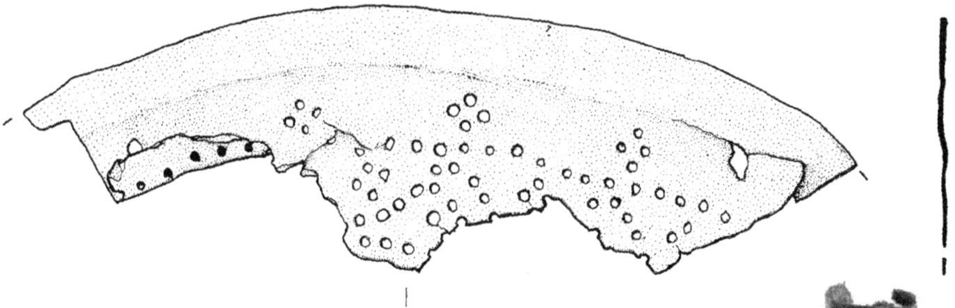

438

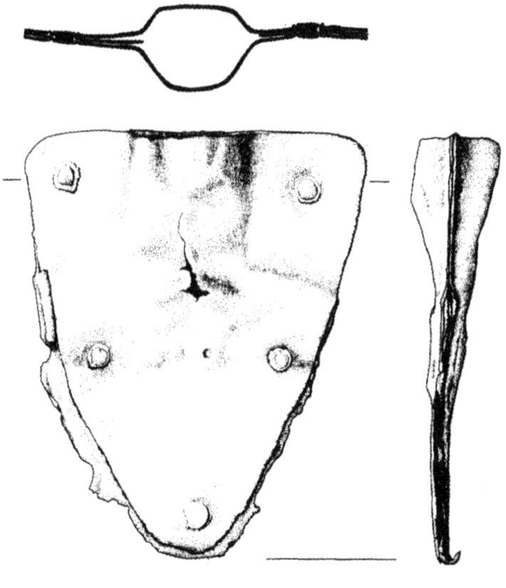

439

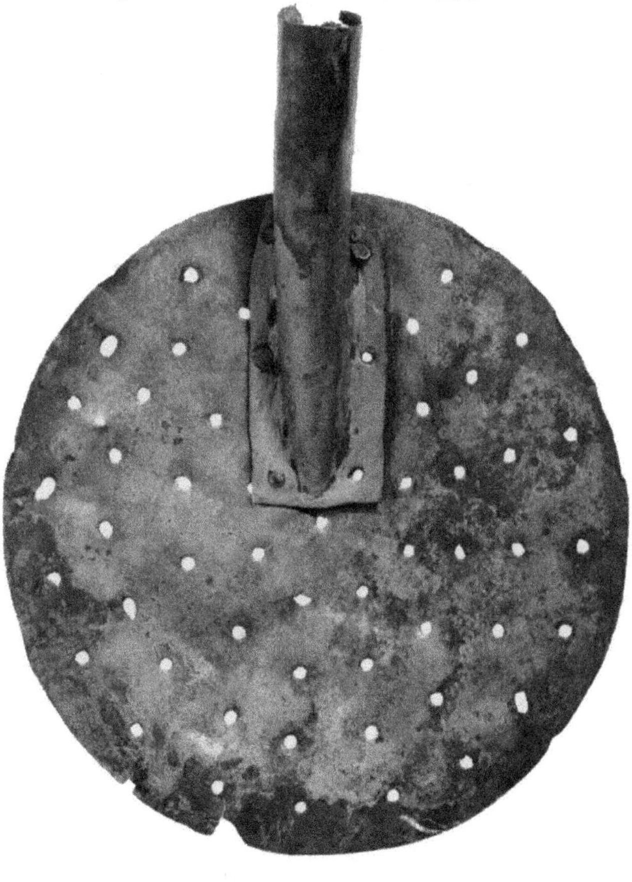

Fig 126   Skimmers: handle attachment plates (1:2) and complete end (MoL acc no 90.45, reduced)

Possible strainer

Copper alloy

440 SWA81 Acc No 3231 (Context 2187) Ceramic
Phase 6 Fig 127

Incomplete sheet (?)disc; d *c*.70mm; roughly pierced
holes from which the metal has not been fully
removed.

It is not known precisely what this item would
have been used for. The lack of neat finishing may
imply that it was some kind of drain filter (a spice
rasp seems less likely in such a crude form at this
date). It is comparable to a find from Sussex (A R
Goodall 1977, 58–9, no 16, fig 18).

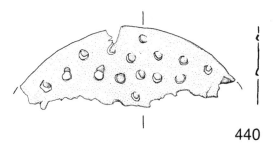

440

Fig 127   Possible strainer (1:1)

Copper-alloy vessels

The manufacture in England of medieval
copper-alloy vessels and the alloys used have
been discussed most recently by Blair & Blair
(1991, 82–5, 93–5; on alloys, see R Brownsword
(ibid. 102–4). Some of the background documentary evidence for the production activities
of London 'potters' (i.e., workers in cast copper
alloys) of the 14th century is discussed by
Unwin (1962, 31–4). There must have been
considerable recycling of metal. See Table 7 for
a probable piece of casting waste from the
excavations considered here.

In addition to items produced perhaps from
the 13th century onwards in this country, there
was a considerable import of copper-alloy vessels etc. (*dinanderie*, so-named from the production area at Dinant near Namur in modern
Belgium, though the industry was found in
many different places around the Meuse Valley,

including part of north-west Germany). See
Unwin (1962, 31–4) for documentary evidence
for Londoners probably trading Continental
vessels in the late 13th/early 14th centuries
and W Hömberg (in Wittstock 1982, 145–79)
for a discussion of some late medieval copper-
alloy vessels in Germany.

Cast, decorative copper-alloy basins (*gemel-
lions* – often used in pairs) seem to have been
relatively expensive. None of these, nor of the
decorated sheet dishes of the kind studied by
Weitzman Fiedler (1981) – known from the
early part of the period considered in this
present volume up to the 13th century – has
been identified among the recently excavated
assemblages (though they have previously
been found in London – e.g., ibid. nos 59, 149,
151, 170–3; cf. Roach Smith (1842), Dalton
(1922, 133–40) and Ward Perkins (1940, 201–4
with references); the gilding claimed to have
survived on one of the London finds has not
been verified by analysis and seems
improbable).

Ewers were used together with basins in the
formal washing of hands at meal times. It
appears from the items listed below that cast
ewers may have been used with sheet-metal
basins in most London households that could
afford metal vessels (cf. Lewis 1987a, 19).

Only one, probably cast, item listed below
(No 441) pre-dates the late 13th century, and

Fig 128   (?)A game involving a tripod ewer and
perhaps a suspended lamp; the supine boy appears
to be balancing a ball or fruit on his mouth (redrawn
from the Luttrell Psalter)

this may have come from a vessel made mainly of another material. The chronological sequence of the recently excavated finds tends to confirm the one for cast copper-alloy vessels in England suggested by Cherry (1987, 147).

The very limited size of most of the fragments recovered means that the majority of diameters suggested must be considered approximate. There seems to be a much higher incidence of identifiable repairs among sheet vessels (seven patches and 17 other fragments) than among cast pieces that are definable as vessels (two repairs as against 26 other fragments). The very incomplete state of the surviving pieces and the possibility of repair patches being made of more than one component (see No 494, Fig 144) may make some inferences based on a simple count unreliable.

A large number of fragments of similar date excavated at Winchester show a similar pattern to that of the following items (Biddle 1990, 947–59; the Winchester pieces attributed to Biddle's groups 'A' and 'B', which are thought to be from the Anglo-Saxon period and are not from vessels, have no obvious parallels among the recent London finds).

Analysis of copper-alloy vessels and candleholders (Nigel Blades)

INTRODUCTION

Fourteen excavated objects, mostly vessel fragments and candleholders from 13th–15th-century contexts were quantitatively analysed. Although this is a more time-consuming process than qualitative analysis, much more information is obtained. The exact amount of alloying metals are measured, the proportions of which can be indicators of different periods and of different methods of fabrication (e.g., casting or wrought working). Also, a range of impurity elements is measured, which can give a clue as to the alloy's origin. Obviously, with the small number of analyses carried out here, it is not possible to come to any conclusions about the pattern of copper-alloy use in London during the medieval period, but the results can

be presented in the light of what is already known about medieval copper alloys.

ANALYTICAL METHOD

Quantitative analysis was carried out at Royal Holloway and Bedford New College, University of London (RHB), using inductively coupled-plasma spectrometry (ICPS). The elements sought were: copper, zinc, lead, tin, iron, nickel, arsenic, bismuth, antimony, phosphorus, sulphur, cobalt, chromium, manganese, vanadium, cadmium, silver and gold. The technique requires the removal of a small sample, typically 5–10mg, which is dissolved in aqua regia, and the resulting solution is pumped into the ICPS system. Sampling is carried out either by drilling or, in the case of sheet metal, by cutting away a small piece. This must then be filed clean of corrosion products to expose good metal. These methods ensure that the sample of the core metal obtained can be reasonably assumed to represent the original composition of the artefact.

NOMENCLATURE

The alloy names used in the report follow the guidelines set out by Bayley (in Egan & Pritchard 1991, 13–17; cf. Blair & Blair 1991, 81–5).

Bronze An alloy of copper and tin. If zinc is present, it is at a level of less than one-third the tin.
Brass Copper with zinc. If tin is present, it is at a level of less than one-quarter the zinc.
Gunmetal An alloy of copper with both tin and zinc as alloying components (some workers use the name *latten* for medieval copper/tin/zinc/lead alloys, particularly those with more zinc than tin).
'Leaded' This term is applied to any of the above containing more than 4% lead.

RESULTS

The analytical results are given in Table 7. In order to depict the alloy compositions a ternary

Table 7:   ICPS analysis of cast copper-alloy objects

Object	Catalogue no	Ceramic phase	Cu	Zn	Pb	Sn	Fe	Ni	As	Bi	Sb	P	S	Co	Cd	Ag	Au	Total
Candleholder	424	9	80.6	11.77	1.86	5.01	0.94	0.04	0.40	0.07	0.26	0.00	0.09	0.007	0.003	0.074	0.002	*101.1*
Candleholder	425	9	76.0	11.99	1.55	6.65	0.95	0.04	0.50	0.08	0.31	0.00	0.17	0.007	0.001	0.080	0.002	98.3
Candleholder	426	11	69.3	3.78	18.67	5.33	0.46	0.06	0.37	0.06	1.74	0.00	0.13	0.008	0.000	0.110	0.005	*100.1*
Spout	441	6	71.6	0.91	14.96	9.49	0.23	0.04	0.04	0.00	0.18	0.00	0.10	0.002	0.000	0.045	0.004	97.6
Vessel foot	453	8+	80.8	0.04	11.44	4.26	0.01	0.03	0.34	0.03	0.24	0.00	0.02	0.002	0.000	0.039	0.002	97.2
Vessel foot	456	11	74.3	14.73	3.42	2.26	1.15	0.03	0.30	0.05	0.19	0.00	0.07	0.003	0.001	0.053	0.000	96.5
Vessel foot	457	11	76.4	0.00	7.07	1.25	0.03	0.09	1.27	0.03	1.98	0.03	0.20	0.008	0.000	0.098	0.003	88.4
Vessel foot	458	11	76.5	0.00	8.31	0.59	0.04	0.09	0.87	0.04	2.62	0.17	0.07	0.000	0.000	0.108	0.002	89.4
Vessel foot	459	12	68.2	9.82	16.44	0.22	0.40	0.03	0.17	0.10	2.66	0.00	0.04	0.004	0.000	0.101	0.002	98.2
Vessel foot	462	unstratified	60.2	0.00	26.09	1.02	0.13	0.54	1.41	0.04	7.26	0.01	0.43	0.011	0.000	0.096	0.002	97.3
Cast repair	465	9	74.1	0.37	18.04	4.44	0.14	0.02	0.45	0.06	0.25	0.00	0.07	0.013	0.000	0.041	0.002	98.0
Cast repair	466	10	63.7	29.98	2.15	1.17	0.64	0.12	0.10	0.00	0.10	0.00	0.02	0.000	0.007	0.023	0.002	98.1
(?)Figurative fragment	469	7	68.0	0.00	25.15	6.95	0.02	0.02	0.15	0.00	0.21	0.00	0.01	0.002	0.000	0.032	0.002	*100.6*
(?)Casting waste – (see p. 162)		11	67.0	0.00	24.35	4.48	0.05	0.03	0.24	0.00	0.16	0.00	0.06	0.003	0.000	0.037	0.002	96.4

Also sought, but not detected: chromium, manganese, vanadium.

diagram was plotted. This is obtained by plotting the relative percentages of the major components, zinc (zn), tin (sn) and lead (pb), on a triangular graph, where each of the apices represents a maximum for that alloy component. Thus, a point plotted at the zinc apex indicates an alloy of copper with zinc, containing no lead or tin, whilst a point in the centre of the triangle represents an alloy with equal amount of zinc, tin and lead. Fig 129 top shows the alloys which correspond to different areas on the ternary diagram. It should be noted that this method plots relative compositions, not absolute ones. Thus two coincident points do not necessarily contain the same amounts of each alloying metal, but they do have these in the same ratio. However, by plotting only alloys with similar copper content on any particular graph, it can be ensured that coincident points are reasonably similar in composition. Fig 129 bottom shows results of the analyses.

Even among such a small number of samples there are clear differences in the alloys used to make different objects. The vessel feet, with

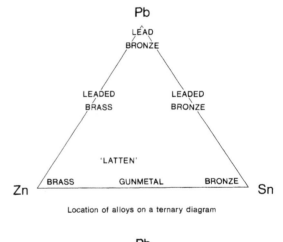

Location of alloys on a ternary diagram

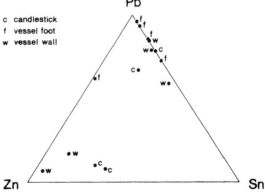

Fig 129   Ternary diagrams of alloys (top) and results of analyses for copper-alloy vessels (bottom)

the exception of No 453, are all made of a heavily leaded alloy, rich in arsenic and antimony. Tin content is uniformly low, less than the antimony in every case. Zinc is present at negligible levels, apart from in No 459. The repairs etc. are of varied composition: spout No 441, repair No 467 and the piece of casting waste are of heavily leaded bronze; repair No 468 is a high-zinc brass and foot (?repair) No 456 is an impure brass with a significant amount of lead and tin. Of the candleholders, No 426 is a heavily leaded gunmetal and Nos 424 and 425 are zinc-rich gunmetals. These last two items are strikingly alike in composition. It could be that they are from a common supply or even from the same piece of metal (although from different sites, the two are attributed to the same period, ceramic phase 9, *c*.1270–*c*.1350).

INTERPRETATION

The vessel feet and the leaded gunmetal candleholder No 426 all contain significant amounts of antimony and arsenic. This is characteristic of metal made from *Fahlerz*, a copper ore, which contains the minerals tetrahedrite (Cu_3SbS_3) and tennanite (Cu_3AsS_3). In antiquity, great value was placed on these ores because of their very high copper content, which was of the order of 30–40% (Tylecote 1986, 13–16). It is believed that during the medieval period the principal source of these ores was in north-west Europe (Lewis 1984, 334) in the Harz mountains area of Germany, and this was probably the source of the ores for these artefacts. The impression given by the vessel feet is one of cheapness: the ore was smelted to obtain the maximum weight of metal, and this was, without purification, alloyed with a large amount of lead (historically lead has always been cheaper than copper, zinc or tin). The resulting alloy is brittle and prone to fracture and corrosion along the grain boundaries where the insoluble lead segregates. It was unsuitable for wrought working, but perfectly satisfactory as a low-performance casting alloy.

The lack of high antimony/arsenic levels in the other alloys examined does not rule out a Harz mountains origin for the copper. For smaller, finer castings a better quality alloy is needed, the copper for which may well have been purified at some stage between smelting and casting. The two candleholders of near-identical composition are both of zinc-rich gunmetals with a small amount of lead (Nos 424, 425). Assuming they are of the same metal, it is probable that they were made either in the same workshop or from a common supply distributed to several workshops. It is possible, however, that they do not share a common origin but are made from a standard alloy. A gunmetal composition, believed to have been widely used in the late medieval period for small cast objects, such as candlesticks, was known in the medieval period as 'latten' (Cameron 1974, 225–30). A candlestick of a zinc-rich gunmetal or latten, similar to the alloy used for the two mentioned above, is published in Brownsword & Ciuffini (1988, 115), although that one is believed to be from the early 15th century rather than the late 13th/mid-14th-century period to which the candleholders considered above have been attributed.

Copper-alloy vessels catalogue

CAST VESSELS

Few of the wall or rim fragments listed below are large enough to determine for certain the original form of the vessel, though it can be suggested tentatively in some instances (often with reference to von Falke & Meyer 1983 and Theuerkauff Liederwald 1988 in the case of cast items).

Tripod cauldrons (see Fig 131 and Cherry 1987) or tripod ewers and long-handled skillets (Fig 130 top) seem to be the most commonly represented forms, and fragments from spouted lavers and ornate *aquamanili* and flagons may possibly also be present. Some of the cast feet seem to be diagnostic of particular vessel forms. No clear parallel has been traced for plain rim or base No 443, and the category of object from which it came is very uncertain. Though they have been retrieved elsewhere (e.g., Lewis 1987a, 4–5, fig 8A), none of the animal-headed spouts from the later part of the appropriate period have been found at the sites considered.

A fragment of what appears (despite its superficial similarity to a handle) to be casting waste, probably from a vessel or a bell, from a deposit attributed to ceramic phase 11, has been analysed. It provides a specific point of reference for one of the alloys used in casting hollow wares in medieval London (BWB83 acc no 2050 of leaded bronze – see Table 7).

See also taps Nos 745–6, the latter possibly of post-medieval date. (Nos 747–8 may perhaps also have been for copper-alloy vessels.)

Spout

441 SWA81 Acc No 3439 (Context 2176) Ceramic Phase 6 Fig 130

Leaded bronze (RHB, Table 7); probably cast; almost complete and somewhat corroded; tubular spout l 33mm, d 15mm with oblique mouth; integral triangular attachment plate with further, incomplete upper part and two (?of original three) rivet holes, one in basal lobe; wear at mouth of spout.

Probably from a wooden vessel, the form of which is uncertain.

A similar, less complete spout excavated at Winchester is described as beaten metal and tentatively dated to the 11th/12th century (Biddle 1990, 957–8, no 3408, fig 294).

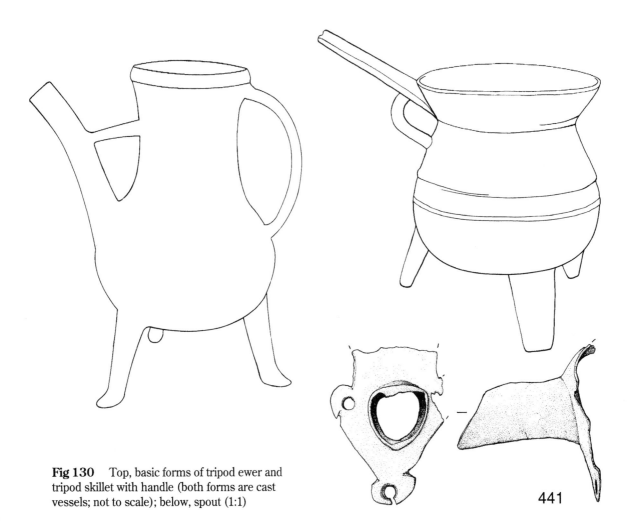

Fig 130 Top, basic forms of tripod ewer and tripod skillet with handle (both forms are cast vessels; not to scale); below, spout (1:1)

441

B

Plate 1 A: Flattened
padlock case of brazed
iron, No 246 (1:1)
B: Ivory writing tablet with
crucifixion scene, No 912
(enlarged)

A

Plate 2 Lead candlestick
No 366 (enlarged)

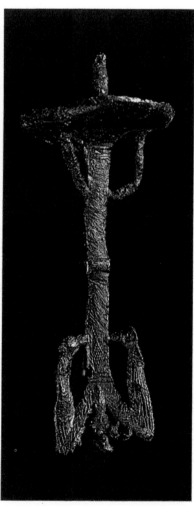

Plate 3 A: Tap No 745
B: Spoon No 769 (both 1:1)

A

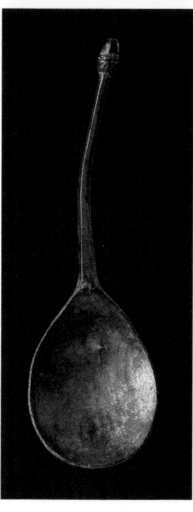

B

A

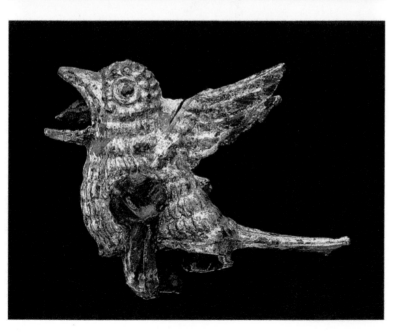

B

Plate 4 A: Peacock feather,
late 14th century, BC72
acc no 2632 - see p. 12
B: Toy bird No 931 (enlarged)

A

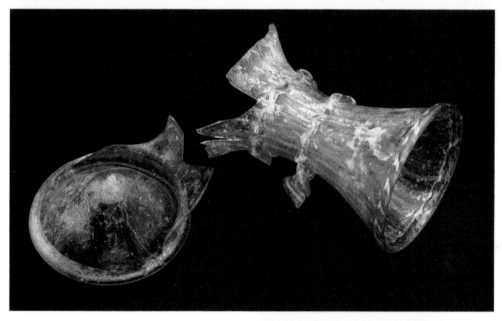

B

Plate 5   Glass vessels
A: Nos 643, left, and 703 (reduced)
B: Flask, LBT86 acc no 14 (reduced)
C: Enamelled Near Eastern fragment
No 695 (enlarged)

C

A

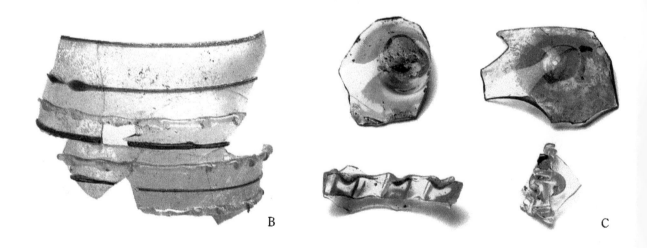

B   C

Plate 6   Glass vessels
A: Drinking glasses, LBT86 acc nos 736 & 8 (reduced)
B: Drinking glass rim, LBT86 acc no 9 (approx 1:1)
C: Lead-glass fragments Nos 657-60 (enlarged)

Plate 7 White glass fragments: left, Nos 693-4 and 689; right, MoL acc nos A17246 and A17160 (reduced)

Plate 8 Enamelled drinking glasses, OST82 acc nos 155 and 128 (top), 129 (middle left) and 130 (bottom right), and detail of latter (lower left) – enlarged to various scales, except middle left and lower right reduced

Fig 131 Fragment of cast (?)tripod cauldron with wrought-iron handle (reduced) and suggested original form

Rim fragments

442 BWB83 Acc No 2371 (Context 10) Ceramic Phase 9
Everted rim; d *c*.170mm; th <1mm; thickened, angled edge.

443 BWB83 396 (263) 9
D estd *c*.380mm; th 5mm; plain vertical rim or base with flat edge; turning marks on interior face.

The form of this fragment is most closely comparable with the footrings of jugs (e.g., Ward Perkins 1940, 200, pl 52), though none of the surviving examples traced approaches a similar size.

444 BC72 2130 (81) 10–11
Everted rim; d *c*.260mm.

445 BWB83 5186 (110) 11
Two joining fragments of everted rim; d at thickened lozenge-section edge band *c*.160mm; th of wall *c*.2mm.

446 BC72 2761 (83) 11 Fig 131
Three (non-joining) fragments of cauldron with everted rim and one surviving vertical angled loop, d at edge *c*.185mm; the loop retains a substantial semicircular pivoting handle of solid iron, l *c*.200mm, with looped ends having asymmetrically expanded terminals.

447 TL74 1529 (1956) 11
Distorted; everted rim; d at edge approx 250mm.

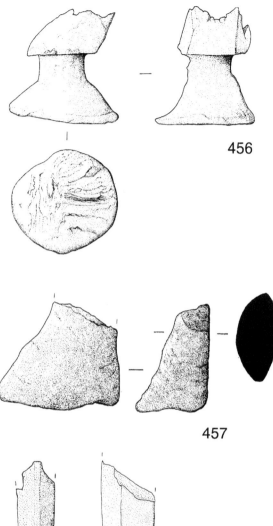

456

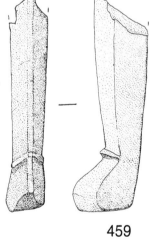

457

448 BWB83 1930 (308) 11

Everted rim; max surviving d *c*.350mm; th of wall *c*.2.5mm; thicker at rim with acute-angled edge.

Vessel wall fragments

449 BWB83 Acc No 1313 (Context 129) Ceramic Phase 11

Max d *c*.180mm; max th *c*.3mm.

450 BWB83 7035 (207) 11

D estd 220mm.

451 BWB83 3000 (330) 11

Max d *c*.320mm; th *c*.1.5mm; ridge horizontally.

452 BWB83 4227 (359) 11

Ridge 9mm w, flanked by two narrower ones on concave side; th 4mm.

The curvature would suggest an original d of approx 300mm, but this fragment may be distorted or from an area other than the body of a vessel of complicated form.

Feet

All of the following were set at an angle; lengths given are of the foot portion only, exclusive of any stub.

Number 453, probably the earliest, has a mortise for joining to the main part of the vessel, while No 456 has a tenon – this may be a repair (cf. certain repair No 465).

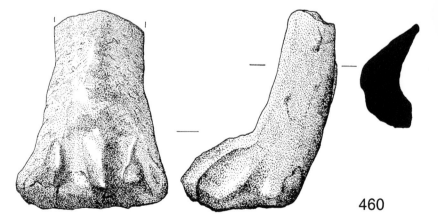

459

Fig 132 Feet from cast vessels (1:1)

460

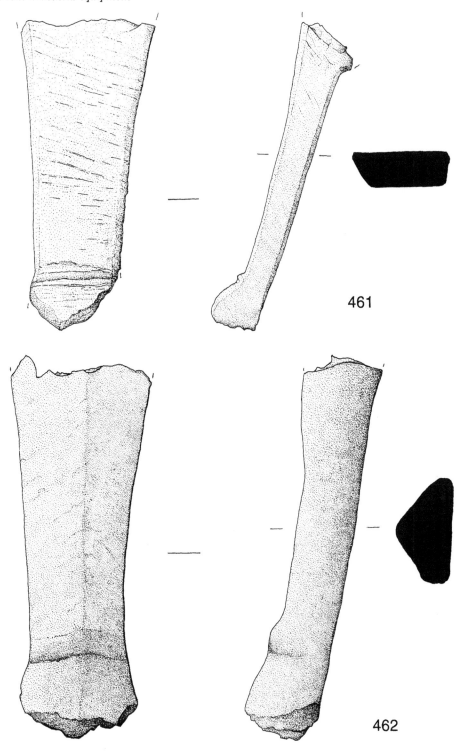

Fig 133   Feet from cast vessels (1:1)

453 BIG82 Acc No 2639 (Context 2591) Ceramic
Phase 8 (deposit possibly contaminated)
Leaded bronze (RHB, Table 7); incomplete; sub-
rectangular section; angled basal end; mortise for
attachment at top; h 80mm.

454 SWA81 2591 (2062) 9
Incomplete, rectangular section; angled basal end;
surviving h 30mm.

455 TL74 1393 (1634) 10
Corroded; fragment with paw-shaped basal end (?five
toes); concavo-convex section; surviving h 52mm.
    (Larger than No 460.)

456 BWB83 4246 (359) 11 Fig 132
Brass (RHB, Table 7); crude oval base expanding
from sub-trapezoidal joining tenon; h 28mm.

457 BWB83 384 (377) 11 Fig 132
Leaded bronze (?)or leaded copper (RHB, Table 7);
fragment of crude foot; plain, expanded basal end;
plano-convex section; surviving h 33mm.

458 BWB83 5386 (305) 11
Leaded copper (RHB, Table 7); incomplete; flat-
section; biconcave on one face; surviving h 39mm.

459 BWB83 7015 (310) 12 Fig 132
Leaded brass (RHB, Table 7); pentagonal-section;
angled base with transverse ridge in the angle;
h 45mm; well-finished surface.
    Probably from a tripod ewer.
    Compare Lewis et al. 1987, 85–9, fig 2, no 6 (for
which analysis of the metal suggests an English
origin) and Biddle 1990, 955–6, no 3397, fig 293.

460 TL74 1319 (1457) 12 Fig 132
Fragment; paw-shaped basal end (?five toes); concavo-convex section; surviving h 50mm.

461 TL74 1387 (1457) 12 Fig 133
Fragment; trapezoidal section; angled near broken-
off basal end, with transverse ridge in corner; surviving h 79mm; fragment of body of vessel is attached
at top.

462 SWA81 3661 (Unstratified) Fig 133
Leaded bronze (RHB, Table 7); triangular section;
transverse ridge at narrowest point; h 102mm.

Handles

463 BWB83 Acc No 2290 (Context 108) Ceramic
Phase 10 Fig 134
Fragment; sub-triangular section, with central flange
on lower side; surviving l 57mm.

Compare the skillet in Fig 130 top right.

464 TL74 585 (414) 11 Fig 134
Incomplete, surviving l 100mm; sub-trapezoidal section handle with narrowed terminal, presumably
angled to improve the grip.
    Probably from a skillet or ewer.

Compare Theuerkauff Liederwald 1988,
282–95, nos 237–70 for a range of vessels of
appropriate form.

Cast repairs

The everted rims suggest these repairs are
most likely to be from cauldrons with two loops
for handles, as No 446, or from two-spouted
hanging lavers (cf. Figs 131 and 137). See also
feet Nos 453 and 456.

465 BWB83 Acc No 2205 (Context 155) Ceramic
Phase 11 Fig 135
Leaded bronze (RHB, Table 7); everted rim; d at
edge *c*.130mm; irregular overlaps from join with
broken part of original vessel.

466 TL74 2323 (1955) 11 Fig 135
Leaded brass (RHB, Table 7); d at edge of everted
rim *c*.160mm; slight, irregular overlaps from join
with broken part of original vessel; body portion
appears to be a thin cover for the original metal; the
edges of the rim portion have tabs (tenons), probably
for secure keying into grooves filed at the sides of
the break in the original vessel; prominent
scratches/file marks on interior face of rim.
    Compare a more extensive repair having keying
tabs within the overlaps excavated at Leicester (Clay
1981, 130, 132, fig 46, no 8).

Possible chafing dish projections

The following two enigmatic items (not counted
as vessels in Table 1) seem too well finished to
be vessel feet. They could perhaps be thumb
pieces from lids (cf. lead/tin lid No 529, Fig
153, and Homer 1991, 76, fig 38, both attributed
to the 14th century or earlier; for copper-alloy
examples see Theuerkauff Liederwald 1988,
247–8, 316–17, nos 321–8, though these ornate
flagons are dated to the mid-15th century). The
two present fragments could be from broadly

similar vessels from the 14th century or even earlier, complete examples of which have apparently not survived in copper alloy. A more likely possibility is that they are the upper, vertical projections on chafing dishes for supporting vessels to be heated (No 467 in particular is closely similar to some versions), but, again, surviving complete parallels in metal appear far later in date (e.g., Lewis 1987, 35, no 43; the form is, however, known in ceramic in the mid-14th century in London-type ware – e.g., Pearce et al. 1985, 44–5, 114, fig 73 – no 400 has projections in the form of human heads; the author is grateful to Lyn Blackmore for discussion of this point).

Fig 134 Handles from cast vessels (1:1)

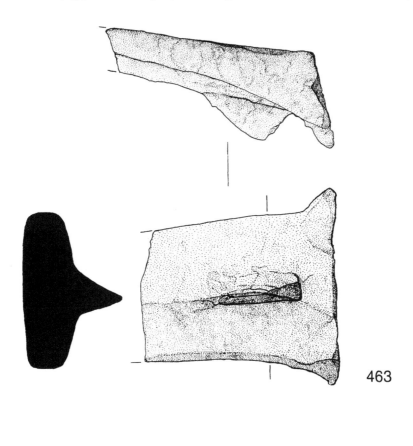

463

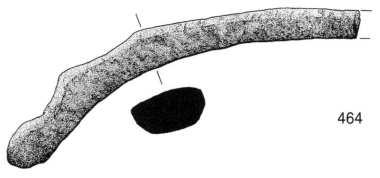

464

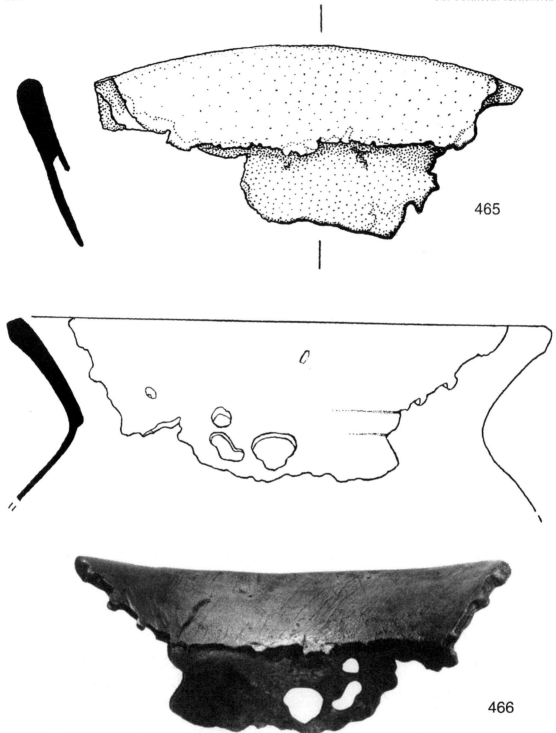

Fig 135   Cast repairs (?)for cauldrons/skillets (1:1)

467 BWB83 Acc No 2331 (Context 118) Ceramic Phase 9 Fig 136
Rectangular section; surviving l 24mm.

468 BWB83 2261 (108) 10 Fig 136
Lentoid section; surviving l 29mm.

The subtle curves imply that this fragment is from a high-quality object.

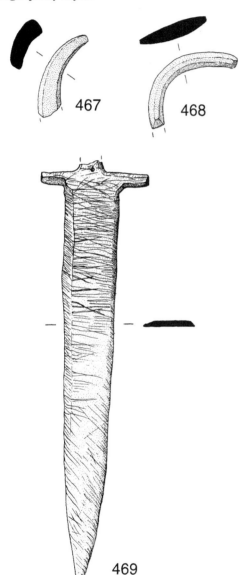

Fig 136 Possible support projections from chafing dishes, and sword perhaps from an elaborate vessel (1:1)

Possible part of ornate vessel

469 BIG82 Acc No 2096 (Context 3204) Ceramic Phase 7 Fig 136
Leaded bronze (RHB, Table 7); incomplete cast sword; l 112mm; broken off at hilt; plain cross guard; prominent transverse file or abrasion marks along edges of blade and, less universally, on central part.

This may not be a toy but part of an elaborate candleholder or a vessel like an *aquamanile* which featured an armed knight (cf. von Falke & Meyer 1983, 114, 117, nos 262, 269; see also Ward Perkins 1940, 288–9, fig 89 for a rather rougher sword hilt on a similar scale – there thought to be a toy, but it is perhaps from the same kind of vessel etc. as suggested for No 469). (Not counted in Table 1.)

Possible suspension rings

Some plain cast rings of d 40mm upwards are buckle frames (as examples complete with pins show, e.g., Egan & Pritchard 1991, 57–8, no 36, fig 36); others are from horse harnesses and very large examples may even be from elaborate door knockers (Mende 1981; the only London find of the last category has lost its ring – Ward Perkins 1940, 290, pl 83). Well-made examples of medium size and appropriate alloys could perhaps alternatively be elements from the swivelling handles or suspension chains of cast copper-alloy hanging vessels of various forms (e.g., rings acc nos 1208 and 2654 from the TL74 site, both from context 368 attributed to ceramic phase 12 – the former is in Fig 137 top), though the rings surviving as parts of vessel handles that have been examined are all of iron. See Fig 137 and Theuerkauff Liederwald (1988, 424–75 *passim*, nos 489 and others) for a range of double-spouted vessels suspended from rings.

SHEETING VESSELS

The original forms of vessels from which miscellaneous wall fragments are found are virtually impossible to identify with certainty, and a number of items of this general character are omitted. See Fig 139 for a sheet cauldron, d 350mm at rim, dated to the late 15th century, found in London (MoL acc no 90.108); cf. Fig 44 top right, where a similar vessel is being used to fill a bath.

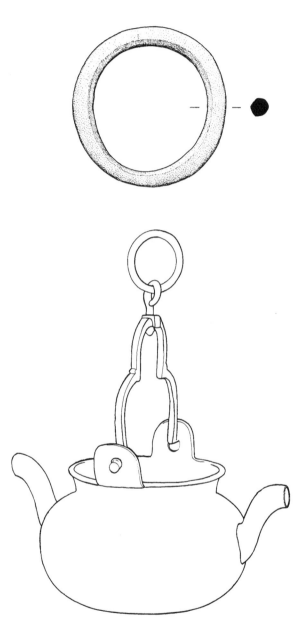

Fig 138   Grotesque monster with armour including cauldron helmet (redrawn from the Luttrell Psalter)

Fig 137   Ring, top, possibly for suspending a vessel (1:1) and suggested use, below (not to scale)

Horizontal rims

These are probably from flat-bottomed dishes essentially similar in form, though not as angled, as lead/tin Nos 501 and others – cf. Ward Perkins 1940, 202–3, figs 65–6 and Gaimster & Verhaeghe 1992, 314–15, figs 8–9.

The fragments listed below are identified as rims by the curvature of the perimeter, which is to a greater or lesser extent thicker than the rest of the wall in each case. The other edges are roughly torn, unless otherwise stated. Distortion and the limited size of most of the fragments mean that estimates of original diameters should be treated as only an approximate indication.

470 SWA81 Acc No 1127 (Context 2130) Ceramic
Phase 7
Distorted; d estd approx 320mm; w of flange *c.*18mm;
roughly cut from the vessel.

471 SWA81 548 (888) 9
Distorted; d estd approx 200mm; w of flange 19mm;
holes for two rivets.

472 BWB83 4222 (359) 11
D *c.*300mm; markedly thickened perimeter; w of
surviving portion, which has been cut from the
vessel, 14mm.

473 BWB83 2298 (144) 11
D *c.*320mm; w of surviving portion, which has been
cut from the vessel, 14mm.

474 BWB83 4221 (359) 11
D estd approx 320mm; w of flange 15mm.

475 BWB83 5397 (298) 11
Distorted; d approx 300–40mm; w of flange 15mm.

476 BWB83 370 (399) 11
D *c.*380mm.

477 BWB83 4733 (283) 11
D *c.*380mm; w of flange *c.*15mm; the surviving portion has been cut from the vessel.

478 BWB83 5237 (306) 11 Fig 139
Distorted; d estd approx 400mm; w of flange, which
is markedly thickened, 11mm.

479 BC72 2005 (79) 11 Fig 139
Distorted (original shape restored in illustration);
d estd approx 400mm; partly cut, partly torn from
vessel.

480 TL74 564 (415) 11
D approx 550mm.

Fig 139 Complete late-medieval cauldron with iron rim support and handle (MoL acc no 90.108, reduced)
and rim fragments from copper-alloy vessels of hammered sheeting (1:1)

481 BWB83 7107 (310) 12
Distorted and folded; d estd approx 280mm; w of rim
*c.*18mm; the fragment, which has been roughly cut
from the vessel, retains up to 30mm of its wall.

482 BWB83 5414 (310) 12
Distorted; d approx 340mm; w of surviving portion
22mm.

Round lids, etc.

483 BWB83 Acc No 1134 (Context 362) Ceramic
Phase 9 Fig 140
Very corroded sheeting; d *c.*75mm; convex, spirally
fluted towards missing centre; flat rim.

Possibly the top of a lantern, though holes to allow
heat and smoke to escape are usually present (see
on No 427).

484 BWB83 3592 (357) 11 Fig 141
Slightly convex; unevenly cut perimeter; d *c.*86mm;
two unevenly cut strips w *c.*13mm, attached on each
face by two crude rivets, are torn off near the edge
and the one on the upper side is roughly folded back
twice (perhaps originally joined by folding around
the edge to form a hinge, as on No 486).

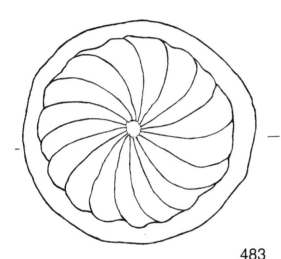

483

485 BWB83 4597 (318) 11
Cast strip, broken off at transverse ridge and with
superfluous hole, partly drilled; attached by two
rivets to fragment of sheeting with edge at same
point as ridge on strip.

Probably analogous to Nos 484 and 486.

486 BWB83 5139 (Unstratified) Fig 141
Slightly convex; d 99mm; holes at centre and perimeter, the latter opposite a neatly finished sheet
hinge, which is folded at the centre around a pivotal
rod and attached by a rivet; engraved sexfoil within
a frame of six concave sides.

A similar but smaller lid (also decorated with
engraved curved lines), retaining a swivelling hook
attached near the centre, survives on a late 15th-
century round, flat box made of sheet-metal,
d 46mm, h *c.*13mm, which retains its original contents of a folding balance and coin weights (Fig 142
– found at Roche Abbey, Yorkshire – Rigold 1978,
371–4; cf. an earlier plano-convex box with similar
contents found at Novgorod in Russia – Hanse 2
1989, 181, no 9.7).

Fig 140   Possible lantern top and reconstruction
(1:1)

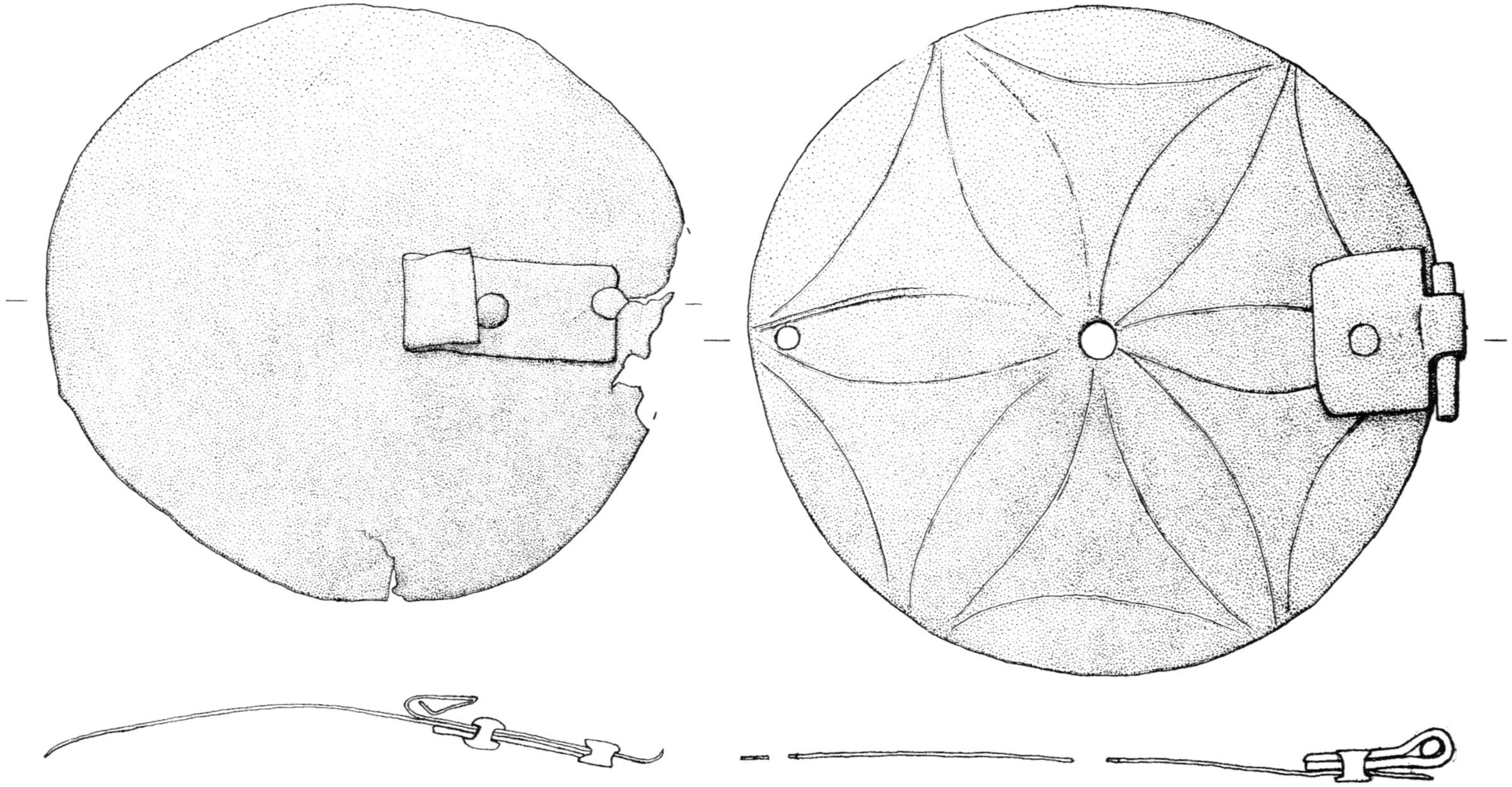

Fig 141 Lids (1:1)

Fig 142   Sheet box for scales and coin weights from Yorkshire (drawing HBMC(E); 1:2)

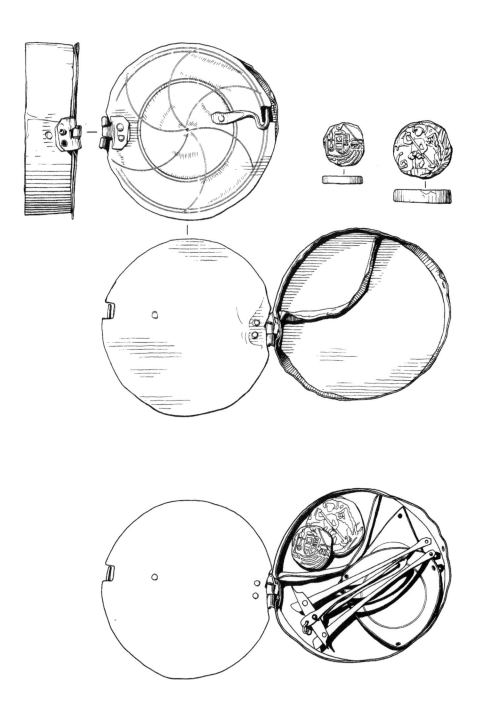

Fig 143   Repaired handle (1:1) and similar handles on sheet vessel (not to scale)

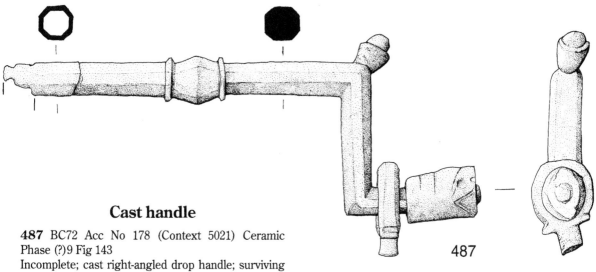

Cast handle

487 BC72 Acc No 178 (Context 5021) Ceramic
Phase (?)9 Fig 143
Incomplete; cast right-angled drop handle; surviving
l 127mm; main horizontal shaft has octagonal section
and central, bifacially bevelled knop with eight facets
and defined by a ridge to each side; angled acorn
knop at corner with the surviving vertical octagonal-
section shaft; other corner broken off; surviving
horizontal attachment end has separate heavy terminal collar in the form of a crude animal head,
which is held on by a rivet, securing an (originally
freely movable) attachment loop with shoulders and
a riveted end; crude repair has been made by placing
a piece of sheeting around the other, broken, end of
the main part of the shaft, with tabs to hold the
missing vertical part. It is unclear how effective the
repair was prior to the discarding of the object.

Probably from a sheet vessel.

(Not counted in Table 1.)

A similar handle survives from an original pair on
a shallow sheet bowl, d *c*.450mm, from a hoard of
14th–16th-century metalwork found in Wales (see
Fig 143 bottom, which restores the second handle;
Hemp 1918/19, 215–16). Compare also handle MoL
acc no 7908. Such handles might have come from a
range of other kinds of objects (e.g., caskets – see
Nos 240–1, Fig 62; robust iron examples are known
on chests, e.g., J Geddes in Alexander & Binski
1987, 175, fig 121; P Tudor Craig & J Geddes in ibid.
347, no 345). The present example is included here
among the vessels because of the close parallel from
Wales.

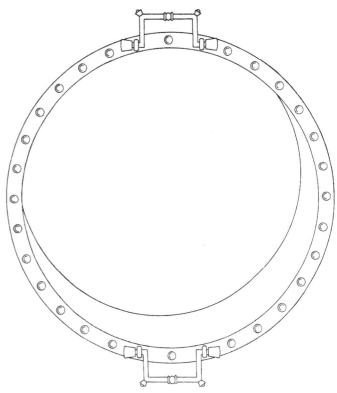

487

Sheet repairs

Sheet rivets, with their characteristic uneven hexagonal outline, folded from cut lozenges (see Fig 144), were used alone to fill small splits in sheet vessels (there is one on the sheet cauldron dated to the late 15th century in Fig 139), and together with sheet patches to repair larger areas of damage, as with Nos 493–4. A folded rivet of this kind appears in a piece of sheeting from the early to mid-12th century (Pritchard 1991, 152, 255, no 115).

FOLDED RIVETS

Dimensions are given in the order A×B (see Fig 144).

488 SWA81 Acc No 3252 (Context 2141) Ceramic Phase 9
13×7mm.

489 SWA81 3375 (2134) 9 Fig 144
29×16mm.

490 BWB83 1199 (113) 11
22×10mm; apparently cut off obliquely at one side.

491 BWB83 3489 (162) 11
31×12mm.

492 BWB83 1925 (313) 12
13×8mm.

PATCHES

493 BWB83 Acc No 1172 (Context 361) Ceramic Phase 11
Incomplete; folded patch; surviving portion *c*.40×*c*.20mm; held by a folded rivet to a fragment of metal that is of a visually similar alloy to the other components.

Presumably a repair to the edge of a vessel.

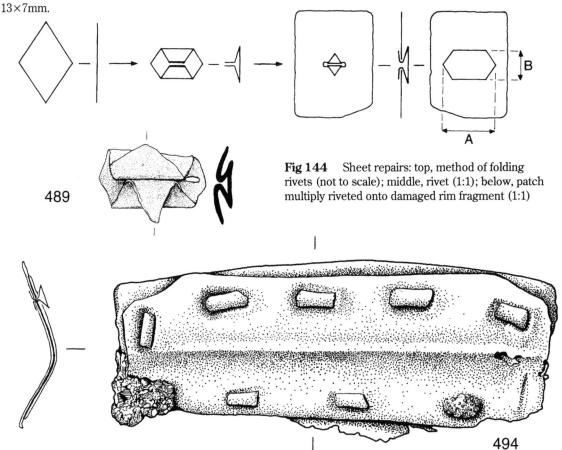

Fig 144 Sheet repairs: top, method of folding rivets (not to scale); middle, rivet (1:1); below, patch multiply riveted onto damaged rim fragment (1:1)

489

494

494 BWB83 6038 (305) 11 Fig 144
Roughly rectangular patch, 115×40mm; angled along the middle; held by eight folded rivets around perimeter to a damaged edge fragment of a vessel, covering both rim and wall; w of rim *c*.24mm; d of vessel approx 500–50mm.

The angle is almost certainly an original feature.

Another crudely attached (?)patch, not necessarily from a vessel, is held by three similar rivets to an irregular fragment of sheeting from a deposit attributed to ceramic phase 8 (BIG82 acc no 2323).

Iron vessels and vessel parts

No medieval iron object excavated at the sites considered in this volume has been identified as a vessel (despite the appearance of an iron 'frying pan' in the 14th-century London inventories at the start of this chapter; see I H Goodall in Biddle 1990, 820–1, no 2544, fig 241 for an excavated example dated to the late 9th/early 10th century; fragments of an 'iron cauldron' among medieval finds from the TL74 site – M Rhodes in Milne & Milne 1982, 89 – could not be identified for the present publication).

A military helmet of iron from the 14th century, found in Southwark and now in the British Museum, had been adapted with an iron handle and a chain, presumably for suspension inverted over a fire as a cooking vessel (Roach Smith 1854, 149, no 735). See also No 422.

LOOPED MOUNTS FOR HANDLES

Iron
These mounts were for sheet copper-alloy vessels, and perhaps also for iron and wooden ones – they consist of a loop attached to a riveted plate or plates.

Compare MoL acc no 83.422/1 for a complete survival of a wrought handle of this kind, probably of late medieval date (see Fig 145 – this handle has a span of 348mm; there is also one on the vessel in Fig 139).

Simple pierced loops

495 SWA81 Acc No 1632 (Context 2185) Ceramic Phase 6
Corroded; (?)rectangular plate; total 37×17mm; single rivet hole; curved profile.

496 BWB83 3105 (285) 9 Fig 145
As preceding item, but broken off at end and no surviving rivet hole; 50×22mm.

497 BWB83 485 (156) 11
Incomplete; as preceding item.

Loop with terminals superimposed

498 SWA81 2313 (2270) 9 Fig 145
Bent bar with flattened, round terminals that have been superimposed and pierced with a tack or rivet; 32×24mm; tin coating; traces of iron to which the handle was attached survive between the terminals.

The metal between these terminals may be from binding strips around copper alloy (cf. Fig 139) or wood; i.e. the entire object may not have been of iron.

See Henig 1974, 191–2, fig 38, no 65 for a pair of loops similar to No 498 and set on an oval iron chain loop together with a swivel, as on No 499; object not traced for the present publication.

No corresponding handle has been recognised from the sites included in this survey, but see the more robust No 446 in Fig 131. It is surprising in view of the large number of medieval wells excavated in the City that more bucket handles have not been recovered from them (if indeed that form of vessel was widely in use in London at this time – ceramic pitchers may have been more common for the everyday task of drawing water).

SUSPENSION CHAIN

Iron
499 BWB83 Acc No 626 (Context 308) Ceramic Phase 11 Fig 146
Corroded; oval link l 63mm, with swivelling, riveted hook through hole at one end; oval links, each l 57mm and with sides bent in towards middle, attached to the hook; two sets of links attached to a larger one (four links survive in one of the sets).

Probably used to hold the two handles of a cooking vessel suspended over a fire.

Compare a sheet copper-alloy vessel, d 240mm, retaining such a chain found in London (Fig 146 – Ward Perkins 1940, 207, pl 54; acc no A9935); two similar chains excavated in County Durham (I H Goodall in Austin 1989, 127, 130, nos 62A and B, fig 55) and another from Winchester (Cunliffe 1964, 156–7, fig 54, no 5).

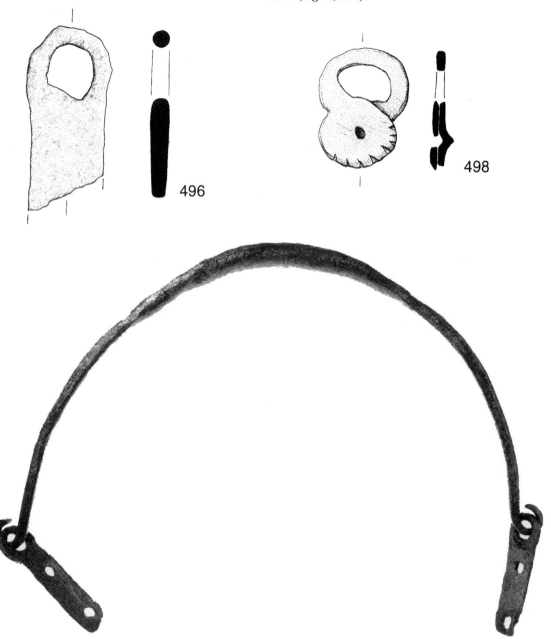

Fig 145   Looped mounts for handles (1:1) and handle with similar mounts (MoL acc no 83.422/1, reduced)

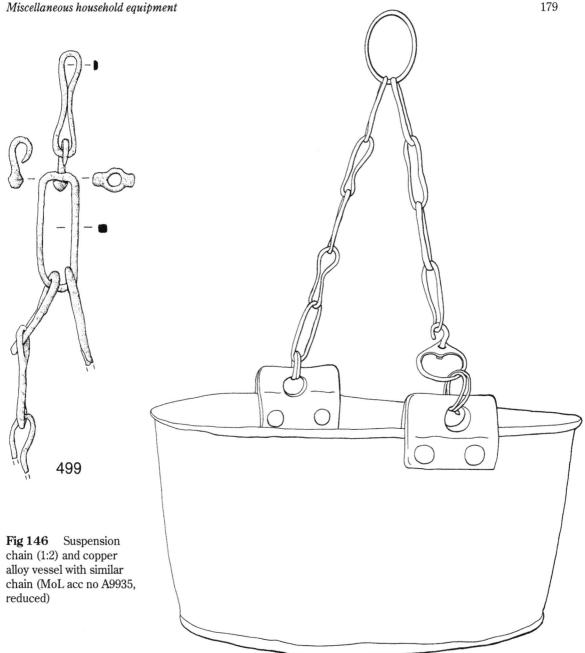

499

Fig 146 Suspension
chain (1:2) and copper
alloy vessel with similar
chain (MoL acc no A9935,
reduced)

Lead/tin vessels

There is no complete vessel among the items
of these metals listed below, and the entire
form of only No 501 can be restored with
confidence (lid No 530 is complete, but the
accompanying vessel has not survived). This
pattern of survival in the ground of mainly
small fragments is probably an indication of the
efficiency of contemporary lead/tin recycling
(cf. Homer 1991, 78). The variety of forms
represented is, nevertheless, extensive, and the

dating provides some valuable new pointers and extends the information available from the meagre survivals of complete pieces from the medieval period (cf. ibid. 79; Hatcher & Barker 1974, 30–6). A few of the vessel types represented cannot readily be paralleled. (It is quite possible that further forms from this period still await discovery and recognition – for a lead/tin *aquamanile* found in Göttingen, Germany, and still unparalleled in Britain, see Grupe 1984, 22, fig 27).

No written record in England of domestic pewterware prior to 1290 (cf. ceramic phase 9) has been traced (Homer 1991, 67) but there were 19 master pewterers in London by 1304 (Hatcher & Barker 1974, 36). With the few items listed below which are attributed to earlier phases (Nos 500 and 518) it is not possible to be sure whether they are domestic or ecclesiastical items, but lead candlestick No 366 from a ceramic phase 7 deposit is likely to belong to the former category (see No 500 for a possible example of the latter). No maker's mark has been noted on the items listed below.

None of the sites considered for this catalogue produced primary evidence for the actual manufacture of pewterware in London. A small decorative and faceted conical lid of medieval date from the VRY89 site (ref V395) is paralleled by one element of a stone mould for making lids of similar form found in the Thames there (private collection; its decoration is slightly different). These lids are smaller than the one in Hornsby et al. 1989, 53, no 16).

Analysis of lead/tin alloy objects (Justine Bayley, Cath Mortimer)

A total of 45 objects and fragments were analysed qualitatively by energy dispersive X-ray fluorescence (XRF). This method was chosen because it was quick and completely non-destructive, though it can provide only a general indication of the alloy. Obtaining accurate percentage compositions is far more time consuming and would not have been undertaken

for this number of objects. It also necessitates cleaning an area of the surface, or removing small samples from the objects, as was subsequently done for a few pieces (see below). XRF is a surface technique, so that when it is applied, as here, to corroded or patinated surfaces, it detects not only the elements in the bulk metal but any that have been deposited on the surface from the environment in which the object was buried. The relative amounts of elements present in the bulk of the metal will not be the same as at the surface, since corrosion (patination) does not normally affect all elements equally. The strength of the signal (peak height) for each element is also affected by the shape and surface texture of the object so multiple analyses of different areas on the same object do not normally give identical results.

The only elements detected in significant quantities were tin, lead, copper and iron. The presence of the latter two elements was thought to be due to burial in anaerobic (waterlogged) conditions which had encouraged deposition from the ground water. They were thus ignored in assessing alloy composition, though it is possible that the objects contain minor amounts of copper and/or iron in the bulk metal. It was thus assumed that the alloys used to make the objects were effectively binary ones of lead and tin; the XRF peak heights for these two elements were recorded and appear in Table 8.

Calibrating these numbers to correspond to percentage compositions is not possible. However, the ratio of lead to tin peak heights ('lead:tin' in Table 8) gives an approximate indication of composition. High numbers indicate relatively high concentrations of lead, while low numbers indicate relatively low amounts of lead and corresponding high amounts of tin. Broadly similar ratio figures indicate broadly similar compositions. Three lead-tin objects of known composition were analysed in the same way as the other objects to provide an approximate calibration of the results. The quantitative SEM analyses provide further cross-checks.

The values of the lead-tin ratio have been plotted in Fig 147 as frequency histograms for the various object categories analysed. It can

Table 8:   X-ray fluorescence analysis of lead/tin alloy objects

Catalogue number		Ceramic phase	Lead	Tin	Lead: Tin (lead reading: tin reading)
Candleholders					
366		7	4137	1	4137.00
368		11	4110	2981	1.38
369	(?'square ware')	11	4008	4068	0.99
372		11	829	689	1.20
376	(stem)	11	1027	770	1.33
376	(cup rim)	11	536	700	0.77
Vessels					
500	flatware	6	1142	4100	0.28
501	flatware	11	58	868	0.07
503	flatware	11	932	4060	0.23
504	flatware	11	4039	1624	2.49
506	flatware	11	4137	2131	1.94
510	flatware	11	504	722	0.70
512	flatware	(?)11	137	1775	0.08
513	flatware	12	389	3996	0.10
514	flatware	12	116	2126	0.05
515	flatware	12	43	598	0.07
516A	flatware	12	96	1646	0.06
516B	flatware	12	228	2783	0.08
523	hollow vessel	11	4133	580	7.13
525	(?)flagon	11	287	342	0.84
529	lid	9	3973	2684	1.48
529	(dark area)	9	4178	1982	2.11
530	lid	11	793	1007	0.79
532	lid thumb piece	9	2010	1496	1.34
533	lid thumb piece	11	2009	1466	1.37
534	lid thumb piece	12	4021	9160	0.44
535	lid	11	4065	3319	1.22
537	lid	11	3972	280	14.19
538	handle	11	4048	665	6.09
539	base	6	1857	2031	0.91
541	'square-ware' foot	11	1	427	0.00
542	miscellaneous fragment	12	223	1839	0.12
545	flower (possible vessel)	12	1857	2031	0.91
Spoons					
749		7	2064	426	4.85
750		9	2051	794	2.58
751		9	2058	900	2.29
753		9	2049	979	2.09
754		9	2000	332	6.02
755		9	550	346	1.59
756		9	2020	613	3.30
757		10	2077	412	5.04
759		11	2006	544	3.69
769		12	2052	799	2.57
770		12	612	855	0.72
772		12	112	2050	0.05
775		12	752	693	1.09
776		unstratified	193	2038	0.09
Stand for figurine					
971		11	2070	707	2.93

be seen that most of the vessels are high-tin alloys, though there are a few exceptions. From comparison with the 'calibration' it is likely that these high-tin alloys contain over 80% tin, and

some may be nearer 100%; those with lead/tin peak height ratios under 0.5 have been identified as 'tin' rather than 'pewter', the same cut-off point as that used by Heyworth (in Egan & Pritchard 1991, 390, fig 262).

The lids, on average, contain a little less tin; No 537, with the highest ratio (lowest tin con-

Candleholders

+ divergent readings from two areas of No. 376

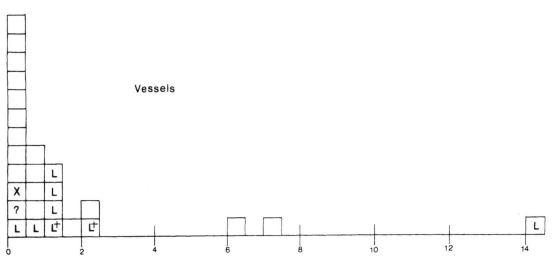

Vessels

L   lid

X   two similar readings from fragments, possibly from same object (Nos. 516A & B)

?   possible vessel No. 542

+   divergent readings from two areas of No. 529

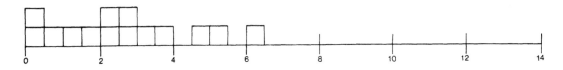

Spoons

Fig 147   Histogram of results of analyses of lead/tin vessels etc.

tent) is probably well under 50% tin. Most of the candleholders are of similar composition to the main group of lids; the exception is candle-holder No 366, which is pure lead.

The spoons present a quite different picture, with a range of compositions from high-tin alloys like the vessels, down to around 50% tin; the small sample gives no indication of pre-ferred compositions within this range.

SCANNING ELECTRON MICROSCOPE AND ENERGY-DISPERSIVE X-RAY ANALYSIS

Since it was thought that some of the lead/tin objects might contain significant amounts of copper, added to harden the metal, samples were removed from five items, two of which are angled (? = 'square' in medieval documents; cf. Homer 1991, 73). These would have been more difficult to restore to their original shape, if knocked, than round turned items and might therefore have tended to be made of a harder, more robust alloy than turned items. The five objects were cleaned and the prepared surfaces were analysed by Cath Mortimer (see below). It was thought that Nos 369 and 541 might contain copper as they appear to be 'square ware'; the other three were not expected to show copper content. The quantitative analyses showed that No 541 contains 4% copper, but No 369 contains no copper; and two of the other objects have up to 2% copper.

Brownsword & Pitt (1983) note that the 1348 ordinances of the London Pewterers' Guild include instructions for making 'fine pewter, with the proportion of copper to the tin, as much as of its own nature, it will take'. The level of addition this implies has been much discussed, but it is not thought to be more than a few per cent. Analyses of 36 items of medieval pewter flatware by Brownsword & Pitt (1984) have confirmed this figure: the mean copper content was found to be 1.7%, with only one item having more than 3% and six having under 1%. Five further items of flatware were analysed and found to have rather higher copper con-tents: their mean composition was 95.1% tin, 0.6% lead and 3.5% copper (*idem* 1985).

Since medieval smelting of tin and lead ores produced metal of high purity, the copper detected in the analyses below is likely to be a deliberate rather than an accidental addition, even when it is present only at low levels. Its presence in No 541, presumably a fine-pewter/ 'square-ware' object, has been demonstrated, as has its absence at a detectable level from No 369. It is possible that the lower levels found in Nos 535 and 521 result from the recycling and mixing of pewter of varying qualities, and it is notable that these two objects contain apprecia-ble quantities of lead. The variations in compo-sition may instead reflect chronological differences or manufacture in different places, as suggested by Brownsword & Pitt (1984).

Cath Mortimer writes:

Small samples were removed from the five selected objects and prepared for scanning elec-tron microscope examination and energy-disper-sive X-ray analysis by mounting in a resin block. The materials concerned, high-purity tin and lead-tin alloys, are very soft and easily scratched. It was not practical to get a smooth, regular surface since polishing would simply smear; surface preparation was therefore limited to grinding on 400 silicon-carbide papers. No lead-tin standards were avail-able to check the accuracy of calibration. Given these factors, it was sensible to calculate normal-ised percentage weight with reduced quoted pre-cision (nearest whole number) using the LINK AN10000 system. Average values from two areas in each sample are presented in Table 9.

Two of the samples, Nos 521 and 535, are pewter, with 1–2% copper. Two pieces are high-purity tin, with small amounts of copper in the case of No 541 and of lead in No 369. Plate No 501 has extremely low levels of all elements except tin.

Lead/tin vessels catalogue

FLAT VESSELS

(Plates and other shallow vessels with a more or less horizontal rim)

(The term 'dish' is avoided; vessels described elsewhere as 'deep dishes' are categorised here as 'bowls', while 'shallow dishes' are termed

Table 9:   Scanning electron microscope and energy-dispersive X-ray analysis

Catalogue number	Ceramic phase	Copper %	Lead %	Tin %	(Iron %)
369 ?'square-ware' candleholder	11	untraced	2	98	(untraced)
501 plate	11	untraced	untraced	100	(untraced)
521 hollow vessel	9	2	31	67	(untraced)
535 lid	11	1	20	79	(untraced)
541 'square-ware' foot	11	4	untraced	96	(untraced)

'plates' here – the two classes are quite distinct in the catalogued material; cf. the use of 'bowl' for wooden vessels in which the height:width ratio is between 1:2 and 1:6; 'plate' for those in which this ratio is 1:6+.)

A few surviving complete medieval plates have been published (Hornsby et al. 1989, 52, no 13 and 53, no 14, found in London and attributed to the 14th century; R F Michaelis in Platt & Coleman Smith 1975, 250–1, excavated in Southampton and dated to *c*.1290; A R Goodall in Allan 1984, 343, 345, fig 192, no 157, excavated in Exeter and dated to the 14th century).

The majority of flatware items below (Nos 500–18) are small rim fragments. Unless other-wise stated, they have an edge fillet for strengthening the perimeter. The complete early plates excavated in Southampton and Exeter and one of those from London differ from later vessels of this form – the latter have the fillet on the lower side of the rim while the former have it on the upper side of the rim. The rim fragments listed below vary between 17mm and 50mm in length. It is frequently difficult with such small pieces to decide which face is the upper and which is the lower. Where it is possible to determine this, fragments with turning marks apparently confined to one face may have these either on the upper face (e.g., No 507; cf. hollow vessels Nos 519, 522) or on the underside (e.g., No 509; cf. hollow vessel No 521). Hollow vessel No 523 has such marks almost all over the surviving portion, on both faces). No 500, attributed to ceramic phase 6, is drawn with the 'fillet' uppermost because of the position of this feature in the earlier com-plete plates (wooden vessels Nos 553 and 555, respectively from deposits attributed to ceramic phases 7 and 8 and with fillets similar to contemporary lead/tin fashions, reinforce the early dating for this trait). Most of the lead/tin flatware rims with a fillet and attributed to later phases are drawn with this on the lower face, though Nos 501, 503 and 507 – fragments from deposits attributed to the late 14th century – clearly have it on the upper one. Number 520, a small fragment which could be seen as having 'fillets' on both faces, might possibly be con-sidered a transitional flatware profile, although it is listed with the hollow vessels. This last item illustrates the difficulties often confronted in trying to establish original forms from such limited evidence (it is not counted in Tables 1 and 4).

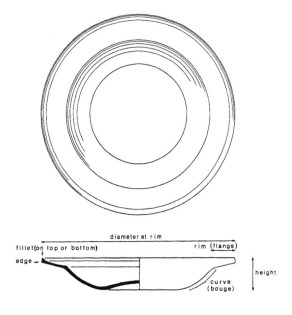

Fig 148   Terminology for flat vessels

For fragments less than 30mm long, the original diameters of the vessels are extremely difficult to estimate accurately (marked * in the following list).

500 BWB83 Acc No 6014 (Context 211) Ceramic Phase 6 Fig 149
Tin (AML, Table 8); thickened, wedge-shaped rim, with perimeter grooves internally and externally and along edge; d estd approx 350mm+.

The two prominent grooves differentiate this early enigmatic fragment (??perhaps an ecclesiastical paten as it antedates the period when domestic pewterware is conventionally thought to have been available in London) from all the others listed; no clear parallel has been traced (including among Roman items – see No 505 for a single groove in a late fragment and No 512 for one with a pair of small grooves).

501 TL74 745 (414) 11 Fig 149
Tin (AML, Table 9; cf. Table 8); almost half of a plate; d 144mm; fillet on upper face; angles between side and both flange and slightly convex base; missing portion has been irregularly broken off, and there are traces of melting at one point (?an accident, or possibly for use as solder etc.).

This is the most complete of the flat lead/tin vessels included in this survey.

502 BWB83 7062 (136) 11
Rim fragment with fillet; d *c.*130mm; cut off with a bladed tool.

503 BWB83 1439 (157) 11 Fig 149
Tin (AML, Table 8); d *c.*180mm; right angle between fillet (on upper face) and flange; turning marks on underside; melted at one end.

504 BWB83 5021 (389) 11 Fig 149
Pewter (AML, Table 8); d *c.*190–210mm*; thickened, angled flat edge; turning marks on one face.

505 BC72 4185 (88) 11
Wedge-shaped edge defined by groove on one face; d *c.*200mm.

506 BWB83 4903 (117) 11 Fig 149
Pewter (AML, Table 8); two distorted, joining fragments of vessel; d *c.*240mm; internal angle defining a flange w 16mm; thickened, wedge-shaped rim; smooth externally, turning marks internally.

507 TL74 2373 (1955) 11
Corroded fragment of flange and part of centre; d 260mm; angled fillet and turning marks on upper face; two small round holes may indicate that this plate was adapted as a strainer/steamer.

(Compare Nos 437–9 of copper alloy.)

508 BWB83 4040 (293) 11 Fig 149
D *c.*260mm; rim fragment with angled fillet (?on lower face).

509 BWB83 2403 (117) 11 Fig 149
D *c.*260mm; flange survives; flat edge; turning marks on underside; hack marks from a blade at point of breakage.

510 BWB83 5976 (291) 11 Fig 149
Pewter (AML, Table 8); original edge missing; d *c.*290mm+; a rabbet marks the (?)flange; th at centre >1mm, at rim *c.*0.5mm; fragment cut straight along one side.

Presumably from a vessel, but made of very thin metal relative to other items included in this present category.

511 BC72 4397 (89) 11 Fig 149
Folded (shown flat in illustration); rounded fillet at edge; original d uncertain.

512 BWB83 3677 (300) ?11 Fig 149
Tin (AML, Table 8); d *c.*220mm; angled fillet and pair of perimeter grooves on one face.

513 SWA81 3409 (2082) 12 Fig 149
Tin (AML, Table 8); d *c.*240mm; fillet on one face (shown in illustration as if on upper face, though dating suggests it may well have been on the lower one).

514 SWA81 2893 (2103) 12 Fig 149
Tin (AML, Table 8); d *c.*270mm; fillet on one face, turning marks on the other.

515 BWB83 7023 (309) 12
Tin (AML, Table 8); d *c.*380mm*; fillet on one face, turning marks on the other.

516 SWA81 2946A (2109) 12
Tin (AML, Table 8); fillet on one face; d uncertain*.

Acc No 2946B (Tin – AML, Table 8) is a wall fragment thought at the time of accessioning to be from the same vessel; although the analytical results differ slightly between the two fragments, this remains possible (JB).

517 SWA81 1471 (2113) 12
As preceding item*, tin.

518 SWA81 733 (2085) 12
As preceding item*.

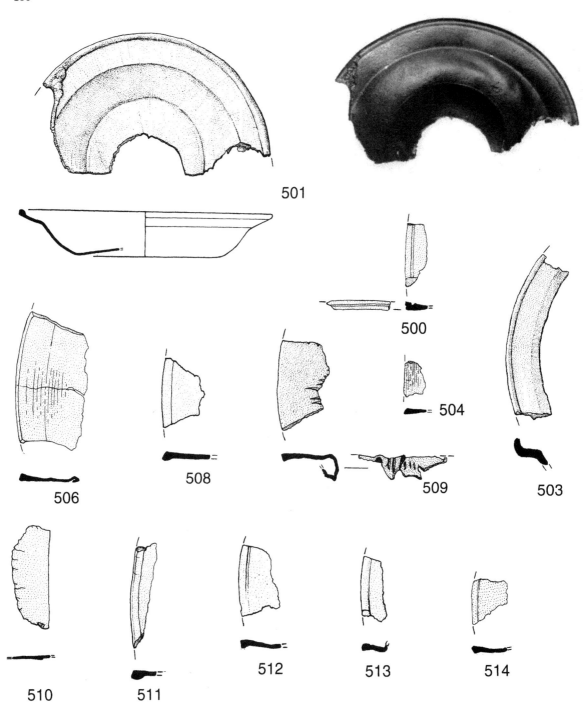

Fig 149   Lead/tin flatware (1:2)

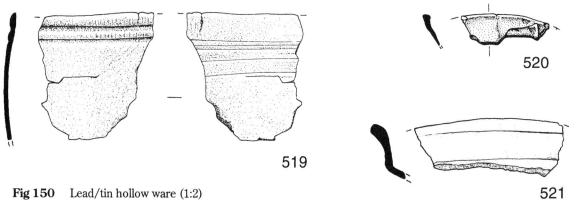

Fig 150   Lead/tin hollow ware (1:2)

HOLLOW VESSELS

Relatively deep vessels (see above on flat vessels), usually with sides at approximately a right angle to the base, e.g., deep bowls and flagons.

519 SWA81 Acc No 1232 (Context 2198) Ceramic Phase 6 Fig 150
Flattened rim fragment, probably originally vertical sided or nearly so (original d uncertain); two grooves near rim externally; turning marks internally.

This could be from a mouth, or a splayed foot of a vessel (?cf. No 527). It antedates the period when domestic pewterware is conventionally thought to have been available in London.

520 BWB83 1480 (362) 9 Fig 150
Base or rim fragment with T-like profile; d *c*.120mm.

This could be from a flagon-type lid like No 529 (not counted in Table 1).

521 BWB83 5309 (221) 9 Fig 150
Pewter with added copper (AML, Table 9); distorted; d *c*.420mm; robust, everted rim with slightly curved profile and groove internally at angle (which may be seating for a lid); turning marks externally.

Probably from a cauldron-type vessel of a form more familiar in copper alloy (the present alloy might be more liable to melting if placed in the fire).

522 BWB83 5495 (399) 11 Fig 151
Distorted, base fragment of flat-bottomed vessel (profile shown as flat in illustration); d at separate, soldered base 72mm; angle of wall uncertain (shown as if from a beaker-like vessel in reshaped section

drawing); original h of surviving portion estd *c*.160–75mm, turning marks internally.

A contemporary parallel is difficult to find, though the form is close to that of round-bodied flagons usually attributed to the late 15th century (Verster 1958, pl 13) and to the post-medieval period (e.g., MoL acc no 8148, see Fig 151).

523 BWB83 5085 (359) 11 Fig 152
Pewter (AML, Table 8); distorted basal fragment (profile tentatively restored in illustration) with slight foot-ring at soldered join with side, and ridge near surviving top; d at base *c*.80mm; external ridge near surviving top; turning marks on side internally and externally and on base externally.

An unstratified fragment from the same site (acc no 4477), pierced several times by a knife, may be from the same vessel.

524 BC72 4675 (225) 11
Complete rim of vessel or base, d *c*.90mm, with groove on one side and angled edge on the other; part cut, part torn from the rest of object; maximum w of surviving portion 10mm.

The removal of such a flimsy ring in one piece without breakage would probably have been quite difficult to effect.

525 BWB83 3241 (117) 11
Pewter (AML, Table 8); folded in half; too distorted for accurate estimate of original d; lower part of side, with trace of separate base that has been cut away with a sharp instrument; turning marks on (?)internal face.

Perhaps from a flagon-type vessel.

526 SWA81 2946 (2109) 12
Two similar fragments of rim with fillet; d *c*.280mm.

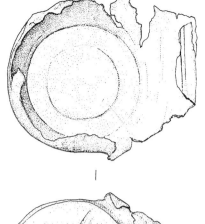

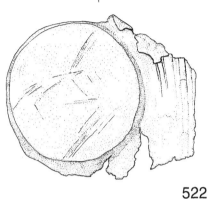

522

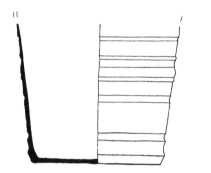

Fig 151   Lead/tin hollow vessel with possible original profile (1:2) and complete flagon (MoL acc no 8148, reduced)

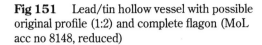

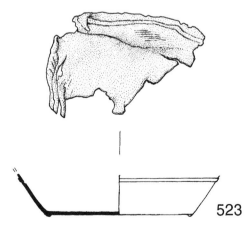

523

527 TL74 2482 (368) 12 Fig 152
Flaring base fragment (unlikely to have been a rim); d *c*.98mm; flange at bottom and triple rabbet near surviving top; turning marks internally, smoothly finished on outside; found folded and flattened.
    Probably from a flagon-type vessel.

528 BWB83 7056 (309) 12
Rim fragment, with external, angled fillet; d *c*.150mm.

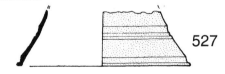

527

Fig 152   Lead/tin hollow-ware bases

Lids

FLAGON-TYPE

OPENING PART COMPRISING ENTIRE TOP

529 SWA81 Acc No 2111 (Context 2081) Ceramic Phase 9 Fig 153
Pewter/lead-tin (AML, Table 8/MLC); nearly complete, slightly distorted, circular lid; d 60mm; flattish, convex top with angled side and horizontal rim having rabbet at base to fit the vessel's body; turning marks internally; separate flat, flaring thumb piece (distorted), probably originally at a right angle to the strap-like attachment tab, and with pierced disc for hinge; two discrete areas on the interior (in the centre and at the point of attachment of the thumb piece) have the imprint of a coarse textile where a damp cloth was held against the inside of the vessel to absorb excessive heat, avoid melting and make the joint smooth while the separate elements were soldered onto the outside (see Nos 739 and 744; cf. Salzman 1952, 277 for a related practice in plumbing in the 16th century); Hero Granger Taylor comments: The worn imprint in the top of the lip has *c*.13 threads per 10mm in one system, perhaps the warp, and *c*.10 per 10mm in the other, and the weave appears to have been tabby; the former presence of a finial (now missing) on the top is also marked externally by a darker sub-circular area, max d 19mm.
(?)Cf. No 520.

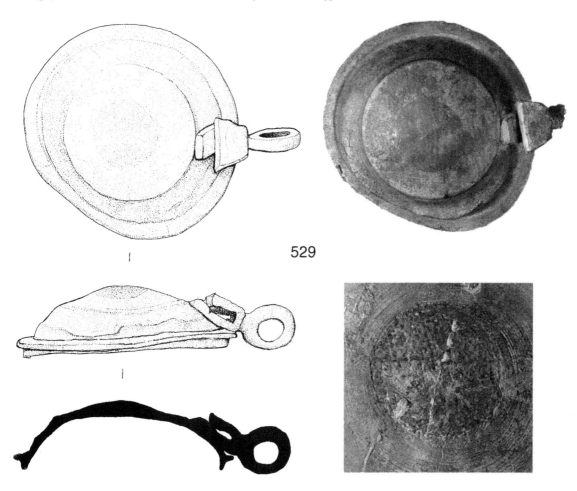

529

Fig 153   Flagon lid (1:1) with detail (enlarged) showing textile mark on the inside

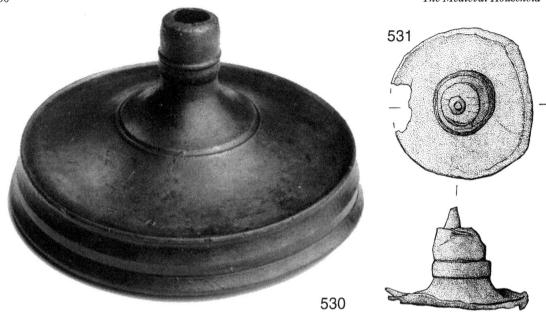

531

530

Fig 154   Lids (1:1)

530 BC72 2255 (83) 11 Fig 154
Pewter (AML, Table 8); complete; d 92mm; h 47mm;
rabbeted at base to fit body of vessel; two angled
rabbets above; slightly flared top has groove defining
an expanded ridged knop from which some kind of
decorative element is missing at the apex; turning
marks internally; the shaft inside the knop has an
octagonal section from the chuck.

No close contemporary parallel is known for this
non-hinged lid.

531 BWB83 5320 (Unstratified) Fig 154
Incomplete; d 41mm; slightly upturned near rim;
central knop with collar and flat top has a conical
projection, which is slightly (?)worn (almost faceted)
around the flat part, suggesting there was once a
separate finial here – a spiralling mark suggests this
was twisted off; portion of rim torn off, probably
where a hinge was attached; central hollow in the
underside appears to have been part-filled with
solder, perhaps to provide additional weight.

No close parallel has been traced.

FRAGMENTS

Numbers 532–4 are too substantial to have
been knops from spoon handles. The dating for
No 532 suggests that this kind of lid was
manufactured from at least the early 14th
century.

532 BWB83 1286 (124) 9
Pewter (AML, Table 8); one acorn from a thumb
piece originally comprising a pair (see No 534).

533 BWB83 4978 (376) 11
Pewter (AML, Table 8); as preceding item.

534 BWB83 3251 (265) 12 Fig 155
Tin (AML, Table 8); pair of opposed acorns from
thumb piece of a vessel lid, probably like that on a
14th-century flagon found in Kent – see Fig 155 (A
North in Alexander & Binski 1987, 281, no 211;
Hornsby et al. 1989, 52, no 12).

OPENING PART COMPRISING ONLY A PORTION OF THE TOP

Circular flat lids

535 BWB83 Acc No 1251 (Context 138) Ceramic
Phase 11 Fig 155
Pewter with added copper (AML, Tables 8 and 9);

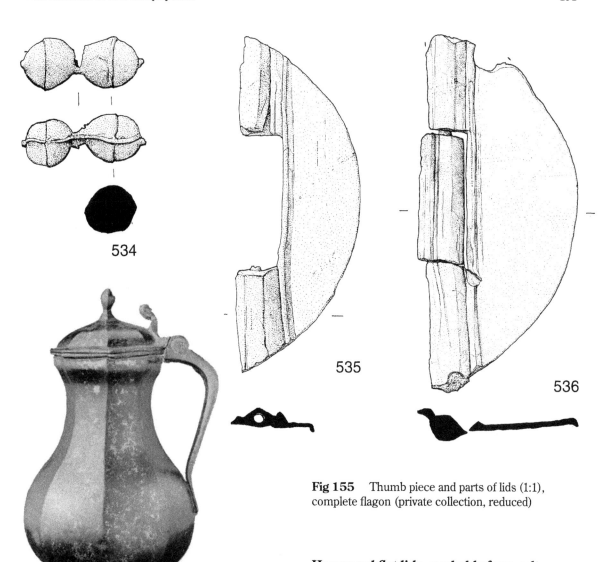

534

535

536

Fig 155 Thumb piece and parts of lids (1:1), complete flagon (private collection, reduced)

Hexagonal flat lids, probably from salts

537 BWB83 Acc No 4957 (Context 359) Ceramic Phase 11 Fig 156
Pewter with high lead content (AML, Table 8); slightly irregular, hexagonal lid; max w 87mm; hinged, dividing the area of the top roughly 2:1 by area, with 2 // 3 faceted hinge loops, defined by angled ridges which are continuous on the upper side and imitate separate folded tabs on the underside; the handle is formed by a separate, rather crude, figure of a squatting dog (spaniel?), h 31mm, with cross-hatching and a square void in the centre of the back, cast in the round in a three-part mould, and attached by solder.

smaller, fixed part of a round lid; d *c.*100mm; two cast angled pivots, defined by a ridge; part of iron hinge rod survives.

536 TL74 269 (306) 11 Fig 155
Fragment d *c.*110mm with 2 // 1 rounded pivots defined by angled ridges and dividing the top roughly 2:1 by area; iron hinge rod.

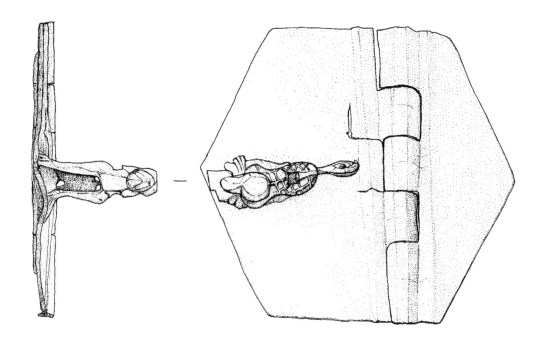

Fig 156 Lids with canine
handles (1:1) and, below complete
salt (Victoria and Albert Museum
acc no 4474–1858, reduced)

537

538 BWB83 1902 (401) 11 Fig 156
Pewter (AML, Table 8); squatting, open-mouthed
dog, h 34mm; with trefoil and dot motifs and hint of
collar with bell; the looped tail is transversely
hatched; from a two-part mould.

Less naturalistic than the one on the preceding
item, but presumably part of a similar lid.

The distinctive canine handles can be compared with others surviving on the lids of some
of a series of varied, highly decorated hexagonal 14th-century containers, one excavated at
Kalmar in Sweden and the other formerly in a
collection in Vienna (Tegnér 1984, figs 1, 9).
Further vessels of a similar character, sometimes with different finials, are noted by Tegnér

537

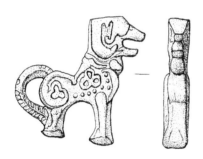

538

(both lacking the handles) have a Latin legend including CUM SIS IN MENSA PRIMO DE PAPAVERE PENSO ('when you are at the table think first of the poor'), suggesting they were for the dining table, probably serving as salt containers. Salts of pewter in London are mentioned in 1307 (Hatcher & Barker 1974, 34). A sitting dog forms the central handle on a round, early 16th-century salt made in Rotterdam (Dufour et al. 1979, 290–1, no 301). It is not known whether the dog had any special significance (?symbolic guardian of salt/preserver of food). Twenty salt cellars were among pewter items seized by the authorities in London in 1350 for having too high a lead content (Riley 1868, 259–60).

Number 537 is a plainer lid than those published by Tegnér and presumably represents a somewhat cheaper version of the same article.

MISCELLANEOUS ITEMS

539 BIG82 Acc No 2872 (Context 4659) Ceramic Phase 6 Fig 157
Pewter (AML, Table 8); flaring base; d *c*.55mm, h approx 15mm; surviving top has been partly rolled over and has a series of torn (?)pin holes around the perimeter, which appears to be an original edge; an irregular series of vertical lines rises from the apices of an irregular running zigzag defined at the base by a perimeter line – all this decoration being executed in paired lines of opposed punched triangles (see Egan & Pritchard 1991, 28, 30, fig 15B and C); found flattened.

Another was found in spoil deriving from the VRY89 site (ref no V235), and a similar item from the BUF90 site retains a small copper-alloy nail (acc no 152). Marian Campbell suggests that the missing cups of the vessels would have been of a prized organic material (perhaps a decorative wood) held by the nails. See Lightbown (1978, pl 17, top) for one category of medieval composite vessel – a covered bowl with a wooden cup and a foot in precious metal, from the early 15th century – though this is a later and much finer object. A closer parallel for this form of base in terms of date may be furnished by a fine enamelled example, d 69mm, from a (?covered) cup found in Denmark but of English workmanship and perhaps attributable to the early 12th century (N Stratford in Zarnecki et al. 1984, 260, no 274; the

in France, Germany and the Netherlands, as well as an example with religious motifs, but lacking the finial, found in London (ibid., fig 13; BM MLA acc no 56, 7–12,17S; see Fig 156 right for a canine-headed lid on a complete, shallow three-footed, hexagonal container, in the Victoria and Albert Museum (acc no 4474–1858, h 64mm; also published by A North in Alexander & Binski 1987, 239, no 118, and Homer 1991, 76, fig 39, respectively described as a pyx and a chrismatory; canine finials on flagons are also noted by North).

Part of a stone mould, apparently for producing similar vessels, was found at Visby on the island of Gotland, Sweden (Tegnér ibid, 295, fig 15). Two of this widespread group of vessels

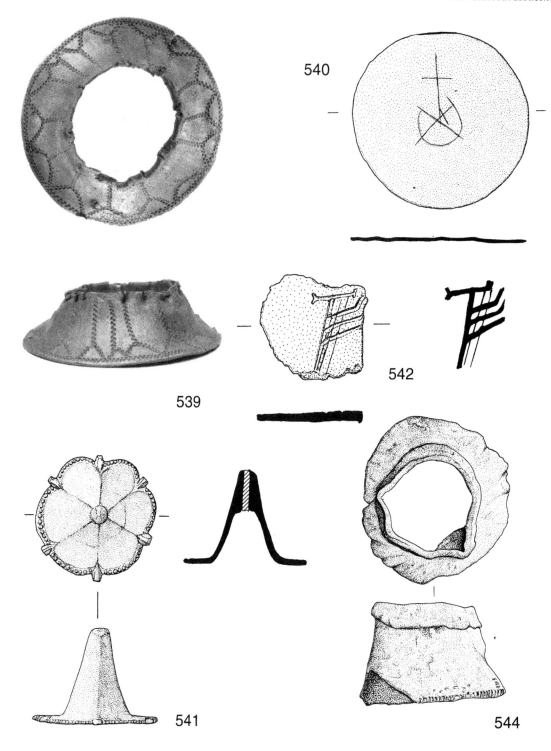

Fig 157   Bases and fragments probably from vessels (1:1)

missing part of this particular vessel is also likely to have been of enamelled copper alloy).

540 BWB83 4583 (285) 9 Fig 157
Disc; d 47mm; th *c*.0.5mm; scratched privy mark in centre.

Probably a base, despite its flimsiness.

541 BWB83 6062 (308) 11 Fig 157
Tin with added copper (AML, Tables 8 and 9); distorted, six-lobed, faceted foot (?)from decorative cup-like vessel (shape of surviving portion restored in drawing); d at base *c*.31mm; surviving h *c*.26mm; cusps in the spandrels; beaded border; trace of iron pin for attaching (?)cup.

The form can be most closely paralleled among precious metal chalices (it is also known for the feet of some crucifixes), though this smaller version was presumably a domestic item. This piece probably represents the only excavated vessel from the recent sites that would have been classified as 'square ware' (i.e., of angular, 'Gothic' form; cf. Homer 1991, 67, 73; see under Analysis of lead/tin alloy objects).

542 BWB83 2392 (150) 11 Fig 157
Tin (AML, Table 8); fragment 28×27mm of (?)vessel base or possibly wall, with incomplete engraved privy mark.

543 SWA81 2605 (2115) 12
Small fragment roughly cut from an angled part of a vessel; d of surviving piece approx 130mm.

544 SWA81 1410 (Unstratified) Fig 157
Battered and corroded; flaring base or possibly rim from composite (?)vessel; max d *c*.40–5mm; folded over at narrow end; engraved zigzag around wide end.

It seems remarkable that there are so few recognised plain wall or base fragments among the excavated material (see Nos 516 B and perhaps 542). The great majority (about seven out of eight) of the plainer fragments listed above (not counting lids or the near-complete No 501) include the edges of rims or the joins of sides with bases. Numbers 510, 540 and 542–3 are the only exceptions (of these, Nos 540 and 542 may have been selectively removed because of their identifiable marks); two plain fragments from sides or bases have been omitted from the listing (SWA81 acc nos 1079 and 1471B, both from ceramic phase 12 deposits). The striking emphasis on relatively small edge parts may be (as Anthony North suggests) because the pieces recovered were mainly fragments removed from damaged or unwanted vessels when they were broken up in the preparation

for recycling via the melting pot. This suggestion finds support in the cut marks on Nos 509–10 (a 15th- or 16th-century fragment from the BOY86 site appears to have the mark of a gripping tool, with which it may have been broken from the rest of the vessel, acc no 703).

See also lead/tin Nos 372–3 listed under Candleholders.

Decorative fragment, possibly from an ornate vessel

545 SWA81 3402 (2082) 12 Fig 158
Pewter (AML, Table 8); five-petalled double flower (cf. heraldic rose) in the round, with opposed oblique hatching on sepals and bulbous pedicel; l 27mm; max d *c*.20mm; broken off at stem; from a three-part mould. The external and internal moulding indicates the flower was intended to be seen from more than one angle.

Perhaps part of an ornate vessel or other decorative item. (Not counted in Table 1.)

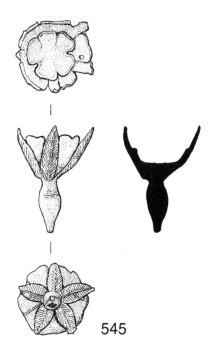

Fig 158 Lead/tin flower (1:1)

Wooden vessels
Lynne Keys

The advice of Carole Morris during extensive revision of the section on wooden vessels, including the catalogue groupings, is gratefully acknowledged.

From manuscript illustrations it is known that wooden vessels were in common use during the medieval period. Because the material requires wet anaerobic conditions for preservation, vessels only survive at waterfront sites and in moist ditch and pit fills etc. Numerous wooden objects were found by excavators in the last century and earlier in the present one, but for want of adequate conservation techniques most of these items perished very soon after being removed from their deposits (e.g., Dunning 1937, 416, where the vessels excavated from a well at the Bank of England site in 1929 survived only long enough for drawings to be made). Excavations elsewhere in Europe have drawn attention to the variety of wooden objects which were in use in the early and high medieval periods (Thompson 1967, 97–8; Schietzel 1970, 77–91; Neugebauer 1975; Kolchin 1989) but until fairly recently the study of wooden objects was not prominent in Britain (Ford 1987, 141–7; M Foreman in Armstrong et al. 1991, 175; C Morris & D H Evans in Evans & Tomlinson 1992, 189–90, 193–5; Morris forthcoming). Pritchard deals with material from London which represents the precursors of the items discussed below (1991, 240–2, 275–6, nos 367–72), and Egan (forthcoming a) describes an assemblage of at least 18 turned wooden vessels from a pit at a medieval religious institution in London.

The wide range of fragments from medieval bowls, dishes and other wooden objects that has been recovered in London from sites investigated between 1972 and 1983 provides useful information on forms in use over the 300-year period considered. A distinction is made between lathe-turned and composite stave-built vessels, reflecting the different crafts of the turner and the cooper in the medieval period (J Munby in Blair & Ramsay 1991, 400–1).

Examination of the recent finds of wooden vessels in London reveals that the genera used changed over the medieval period (see Table 10). Maple was much used in the Saxon period (Pritchard 1991, 240–2) and it occasionally appears later. Ash, a flexible, easily turned and water-resistant wood, began to eclipse all others from the early 13th century onwards in London as elsewhere (cf. Morris forthcoming), and from the latter half of the 14th century it was the most popular wood for bowls and dishes. Ash also has a particularly decorative grain for turned vessels, as was recognised in the medieval period (Kolchin 1989, 20–1). Numbers 564 and 588 (Figs 164 and 168) in their present state exhibit this characteristic more than most of the other excavated vessels. The attractive grained pattern could be why the former was repaired and not discarded when first broken (the present prominence of its markings is due, in part at least, to polishing after retrieval). Alder, also water resistant and easy to turn, was the second most popular wood for turned vessels in medieval London (again, a trend observed widely in England – Morris forthcoming), but it appears to have declined in use towards the end of the period considered. Beech seems to have been used for small turned boxes until the late medieval period, but it was little used for bowls if the recently excavated finds are representative (though the seven recovered from a well at the Bank of England site in 1929 were identified as beech – Dunning 1937, 416). At Southampton, 18 turned wooden bowls from 13th-century deposits comprise ten of birch, seven of ash and one of beech (Platt & Coleman Smith 1975, 228–30). Oak, which is readily split longitudinally, is suitable for making stave vessels such as barrels, buckets and tubs.

The two largest assemblages of wooden items listed below comprise, in the one case, eight bowls (Nos 554, 562–4, 566, 597–8 and 600) together with a box and an unusual lid (Nos 614 and 623) from a mid-13th-century pit at the MLK76 site and, in the other case, seven bowls from an early 15th-century deposit at the TL74 site (Nos 586–7, 589, 591 and 609–11), a fragment from a stave vessel (No 636) and a small, carved vessel (No 638). Other groups found at the BC72 site are dated to the mid-14th century (vessels Nos 558, 578–9 and 603, and probable lid 626) and to the late 14th

Table 10:   Genera of wooden vessels
(L=lid, S=stave, B=base)

Ceramic phases	6	7	8	9	10	11	12
Turned							
Ash	1	3	10	6, 1L	1	9(?+1)	7(?+1)
Maple	3	–	2, (?)1L	2	1L	–	?1
Alder	–	1	1, 2L	5(?+1)	2, 1L	–	2
Beech*	–	–	2	3	–	2(?+1), 1L	–
(?)Ash/hazel	–	–	–	–	–	1	–
(?)Poplar/willow	–	–	–	–	–	1L	–
Oak	–	–	–	?2, ?1L	–	–	–
Unidentified	1L	–	1	1L	–	–	–
Coopered							
Hazel	1S	–	–	–	–	–	–
Oak	–	–	–	1S	–	1S, 2B(?+1)	2S
(?)Cedar/silver fir	–	–	–	1S	–	–	–
Unidentified	–	–	–	–	–	1S	–
Hand-carved							
Oak	–						1

* especially used for boxes

(Possible lids Nos 639–40, which are not turned, are omitted.)

century (Nos 559–60, 582–3, 607, 620 (a box), and 635 (from a stave vessel). Two groups at the LUD82 site are dated to the late 13th/mid-14th century (respectively Nos 569, 575 and 601–2; and Nos 568, 570, 573–4 and 576); two at the SWA81 site are dated to the late 13th/ early 14th century (vessels Nos 571–2 and, from another context, boxes Nos 615–16); and two undated items at the LH74 site (Nos 592–3) were also found in close association. This concentrated grouping of finds may be due as much to deliberately deciding on disposal (rather than to use the wood as fuel) as to factors of survival and retrieval.

Five vessels are marked, three by branding and two with incised lines: bowls Nos 554 and 563 (from the same pit at the MLK76 site) both have an S-like mark burnt into their bases, an indication that they probably once belonged to the same household; No 602 has a burnt cross; and Nos 593 and 599 have incised cross-like motifs. Three bowls had been repaired, Nos 546 and 583 with staples and No 564 by sewing in two places (perhaps using thin wire – cf. Hume 1863, 309, cited in Morris forthcoming).

The five turned boxes, Nos 613–17, are very similar in form to those from sites elsewhere in Britain and on the Continent (e.g., Neugebauer 1975, fig 25; Kolchin 1989, pl 55). At Novgorod in Russia they were used for holding cosmetics, ointments and jewellery (Kolchin 1989, 62) and the London examples may have served a similar range of purposes. They all have a rabbet to take a lid, but in no instance does a lid survive in association. No 620, interpreted as a (?)re-used lid, was found containing a yellow substance, possibly paint. The seven larger lids recovered (Nos 621–7) have no obvious corresponding wooden vessel forms to which they can be attributed among finds from the sites considered; they may have been for ceramic containers. Several items from CUS73 published by Henig (1974, 1975) were not located for the present catalogue.

All grooves noted are turned and on the exterior, unless otherwise stated (only No 570 has one on the interior), and all marks of ownership etc. are on the exterior.

Dimensions of the catalogued vessels, where there is appropriate survival, are set out as follows:

rim diameter; base diameter; maximum surviving height (– indicates that no meaningful measurement can be obtained).

Morris (forthcoming) terms vessels in which the height:width ratio is between 1:2 and 1:6 'bowls' and those in which it is 1:6+ 'plates'. Dimensions are often very approximate owing to distortion/drying of the wood.

A measurement with '+' indicates the surviving dimension of an incomplete part of the vessel.

LATHE-TURNED VESSELS

Bowls

These are divided into large examples with thick walls (presumably all turned), those with flanged rims and those with plain rims.

Some of the vessels are nearly hemispherical, while others have more outsplayed sides and No 577 has a seemingly inverted rim (possibly distortion), but these differences seem to have no chronological implication. Similarly, the other typological divisions used below have no apparent chronological significance, and vessels of different categories were sometimes found together.

The sizes of the bowls catalogued cover a great range, from large heavy vessels (No 548 was over 310mm in diameter) to No 581 at 60mm. (There are none listed to compare with a London vessel which apparently has a diameter of over 525mm – Dunning 1937, 417, fig 3, no 1).

Turned wooden vessels of similar date excavated at Winchester (D Keene in Biddle 1990, 959–65, nos 3420–6, figs 217–26) had been made (where it is possible to determine) from tangentially split or sawn boards (half-log sections of roundwood), with the bases towards the sapwood and the rims towards the heartwood for strength (sometimes incidentally producing the attractive, regular pattern evident in Nos 564 and 588 below). A similar tendency appears in the use of the timber in the London finds, apart from lid No 623 (Damian Goodburn pers comm, from a rapid examination of only some of the items). Face turning – i.e., with the grain at a right angle to the rotation axis of the lathe – was the norm, using green wood (Morris forthcoming). The blackened interior of some of the listed vessels is thought to be an accumulated deposit resulting from holding heated greasy foods.

HEAVY, PLAIN VESSELS

Most of these are round-bottomed, or nearly so. The walls vary in thickness, sometimes narrowing towards the rim, and are over 10mm thick at the centre and/or side. Bowls of this kind are generally plainer as well as being more robust than Nos 551–93. The better preserved examples are turned, but, as these particular

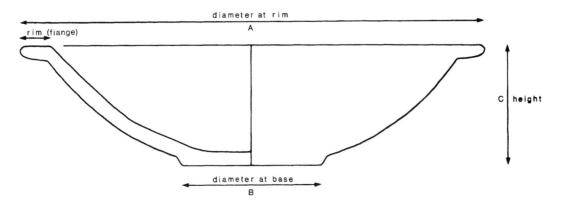

Fig 159   Dimensions for wooden vessels

546

items are usually represented by abraded fragments, the method of manufacture is often difficult to determine. Vessels of this form are likely to have been used in food preparation, for serving stews and also in the dairy (cf. Morris forthcoming).

546 MLK76 Acc No 989 (Context 1193) Ceramic Phases 4–6 Fig 160
Fragments; d at existing perimeter 230mm+ (perhaps originally about double this; *or* more than one vessel may be represented); d at base –; h 139mm+; *Fraxinus* sp (ash); burnt on interior and to a lesser extent on exterior; split repaired with iron staple. Damian Goodburn points out that the graining of the two pieces photographed does not match, i.e., apparently a different piece was used in the repair.

Fig 160 Wooden vessel fragments (bottom reduced); detail at top shows repair (slightly enlarged)

549

Fig 161   Wooden vessel (photographs reduced; drawing 1:2)

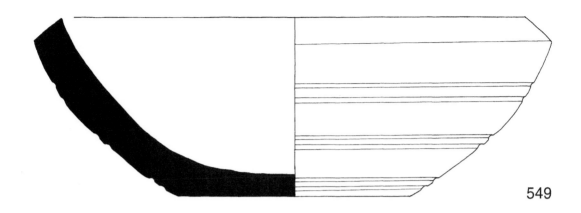

549

547 BC72 1983 (83) 11
Distorted; two fragments, including rim; pair of turned ridges; approx 300mm; –; –; *Fraxinus* sp (ash).

548 BYD81 9 (17) 11–12
Thick, slightly curved base; 310mm+; 105mm; 65mm+; one groove; *Alnus* sp (alder).

549 BYD81 2 (5) Medieval Context Fig 161
Almost complete; thick side; three paired grooves; 270mm; 130mm; 96mm; *Ulmus* sp (elm).

550 MM74 41 and 42 (166) Medieval Context
Fragments; measurements unobtainable; ?*Ulmus* sp (?elm).

Compare No 577.

FLANGED RIMS

551 MLK76 Acc No 319 (Context 1082) Ceramic Phases 5–6 Fig 162
D at rim *c*.255mm; d at base 80mm; h *c*.45mm; w of flange 25mm; *Acer* sp (field maple); blackened interior.

552 MLK76 253 (1089) 5–6
Fragment; 255mm; –; –; w of flange 27mm; *Acer* sp (field maple); blackened interior.

553 SWA81 2640 (2266) 7 Fig 162
Rim fillet on upper face; *c*.190mm; 90mm; (?)45mm; distorted, but appears to have been flanged; *Fraxinus* sp (ash); blackened interior.

554 MLK76 496 (3061) 8 Fig 162
112mm; 55mm; 28mm; w of flange 9mm; *Acer* sp (field maple); S-shaped burnt mark on base.
  (See also No 563.)

555 BIG82 2151 (2012) 8 Fig 162
Rim fillet on upper face; 150mm; (?)70mm; (?)26mm; w of flange 24mm; *Fraxinus* sp (ash).

556 CUS73 610 (VII,10) 9 Fig 162
Fragments; 110mm; 78mm; 20mm; w of flange 11mm; *Fraxinus* (ash).
  (Not in Henig 1974.)

557 CUS73 854 (I,12) 9 Fig 162
180mm; 85mm; (?)15mm; w of flange 22mm; *Alnus* sp (alder).
  (Not in Henig 1974.)

558 BC72 3673 (250) 10 Fig 162
Fragments; distorted rim; (?)105–135mm; 62mm; 28mm; w of flange 14mm; ?*Quercus* sp (?oak).

559 BC72 4788 (150) 11
Distorted rim; (?)90mm; – ; wood unidentifiable.

560 BC72 4239 (150) 11 Fig 162
(?)*c*.120mm; 60mm; 26mm; w of flange 15mm; wood unidentifiable.

PLAIN RIMS

In some worn examples the original rim may not have survived.

561 SH74 Acc No 204 (Context 484) Ceramic Phase 7 Fig 163
Fragments; paired grooves; d at rim *c*.190mm; d at base (?)90mm; h 70mm; *Fraxinus* sp (ash).

562 MLK76 505 (3061) 8
Fragments; *c*.120mm; 56mm; (?)50mm; *Fraxinus* sp (ash).

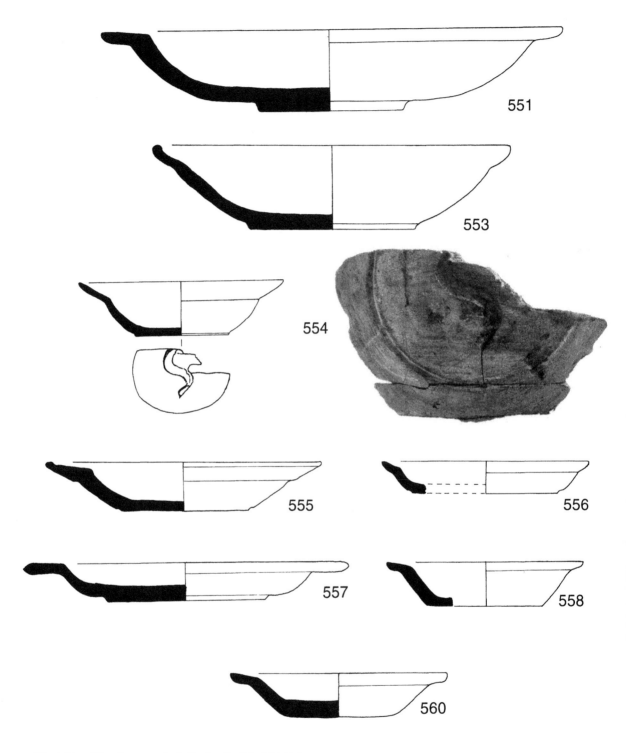

Fig 162   Wooden vessels (1:2); detail of No 554 (1:1)

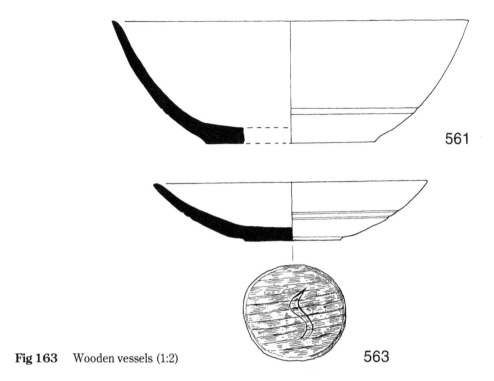

Fig 163   Wooden vessels (1:2)

563 MLK76 488 (3061) 8 Fig 163
Distorted; paired grooves; *c*.150mm; 55mm; (?)*c*.27mm; *Fraxinus* sp (ash); S-shaped mark burnt into base.
    (See also No 554.)
564 MLK76 487 (3061) 8 Fig 164
180mm; 60mm; 46mm; *Fraxinus* sp (ash); tiny paired holes either side of two cracks indicate sewn repairs.
565 BIG82 2194 (2242) 8 Fig 165
c.170mm; 61mm; 34mm; *Fraxinus* sp (ash); blackened interior.
566 MLK76 504 (3061) 8
Paired grooves; *c*.200mm; 90mm; 45mm; *Fraxinus* sp (ash); blackened interior.
567 LUD82 28 (516) 8
(?)*c*.220mm; –; –; *Alnus* sp (alder).
568 LUD82 59 (1078) 9 Fig 165
Distorted; paired grooves; (?)*c*.210mm; 80mm; (?)45mm; *Acer* sp (field maple).
569 LUD82 58 (1060) 9 Fig 165
c.160mm; 40mm; 45mm; *Alnus* sp (alder).

570 LUD82 467 (1078) 9 Fig 165
Distorted; *c*.170mm; *c*.48mm; *c*.42mm; internal groove at base; *Fraxinus* sp (ash); interior charred.
571 SWA81 2644 (2134) 9 Fig 165
One groove; (?)170mm; (?)100mm; 42mm; *Fraxinus* sp (ash); charred interior and exterior.
572 SWA81 4737 (2134) 9 Fig 166
One groove; (?)200mm; 125mm; 32mm; *Fraxinus* sp (ash).
573 LUD82 57 (1078) 9 Fig 166
215mm; 80mm; 50mm; *Alnus* sp (alder); blackened interior.
574 LUD82 251 (1078) 9 Fig 166
c.220mm; *c*.100mm; (?)40mm; *Fraxinus* sp (ash); charred inside base.
575 LUD82 249 (1060) 9 Fig 166
Distorted; *c*.240mm; –; –; paired grooves; *Alnus* sp (alder); charred interior and exterior.
576 LUD82 301 (1078) 9
Rim and side fragment; 300mm+; –; –; *Alnus* sp (alder); blackened interior.

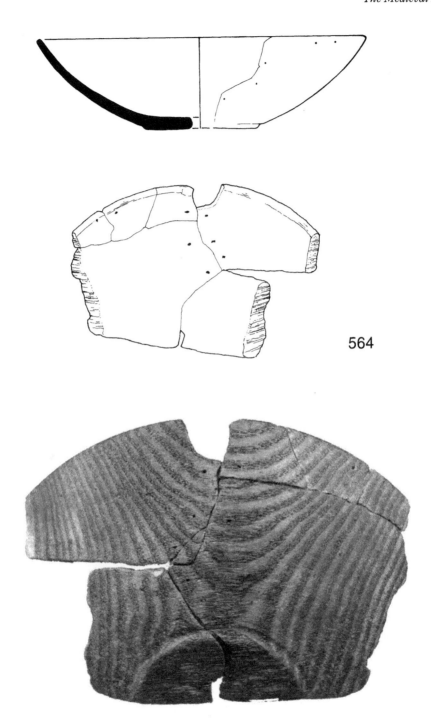

564

Fig 164 Wooden vessel with sewn repair
(drawings 1:2; photograph slightly reduced)

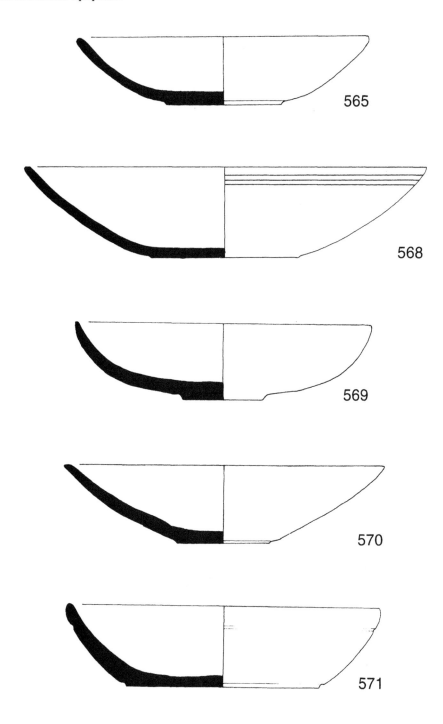

Fig 165   Wooden vessels (1:2)

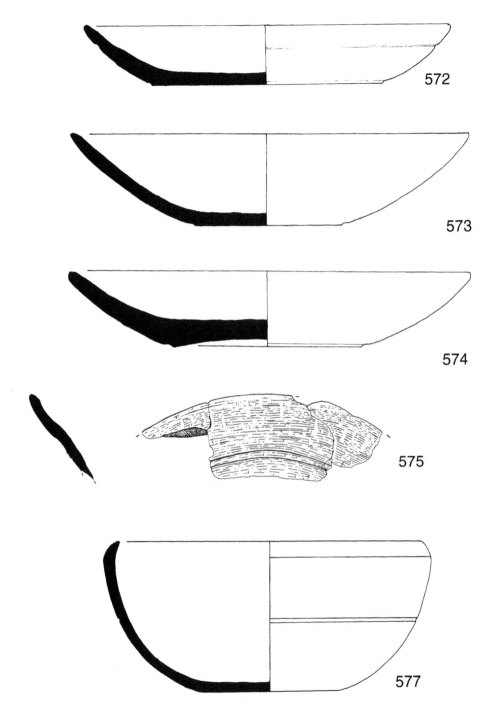

Fig 166   Wooden vessels (1:2)

577 SWA81 1732 (?2018) ?9 Fig 166
(?)Inverted rim (possibly distorted); single groove; (?)180mm; (?)75mm; 80mm; wood unidentifiable.

578 BC72 2896 (250) 10 Fig 167
(?)135mm; 37mm; (?)40mm; *Alnus* sp (alder); three grooves.

(?)Relatively a deeper vessel than the others listed here.

579 BC72 2897 (250) 10 Fig 167
Distorted; 185mm; 80mm; (?)30mm; *Fraxinus* sp (ash); interior and exterior blackened.

580 BC72 2906 (119) 10–11
Fragments; 240mm; –; –; *Fraxinus* sp (ash).

581 BC72 4106 (88) 11
60mm; –; (?)8mm; *Fraxinus* sp (ash).

This is the smallest turned bowl from the sites considered here.

582 BC72 4034 (150) 11 Fig 167
240–65+mm; 114mm; 48mm; *Fraxinus* sp (ash); interior blackened.

583 BC72 5339 (150) 11
300mm; –; 44mm+; *Fraxinus* sp (ash); crack repaired with two iron staples.

584 BC72 2351 (79) 11
Measurements unobtainable; *Corylus* sp/*Alnus* sp (hazel/alder).

585 BC72 4408 (89) 11
Measurements unobtainable; *Fraxinus* sp (ash); blackened internally and externally.

586 TL74 1160 (368) 12
Distorted; *c*.140mm; 67mm; –; *Fraxinus* sp (ash).

587 TL74 490 (368) 12 Fig 167
Fragments; 150mm; 66mm; 26mm; *Fraxinus* sp (ash).

588 TL74 491 (364) 12 Fig 168
c.170mm; 70mm; 37mm; *Fraxinus* sp (ash); blackened interior.

589 TL74 1087 (368) 12 Fig 168
(?)*c*.175mm; 78mm; 43mm; *Alnus* sp (alder).

590 TL74 1078 (275) 12 Fig 168
180mm; 100mm; 35mm; *Fraxinus* sp (ash).

591 TL74 1158 (368) 12
210mm; 80mm; 40mm; *Fraxinus* sp (ash).

592 LH74 40 (F90) Medieval Context
Fragments; (?)*c*.240mm; –; –; *Alnus* sp (alder).

593 LH74 170 (F90) Medieval Context
Base and fragments of side; 180mm+; 56mm; –; *Fraxinus* sp (ash); incised cross near base.

FRAGMENTS FROM WHICH THE RIMS ARE MISSING

Rim diameters have not been estimated because of potential gross distortion in many of the items. Several small fragments have been omitted.

594 BIG82 Acc No 2340 (Context 2505) Ceramic Phase 7
Pronounced base and part of side; d of base 78mm; h –; *Acer* sp (field maple).

595 SH74 726 (484) 7
–; (?)65+mm; *Fraxinus* sp (ash); blackened interior.

596 SWA81 4673 (2278) 7
Measurements unobtainable; *Alnus* sp (alder); interior charred.

597 MLK76 1715 (3061) 8
Base and side fragments; *c*.60mm; –; *Fraxinus* sp (ash).

598 MLK76 498 (3061) 8
Base and side fragments; *c*.90mm; –; *Fraxinus* sp (ash).

599 SH74 141 (386) 8
Base and part of side; 65+mm; –; wood unidentifiable; cross of two incised lines at right angles on base.

600 MLK76 501 (3061) 8
Fragments; measurements unobtainable; *Fraxinus* sp (ash).

601 LUD82 250 (1060) 9
c.70mm; –; *Fagus sylvatica* (beech).

602 LUD82 60 (1060) 9 Fig 169
Base and side fragments; 50mm; 12mm+; *Acer* sp (field maple); cross burnt on base; interior blackened.

603 BC72 2898 (250) 10
Measurements unobtainable; *Alnus* sp (alder).

604 BC72 3716 (255) 11
70mm; –; *Fraxinus* sp (ash).

605 TL74 116 (306) 11
70mm; –; *Fraxinus* sp (ash).

606 BC72 1874 (79) 11
84mm; –; *Fraxinus* sp (ash).

607 BC72 3686 (150) 11
130mm+; –; smooth interior, rough exterior; (?)*Fraxinus* sp (?ash).

608 BYD81 6 (17) 11–12 Fig 170
Two grooves; pronounced, everted base; *c*.55mm; 45mm+; *Alnus* sp (alder).

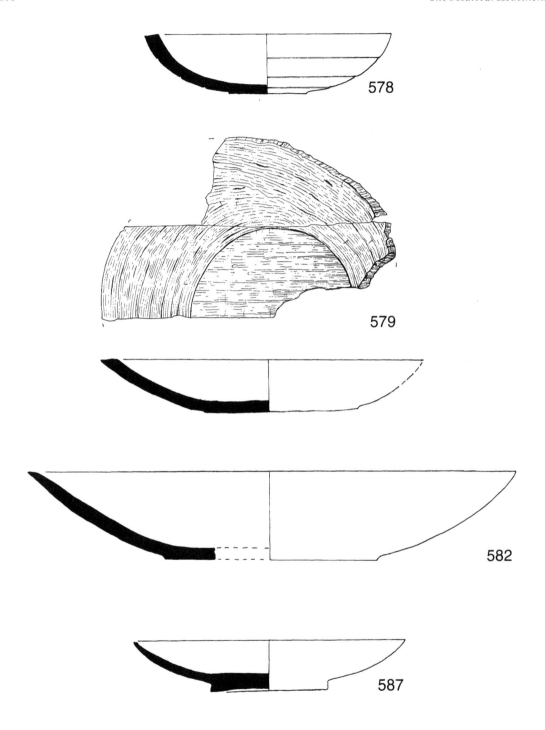

578

579

582

587

Fig 167   Wooden vessels (1:2)

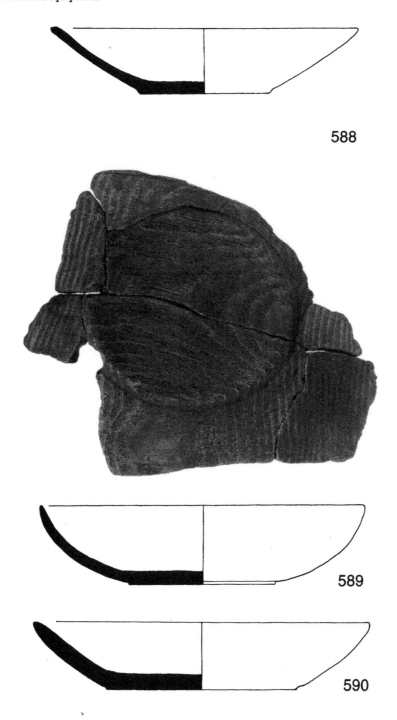

588

589

590

Fig 168   Wooden vessels (1:2;
detail of No 588 not to scale)

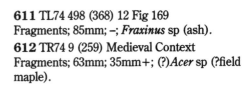

611

Fig 169   Wooden vessels (1:2)

602

609 TL74 385 (368) 12
Fragments; (?)*c*.40mm; –; *Fraxinus* sp (ash).
610 TL74 3233 (368) 12
Distorted fragments; *c*.80mm; –; *Fraxinus* sp (ash).

611 TL74 498 (368) 12 Fig 169
Fragments; 85mm; –; *Fraxinus* sp (ash).
612 TR74 9 (259) Medieval Context
Fragments; 63mm; 35mm+; (?)*Acer* sp (?field maple).

Turned boxes

(Containers with vertical or nearly vertical sides)

These are rabbeted at the top to take a lid. Some may have been slightly waisted in profile, perhaps corresponding with the ceramic (majolica) form from the end of the medieval period. Acc no 534 from the VRY89 site is a wooden box of this form which retains traces of painted decoration, thus emphasising this connection. A tendency in some of the excavated wooden vessels to narrow slightly towards the top is probably attributable to distortion of the thinnest part. Diameters given below are measured at the base.

Boxes of this kind are known, mainly from the 12th to 15th centuries, from several towns (e.g., C Morris in Margeson 1993, 96, fig 53, no 598, a matching vessel and lid from Norwich, with references to finds elsewhere). The form of vessel is familiar from artistic representations of Mary Magdalene holding an alabaster container of similar shape for the costly oil with which she anointed Christ's feet.

613 SH74 Acc No 95 (Context 386) Ceramic Phase 8 Fig 171
Distorted; base and side fragments; d *c*.40mm; h 46mm; *Fagus sylvatica* (beech).

608

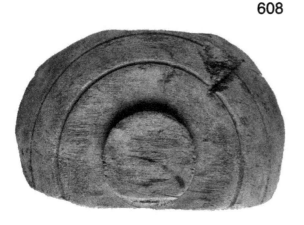

Fig 170   Wooden vessel (1:2)

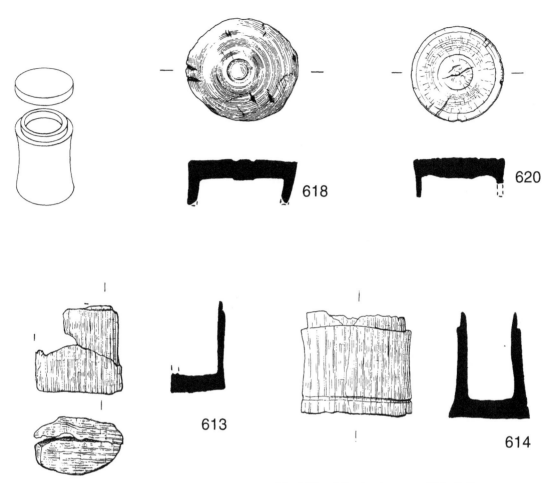

Fig 171 Wooden boxes and lids (1:2);
reconstruction, top left (not to scale)

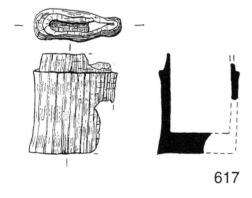

614 MLK76 497 (3061) 8 Fig 171
Distorted; one groove; d *c.*52mm; h 52mm; *Fagus sylvatica* (beech).

615 SWA81 4721 (2065) 9
Incomplete and distorted; lower part; one groove near base; d *c.*120mm; surviving h 49mm; *Fagus sylvatica* (beech).

616 SWA81 4723 (2065) 9
Distorted fragment; – ; h 70mm+; *Fagus sylvatica* (beech).

617 SWA81 1173 (2112) 12 Fig 171
Distorted; d (?)*c.*35mm; h 51mm; *Alnus* sp (alder).

SMALL TURNED LIDS

(These presumably went with boxes like the preceding ones.)

618 SWA81 Acc No 1704 (Context 2055) Ceramic Phase 9 Fig 171
D 60mm; h 22mm; *Fagus sylvatica* (beech).

619 CUS73 668 (IV,48) 9
D 60mm; h 23mm; (?)*Quercus* sp (?oak); charring on all but base.

Published as a box (pyx) by Henig (1975, 152–3, no 9, fig 25).

620 BC72 4119 (150) 11 Fig 171
D 47mm; h 19mm; (?)*Populus* sp/(?)*Salix* sp (?poplar/?willow); found (?re-used) containing a yellow deposit with a fine hair in it.

The deposit could be paint, and the hair could perhaps be from a brush.

Other turned lids

These are all larger than boxes Nos 613–17; no straight-sided wooden vessel of corresponding size has been recognised among the finds from the sites included in this survey. These lids may have been intended for vessels of other materials (coopered vessels seem unlikely, in view of the traditional division of the two woodworking crafts) or perhaps for round-sided bowls.

The hole in No 621 may have been for a string or a chain to prevent loss (cf. No 641).

621 SWA81 Acc No 1341 (Context 2209) Ceramic Phase 6 Fig 172
Fragment; d 100mm; central hole; seating rim at perimeter; oblique hole between top and side; wood unidentifiable.

622 BIG82 2148 (2053) 8
Fragment; original d (?)c.100mm, h 12mm; (?)*Acer* sp (?field maple).

623 MLK76 320 (3061) 8 Fig 172
Distorted fragment; vertical side; right-angled rabbet at base; thickens towards centre; d estd c.250mm; h 51mm; series of concentric grooves on top; *Alnus* sp (alder). Damian Goodburn observes that this object was turned in the round ('spindle turned') – i.e., with the grain running vertically, rather than horizontally as was usual (turning in the round is generally

avoided because of the risk of splitting the block – in the present instance a particular graining effect may have been desired).

624 MLK76 1128 and 1129 (25) 8
Fragments, probably from same object as preceding item; *Alnus* sp (alder).

625 LUD82 410 (1060) 9 Fig 172
Fragment; d 80mm; seating rim at perimeter; conical centre on top, possibly where a knop has broken off; wood unidentifiable.

626 BC72 3734 (250) 10 Fig 172
Fragment; flat, circular object with possible seating ring at perimeter; d c.190mm, h 26mm; tapers towards centre; *Acer* sp (field maple).

Probably a lid.

627 BIG82 2583 (4045) 11 Fig 172
Fragment; d c.100mm; seating ring away from the perimeter, d 55mm; *Alnus* sp (alder).

Stave-built composite vessels

These coopers' products are represented either by a stave from the side (sometimes parallel-sided, sometimes slightly flaring towards one end or the middle) or by part of an end disc (head). The inner face of the stave has a horizontal groove (or grooves) near the end(s) to hold the head(s) in position. Barrels (casks) would have had the latter at both ends; open vessels like No 629 would have had them only at the base. It is not possible to be sure of the form of the complete vessels, since in all cases only a single main element survives. Binding hoops survive in association with the stave in No 628.

The larger items among the following may be from casks, buckets, tubs and churns; the smaller ones from bowls, flagons and jugs. Six discs or pieces from discs (diameters between 14mm and 450mm) may have been the bases of containers of this kind; the smaller ones could be from flared vessels. Oak predominates, though among the staves No 628 is of hazel and No 630 is of cedar or silver fir.

Flared staves from small bowls and cups are known from excavations in Britain (Platt & Coleman Smith 1975, 230–1, fig 228, no 1630; Curteis & Morris forthcoming) and in Germany, Denmark, the Netherlands and

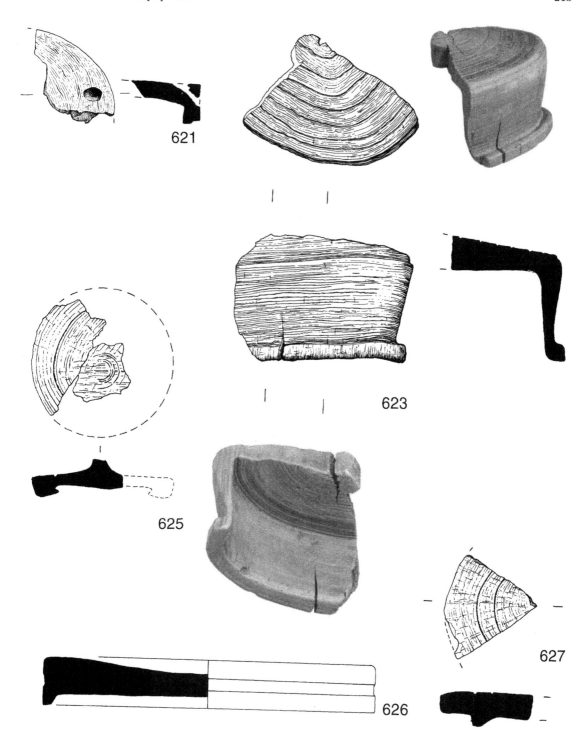

Fig 172   Wooden lids (1:2)

Russia (e.g., Neugebauer 1975; Kolchin 1989). Number 629 is from a large vessel of this kind. Their general rarity in Britain has been noted by Ford (1987, 143).

STAVES

(All of the following have internal grooves to hold end discs.)

628 SWA81 Acc No 4677 (Context 1354) Ceramic Phase 6

Incomplete; h 230mm+; w at (?)base 112mm; *Quercus* sp (oak); surviving hoops with bark, semi-circular in section, *Corylus avellana* (hazel).

629 SWA81 4815 (2134) 9 Fig 173
Slightly flared; h 248mm; (?)basal w 79mm; (?)top w 86mm; *Quercus* sp (oak).

630 SWA81 1728 (2018) 9 Fig 173
Incomplete; surviving h 249mm; surviving w 35mm; *Cedrus* sp (cedar) or *Abies alba* (silver fir).

631 TL74 2077 (291) 11
Incomplete; surviving h 259mm; w 62mm; *Quercus* sp (oak).

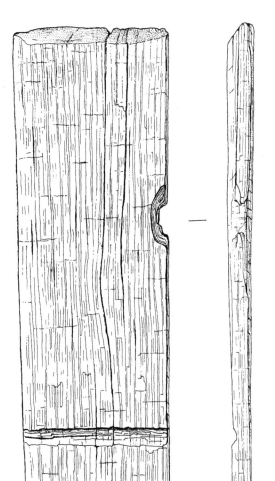

629

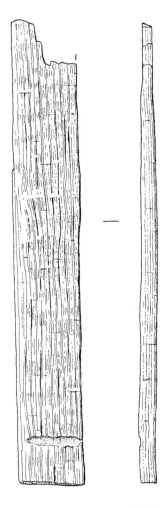

630

Fig 173   Wooden vessel staves (1:2)

END DISCS (heads/bases)

Half of these have plain edges. In the others, the chamfered edge of the disc (chime), shaped to fit into the groove in the stave, either has both the upper and lower faces chamfered or is only modified in this way on one side (cf. Kolchin 1989, 42, pl 34, nos 6, 7, 9).

632 BC72 Acc No 4104 (Context 88) Ceramic Phase 11 Fig 174
Two fragments; d 38mm; plain edge; *Quercus* sp (oak).

Possibly a vessel base.

633 BC72 3717 (255) 11 Fig 174
Fragment; d of vessel 140mm; surviving l 117mm; surviving w 37mm; plain edge; wood unidentifiable.

634 TL74 3276 (414) 11
Fragment; d of vessel 420mm; surviving l 208mm; surviving w 35mm; both faces chamfered; *Quercus* sp (oak).

635 BC72 3102 (150) 11 Fig 174
Fragment; d of vessel *c*.450mm; surviving l 259mm; surviving w 54mm; both faces chamfered; *Quercus* sp (oak); burnt.

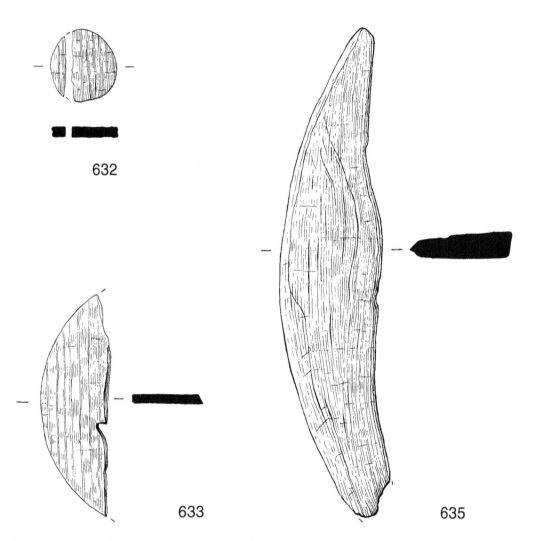

632

633

635

Fig 174 Discs probably from wooden stave vessels (1:2)

636 TL74 1157 (368) 12
Fragment; d of vessel (and l) 140mm; plain edge;
Quercus sp (oak).

637 TL74 1630 (275) 12
D of vessel 280mm; surviving l 223mm; max w 80mm;
(?)chamfered on one face only; *Quercus* sp (oak).

HAND-CARVED VESSEL

638 TL74 Acc No 1150 (Context 368) Ceramic
Phase 12 Fig 175
Roughly made; d at rim 45mm; d at base 26mm;
h 20mm; *Quercus* sp (oak); traces of red paint on
rim and sides.

This small vessel is not the product of a craft wood
worker. It may perhaps have been a plaything.

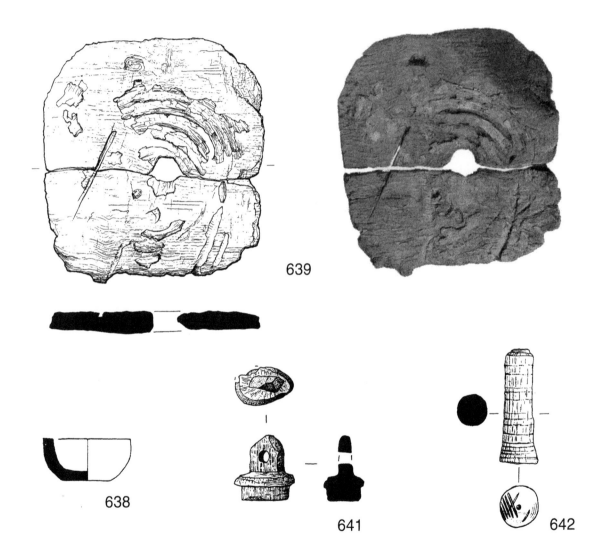

639

638

641

642

Fig 175   Possible wooden lid, carved wooden vessel, stopper and turning waste (No 639 1:4; remainder 1:2)

POSSIBLE CASK HEADS
(not turned)

The central hole may have been for lifting the lid with an inserted finger. These objects may not have gone with wooden vessels. Compare the oak items found at Beverley and identified as cask heads (C Morris & D H Evans in Evans & Tomlinson 1992, 195–6, nos 623–4, fig 93).

639 SWA81 Acc No 2643 (Context 2257) Ceramic Phase 7 Fig 175
Abraded and in two pieces; riven; squarish, with rounded corners, 255×240mm; central hole d *c.*25mm; *Quercus* sp (oak); traces of at least six concentric rings of flimsy, unidentifiable wood/reeds on one face; burnt at side.

The rings could be from some kind of basketry, but their precise relationship to the main piece is unclear.

640 SWA81 1722 (350) Medieval Context
D 223mm; riven; central hole d 21mm; *Quercus* sp (oak); burnt at perimeter.

STOPPER

641 BIG82 Acc No 2413 (Context 2938) Ceramic Phase 8 Fig 175
Partly carved (?possibly also turned); head has flat tab with angled top and perforation; l 30mm; *Acer* sp (field maple).

The perforation was probably to take a string or a chain (cf. No 621).

TURNING WASTE
(Identified by Carole Morris)

642 SWA81 Acc No 1340 (Context 2209) Ceramic Phase 6 Fig 175
Cylindrical; l 60mm; d of expanded end 23mm; d of remainder 13mm; *Buxus* sp (box).

This central rod remained in place while a vessel was being hollowed out by turning on the lathe; it was then discarded.

Glass vessels
Lynne Keys

INTRODUCTION
Geoff Egan

The catalogue of excavated glass, below, covers a wide range of compositions (metals) and different vessel forms. Although there are no complete objects, for the first time some idea of the variety of glassware available in medieval London is provided, including that for the early 15th century (cf. ceramic phase 12), which was hitherto particularly poorly understood in Britain (Charleston 1984, 42). An increase in glass consumption through the period considered, at least up to *c.*1400, is reflected in the number of datable finds recovered (see Table 1).

Many of the catalogue items are from rubbish pits which produced fragments of more than one vessel. It is not possible in the present state of knowledge to identify for certain the place of manufacture of any individual item, but it seems likely that the majority may be imports (with the probable exception of glass lamps and urinals, which are catalogued elsewhere in this volume). Some of the potash vessels in this present section could well be English (though this formula was used on the Continent too), as could items in other metals (see Table 12), but there is no clear evidence at present.

Several items have close Continental parallels, and at least one (No 695, Col Pl 5C) appears to be from the Islamic world. Most of the forms are well known elsewhere (see Baumgartner 1987, 116–19, Foy & Sennequier 1989, 361–425, for suggested chronologies of some types of vessels), though the fragments of an elaborate (?partly) figurative vessel (No 703) are difficult to parallel. Both the metal and forms of opaque white glass lids and a (?)handle (Nos 691–4) appear so far to be unknown outside London at the date suggested (No 689, the base of a (?)drinking glass of the same metal, is at least a familiar medieval form). The heavy, yellow lead glasses stand out as a group (Nos 657–60), and other groups are defined by the results of analyses by Cath Mortimer. Table 13 traces the rise of soda glasses through the period considered and, more arguably, may reflect a decline in potash glass at its end. Some categories of medieval glass known from other excavations and finds in London are not represented below (e.g., a fragment painted with (?)heraldic devices – Baumgartner & Krueger 1988, 285–6, no 324, and the opaque red glasses found in a deposit attributed to the late 13th century – Nöel Hume 1957, no 1, and also at the BA84 site – acc no 978; cf. Baumgartner 1987, 44–5 and front cover, no 15 for a complete vessel of this material in Germany).

A small number of fragments of distilling vessels from the appropriate sites are not included below, though these 'industrial' items may have had a domestic usage in the preparation of liqueurs etc. for home consumption in affluent households.

DISCUSSION
Lynne Keys

It is now recognised that excavated glass, though rarely furnishing complete vessels, provides the chance to reassess the range of available forms and their significance in the medieval period (R Charleston in Biddle 1990, xxviii, 235).

Several specialists have written extensively on medieval glass: in England, Harden (1968; 1972; 1975; 1978) and R Charleston (in Platt & Coleman Smith 1975; 1984; in Biddle 1990, 934–7), and on the Continent, Baumgartner (1987), Foy (1985; 1988), Foy and Sennequier (1989) and Henkes (1994). The little evidence that has been discovered for the manufacture of vessels in England has been discussed by Charleston (1991, see esp 252, 257–60). The volume by Baumgartner & Krueger (1988) is the most comprehensive survey of medieval glass undertaken and includes several examples from London in its catalogue. In contrast, very little that is site-specific has previously been published on London finds: see Nöel Hume 1957 for some bottles of appropriate date for this present volume (though most of those discussed there are slightly later); Cook 1967 for a summary description of glass dated to the early 15th century (cf. ceramic phase 12) found in a pit excavated at Cannon Street

Station; Clark (1983) for a group of enamelled drinking glasses (cf. Col Pl 8), and *idem* (1986) for drinking-glass fragments found just north of the City. Tyson & Clark illustrate an otherwise unpublished assemblage from Post Office Court, London (1994, front cover).

By the 11th century, potash (potassium carbonate) was being used as the fluxing agent for the manufacture of glass. As potash was derived from the burning of wood (beech, in particular), which was also needed for the furnace fuel, the industry became established in regions of extensive woodland in north-west Europe. In England, the Sussex Weald was a major production area, with both documentary and archaeological evidence indicating that glass makers moved from place to place as wood supplies became exhausted (Winbolt 1933; Kenyon 1967). As a result of this dependence on wood fuel, potash glass is sometimes referred to as 'forest' glass. The increasing amount of glass used in medieval England was often of this kind, though Table 13 (below) suggests an increase, particularly in soda metal, at the end of the period considered in this present volume. Forest glass can be reliably identified visually among the listed fragments where it has a dark green colour (paler green pieces may be of this category or of another), while lead glass, of yellow or green colour, usually stands out because of its relative heaviness. At least three kinds of glass – potash, lead and soda – have been identified among the material considered below (lime glass No 682 may well be intrusive).

The rate of decay ('weathering') may be affected by outside influences as well as by internal decomposition (Harden 1956, 333–5). Although in general potash glass is less stable than other categories, analysis is required before individual identifications can be made. It is almost certain that specific burial conditions have an effect on the rate of decay.

Glass containing over 50% lead oxide (see discussion below of translucent lead glasses) was used in north-west Europe, including England and Russia, from about the 9th century onwards for small objects such as finger rings, jewellery and gaming pieces (Bezborodov 1957, 168; Baumgartner & Krueger 1988, 161; Pritchard 1991, 172–3) and perhaps slightly later for pinheads (Egan & Pritchard 1991, 304, nos 1468–9, both from late 12th-century contexts) as well as for vessels. It is noticeably heavier, sometimes double the density of other glasses. All the examples of this catalogued below are yellow (as is a 13th- or early 14th-century stemmed drinking-glass fragment found at Nicholas Lane in London, MoL acc no A25270; cf. Baumgartner & Krueger 1988, 161–75 – no 135 is the London find, other similar items are from Germany and elsewhere on the Continent; Tyson 1996 draws together all the known finds of vessels of this glass in Britain).

NB: a fragment of yellow lead glass with a berry prunt, published by Baumgartner & Krueger (1988, 174, no 140; see also Tyson 1996, 2) as a find from the SWA81 site, does not correspond with the original record-card drawing of the item with the accession number in question. The accession details attributed to the previously published item are identical to those of No 782 in this catalogue (which is green and does correspond with the drawing on the card). Thanks to Rachel Tyson for pointing out this anomaly, the origin of which now appears impossible to identify.

The manufacture of vessels was originally a small offshoot of an industry mainly geared to producing coloured window glass. The 12th-century writer Theophilus, after describing the manufacture of window glass in some detail, discusses the making of vessel glass as a secondary activity (Dodwell 1986, 36–60; Charleston 1984, 30). A number of different techniques were used to decorate medieval glass vessels. Applied trails, which had been one of the main ornamental features of Frankish, Merovingian and Saxon glass, were obtained by fusing pieces of self-coloured (i.e., the same colour as the vessel) or differently-coloured glass wholly or partly to the surface of a vessel. The same method was used to attach handles. Many of the other techniques which made their appearance in Europe in the medieval period had been in use in the Middle East since the Roman period (Harden 1956, 338–43). 'Mould-blowing' is the process during which the paraison (the gather of glass on the end of the blowpipe which contains the first inflation) is blown into a plain or decorated mould to fashion its shape and/or to add decor-

ation. A further process is where a paraison is blown first into a high-relief mould, then removed and further freely inflated to produce low-relief decoration or a particular surface texture (Nos 669, 671, 710; cf. Baumgartner & Krueger 1988, 228–30; the term 'optic blown' was used by Harden and others to distinguish vessels made in this way from those that were mould-blown with a single inflation).

The relatively small amount of glass recovered from excavations in London is probably not indicative of the amount actually in use there in the medieval period. The scarcity of excavated glass may be due in some measure to the use of unstable potash glass, which is affected by weathering (leading sometimes to its total degradation), and also to the recycling of glass as cullet (i.e., to act as a nucleus around which new glass would form during manufacture) thus helping to eliminate impurities in the batch (Hodges 1976, 55). It is extremely difficult to assess the range of vessels in use or how common they were. A rare recorded price for 'London glassez' at 4 pence for six in 1444 is cited by Celoria in a discussion of vessels (1974, 17); whatever these items were – and assuming they were not spectacles or mirrors – this does not seem prohibitively expensive at the end of the medieval period. For the later period (*c.*1350–*c.*1450, ceramic phases 11 and 12) when one might expect the prunted beakers of Germany, which were made of more stable glass, to make their appearance in some numbers in London, the fragments recovered from excavations are not sufficient to make up a single vessel of the type. They become more common in the early post-medieval period. Vessel types that are common abroad are often little represented in, or completely absent from, the London material. Londoners may not, therefore, have been using glass quite as much as their Continental counterparts.

With the possible exception of Nos 643, 679 and 697, no medieval vessels from the sites considered here have been recognised to be earlier than the beginning of the 13th century. The number begins to increase from the mid- to late 13th century and the majority of the vessels belong to the period from the mid-14th century onwards. This could be explained in any one or all of three ways: activity in the later medieval period may have destroyed the fragile potash glass in earlier deposits; an improvement in glass recipes may have contributed to the survival of glass from the later period; and/or the increase in the number of fragments over the period may indeed reflect an increase in the use of glass in London from the 14th century onwards. Harden notes that glass was not common in the late 11th century and rarely appears in 12th-century manuscript illustrations (1968, 101).

The Church is likely to have made regular use of glass vessels long before they were available to medieval society at large. On the Continent, glass from the early medieval period has frequently been found in tombs and crypts and on the altars of churches (Harden 1968, *passim*). Parallels for the early examples Nos 643 and 679 have been found in churches in Germany (Baumgartner & Krueger 1988, 106–13), where they may have been used for holding relics, though the London finds considered here are not from sites of ecclesiastical buildings (some of the parallels cited for opaque white glasses Nos 689 and 694 are from such sites, but other parallels are not – the significance of these limited religious associations is as yet uncertain). When glass did become more frequent in London, it was being used for stemmed glasses, flasks and jugs (see below), lamps (Nos 344–55 above) and urinals (Nos 777–85). This increase may partly have come about in response to a demand created by familiarity with glass vessels from southern Europe and the East as a result of the Crusades.

The more resilient lead glasses Nos 657–60, Near Eastern fragment No 695 and (less certain to be from the same area of origin as the last) No 696 are dated to the late 13th/14th centuries; this corresponds with dating for similar exotic enamelled glass found in excavations elsewhere in England (Wenzel 1984).

Analysis of glass vessels (Cath Mortimer)

Quantitative analysis of 33 of the excavated glass vessel fragments shows a wide range of glass compositions. Both soda and potash were used as alkalis among the lightly tinted glasses. One high-lime glass may well be intrusive from the post-medieval period (No 683). Six pieces of lead glass (more accurately, lead-silica glasses) were analysed quantitatively, of which four are white, opacified with tin oxides (Nos 689, 692–4), and two are transparent yellow (Nos 659–60). Some pieces, the forms of which have strong typological associations, were found to have closely similar compositions. Qualitative analysis shows that enamel and in one case gold were used on fragments of Near Eastern type glass (Nos 695–6).

THE SAMPLE

The glass from the sites considered here represents a cross-section of many of the important compositional varieties found in medieval contexts in England. Amongst the fragments are examples of many different colours as well as of varying degrees of colour strength and opacity. Such features are the result of a combination of factors: primarily the raw materials, their supply and management, and the control of furnace atmosphere. By combining information relating to these factors, together with typological attributes, other visual traits and compositional information, much can be revealed about the systems that produced these objects and the range of techniques known to the glass workers of the period.

Some of the categories under consideration have strong Continental associations. It is often stated as a general theory that the fine transparent glass of this period was made in Italy or Spain, whereas the heavier darker glass originated in the glasshouses of northern Europe (including England). Products from these two regions are thought to have very different technical characteristics, notably reflecting the adoption of potash as a flux in northern Europe and the continued use of soda as the main alkali source in the Mediterranean region (Harden 1971, 104). However, recent publications have emphasised that 'virtually colourless glass was made in (north-western) Europe in the 13th and 14th centuries and probably earlier' (R Charleston in Biddle 1990, 934).

It is now important to characterise accurately (i.e., by chemical analysis) the compositions of medieval glasses found in Britain. Chemical analysis can identify the kinds of glass used for different vessels, identify colourants, opacifiers etc., and give an understanding of the degree of compositional variability within groups. Although little comparative chemical data is yet available, further research in this area may be stimulated by this kind of study.

METHODS

Two methods of chemical analysis were used, scanning electron microscopy (SEM) with an energy-dispersive X-ray analysis (EDX) attachment and non-destructive X-ray fluorescence analysis (XRF) – see Tables 11 and 12. For SEM/EDX work, small samples were detached from the edges of the artefacts, mounted in cold-setting resin and ground and polished. X-ray fluorescence was performed using a 3×5mm X-ray beam. This allowed some preliminary information to be gained about the kind of glasses concerned, but the analyses largely represent the situation at the surface only (i.e., with products of decay). Several of the pieces were covered in thick crusts of weathering products, and others are likely to have suffered considerable changes, even if this cannot be observed visually. Even on relatively clear areas

of glass, without a vacuum being applied (inadvisable for several of the pieces), it is not routinely possible to detect either silicon (whose oxide forms the major component of most glasses), or sodium (which is also likely to be present). Hence the XRF results presented here are qualitative only.

COLOURLESS AND LIGHT-COLOURED GLASSES

The results of XRF analysis of ten colourless or lightly tinted fragments (see Table 11) show that calcium, manganese and iron are frequently present, presumably at high levels (i.e., 1% or more). Lower (trace) levels of copper, zinc, titanium, potassium, nickel and lead were also often detected. From this it can be assumed that these glasses were made from a lime-containing sand and an alkali. Whether the latter is potash or soda cannot be determined from the XRF results, as sodium is not detectable under the conditions of the analysis. Lime may have been added, deliberately in some cases, to supplement the natural lime content of the sand used. Manganese is a powerful decolouriser, but other elements often give the glass a slight tint when present at low levels. Other elements may have been added deliberately to give colour. Iron, which was also

Table 11: X-ray fluorescence analysis of glass vessels

Catalogue number	Ceramic phase	Major peaks	Minor peaks	Trace, or possibly present	Comments
643	6–7	Mn Fe	Zn Ti Ca K	(?)Ni (?)Pb	decayed
644	9	Fe	Zn Ca Ti	Mn Ni Cu Pb (?)K	decayed
672	12	Ca Fe	Mn K	Ti Cu Pb (?)Ni	blue-green
673	12	Mn Fe Ca	K Cu Ti	(?)Zn Pb	very pale green
674	12	Ca Fe	K Mn	Ti Cu	blue-green
679	(?)6	Mn Fe	Cu Ti Ca	Zn K	green (decayed surface)
703	8–11	Mn	Fe Ca	Ni Cu Zn Pb Ti	heavily decayed
717 (wall)	(medieval)	Ca Mn Fe	–	Ti Cu Pb K	colourless body
717 (trail)		Fe Cu Ca	Mn Ni	Pb K	blue (enamel)
LBT86 acc no 9 (See p. 225, Col Pl 6B)	(medieval)	Ca Mn Fe	K	Ti Cu Zn	colourless body
LBT86 acc no 9 (trail)		Fe Ca	Cu Zn Mn	K Pb	blue (enamel: Cu% > Zn%)
LBT86 acc no 736 (See p. 230)	(medieval)	Ca Fe Mn	–	(?)Ti (?)Cu	pale green

Table 12: Glass compositions as determined by energy-dispersive X-ray analysis

Catalogue number	Ceramic phase	Colour	Na₂O	MgO	Al₂O₃	SiO₂	P₂O₅	S	Cl	CaO	K₂O	TiO₂	Cr₂O₃	MnO	Fe₂O₃	CuO	SnO₂	PbO	Total
Colourless and light-coloured glasses:																			
Potash glasses																			
655	10	pale green	2.4	6.5	1.5	50.9	3.5	nd	0.2	11.7	11.9	0.4	nd	0.9	0.9	nd	nd	nd	90.8
664	11	pale green	1.9	6.1	0.9	57.5	3.6	0.1	0.2	14.4	9.6	0.3	nd	1.1	0.7	nd	nd	nd	96.4
666	11	colourless	2.0	6.9	1.3	57.9	3.6	0.1	0.2	15.9	11.2	0.3	0.1	1.2	0.8	nd	nd	nd	101.5
668	11	pale green	2.3	6.7	1.6	55.2	3.5	0.1	0.2	17.2	12.2	3.0	0.1	1.5	1.0	nd	nd	nd	104.6
678	–	(residual) blue-green	0.5	3.4	1.3	58.5	3.4	nd	0.2	16.6	13.3	0.4	nd	1.0	0.8	nd	0.3	0.1	99.8
688	12	originally colourless	4.7	7.3	1.3	48.5	3.9	0.1	0.1	13.3	11.1	0.1	nd	1.1	1.3	nd	nd	nd	92.8
Soda glasses																			
648	11	colourless	12.1	3.9	1.0	67.4	0.4	0.1	0.4	10.8	2.1	0.1	0.1	1.0	0.5	nd	nd	nd	99.1
649	12	green (decayed surface)	11.4	3.9	1.1	70.9	0.4	0.1	0.4	9.9	2.5	nd	0.1	0.9	0.5	nd	nd	nd	102.1
651	12	colourless	11.3	4.0	1.0	67.0	0.4	0.1	0.3	10.9	1.9	0.2	nd	0.8	0.7	nd	nd	nd	98.6
652	12	green	13.1	4.2	0.9	71.9	0.5	0.1	0.4	6.5	3.4	nd	0.1	0.5	0.4	0.1	nd	nd	102.1
661	11	colourless	13.2	3.3	0.5	71.5	0.3	0.1	0.3	9.3	2.6	0.1	nd	0.3	0.3	nd	0.3	nd	102.1
662	11	pale green	10.2	4.5	1.2	66.1	0.3	nd	0.3	13.5	2.1	nd	0.1	0.5	0.5	nd	0.2	0.1	99.6
665	11	colourless	10.6	4.7	1.6	66.3	0.4	0.1	0.3	3.6	2.1	0.1	0.1	0.5	0.7	nd	nd	nd	99.1
670	12	pale green	12.2	2.4	0.5	69.6	nd	0.1	0.4	8.7	2.3	0.1	0.1	1.1	0.4	0.1	0.1	0.2	98.3
671	12	colourless	12.6	4.2	1.2	68.5	0.4	0.1	0.4	10.1	2.8	0.1	nd	1.1	0.7	nd	0.4	nd	102.6
675	12	colourless	11.9	3.1	1.1	70.8	0.5	0.1	0.3	10.8	2.5	nd	nd	0.9	0.4	nd	nd	nd	102.4
676	12	blue-green	11.5	4.4	1.3	68.2	0.3	0.1	0.3	9.7	2.3	0.1	nd	0.3	0.8	nd	nd	nd	99.3
677	12	colourless	10.6	4.1	1.2	69.0	0.4	0.1	0.3	12.0	2.2	nd	0.1	1.0	0.7	nd	0.4	nd	102.1
712	11	colourless	12.8	4.2	1.0	70.0	0.2	0.1	0.4	11.2	2.2	0.1	nd	0.9	0.5	nd	nd	nd	103.6
716	12	colourless	11.7	3.1	0.9	71.8	0.5	0.1	0.3	10.8	2.4	nd	nd	0.1	0.5	0.1	nd	nd	102.3
718	11	colourless	12.6	4.5	1.4	68.8	0.3	0.1	0.4	11.0	2.6	0.1	nd	0.8	0.8	0.1	nd	nd	103.6
LBT86 acc no 777		colourless	13.1	4.6	1.2	61.5	0.1	0.1	0.3	8.6	2.1	nd	nd	0.8	0.7	0.2	nd	0.2	93.5
(late medieval – see p. 223)																			
Lead glasses																			
659	9	yellow	0.2	0.2	0.2	27.6	nd	nd	nd	0.1	nd	0.1	nd	nd	0.3	nd	0.1	74.8	103.6
660	10	yellow	nd	nd	0.1	24.8	nd	0.5	0.1	nd	nd	nd	nd	nd	nd	0.3	nd	nd	68.1	93.9
[**Lime glass** NB: this item is almost certainly of post-medieval date, intrusive in the context to which it is assigned																			
682	11	green	2.9	3.1	2.6	60.3	2.6	0.1	0.4	21.8	2.8	0.3	nd	0.5	1.3	0.3	0.1	nd	99.1]

Categories based on colour and form:

No.	Cat	Description																Total
Opaque white glasses																		
689	12		10.0	2.4	0.5	nd	59.8	nd	nd	1.5	5.6	nd	0.2	nd	nd	4.5	12.5	97.0
692	11		8.2	2.2	0.1	0.1	51.5	nd	nd	1.2	5.4	0.4	nd	0.2	0.1	6.5	22.6	98.5
693	11+		9.9	2.2	0.7	0.3	60.8	0.1	0.1	1.5	7.0	0.3	1.0	0.2	0.2	4.6	12.2	101.1
694	12		9.5	2.5	0.7	nd	60.2	0.1	nd	1.6	7.7	0.3	0.8	0.5	nd	5.2	12.8	102.1
Urinals																		
778	9	blue (soda)	16.6	0.4	2.2	0.1	69.3	0.1	0.1	0.6	6.8	0.3	0.7	0.7	0.1	nd	0.1	98.0
782	9	pale green (potash)	2.6	7.1	1.9	4.8	53.6	nd	0.1	14.0	10.3	0.2	0.7	1.3	nd	nd	nd	97.1
785	11	blue-green (potash)	3.0	7.3	1.1	3.4	54.1	0.1	nd	10.8	16.5	0.2	1.1	0.7	nd	nd	nd	98.5
Multicoloured enamelled glasses																		
695	9	colourless wall	13.4	3.0	0.7	0.4	70.9	0.1	nd	2.9	6.0	0.4	1.2	0.4	0.1	0.1	nd	99.6
696	11	colourless wall	14.2	3.4	0.5	nd	67.2	0.1	0.1	2.5	9.3	0.4	1.0	0.3	nd	0.3	nd	99.5
696	11	blue enamel	14.0	1.3	1.7	0.7	62.0	0.2	nd	1.0	7.5	0.4	0.8	2.6	nd	nd	2.2	95.2

nd = not detected

consistently detected by XRF, can cause tinting on its own, depending on the state of reduction/oxidisation in the furnace.

QUANTITATIVE ANALYSIS AND MICROSCOPY RESULTS

Of 20 fragments of glass selected for a general review, five proved to be potash, 14 soda, and one, which has high levels of lime and low levels of both potash and soda, is probably intrusive from a later period. The different tints of these glasses (green, blue and brown) must be attributed to the presence of various trace elements, chiefly iron and manganese. Four of the vessel forms can be dated reasonably precisely. Number 666, a potash glass, is attributed to the late 14th century. Two fragments from early 15th-century flasks with fluted necks were shown to be fluxed with soda (No 651 and LBT86 site acc no 777 – not in catalogue). Both pieces are of similar composition despite the colour difference (the former is colourless and the latter retains a greenish tint despite some decay). The explanation must lie in the reducing/oxidising environments in which the glasses were made. Fourteenth-century potash glass jug No 655 is pale green (closely comparable jugs cited below from outside London have not been analysed).

Chronological ordering of these analyses by the ceramic phasing of the deposits illustrates an apparent shift in the alkali used, from potash to soda, during ceramic phases 11 and 12, i.e., the late 14th and early 15th centuries (Table 13). Further analyses would be helpful in confirming this pattern.

The compositions of the soda glasses appear to be quite similar to those for 12th- to 15th-century soda glass vessel material from France and Italy, in which up to 5% potash is common (Foy 1985; Veritá 1985). Close parallels for the potash glasses from London are found in window-glass material from York Minster (Bimson & Freestone 1985, table 2).

Number 682, with low levels of potash and soda and a particularly high lime content (c.22%), is probably intrusive from the 17th/18th century. Increasingly high levels of lime have, nevertheless, been noted in European

Table 13:   Colourless glasses as defined by principal alkali (oxide)

Ceramic phase	Potash	Soda	Lime*	Totals
10	1			1
11	3	5	1*	9
12	1	9		10
Totals	5	14	1*	20

* NB: This item is almost certainly intrusive from the post-medieval period

glass of the 14th and 15th centuries (Muller & Bochynek 1989). High-lime glass is found relatively frequently at English glasshouse sites of the medieval and late medieval periods, and in many types of utilitarian vessels (Kenyon 1967, 39; Crossley & Aberg 1972; Vose 1980, 202–3; Cable & Smedley 1987; Green & Hart 1987, table 1).

It is interesting to observe the relative degrees of decay amongst these pieces. On the whole, the potash glasses are much more decayed than the soda glasses, with surface deposits ranging from pitted and 'sugary' (e.g., No 678) to thick and crusty (No 688). However, some potash glasses are comparatively well preserved (e.g., urinal No 782).

TRANSLUCENT LEAD GLASSES

The surprisingly heavy weight of the lustrous fragments listed below initially brought them to attention as a group. EDX analyses on fragments Nos 659 and 660 show that there is up to 75% lead oxide in these glasses, and the balance is mainly silica. Other elements are found at only very low concentrations. Previous researchers have pointed out the difficulties of detecting trace elements when analysing high-lead glasses (e.g., Bimson & Freestone 1985, 216, 219; see Wedepohl et al. 1995 for analysis that suggests some of these vessels were made in Germany).

The analyses provide no evidence for deliberate addition of alkalis, probably because further fluxing materials are not necessary for glasses with such high concentrations of lead (see, e.g., Brill & Hoffman 1987; Henderson in Armstrong et al. 1991, 124 and fiche).

These glasses would have had a low softening point when heated, making them easily workable at low temperatures. Litharge and sand could have been added together in a 2:1 or 3:1 ratio to achieve these proportions.

There is plentiful evidence from all over Europe for glasses from the 9th to 15th centuries with lead-oxide contents of between 60% and 80%, which were used to manufacture accessories such as beads and rings (Ullrich 1989, 94–6; Brill & Hoffman 1987, 397; Baumgartner & Krueger 1988, 163–75; Henderson 1991; *idem* forthcoming). The colour of medieval lead glass varies from golden yellow to green. Both the glasses examined, Nos 659–60, are yellow (Col Pl 6C). It is thought that copper alloys had to be added to give a green colour (brass was used according to the Roman writer Heraclius – Merrifield 1967, 216; cf. Bayley 1987, 251). Varying the lead content may also have produced colour changes (Baumgartner & Krueger 1988, 162). Fragment No 657 is dated to the late 13th or early 14th century (as are many Continental examples; Baumgartner & Krueger 1988, 161ff). Lead-silica-potash glasses became very popular in the post-medieval period because of their brilliant appearance.

OPAQUE WHITE GLASSES

The close compositional similarity between the analysed pieces (Nos 689 and 692–4, Fig 184) which are attributed to late 14th/early 15th-century contexts means a single source can be suggested for all four. XRF analysis indicates that these unusual glasses have high levels of lead and tin. Quantitative analyses demonstrate that all four have a high lead content, with low trace element ('impurity') concentrations (see Table 11). The glasses were rendered opaque by the presence of tin oxide inclusions. Some of the larger inclusions were analysed and found to contain about 40% tin oxide. Control of the lead-oxide to tin-oxide ratio effectively allows control over the colour of the glass, a range from pure white to yellow being achievable (Freestone 1991, 275). The use of tin oxide for opacifying glass is thought to have been dominant in medieval Europe, succeeding Roman and earlier traditions using calcium antimonate (pyroantimonate) and other oxides of lime and antimony, and preceding the late and post-medieval use of lead arsenic and calcium phosphorous oxides (phosphoroxides) – Turner & Rooksby 1959; Rooksby 1962). Neither antimony nor arsenic was detected by XRF or by EDX in samples from the current items (fluorine is not detectable by EDX analysis).

Few other analyses have been carried out on opaque white glasses from the late medieval period, but the composition of a white enamel made in England in the late 15th century can be considered (Bimson & Freestone 1985, 217). Some of the chemical differences between the glasses catalogued here and this enamel may be due to differences in the technical requirements of the material used for making vessels and that for making enamels, which had to be more fluid than that for glass.

URINALS WITH STRONG TINTS

Urinal fragments Nos 778, 782 and 785 were analysed (see Table 12). They all have strong green or bluish tints but are otherwise transparent, without bubbles. Two of the analysed pieces used potash as the alkali and have moderately high amounts of lime. Their compositions are very much like those of English window glass from the 14th century (Bimson & Freestone 1985, 218). Number 778, however, is made of soda glass, with very little potash detected, and it has a decidedly blue tint.

GLASSES WITH APPLIED, MULTICOLOURED DECORATION

Two decorated fragments believed to be from the Islamic world, Nos 695 and 696, and other fragments were studied using EDX (Table 12). The wall glass in the two former fragments is transparent and nearly colourless, No 695 being particularly clear. They both show peaks for calcium, potassium, manganese, iron and strontium. The blue enamel on No 696 is a soda-lime-silica glass with the addition of 2.2% lead oxide, 0.7% copper oxide and traces of cobalt

and zinc. Despite the apparently standard soda glass composition, the enamel has an open texture, with many spherical pores. Under the microscope, there is a visual difference between the blues on the two fragments. In the former it is vesicular, in the latter solid. The blue area on No 695 seems also to contain lead, along with traces of copper and zinc, but it is more dense. Cobalt was not noted in this case; it may well have been present at trace levels not detectable by XRF but sufficient for colouring the glass. Other techniques might be employed to detect low levels of cobalt (e.g., ultra-violet fluorescence). Zinc-containing, cobalt-blue enamels have been observed elsewhere in parallels, and the enamel technology found in these forms has been used as evidence for a 'substantial input of Syrian technical knowledge' (Freestone 1991, 52). Copper was also detected in the dark blue, applied trails of No 717 and of LBT86 site acc no 9 (Col Pl 6B). The gold area on No 695 is probably pure (no silver was detected in this area).

SURFACE DETERIORATION

Several pieces of glass with high levels of lead and tin have a dark appearance, although others with similar compositions have decayed to a whitish colour. This difference is most probably due to environmental factors – soil moisture levels, acidity/alkalinity values etc. It suggests that a high-purity, high-lead composition may bring about instability, a fact noted by early producers of high-lead glasses (Vose 1980, 112–14).

CONCLUSIONS

The variation in the items sampled demonstrates the enormous compositional tolerance of glass. A wide range of oxide proportions was discovered in lightly tinted glasses, and an even wider range of compositions was used to make glasses of other kinds. Chemically, the opaque white pieces show fairly strong, within-group cohesion. Soda glasses dominate the analysed items as a whole, and potash glasses are also important components. If potash glasses were more or less exclusively produced in north-west Europe after the 11th/12th century (as claimed by, e.g., Bimson & Freestone 1987, 219), then examples with a high soda content might indicate re-use of glass scrap from earlier periods, or they may have originated from further abroad. Good quality soda glass was produced at this time in the Mediterranean world.

Glass vessels catalogue (Lynne Keys)

The advice of John Shepherd during extensive revision of the following sections on glass, including the catalogue groupings, is gratefully acknowledged; Rachel Tyson kindly provided help with a number of specific points.

Fragments from vessels of identifiable forms are grouped together (opaque white glass lids and (?)handle Nos 691–4, and multicoloured enamelled glasses Nos 695 and 696 are considered separately). Bases from unidentifiable vessels are listed separately (pushed-in bases and foot rings appear in flasks/bottles and also in drinking glasses), and other undiagnostic pieces are also grouped together (Nos 718–30).

For possible trends in the availability of glass and other tableware, see Table 1 (glass fragments that are possibly from the same vessel are counted together there as one item, and Nos 718–30 are omitted).

All items grouped together below are listed as far as possible by increasing major diameter, within ceramic phases.

FLASKS/BOTTLES

The term 'flask' is used here for vessels with narrow necks – at least as long as their bodies are wide – and lacking handles. They were probably used to hold wine and are frequently seen gracing tables in medieval illuminated manuscripts. Theophilus describes how the paraison was swung over the head of the glassblower to draw out the neck of a flask (Dodwell 1986, 44). Sometimes a decorative effect was obtained by twisting a mould-blown, ribbed

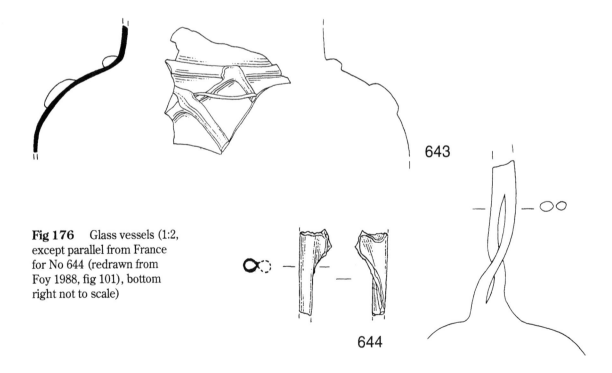

Fig 176 Glass vessels (1:2, except parallel from France for No 644 (redrawn from Foy 1988, fig 101), bottom right not to scale)

643

644

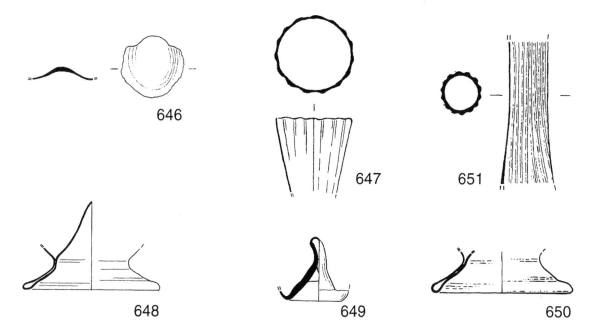

Fig 177   Glass bottles/flasks (1:2)

vessel (cf. Nos 647 and 651) during blowing to make a wrythen (spiral effect) neck. Bottles (including urinals – see Nos 777–85) can be defined as having flanged rims and widened bodies (body and base sherds on their own are impossible to differentiate from flasks etc.). Both categories usually have more or less globular bodies, though the terms are also appropriate for a range of more complicated decorative forms. The LBT86 site has produced more complete items than those catalogued below (see acc no 14 in Col Pl 5B).

643 WAT78 Acc No 492 (Context 4138) Ceramic Phase 6–7 Fig 176 Col Pl 5A
Fragment of neck and globular body d 205mm; applied horizontal and zigzag trails; decayed (Table 11).

For similar, Continental examples dated to the 12th and 13th centuries, see Baumgartner & Krueger (1988, 111–12, nos 56, 57).

644 SWA81 838 (2055) 9 Fig 176
Fragment of two joined neck tubes; decayed; original colour unknown (Table 11).

This is from a vessel of the kind known in Germany as a *Kuttrolf*, the neck of which consists of two or more small tubes wound around each other – see Fig 176 for a parallel found in Avignon, France, and dated to the 14th century (Foy 1988, 241, figs 101–2; cf. Baumgartner & Krueger 1988, 324, no 388, which was found in Nuremberg and dated to the (?)early 14th century). See Charleston (1991, 253) for a hint that the technical difficulties involved in manufacturing these vessels may have been mastered in England as well as on the Continent.

645 BC72 1796 (55) 11
Base d *c*.35mm; green.
Possibly from a flask or bottle.

646 BC72 2772 (83) 11 Fig 177
As preceding item, but decayed.

647 MIL72 112 (502A) 11 Fig 177
Fragment of neck and rim d 40mm; mould-blown fluting; colourless.
Numbers 648, 712 and minor body sherd acc no 145 (not catalogued here) may all be from the same vessel.
Compare No 651, LBT86 acc no 1421, and also vessels found in Southampton (R Charleston in Platt

& Coleman Smith 1975, 218, 220, fig 223, nos 1531, 1536, attributed to the late 15th/16th centuries, the former restored as a long-necked, globular-bodied vessel some 345mm in height); several similar necks have been found in London, e.g., MoL acc no 1946.21, the neck of which is 150mm in length.

648 MIL72 161 (502A) 11 Fig 177
Soda glass (Table 12); pushed-in, folded base; d 75mm; colourless.

See preceding item and cf. the following two items.

649 SWA81 839 (2117) 12 Fig 177
Soda glass (Table 12); pushed-in base fragment; d (?)50mm; green; decayed.

650 TL74 2689 (368) 12 Fig 177
Similar to preceding item; pushed-in, folded base fragment with mould-blown decoration; d 75mm; colourless.

Compare a vessel found in Southampton (R Charleston in Platt & Coleman Smith 1975, 218, 220, fig 223, no 1522).

651 TL74 1178 (275) 12 Fig 177
Soda glass (Table 12); neck fragment; h 78mm+; fluted; colourless.

See on No 647.

652 TL74 2690 (368) 12 Fig 178
Soda glass (Table 12); fragments of two major, joined parts of a vessel; base, probably from ring flask; green.

Compare a more complete example (MoL, ER 1118, acc no 25102, h 117mm, Fig 178 bottom, from a pit containing early 16th-century items). Six other examples of these vessels are known from London, four of them from datable contexts assigned to the late 14th to early 16th centuries (Shepherd in preparation). The form is also known in Islamic glass dated stratigraphically to the 12th/13th centuries (e.g., Pinder Wilson 1991, 161 for a Syrian vessel).

JUGS

(Vessels with globular bodies, a lip at the rim and a handle)

Jugs of glass would not have been common when versions in metal, ceramic and perhaps leather were more durable and probably cheaper. It is likely that they were used only in the wealthiest households, on special occasions. The small number of vessels

652

Fig 178 Glass ring flasks (drawing 1:2; photograph of MoL collection parallel – acc no 25102 – approx 1:2)

recovered is probably indicative of their relative rarity. Numbers 655 and 656 are almost identical in form and date to an example found in Southampton (R J Charleston in Platt & Coleman Smith 1975, 216–17, fig 221, no 1489) and to another found at Battle Abbey, Sussex, from a post-Dissolution phase (*idem* 1985, 143–4, fig 43, no 37, citing further analogous examples). The form is also known on the Continent (e.g., Ruempol & Van Dongen 1991, 44 – found in Germany).

653 SWA81 Acc No 376 (Context 2018) Ceramic Phase 9 Fig 179
Fragment of rim d *c*.60mm; pinched-out lip; two horizontal, applied threads; decayed.

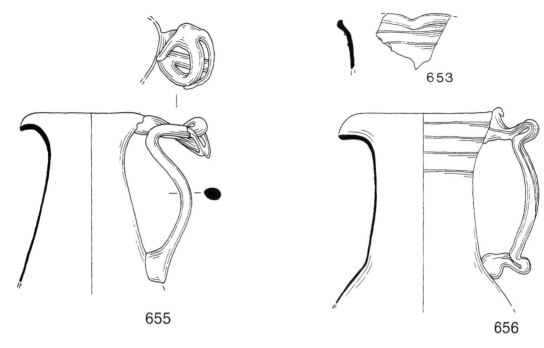

Fig 179 Glass jugs (1:2)

654 TL74 2469 (2532) 9
Decayed fragment with applied pinched and folded trail.
  Probably base of a handle as on following item.
655 POM79 222 (2048) 10 Fig 179
Potash glass (Table 12); rim d 74mm, and neck; rod handle folded and pinched together at top; pale green.
656 POM79 220 (2048) 10 Fig 179
Similar to preceding item; applied spiral trail around neck; handle pinched together at top and bottom; rim d 80mm.

DRINKING GLASSES

These are open vessels whose cups sometimes have a high foot or a stem; those in which the cup begins at the base are here referred to as beakers. Rim and side sherds are generally not diagnostic of the complete form. Beakers, used for drinking wine or beer at table, resemble a modern tumbler with the addition of a pinched foot ring or, less commonly, a raised pedestal foot. They are often decorated with ribs or

applied prunts or by 'optic blowing'. Beakers with rows of tiny prunts are known in Germany as *Nuppenbecher* (prunted beaker), describing their knobbly appearance (Baumgartner & Krueger 1988, 192–217; Henkes 1994, 44–5). On the Continent, prunted beakers were being manufactured by at least the end of the 13th century, while 'optic-blown' beakers are dated from the late 13th century onwards (Baumgartner & Krueger 1988, 229, nos 218–19). Given the small number of London fragments, all of which date from the mid-14th century onwards, it is difficult to assess when the different categories would have made their appearance over here, but the *Nuppenbecher* variety may have come to London soon after this. Beakers with larger prunts (known in Germany as *Krautstrunk* – 'cabbage stalk') were a late medieval development. The relatively small numbers of these found in London is in contrast to the large numbers excavated in Germany and the Low Countries. Near Eastern enamelled fragment No 695 (Col Pl 5C) is possibly a multicoloured drinking glass, but the origin of No 696, which is somewhat similar, is less certain. A

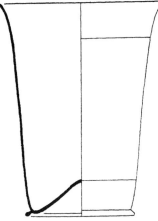 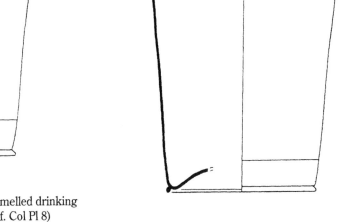

Fig 180   Outline forms of enamelled drinking
glasses from OST82 site (1:2 – cf. Col Pl 8)

group of fragmentary, enamelled beakers found
in a pit at the OST82 site are probably the most
remarkable finds of medieval glass in London
(Fig 180 and Col Pl 8; Clark 1983). See below
on Nos 695–6.

Drinking glasses are likely to have been used
only by wealthy households, for display and on
special occasions. Those listed below date from
the 14th century onwards. The stemmed form
(see Nos 659–60 and 678; cf. No 717) can be
very similar to that of a modern wine glass and
is frequently decorated with knops and other
embellishments. It is quite possible that a
number of those in green metal were made in
the Rhine/Meuse region, where remains of
furnaces and extensive waste heaps of similar
glasses have been excavated (Baumgartner &
Krueger 1988, 31–3); they may alternatively
have been made in southern France. See No
689 (Col Pl 7) for a possible drinking glass of
white metal, perhaps made in Venice. The
mould-blown and prunted beakers catalogued
below were possibly in use for a considerable
time before being discarded. Two prunted
beakers from medieval contexts at the LBT86
site are included in Col Pl 6A (acc nos 8 and
736, the latter from a deposit dated to after
1270). The Museum of London's established
collection includes five fragmentary stemmed

glasses of medieval date (acc nos 14701–3,
A25270 and A25286; the penultimate of these is
of lead glass, which may be compared with Nos
657–60). Besides the items listed below, a
fragment from the LBT86 site (acc no 9, found
in post-medieval debris – see Fig 181, top left,
and Col Pl 6B), with a rim d 85mm, a colourless
body and alternate pinched (colourless) and
smooth (blue) trails, is assigned to the 13th or
14th century by Baumgartner & Krueger (1988,
184, no 154).

657 TL74 Acc No 1456 (Context 1588) Ceramic
Phase 9 Fig 181 and Col Pl 6C
Body sherd of dark-yellow lead glass; d 50mm;
horizontal applied, pinched, self-coloured trail.

(?)From a beaker or stemmed glass.

Also noted by Tyson (1996, 2); cf. Baumgartner &
Krueger 1988, nos 132, 149–53.

658 SWA81 2132 (2030) 9 Fig 181 and Col Pl 6C
Body sherd of dark-yellow lead glass; d c.75–80mm;
applied, pinched, self-coloured trail, with tiny, dark-
blue fragment surviving.

(?)From a beaker or stemmed glass (cf. preceding
item). Also noted by Tyson (1996, 2).

659 TL74 2309 (2472) 9 Fig 181 and Col Pl 6C
Dark-yellow lead glass (Table 12); cup-base fragment
d 40mm+, with pontil mark.

(?)From a stemmed drinking glass.

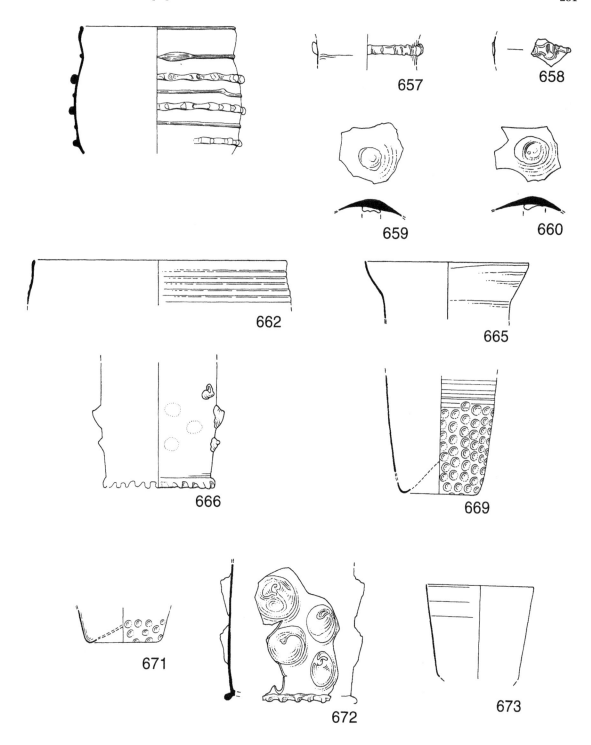

Fig 181 Glass drinking vessels (1:2); top left LBT86 acc no 9

660 TL74 1448 (1783) 10 Fig 181 and Col Pl 6C
Dark-yellow lead glass (Table 12); as preceding item.
  Also noted by Tyson (1996, 2–3, fig 3.4).

661 BC72 2920 (83A) 11
Soda glass (Table 12); fragment of side; colourless.

662 BC72 4378 (88) 11 Fig 181
Soda glass (Table 12); fragment of rim/side,
d c.137mm, with horizontal ribbing; pale green.

663 BC72 4375 (88) 11
Fragment of rim; d c.80mm; similar to preceding
item, but thinner and paler green.
  See following item.

664 BC72 4379 (88) 11
Potash glass (Table 12); fragment as preceding item
(possibly from the same vessel – not counted separately in Table 1).

665 MIL72 144 (502) 11 Fig 181
Soda glass (Table 12); fragments of flared rim;
d 90mm; colourless.

666 MIL72 143 (502) 11 Fig 181
Potash glass (Table 12); fragments of base, d 62mm,
and side; small, applied prunts and pinched foot ring;
colourless.
  Analysis shows that this is not from the same
vessel as the preceding item (from the same
deposit), despite the visual similarity of the
materials.

667 BC72 2771 (83) 11
Fragments of side and foot or rim; d 100mm; green.

668 BC72 4380 (88) 11
Potash glass (Table 12); rim fragment; d 130mm;
pale green.

669 TL74 1455 (2230) 10–12 Fig 181
Fragments; 'optic-blown' rows of roundels below
plain rim; d 60mm; colourless with small bubbles.

670 TL74 2675 (368) 12
Soda glass (Table 12); fragments of pushed-in base;
d 40mm; pale green.

671 SWA81 5015 (2082) 12 Fig 181
Soda glass (Table 12); two body fragments, one with
part of one shoulder or base; d 50mm; 'optic-blown'
decoration of rows of roundels; colourless.
  Similar to No 669.

672 TL74 149 (274) 12 Fig 181
Fragments of pinched base, d 65mm, and body with
applied prunts; blue-green with some bubbles (Table
11).

673 SWA81 842 (2082) 12 Fig 181
Fragment of rim and vertical side; d 60mm; very
pale green (Table 11).

674 SWA81 4698 (2112) 12 Fig 182
Base, d 60mm, with pinched foot ring; blue-green
(Table 11).
  Possibly from a prunted beaker, as No 672.

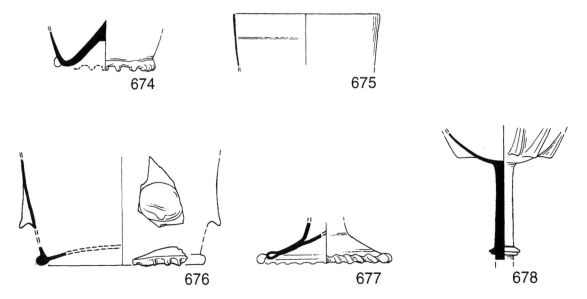

674   675

676   677   678

Fig 182   Glass drinking vessels (1:2)

675 SWA81 787 (2084) 12 Fig 182
Soda glass (Table 12); rim fragment; d 80mm; colourless.

676 SWA81 841 (2082) 12 Fig 182
Soda glass (Table 12); two fragments; one a base, d *c*.90mm, with pinched foot ring; the other from the side, d ?*c*.110mm, and with an applied prunt; blue-green.

677 TL74 405 (364) 12 Fig 182
Soda glass (Table 12); base fragments; d *c*.70mm; folded, pushed-in foot with applied, pinched trail; two concentric rings are formed by air trapped in the fold; colourless.

678 BIS82 290 (920) Residual in post-medieval context Fig 182
Potash glass (Table 12); incomplete stem with knop, and fragments of cup base, d *c*.70mm, with mould-blown ribs; blue-green, with white decayed areas.

A number of fragments from ribbed glasses of similar form are known, including ones excavated in Utrecht and elsewhere in the Netherlands (Isings & Wijnman 1977, 78–80, nos 1–8, fig 1; Henkes 1994, 28–30, 32, nos 4.1, 4.2, 4.7) and in France (Foy 1988, 207, fig 54; Foy & Sennequier 1989, 204ff) and others from Cologne and Nuremberg in Germany (Ruempol & Van Dongen 1991, 45; Kahsnitz & Brandl 1984, 41, fig 19).

FRAGMENTS OF VESSELS OF UNCERTAIN FORMS

The following fragments cannot be assigned with certainty to a particular form of vessel, though in several cases a tentative suggestion can be made. The first group are bases; other groups are defined according to the visual appearance of the glasses.

Bases

(From flasks/bottles, jugs or drinking glasses etc.)

679 GPO75 Acc No 5162 (Context 1398) Ceramic Phase (?)6 Fig 183
Pushed-in base; d *c*.80mm; with applied, self-coloured trails; decayed; originally green; (Table 11).

This was found together with 11th/mid-12th-century pottery.

Possibly from a flask (cf. Baumgartner & Krueger 1988, 111–12, nos 56–7).

680 WAT78 912 (3665) 9
Folded, pushed-in base fragment; d *c*.100mm; decayed.

681 WAT78 1441 (2040) 10+
Decayed base fragments; pontil mark.

Possibly from a urinal (not counted in Table 1).

682 TL74 2310 (2840) [11]
NB: *This item is probably intrusive from the post-medieval period*: lime glass (Table 12); fragment of folded, pushed-in base; d 160mm; green.

Probably from a horticultural cloche for forcing vegetables etc. (cf. Nöel Hume 1974, 62–7, fig 41 for 17th-century examples) or from a bowl (Kenyon 1967, 91, fig 13C for a post-medieval one). The rim form appears to be unknown in the medieval period, and the glass has the appearance (John Shepherd pers comm) as well as the chemical formula (see Table 12) of post-medieval glass.

(Not counted in Table 1.)

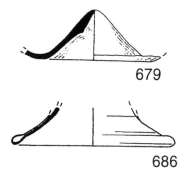

679

686

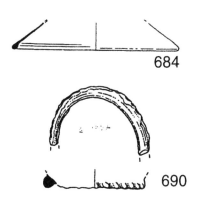

684

690

Fig 183   Glass vessels (1:2)

683 BC72 2873 (150) 11
Fragments of base or rim; d 80mm; surface decayed; light green.

684 BC72 1937 (79) 11 Fig 183
Fragment of simple splayed base or rim; d 88mm; green.

685 BC72 1797 (55) 11
Base fragment; d 90mm; green.
   Possibly from base of stemmed drinking glass, or from a flaring rim.

686 BC72 1935 (79) 11 Fig 183
Fragment of folded base; d 90mm; green.

687 BC72 2694 (79) 11
Fragment of base or rim, d 110mm; green.

688 TL74 527 (364) 12
Potash glass (Table 12); base fragment; d 75mm; folded, pushed-in base; decayed; originally colourless.

689 SWA81 5009 (2107) 12 Fig 184 and Col Pl 7
Opaque-white glass (Table 12); fragment of folded, pushed-in base with applied, pinched band; d 80mm.
   Compare MoL acc no A17160 for a similar item (also Fig 184 and Col Pl 7). A piece of rim, d *c*.90mm, probably from a cup (BA84 acc no 1910 – this fragment, from the site of Bermondsey Abbey in London, appears slightly greenish by transmitted light) may indicate the original form of No 689 (though as this parallel was found in a mid-16th-century context it may be from a later vessel). See Nos 691–4 for other opaque white glasses.

690 Watling House 19 (ER190A) Medieval context Fig 183
Basal ring with pinched band; d 55mm; decayed; (?)probably from a beaker.

Opaque white glasses (*lattimo*)
Geoff Egan

This intriguing group of late medieval (non-decayed) white glass vessels is so far apparently confined to London and its hinterland (Col Pl 7). With more than half a dozen medieval vessels now represented by finds from datable contexts, this distinctive glass was clearly available in the capital in some quantity fully a century prior to the well-known, prestigious Venetian glass imitations of porcelain and tin-glazed ceramic vessels (T H Clarke 1974,

who lists 14 surviving later vessels; cf. Tait 1979, 120–2, no 204; Vose 1980, 69; Charleston 1984, 46–8). The place of manufacture of the present items is open to question. Venice seems a strong contender (although surviving white glass is currently only known there from the late 15th century, the term *làtemo* has been traced in written records relating to Venetian glassmaking from 1420 onwards, and *attimium*, probably referring to white glass mosaic for churches, appears as early as 1360 – Zecchin 1987, 41, 36; 1989, 337–41, 390). Enamels on glasses of the so-called 'Aldrevandin group' virtually always include white (see on Nos 695–6 and Col Pl 8). An isolated find of much earlier medieval white glass from Saint Denis in France (Baumgartner & Krueger 1988, 80–1, no 92) is unlikely to mean that there was a continuing tradition over the intervening centuries. The term 'white glass' in many medieval documents regularly refers to *colourless* metal (e.g., Charleston 1991, 254).

The present category of white glass vessels is unlikely to have been as unusual as might have been implied by its recognition only at this relatively advanced stage of medieval glass studies. It remains to be seen whether the possible religious contexts for the parallels for Nos 689 and 694 are more pertinent than the upper-class milieux implied by some of the other findspots for items in the group, and also whether these fragments will be matched on the Continent. (The author is grateful to Hugh Tait and Ingeborg Krueger for discussion of this material.)

691 BC72 Acc No 2872 (Context 83A) Ceramic Phase 11 Fig 184
Fragments from rim, side and top of a lid; d at rim *c*.60mm; maximum d at base *c*.90mm; surface decayed and stained black.
   (These are the only fragments among those discovered in London with discolouration so marked as to make recognition of the original white colour difficult.)
   Compare a fragmentary lid which provides a complete profile apart from the top of the finial (MoL acc no A17246, Fig 184 and Col Pl 7; this and the parallel for white base No 689 were both found in King William Street, London, and were attributed to the 15th century, presumably from associated pottery.

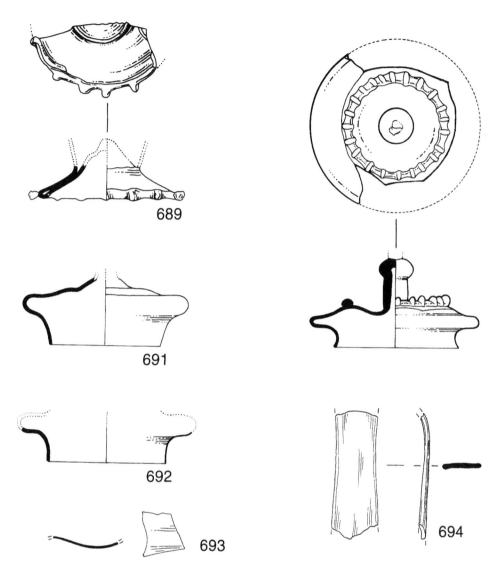

Fig 184 White glass vessels and lids (1:2; upper right MoL acc no A17160)

Although these two items were apparently accessioned by the Guildhall Museum some weeks apart, they may well have come from the same assemblage).

Relatively few lids of glass have been identified from the medieval period (see Baumgartner & Krueger 1988, 440–1, nos 555–6 for one of a different kind found in London, and Dorigato 1986, 20, for a *lattimo* chalice in Venice attributed to the 16th century, the lid of which is surmounted by a cross;

Kahsnitz & Brandl 1984, 203 illustrate another lid of translucent glass, found in Germany and attributed to *c*.1500). Dunning's discussion (1977) of a green glass lid, perhaps for a goblet, found at Portchester Castle in an early 16th-century context and thought to be a Venetian import, refers to several slightly later parallels for the form.

Fragments of four white glass lids apparently similar to No 691 are now known from three sites in London (see following two items). The form of the corresponding vessels remains uncertain; No 689 and its parallels (one of them presumably found together with a lid, as above) seem unlikely candidates in view of the apparent discrepancy in diameter measurements (though see Baumgartner & Krueger 1988, 398, no 499 for a later glass beaker with a lid).

Alternatively, the squatter, broader-lidded, late medieval glass cups of the form known in Germany as *Scheuer* might be considered. Possible handle No 694 below does not seem compatible with those on known glass of the *Scheuer* form (ibid. 381–5).

692 BC72 4766 (255) 11 Fig 184
Analysed (Table 12); similar to preceding item; fragment of plain, vertical rim, d 70mm, and shoulder from lid (no staining).

693 TL74 3366 (416) 11 Fig 184 and Col Pl 7
Fragment probably of a lid similar to preceding two items; analysed (Table 12) (no staining).

694 TL74 699 (364) 12 Fig 184 and Col Pl 7
Flat, pulled strip (?flattened tube); max w 24mm; l 67mm (Table 12).

Presumably a handle; form of vessel unknown.

A similar fragment found at the NEW81 site at Clerkenwell in a post-dissolution context (acc no 23) is more clearly a piece of flattened tubing; it could derive from the late medieval nunnery there.

Multicoloured enamelled glasses

Prestigious vessels of multicoloured, highly decorated glass from the Islamic world (Pinder Wilson 1991, 130–5) were brought to north-west Europe in the medieval period. Syria and possibly Egypt have been suggested as the most likely places of origin. Two fragments from a vessel similar to No 695 are also known in London, from the Pyx Chapel at Westminster (Ward Perkins 1940, 293, pl 84; MoL acc no B211). Thanks are due to Oliver Watson for providing useful comments on the following two catalogue items, including the possible interpretation of the legend on No 695, and for allowing them to be compared with material found in the Near East and now in the Victoria and Albert Museum's collection. For Near Eastern glass in general see Lamm 1929.

Enamelled glasses of the so-called Aldrevandin group were almost certainly developed in Venice in imitation of the earlier tradition men-

tioned above (the former term, 'Syro-Frankish', is now recognised to be a misnomer). Several enamellers (some of whom are known by name from inscriptions on the vessels they decorated, including *magister Aldrevandin* whose name has been used to describe this entire group of vessels) came to Venice from further east in the Byzantine Empire. For recent assessments of this category of glasses see Baumgartner & Krueger (1988, 126–60, indicating the wide area of Europe across which they have been found) and Tait (1991, 151–3).

An excavated assemblage of glasses of this category, found in a pit at the OST82 site (acc nos 128–34 and 155–60), dated to ceramic phase 9, includes at least six, and perhaps eight or more, beakers (see Col Pl 8; J Clark 1983; Baumgartner & Krueger 1988, nos 75–6, 86, 109). These particular vessels are not in the numbered catalogue as they were probably not a household group but shop stock (perhaps awaiting the addition of precious metal mounts at the time they were broken – judging from their having been discarded in the goldsmiths' quarter of London and by the discovery of a crucible with silver residues in the same pit). Also from the area north of Cheapside is a fragment of a glass bowl of the same category as these finds (Cook 1958a).

695 SWA81 Acc No 563 (Context 2051) Ceramic Phase 9 Fig 185 and Col Pl 5C
Fragment of side or body; colourless (Table 12), with externally painted decoration in gold, blue and red enamel; cursive Arabic script (*naskh*) in gold in a blue field – one complete letter and part of two others survive, possibly ... D(A or L) ... (??'the just'). Probably from a drinking glass (cf. Fig 185 right); presumably of Near Eastern origin.

Mentioned by Wenzel (1984, 17).

696 BWB83 3613 (355) 11
Colourless fragment of side or body, with traces of highly decayed red material, presumably applied externally, underneath and between patches of blue enamel.

The red material seems far too decayed to have been a genuine enamel, though it could have been some kind of substitute (see Table 12). The quality of decorated glass in the Islamic tradition of the preceding item deteriorated markedly in products from the late 14th century (Pinder Wilson 1991, 135).

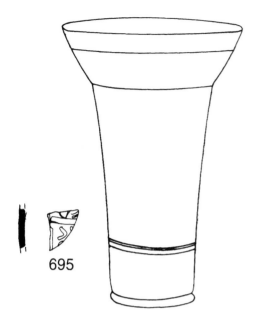

Fig 185 Near Eastern enamelled glass (1:2) with possible form of vessel (not to scale)

Nevertheless, Oliver Watson comments that the present fragment does not have the appearance of most pieces of known Near Eastern origin. Possibly an imitation from Mediterranean Europe (?cf. Baumgartner & Krueger 1988, 156–8, no 116).

Green/colourless and decayed glasses

697 BIG82 Acc No 3283 (Context 4339) Ceramic Phase 7
Decayed fragment with applied thread.

698 SWA81 5011 (2022) 9
Fragment of neck and shoulder; decayed; originally green.

699 BIG82 4017 (2424) 9+
Two rim fragments; decayed.

700 POM79 750 (2048) 10
Fragment; d 60mm; decayed.
  Possibly from a neck.

701 BC72 2745 (250) 10
Decayed fragment; blue (?roundel) applied onto main colourless piece; possibly from a base.

702 Watling House 31, 32 and 35 (ER190C) 10
Rim, d 86mm, and neck; decayed; (?)all from the same vessel.
  Possibly from a urinal, flask or bottle.

703 WAT78 92 (3680) 8–11 Fig 186 and Col Pl 5A
Hollow body of (?)short-tailed quadruped (head and most of legs missing); l 52mm+; applied to vessel (?)neck, which emerges from beneath the animal's belly; a small blob of glass on the back may indicate that there was once a rider; decayed (Table 11).
  The form is difficult to parallel. Though drinking glasses with the fore parts of pig-like animals are known on the Continent in the 16th century (e.g., Baumgartner & Krueger 1988, 399–404), the present fragment does not seem to be from a vessel like those illustrated.

704 BC72 807 (79) 11
Fragment from junction of neck, d 100mm, and shoulder; pale green.
  The form is difficult to parallel.

705 BC72 2696 (79) 11
Base fragment; pontil mark; green.
  Possibly from a urinal.

706 BC72 1936 (79) 11
Rim fragment; d 110mm; green.
  Possibly from a flask or urinal.

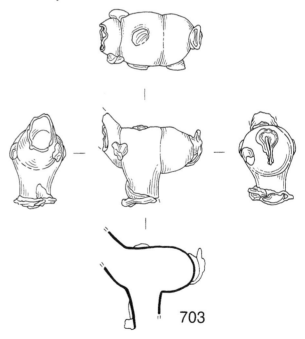

Fig 186 Glass vessel fragment in animal form (1:2)

707 BC72 2921 (83A) 11
Moulded side/body fragment with ribbing; colourless.

708 BC72 4374 (88) 11
Rim fragment; d *c*.60mm; decayed.
　Possibly from a jug.

709 BC72 4376 (88) 11
Rim fragment; d *c*.180mm; decayed.

710 BC72 4490 (150) 11
Side/body fragments; 'optic-blown' decoration of rows of roundels; green.

711 BC72 4494 (150) 11
Base or rim fragments; green.

712 MIL72 115 (502) 11
Soda glass (Table 12); globular side/body fragments with ribbing; d *c*.115mm; colourless.
　Possibly from a flask or bottle. See No 647.

713 BC72 4401 (89) 11

Flaring rim, d 100mm, and neck; green (partly decayed).

714 MIL72 117 (502) 11
Rim, d *c*.100mm, and base fragments; decayed.
　Possibly from a urinal.

715 RAG82 518 (1205) 12
Fragments, including rim, d 140–5mm; green.
　Possibly from a flask/urinal or lamp.

716 TL74 3635 (275) 12
Soda glass (Table 12); fragment of base and body, both d *c*.100mm; colourless.
　Possibly from a bottle.

717 AL74 695 (1247) Residual in post-medieval context
Fragment; colourless; applied dark blue, and pinched, self-coloured trails (Table 11).
　Possibly the base of a wide flat cup from a stemmed drinking glass.

Minor fragments

(Side/body fragments lacking salient features (not counted in Table 1))

No	Site	Acc No	Context	Ceramic phase	Colour	Comments
718	TL74	3634	416	11	colourless	soda glass (Table 12)
719	BC72	951	25	11	originally colourless or pale green	decayed
720	BC72	4488	150	11	pale green	
721	BC72	4489	150	11	pale green	fragments
722	BC72	1859	79	11	green	
723	BC72	2695	79	11	green	
724	BC72	4492	150	11	green	
725	TL74	2676	368	12	(?)originally colourless	d *c*.50mm; decayed; possibly from a flask or bottle
726	TL74	583	368	12	colourless	probably from same vessel as preceding item
727	TL74	2688	368	12	colourless	possibly from same vessel as preceding two items
728	RAG82	871	1205	12	colourless	
729	TL74	2674	368	12	green	
730	TL74	2673	368	12	dark green	

Leather vessels
Geoff Egan

The two items listed below are both from near the end of the period considered (another leather vessel from London, published in a discussion of medieval leather-working, is likely to be of 16th-century date; Cherry 1991b, 312, fig 157). This sparsity of recognised medieval leather vessels, or parts of them, is probably misleading, but there is apparently little direct evidence elsewhere in the form of excavated survivals. Ceramic vessels which imitate leather forms and their stitched seams (e.g.,

S Keene & M Biddle in Biddle 1990, 245, 247, fig 53a for a late Saxon pottery vessel found at Winchester) hint at what has been lost from the earlier part of the period dealt with here.

Shrinkage by an average of between 5% and 10% is to be expected after retrieval from the ground; leather vessels would almost certainly originally have been coated internally with pitch or a similar material to make them leakproof. No trace of any coating has been noted on the following excavated items.

COSTREL

731 BC72 Acc No 1996 (Context 83) Ceramic Phase 11 Fig 187
Main piece from costrel; calf/cattle leather (G Edwards); ends missing; presumably originally barrel-shaped; th of leather up to 7mm; l 200mm; the present h of *c*.195mm includes some increase from distortion (though shrinkage must also be taken into account); estd original d at ends approx 90mm (?perhaps originally oval rather than circular);

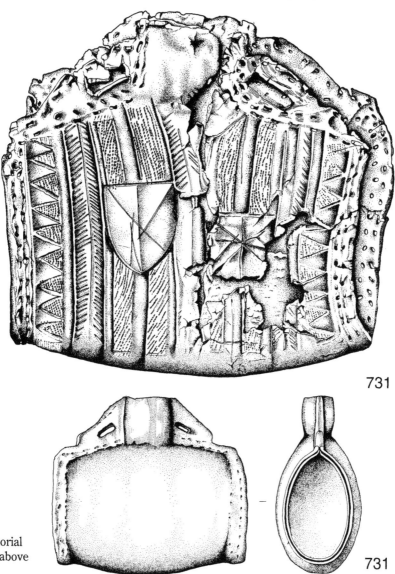

731

731

Fig 187 Armorial leather costrel (above 1:2; below 1:4)

double lines of stitching holes around ends, top and neck, with two relatively unworn slots for attachment to straps; moulded, raised, vertical ribs with scraped, opposed oblique hatching to each side of a central line; running zigzags, the triangular fields in the strip-like end panels being alternately plain and punched with a five-pronged tool; in each of two main central panels are incised vertical lines and a shield – the wider, alternate bands here having punched fields similar to those in the triangles; the shields are roughly incised, that to the right with radiating lines to form eight triangular fields (i.e., *gyronny of eight*), and that on the left vertically (*per pale*) and also with (?)random, oblique lines; the capacity appears to be roughly one quart.

Probably designed to be used mainly while travelling rather than in the home. The arms are probably simple, non-specific decoration, like those which sometimes appear on leather knife scabbards (cf. T Wilmott in Cowgill et al. 1987, 45–57). The five-pronged tool used on the costrel has no exact parallel among contemporary decoration on scabbards from the sites considered for this series of volumes, though scabbard no 403 from a context attributed to ceramic phase 9 is also punched with a five-pronged implement (Cowgill et al. 1987, 44, 130).

Compare Roach Smith 1854 (133, no 660) for a plainer, London leather costrel of uncertain date and Ward Perkins 1940 (195, pl 49) for decorated ones (the one illustrated by the latter is also discussed in Baker 1921, 55–7, fig 22).

VESSEL BASE

732 BC72 2503 (83) 11
Probably cattle leather (G Edwards); incomplete circle; d *c.*155mm; double row of stitching around angled perimeter; incised saltire cross of paired double lines on underside.
   Probably from a flagon or bottle.

Lead plugs

(Repairs for ceramic vessels)

These are makeshift repairs using melted lead to fill holes in damaged ceramic vessels, so as to overlap the broken edges. Some plugs retain pieces of the pottery to which they were attached. Most plugs are roughly circular and very heavy relative to the ceramic they replaced. Some are extremely clumsy, but the textile imprints on Nos 739 and 744 imply at least a basic awareness of one of the techniques used by those working in the pewter/lead crafts (see on lid No 529, cf. Fig 153, bottom right). Comments on the imprints are by Hero Granger Taylor. Compare examples from Northampton (Oakley 1979, 265–6, nos 7–9).

A plug of lead used as a bung-hole stopper in a Coarse Border ware cistern was found at the SUN86 site (acc no 1706, probably 14th century). The following items can be differentiated from that kind of stopper by their perimeter grooves for the broken edges of the pottery.

Ceramic identifications are by Julie Edwards.

733 SWA81 Acc No 1184 (Context 2157) Ceramic Phase 6 Fig 188
Neatly rounded on one face, *c.*20×*c.*18mm; the lead has dribbled in a series of radiating runnels on the other side; retains tiny fragments of vessel of unidentified reddish fabric.

734 SWA81 5097 (2187) 6
32×28mm.

735 BWB83 3549 (354) 7
*c.*25×22mm.

736 BWB83 3301 (362) 9
*c.*20×20mm; retains small traces of vessel of indeterminate fabric.

737 SWA81 2657 (2256) 9
*c.*31×*c.*25mm; retains pieces of vessel of unidentified greyish fabric.

738 BWB83 7054 (260) 9
32×27mm; retains fragments of vessel of unidentified fabric.

739 BWB83 5407 (285) 9 Fig 188
*c.*52×47mm; weighs some 144gms; imprint of a textile (*c.*10 threads per 10mm in one direction, the other has almost a corded appearance; cf. No 744) on external face, against which the repair was poured or built up.

740 BWB83 7053 (356) 11
*c.*35×35mm; retains fragments possibly of London-type ware vessel.

741 BWB83 3527 (387) 11 Fig 188
*c.*48×35mm; max th 23mm; compared with 6mm for
the surviving ceramic, which is early Surrey ware
(manufactured *c.*1050–*c.*1150; the vessel may possibly have been in use in the repaired state at a
somewhat later date, or it may be residual in the
context).

742 BWB83 7055 (341) 11 Fig 188
51×50mm; punched marks from sharp, three-cor-
nered object, perhaps the point of a knife, on
smoother (?internal) side; th of presumed vessel
*c.*8mm.

Possibly not from a ceramic vessel.

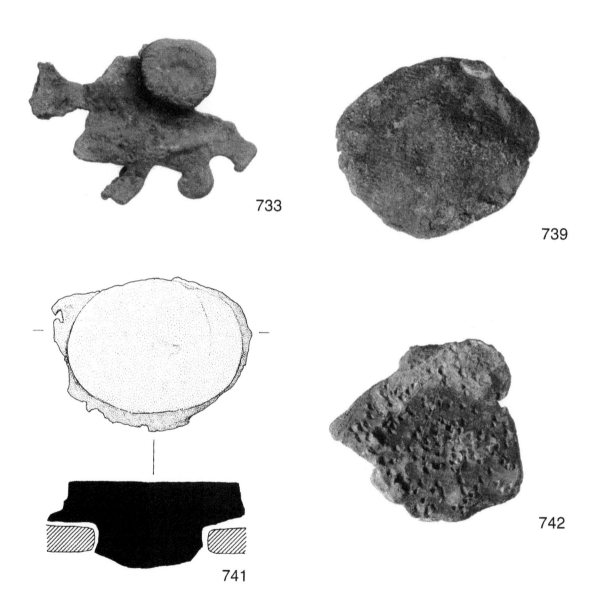

Fig 188   Lead repair plugs for ceramic vessels (1:1); No 739 has a textile imprint

743 BWB83 7061 (314) 12
*c.*57×*c.*30mm, with runnels; retains fragments of
Surrey White ware (possibly Kingston ware or
Coarse Border ware) vessel.

744 SWA81 3949 (Unstratified)
Incomplete; *c.*26mm+ × *c.*23mm; imprint of a textile
(*c.*8 threads per 10mm in one direction, the other is
unclear – possibly a twill; cf. No 739) probably on
internal face; other face has been pared or otherwise
smoothed; retains fragment of vessel of unidentified
greyish fabric.

Taps

(For metal vessels, cisterns etc.)

These are listed here because of their
occasional use on elaborate copper-alloy *aquamanili* (e.g., Von Falke & Meyer 1935, 217–23,
nos 539, 542, 544, 546, 548, 554, 556–8, all these
vessels being dated to the 14th century, though
their taps could presumably include later
replacements). The excavated taps listed below
may include some plumbing fixtures (see
Duncan & Moorhouse 1987, 132–3, nos 187.1
and 187.2, 188, fig 69 for more certain examples
of this from Yorkshire). Taps for coopered
vessels may have been of wood (none was
recovered from the sites considered for this
volume).

Copper alloy

745 BC72 Acc No 2864 (Context 150) Ceramic
Phase 11 Fig 189 and Col Pl 3A
38×31mm; made in two parts: oval handle, and shaft
with transverse hole; the handle has animal-headed
terminals with widely gaping jaws forming triangular
flanges, one of which is engraved to indicate the
mouth (omitted on the other); the shaft appears to
consist of a narrow, central rod with the ends
expanded to the full width (the lower one having the
hole), with three disc-like, transverse flanges of
similar width between, and the gaps have apparently
been infilled by the subsequent casting of the handle
(see X-ray photograph).

The seemingly extraordinary and cumbersome
method of manufacture has no obvious advantage of
function or strength over a one-piece casting (though
the conceit of the animal heads is perhaps slightly
enhanced by the impression of teeth where the disc
flanges join the heads).

A very similar item found in Hampshire has four
transverse flanges, but there is an oval loop at the
opposite end from the handle, with a series of small
projections on its perimeter (Rowland 1994), which
would seem to make use in a simple tap somewhat
questionable.

746 BWB83 198 (305) [11] Fig 189 (probably
intrusive?)
W 35mm; h 73mm; moulded finial somewhat resem-
bling a curtailed fleur-de-lis, with incompletely
stamped black letter P or Y at centre; the lower half
of the tapered, hollow case (below the hole to control
the passage of liquid) has been plugged with lead,
presumably to provide added weight against a significant anticipated flow; d at hole *c.*19mm; there are
signs of wear on one side of the hole. Probably an
import.

The stamp, presumably a maker's mark rather
than one of ownership (it seems unlikely to be a very
early tavern property mark) suggests a background
of guild quality control for these precision objects
(cf. Baart et al. 1977, 352–6, nos 657–68, marked
taps from deposits in Amsterdam attributed to the
16th and 17th centuries). No other marked tap that
is definitely of a date as early as that suggested for
the present example has been traced in Britain (in
view of the later parallels indicated below it may be
intrusive in the late medieval context to which it is
assigned). Drack cites several examples on the
Continent in a survey of the known examples of this
particular form (1997, group D; no 30 from Zurich in
Switzerland has a similar stamp).

Very similar taps, together with their spigots,
which are plain apart from the octagonal tap housing
and a spur near the mouth, have been found at
Butler's Wharf in London (private collection), in
Salisbury (see Fig 189 – Salisbury and South Wiltshire Museum acc no 82/63, published in Shortt
1973, 35, no 82), at Nieuwlande in the Netherlands
(Bos et al. 1987, 48, no 261 – apparently pre-1530),
Lübeck in Germany (Cherry 1980, 175, fig 57). Drack
(1997, 70, 75–6, fig 37, nos 28–32) cites at least nine
further examples from Denmark, Germany, Switzerland (including two with a suggested date of *c.*1460
and another from Geneva from a 16th-century context) and Hungary, showing that these objects occur
from Britain to Central Europe; a spigot of a similar
kind, dated to *c.*1500, was excavated in Exeter (A R
Goodall in Allan 1984, 344–5, fig 193, no 180).

See Micklethwaite 1892 (7–8, fig 6) for another
tap, found at Westminster Abbey and thought to be

Fig 189   Taps (1:1) with X-ray of No 745 and, top left, parallel from Salisbury for No 746 (Salisbury and South Wiltshire Museum acc no 82/63)

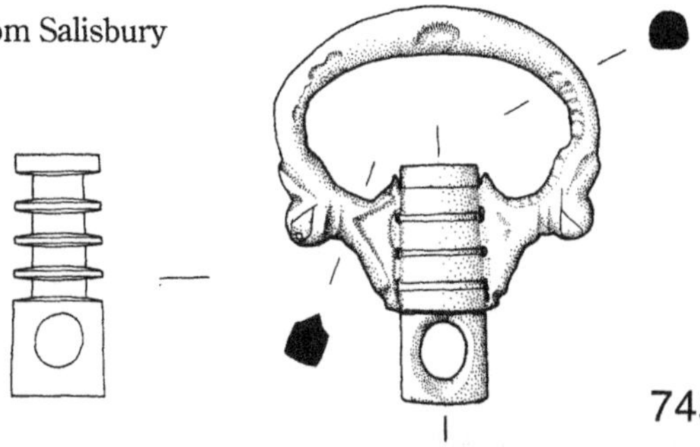

745

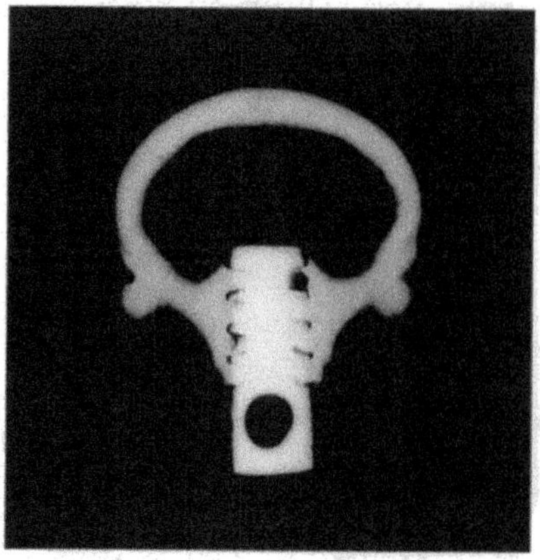

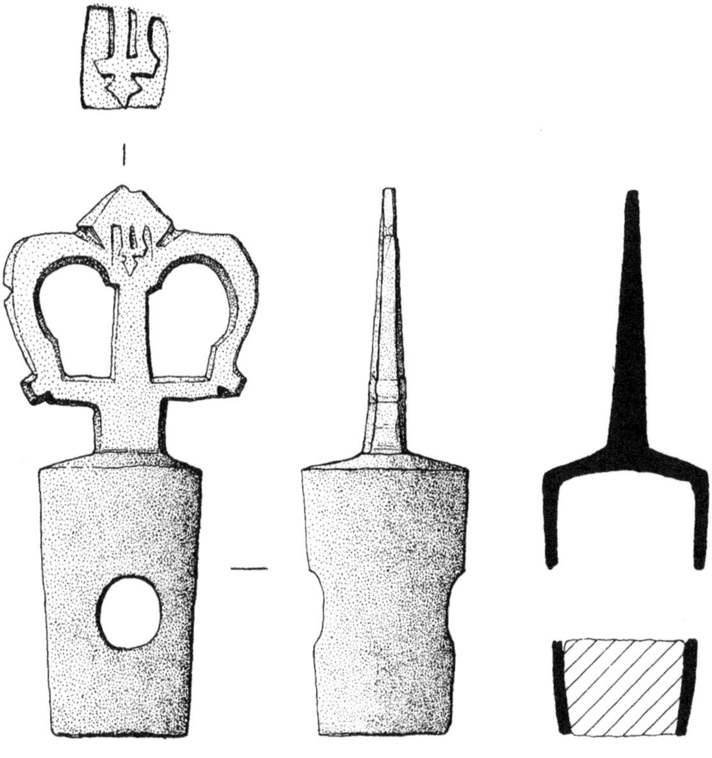

746

from a water-filtering system; cf. also MoL acc nos 8069–72. Salzman lists medieval references to several water-system taps, most of which seem to have been large and quite decorative (1952, 275–6).

Keys for turning pegs with square ends

Copper alloy

The objects to which these items relate have not been identified for certain. The keys may perhaps be too robust and too elaborate to have been used for tightening the square-ended bone keys of stringed musical instruments (though something must have been used and no other tool for this purpose has been identified – see Nos 939–44, all of which have ends too small for Nos 747–8). There appear to be no recognised spigots or other metal items of medieval date with corresponding ends (Marian Campbell and Anthony North pers comm). Tap spigots, nevertheless, at this stage seem possible candidates (?cf. 'a key called *hollow key* for the lock of the water conduit within the privy Palace' at Westminster in 1443 – Salzman 1952, 302; though this was perhaps larger than Nos 747–8, it may have been a similar object).

The two examples described below have triple collars below the ornate handles, and rectangular apertures (internal dimensions are given in brackets) in the expanded ends.

747 BWB83 Acc No 739 (Context 306) Ceramic Phase 11 Fig 190
L 47mm (7×5mm); handle has drooping foliate terminals with a central diamond knop pierced for attachment to a key chain etc.
A similar item comes from the SLH93 site (acc no 3, unstratified).

748 BWB83 4429 (Unstratified) Fig 190
L 54mm (9.5×6mm); handle is an openwork quatrefoil with a stubby cusp at each spandrel, and a central hole connecting with those above and below, this channel being echoed by shallow grooves to each side on both faces.

Spoons

While some medieval spoon bowls are as deep as those in common use today, the flatness of a few of them (e.g., Nos 750, 766–7) raises the question of what precisely these were used for, since this profile cannot be attributed to distortion in every case. Even a perfectly flat bowl would be adequate for use at the table for

Fig 190   Peg Keys (1:1)

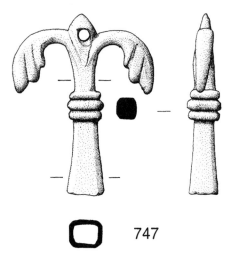

747

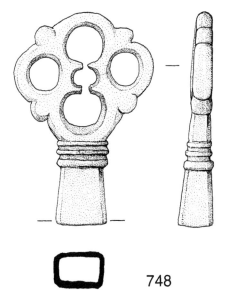

748

mushy foods and for salt (the special significance of which, at least in late medieval etiquette, might have led to the use of such utensils). The 12th/13th-century highly decorated spoons discussed below, like Nos 756 (?)and 759 could perhaps have been for salt; see below, and compare decorated lead/tin salt containers like Nos 537–8 (both from deposits attributed to the late 14th century).

None of the spoons below appears, from testing with a magnet, to have the stem reinforced by an internal iron rod, though this is known in some other examples from the medieval period (Ward Perkins 1940, 129; Hornsby et al. 1989, 54, no 17c).

Eleven lead/tin spoons in the Coventry Museums collection (the only large published medieval group outside London that was found in the field), along with two examples of copper alloy in the same collection attributed to the 13th/14th centuries, are attributed to the same chronological span as those listed below. The only two spoons of comparable date excavated at Winchester are of lead/tin (T Brisbane in Biddle 1990, 833, nos 2625–6). The survey of medieval spoons in the London Museum in 1940, in contrast, covered fewer pewter than copper-alloy ('latten') examples (Ward Perkins 1940, 129; cf. *idem* 1939; see also Hornsby et al. 1989, 54, no 17d). The recent London finds and the Coventry collection indicate that this prominence for copper alloy may be misleading if it is taken to be representative for the period. The absence of copper-alloy spoons from the recent London excavations is also more consistent with the impression over the years from casual finds in the city that these were far less common relative to spoons of lead/tin than even the Coventry figures might suggest (MoL acc no 84.379, a medieval copper-alloy spoon found in spoil deriving from the Billingsgate site, is an exception; a 'bronze spoon' among the medieval finds from the TL74 site – M Rhodes in Milne & Milne 1982, 90 – could not be identified for the present survey). This pattern raises a potential problem with the attribution of tin-coated 'brass' spoons of the 14th and 15th centuries in the Boymans-Van Beuningen collection, Rotterdam, to English manufacture (Ruempol & Van Dongen 1991, 48, 51, 93–4).

A more surprising absence from the listed London lead/tin spoons is any early (12th/13th century) decorated bowl, though see stems Nos 756 and 759 among the listed items and Fig 194 (the human figure finial, defective on the example on the left, is paralleled by several others found in London, like the one on the right from the TEX88 site – acc nos 1978–9 – arguably both men and women are depicted). A finial has also been found in Novgorod in Russia (Thompson 1967, 10 – misidentified in the text as a figure of a pagan god). A number of early spoons of this general category with decorated bowls have now been recovered in London, notably at the VRY89 site, which produced over thirty – probably about as many as the total of all the others now known put together. Similar examples have been found widely in north-west Europe (e.g., at Winchester – T Brisbane in Biddle 1990, 833–4, no 2625, fig 248; at Droitwich – Hurst 1992, no 1, fig 118; at York – Bayley 1992, 780, no 4279, fig 340, a handle, not identified in text; at Beverley – B Spencer in Evans & Tomlinson 1992, 143, 145–6, no 174, fig 77, pl 25, with references to others; at Saint Denis in France – Meyer & Wyss 1985, 101–2, fig 72, no 2; at Bruges in Belgium – Vandenberghe 1988, 175, 177, fig 153; at Bergen in Norway – Herteig 1969, 66; at Lund in Sweden – Mårtensson & Wahlöo 1970, 23, no 25; Mårtensson 1976, 337–8; Hanse 2 1989, 470, no 22.4). A stone mould for similar spoons has been found in Winchester and another, with a design not known in England, is from Magdeburg in Germany (Nickel 1964, 43–4, pl 65 – Ingeborg Krueger kindly provided these references through Judy Stevenson). A recent discussion draws together the twelve known examples from Scandinavia (Horne Fuglesang 1991). These spoons have sometimes been interpreted as having some religious connection ('christening spoons' etc.), from the supposed symbolism of designs with a cross (one of the Vintry examples may depict hands to the sides – i.e., a person wearing some kind of robe with a cross?) or fish on several examples. However, the relatively large numbers that are now known from secular sites suggest that these are most likely to have been domestic utensils (not one, at least in England, appears to be from an indisputable ecclesiastical context, and several include fish motifs, sometimes together with others, for which there is no immediately obvious religious interpretation, as in Fig 194). The significance, if any, of the recurrent motifs has yet to be established. The domestic interpretation is likely to hold true of No 759, despite its religious motto. The suggestion above that these spoons may have been for salt is not influenced one way or the other by the findspot of one of the parallels in the salt-producing town of Droitwich.

There is still no transitional form of spoon bowl (as suggested by Ward Perkins 1940, 128) between the 13th-century pointed ('leaf-shaped') bowl of No 750 and the later, rounder, 'fig-shaped' forms, and it now looks as if the different shapes may well have had separate origins.

The range of surviving knops among the recent finds might be taken to confirm the

established general pattern of domestic spoons becoming more decorative towards the end of the medieval period (among those listed only the ball form is represented prior to the late 14th century; cf. Ward Perkins 1940, 129, citing a reference from 1351 to an early 'acorn' knop), but other London finds of the earlier, highly decorated spoons include several elaborate knops (cf. Fig 194). Two 'diamond' knops (Nos 770 and 775) suggest that the rarity once claimed for this form in pewter (ibid. 129–30) may be open to question. The number of survivals is still relatively small and, as with much else relating to medieval spoons, it is probably too early to draw a firm conclusion.

The probable owners' marks on Nos 769 and 773 are not easily paralleled among other published excavated spoons of medieval date, though they may be compared with marks on some of the metal vessels in this volume.

Almost exactly one half of the listed spoons are broken at the junction of the bowl and stem (No 772 has arguably been broken twice here), showing that this was usually the weakest point. Breakage between stem and bowl may

Fig 191 Spoon dimensions and terminology (overall length A, length of stem B, dimensions of bowl C×D)

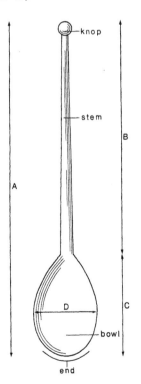

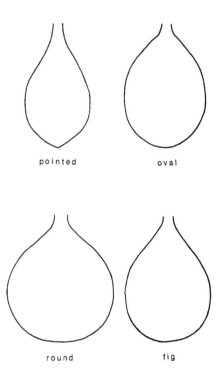

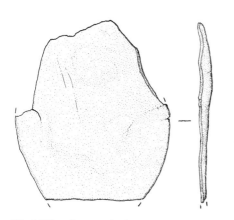

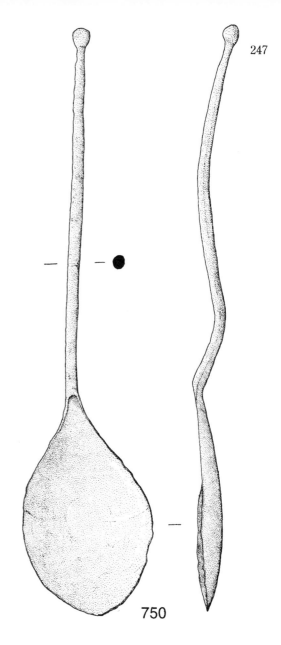

749

750

Fig 192 Spoons (1:1)

well have occasioned the discarding of a large proportion of the spoons included below.

All the 32 medieval spoons recovered at the sites considered in this survey are of lead/tin (this includes four fragmentary bowls not included in the list – one from a ceramic phase 9 deposit and three from ceramic phase 12 deposits). Only three of the listed items, Nos 750 and 769–70, seem to have been discarded in a complete state. Copper alloy, bone and wood are unrepresented, as are the much rarer iron ladles (though copper alloy and wood are present among excavated post-medieval spoons from London). For AML analyses of listed items see Table 8.

Lead/tin

A pewter spoon with a pointed oval bowl, acorn knop and animal head at the base of the stem, dated to *c.*1300, has recently been published as the earliest known English spoon (i.e., post-Roman and of pewter; A North in Alexander & Binski 1987, 281, no 210). This claim cannot be challenged by any of the spoons listed below, though fragment No 749 may be of comparable date, and some of the parallels from the VRY site cited above are probably from the 12th century or even earlier. No 750, which was not deposited until at least the late 13th century, comes closest in bowl form.

See Homer 1991 (66, fig 21) for a part of a stone mould for casting spoons, found in London and attributed to the 15th century (perhaps of slightly later date than the period covered in this present book).

Bowls have round ends unless otherwise stated. The order of dimensions, A–D (Fig 191) follows Muldoon & Brownsword (nd, 9); where only a bowl survives dimensions are given in the order C×D. Where a bowl's original profile seems to be definable, this is stated; the majority are too distorted.

749 SWA81 Acc No 1126 (Context 2130) Ceramic Phase 7 Fig 192
Pewter (AML, Table 8); fragmentary bowl; parts cut off; *c.*47×42mm.

750 SWA81 437 (2018) 9 Fig 192
Pewter (AML, Table 8); l 158mm; 100mm;
59×36mm; ball knop; round-section stem is slightly
distorted; flattish, pointed bowl.

751 SWA81 1976 (2050) 9
Pewter (AML, Table 8); round-section stem is fragmentary; pointed bowl is distorted; l 93mm+;
63×42mm.

752 BWB83 7052 (285) 9
Distorted bowl fragment, c.37×42mm.

753 BWB83 4156 (219) 9 Fig 193
Pewter (AML, Table 8); fragment of deep bowl
c.58×41mm.

753

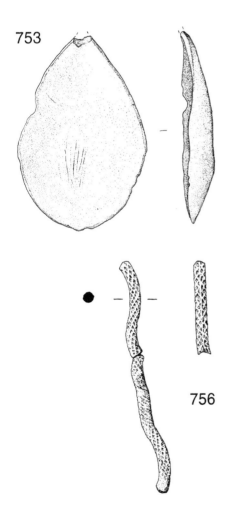

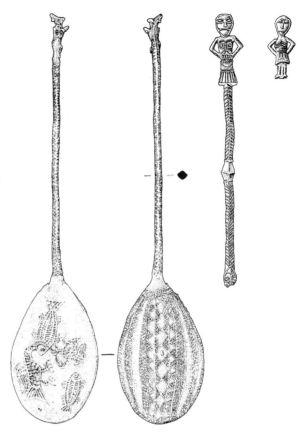

Fig 194 Decorated spoons (left, MoL acc no
89.95/1, reduced, length 154mm; middle and right,
TEX88 acc nos 1978–9; (1:1))

756

Fig 193 Spoons (1:1)

754 BWB83 4551 (274) 9
Pewter (AML, Table 8); 35mm; 59×48mm; incomplete bowl and part of hexagonal-section stem.

755 SWA81 659 (2061) 9
Pewter (AML, Table 8); stem fragment; round section; ball knop; l 64mm+.

756 SWA81 2592 (2062) 9 Fig 193
Pewter (AML, Table 8); stem fragment; broken off
at both ends; round section; l 62mm; oblique cross-
hatching over entire surface.

Identifiable as part of a spoon by comparison with
more complete examples (see Fig 194 for one found
in spoil from the TEX88 site, MoL acc no 89.95/1

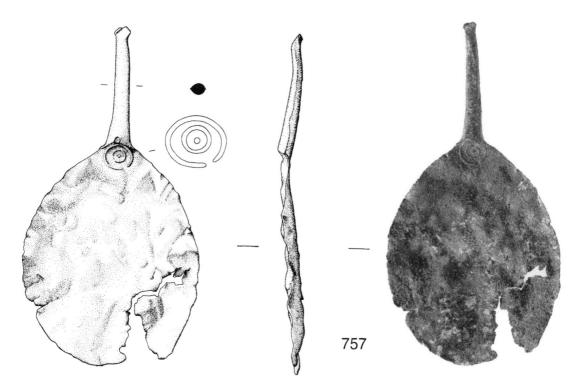

757

Fig 195 Spoon with 'mark' (1:1; detail 2:1)

and others excavated at the same site – acc nos 1978–9; cf. another complete, highly decorated spoon which came from spoil deriving from the Billingsgate site – BM MLA acc no 1984,5–5,3). See fuller discussion of this series of spoons above.

757 BWB83 1405 (108) 10 Fig 195
Pewter (AML, Table 8); l 89mm; 31mm; 58×47mm; round-section stem; damaged oval bowl; cast motif of two concentric circles around central dot.

This, the only spoon with a possible maker's mark from a medieval context at the recent London excavations, would also be the first recorded example on which such a device is integrally cast rather than struck. A spoon found in Salisbury (no context dating) has a very similar but apparently scratched mark in the same position (Egan forthcoming b). The significance of the mark (if such it is) on No 757 is uncertain. Presuming the context to be accurately dated, the find would foreshadow by a century and a half the stamped makers' marks required by Statute 19 Hen VII c6 of 1503, which became part of the quality control system of the Pewterers' Guild (the first ordinances, in 1348, perhaps significantly corre-

spond with the ceramic dating for the present item), though a stamped hammer or a letter P are known on a few surviving pieces of pewter plate from the 14th century (Hornsby et al. 1989, 10–13, 52–3, nos 12–14).

758 BWB83 5032 (108) 10
Fragmentary, distorted round-section stem, with small portion of bowl; l *c*.90mm+.

759 BWB83 4635 (299) 11 Fig 196
Pewter (AML, Table 8); triangular-section stem with end missing; l 63mm+; cross-and-pellets motif, IESVS:NAZARENVS: (Lombardic lettering, using two different kinds of N).

Compare Muldoon & Brownsword (nd, 10–11, no 49/227/208) for a spoon with a round bowl and an incomplete stem and with a different Lombardic letter inscription (legend uninterpreted; found in Coventry).

A similar handle on a spoon illustrated in a sale catalogue has an acorn knop and a pointed bowl decorated with two fish on hooks (Christie's 1993, 10–11, no 37, described as a christening spoon); while the bowl's shape and decoration seem appro-

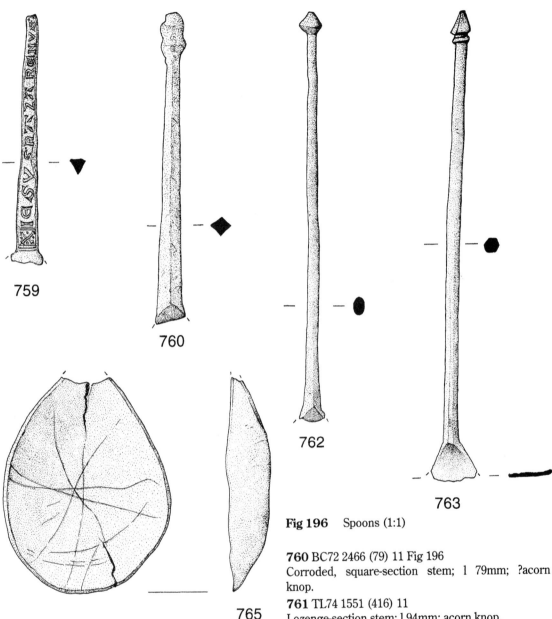

759

760

762

763

765

Fig 196 Spoons (1:1)

760 BC72 2466 (79) 11 Fig 196
Corroded, square-section stem; l 79mm; ?acorn knop.

761 TL74 1551 (416) 11
Lozenge-section stem; l 94mm; acorn knop.

762 BWB83 5962 (298) 11 Fig 196
Round-section stem; l 106mm; conical knop.

763 CUS73 80 (IV,25) 11 Fig 196
Distorted (shape restored in illustration), round-section stem; l c.115mm; conical knop with collar.

764 BWB83 5189 (306) 11
Bowl; 58×43mm; cuts on both faces from a sharp instrument.

priate for the 12th/13th centuries in view of several parallels (see on No 756 and discussion above), the knop has been queried as an original feature (examination of the sale item by colleagues revealed no indication of a recent join. It would be useful to have a more scientific test carried out on the object).

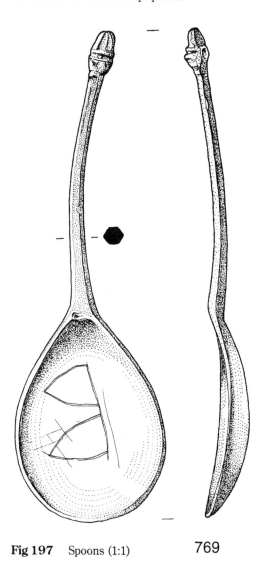

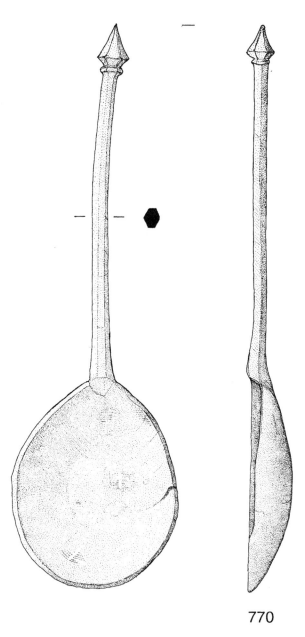

Fig 197   Spoons (1:1)

769

770

765 BWB83 2096 (307) 11 Fig 196
Fig-shaped bowl; 59×45mm; crude scratches on inside.

766 BWB83 1929 (308) 11
Flattish bowl; 58×36mm.

767 BWB83 5076 (338) 11
Flat bowl; 60×43mm.

768 TL74 2165 (378) 12
Bowl; 58×46mm.

769 SWA81 1971 (2109) 12 Fig 197 and Col Pl 3B
Pewter (AML, Table 8); acorn knop; hexagonal-section stem is distorted; l 131mm; 75mm; 41×

55mm; deep, fig-shaped bowl with scratched (?)B on inside.

770 SWA81 914 (2082) 12 Fig 197
Pewter (AML, Table 8); l 152mm; 94mm; 58×46mm; oval bowl; hexagonal-section stem and pointed knop ('diamond knop') with collar.

771 BWB83 5399 (310) 12
Bowl; 39×57mm; fragment of round-section stem.

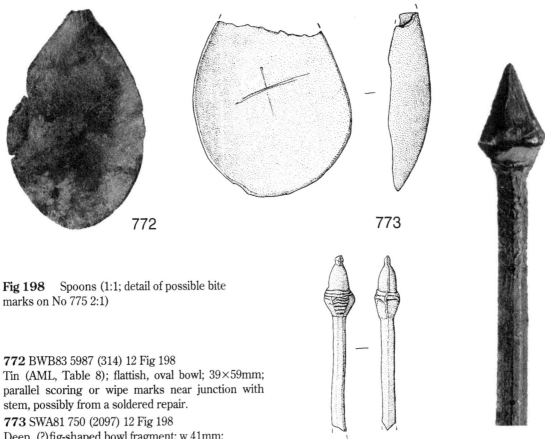

Fig 198   Spoons (1:1; detail of possible bite marks on No 775 2:1)

772 BWB83 5987 (314) 12 Fig 198
Tin (AML, Table 8); flattish, oval bowl; 39×59mm; parallel scoring or wipe marks near junction with stem, possibly from a soldered repair.

773 SWA81 750 (2097) 12 Fig 198
Deep, (?)fig-shaped bowl fragment; w 41mm; scratched cross on inside.

774 SWA81 2049 (2106) 12 Fig 198
Hexagonal-section stem fragment; l 45mm+; acorn knop.

775 SWA81 2048 (2106) 12 Fig 198
Pewter (AML, Table 8); stem fragment; l 85mm+; similar to No 770, but pentagonal section; possible bite marks near knop.

776 SWA81 863 (Unstratified)
Tin (AML, Table 8); round, corroded bowl; 57×64mm; with part of hexagonal-section stem l 61mm+; lead-tin (MLC).

Glass urinals
Lynne Keys

The widespread increase in the use of urinals from about the mid-13th century (Harden 1968, 105) is reflected in the items listed under this category, the earliest being attributed to the period *c.*1230–*c.*1260. They were used for urinoscopy – the examination of the colour and clarity of urine for medical diagnosis. Even in the home this appears to have been their primary function, the first urine of the day being collected for examination by a physician to determine the condition of the patient (Charleston 1984, 32–3; *idem* 1991, 260, 262; see Fig 199 top right). The blue or bluish glass of Nos 778 and 785 (which also appears in some of the drinking glasses, above) may possibly have been intended to aid diagnosis by defining the colour more clearly (or at least by avoiding any enhancement of yellow, which might have happened with some green metals).

Fig 199 Right, urine examination
at the deathbed of Richard Whittington,
from Mercers' Company ordinances
of 1442; left, urinals, including
restored form, top (1:2)

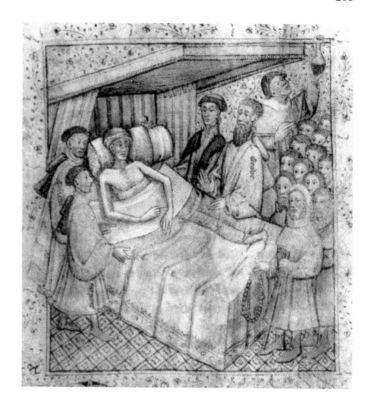

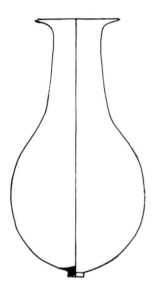

778

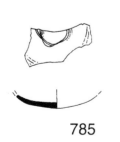

785

Only fragments of these vessels have been
recovered. The form of the urinal remained the
same from the earliest examples listed below
until after the end of the medieval period: a
globular/piriform body with a broad neck and
wide lip (which can sometimes be difficult to
distinguish from flask rim fragments and flaring bases – Rachel Tyson pers comm) and a
rounded base with a pontil mark on the convex
side (Fig 199). Because the glass of the body
was of necessity thin to allow the contents to
be examined, it is the base and, sometimes,
part of the rim and neck which survive in an
identifiable state. In most cases the rounded
base would have prevented urinals from standing upright unsupported, and documentary references indicate that they were often kept in a
metal frame or a basket (Charleston 1991, 260).
The colour of the glass is green, where ascer-
tainable, except for No 778, which is a natural
blue, and No 785, which is blue-green. Number
778, from a deposit attributed to the late 13th/

early 14th century, is of the soda formula and may be an import. The potash-formulae vessels may well have been manufactured in England.

777 MLK76 Acc No 7 (Context 25) Ceramic Phase 8
Base fragment.

778 SWA81 1190 (2149) 9 Fig 199
Soda glass (Table 12); base fragment; blue.

779 WAT78 448 (3665) 9
Base fragment.

780 WAT78 504 (3665) 9
Rim fragment.

781 Watling House 33 (ER190C) 9
Base fragment.

782 SWA81 5012 (2078) 9
Potash glass (Table 12); rim fragments; green; d *c.*90mm.

783 POM79 223 (2048) 10
Rim fragment; d 106mm.

784 WAT78 1016 (2029) 10+
Fragments, including part of rim.

785 BC72 2696 (79) 11 Fig 199
Potash glass (Table 12); base fragment; blue-green.

Items for other activities

GEOFF EGAN

Articles for household maintenance

(NN = wood examined by Nigel Nayling)

BRUSH

786 BC72 Acc No 4209 (Context 150) Ceramic Phase 11 Fig 200

Brush; wood unidentifiable (NN); slightly distorted wooden rod handle and round head (?originally almost hemispherical) with six holes for missing gathers of bristles; present l 163mm; d of head c.40–5mm; the tapering handle has a groove to each side of a transverse hole and a rabbet towards the end (the difference in diameter between the two parts at the break is probably not an original feature).

The hole in the handle may have been for a string etc. by which to hang up the brush. The shape suggests that this was a robust cleaning implement, probably for use in a privy rather than for cleaning vessels used for food preparation.

PEG

787 BC72 Acc No 2635 (Context 79) Ceramic Phase 11 Fig 200

Peg; wood unidentifiable (NN); neatly finished, two-pronged; l 62mm; shaft 8×6.5mm; prongs slightly offset, which would help in fixture.

This could have served a number of different functions in which there was a need to hold textiles securely in place, including the drying of items after washing.

Several items in the waterfront site assemblages are likely to be for household repairs, though they are difficult to differentiate from materials used in manufacturing industries. Two examples of such objects follow.

WIRE

788 BWB83 Acc No 4584 (Context 285) Ceramic Phase 9 Fig 201

Roll of copper-alloy wire; d 89mm; gauge of wire 0.7mm.

ASSEMBLAGE OF NAILS, ETC.

789 SWA81 3650 (Unstratified) Fig 201

Base of Kingston ware baluster jug (max d 107mm) containing a collection of iron objects: nails (including one of a form generally used for horse shoes), a strap loop (see Egan & Pritchard 1991, 229–35), a bladed tool and some tin-coated sheet items.

Kingston ware baluster jugs were current in the late 13th/early 14th centuries (Lyn Blackmore pers comm).

The equivalent, perhaps, of today's old tin or jam jar full of nails etc. in a cupboard or shed.

See also window cames No 49 and lead plugs Nos 733–44.

Articles for textile work

The following items are presumed to relate to work in the home. Pins, widely used in women's headdresses, are discussed elsewhere in this series (Egan & Pritchard 1991, 297–304, nos 1468–88).

SPINDLE WHORLS

These common domestic objects, regularly used by the majority of women and girls in the medieval period, must in many instances have been among the most familiar of personal possessions. As symbols of female work they appear in many contemporary depictions of everyday living both inside and outside the home (cf. Akerman 1857, 87–100).

The materials used, though humble, are relatively diverse compared with many other categories included in this volume. The whorls are of various stones, lead and a (?)resinous material (those made from adapted pottery sherds and bone appear mainly if not exclusively to be earlier, while mass produced stoneware versions imported from the Rhineland are later than those listed here). Although the cheapest (?home-made) whorls of ceramic and bone seem by the start of the period considered here to have been displaced by purpose-made ones of stone, the apparent lack of interest in the later Middle Ages in developing a popular demand for more decorative versions (compare, for example, the glass whorls of the Roman and Saxon periods) or in extending the range of materials commonly used is remarkable. It is a comment on the strength of the rarely questioned assumptions about the role

Fig 200   Brush and peg (1:1)

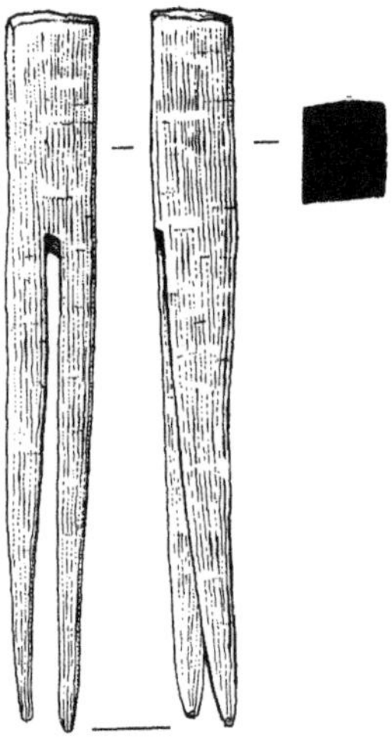

787

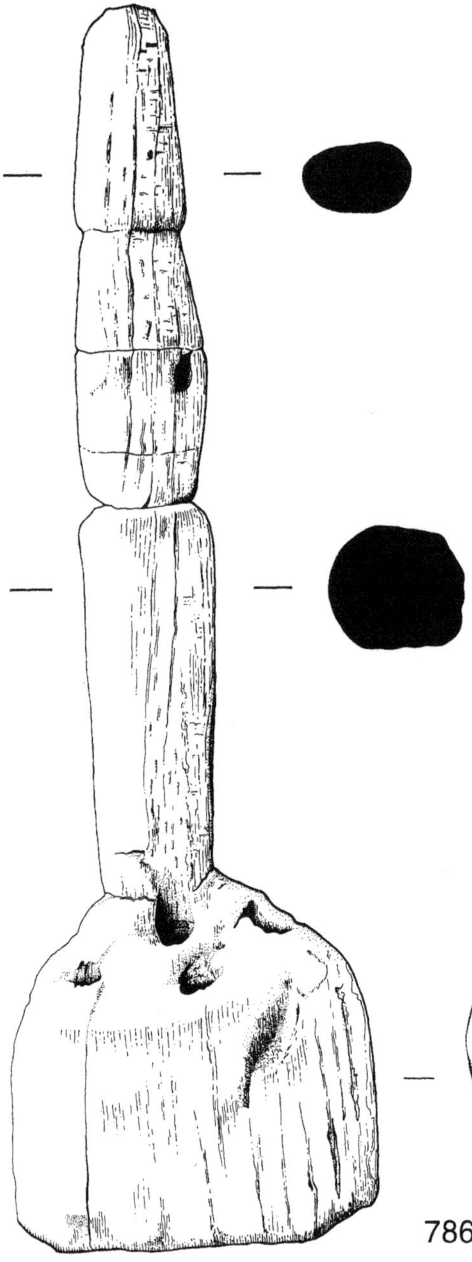

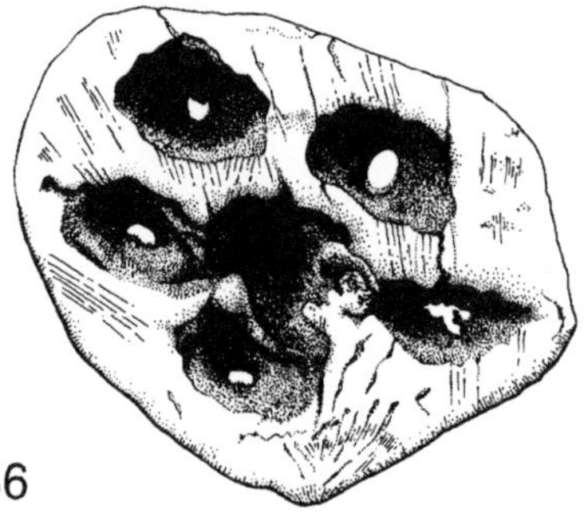

786

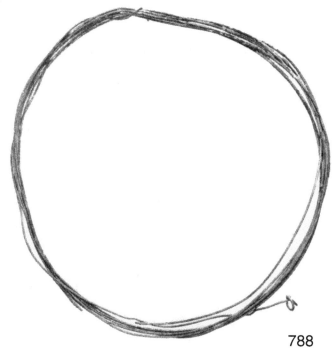

788

Fig 201 Roll of wire and assemblage
of ironwork in pot base (1:1)

789

of women in medieval society that these ubiqui-tous items seem in the period considered here to have carried no implications about the rela-tive wealth of the user in the way that, for example, dress accessories did. A peak in the numbers of spindle whorls recovered at some Norwegian sites (Bergen and Trondheim – see McLees 1990, 137) between the mid-13th and the early 14th century (cf. ceramic phases 8 and 9) is not reflected in the more limited numbers found in London and listed below.

More than half of the whorls catalogued here are of calcareous siltstone/sandstone. This widely occurring material (available, for example, in Gloucester, Hereford and Worces-ter, and Norfolk) was also used for London whorls in the Anglo-Norman period (Pritchard 1991, 165, 259, nos 170–4). Whorls of Jurassic limestone found in Norwich and King's Lynn are of slightly later date than most of the London ones of stone here (Margeson 1993, 185, nos 1442–6), while 'chalk' whorls are common in Winchester up to the 13th century at least (M Woodland in Biddle 1990, 216–25). Any whorls of unusual, non-local stone might have a potential significance as indicators of the movements of individual women around the country, or even beyond (see No 800 of a stone from northern France; it is not clear whether this whorl was made on the Continent or was adapted in England from a piece of building stone). The finds of stone listed below (Nos 790–802) suggest, instead, a pattern of mass production from a limited range of geo-logical sources, possibly with occasional ad hoc supplements. More information is needed about trade mechanisms of production and distribution of these simple objects before any firm conclusions can be drawn.

Stone

Calcareous siltstone/mudstone whorls are light grey and fine grained unless otherwise stated. Weights given are to the nearest 0.5gm. Geo-logical identifications are by Ian Betts.

790 BIG82 Acc No 5372 (Context 5400) Ceramic Phase 6 Fig 202
Incomplete; calcareous siltstone/mudstone; plano-convex; d 28mm; h 13mm; turning lines; estd *c*.11.5gms.

791 BIG82 2656 (4209) 6 Fig 202
Calcareous siltstone/mudstone; biconvex; d 28mm; h 18mm; turning lines; stone cracked; 16.5gms.

792 BIG82 3149 (5229) 6
Calcareous siltstone/mudstone; biconvex; d 37mm; h 20mm; turning lines; blackened by ?burning; 31.5gms.

793 NFW74 213 (84) ?7
Calcareous siltstone/mudstone; plano-convex; d 39mm; h 19mm; turning lines; 29.0gms.

794 GPO75 357 (1125) 6–8 Fig 202
Incomplete; biconvex; d 32mm; h 16mm; cream-coloured, fine-grained calcareous siltstone/mud-stone; turning lines; *c*.15gms.

795 BIG82 5370 (2598) 8 (post-1250) Fig 202
Calcareous siltstone/mudstone; biconvex; d 27mm; h 16mm; turning lines; 16.5gms.

796 BIG82 1183 (1178) 9
Calcareous siltstone/mudstone; biconvex; d 29mm; h 20mm; turned; 25.0gms.

797 BWB83 6008 (195) 9
Incomplete; calcareous siltstone/mudstone; bicon-vex; d 36mm; h 21mm; turned; estd *c*.30 gms+.

798 TL74 597 (416) 11 Fig 202
Light-grey, fine-grained stone of uncertain category (not calcareous); biconvex; d 26mm; h 16mm; turn-ing lines; 13.5gms.

799 TL74 812 (414) 11 Fig 202
Probably chalk; biconvex; d 40mm; h 21mm; turning lines; 31.0gms.

800 BWB83 6009 (154) 11 Fig 203
Incomplete; Caen stone; plano-convex; d *c*.60mm; h 33mm; turning lines; estd 150gms+.

Perhaps made in London from building stone.

801 GPO75 1135 (1087) 11–12+ Fig 203
Calcareous siltstone/mudstone; plano-convex; d 19mm; h 13mm; turning lines; 6.0gms.

802 BG76 1 (4) ?Late 14th–late 16th century context
Incomplete; calcareous siltstone/mudstone; bicon-vex; d 27mm; h 20mm; turned; estd *c*.22.5gms.

Presumably, by comparison with the above whorls, of medieval rather than post-medieval date.

Lead

Neither of the finds listed below is particularly neatly finished. They would, nevertheless, have been perfectly functional as whorls, though neither approaches even the aesthetic qualities of crudely decorated whorls of lead, like the

Fig 202 Spindle whorls of stone (1:1)

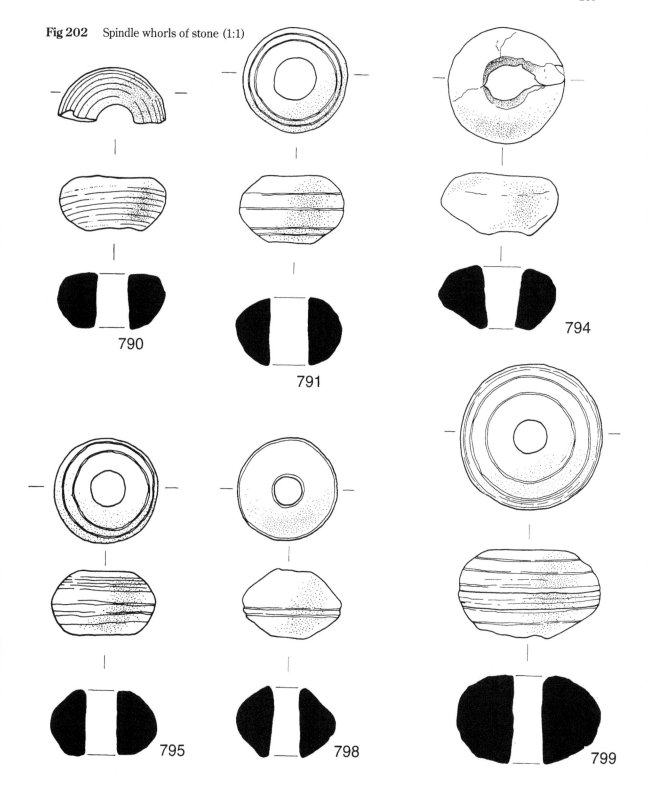

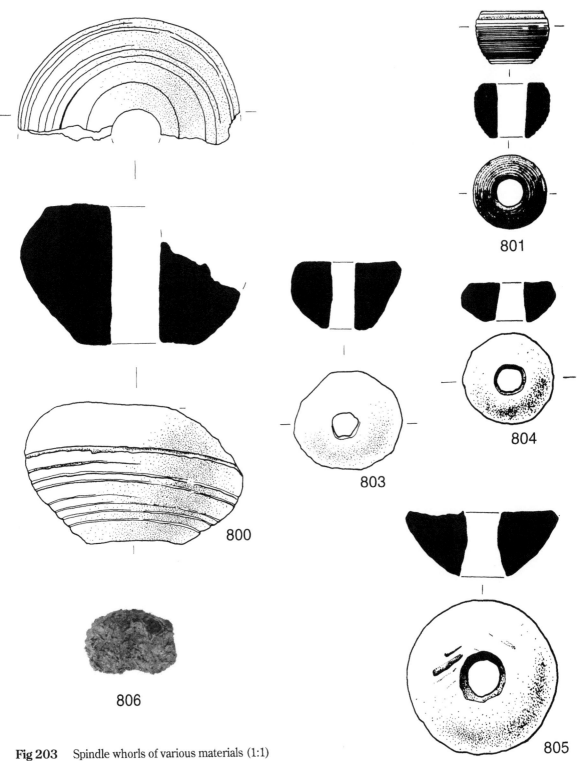

801

800

803

804

806

805

Fig 203   Spindle whorls of various materials (1:1)

one retaining its oak spindle that was excavated in Leicester (P Clay in Mellor & Pearce 1981, 139–40, no 70, fig 51).

It would be misleading to claim an introduction of lead whorls to London from the late 14th century onwards based on the two following finds; earlier examples are known from the city (e.g., from the VRY89 site). There may, nevertheless, have been an increase in the use of heavier whorls in the late medieval period to cope with thicker yarn. The published whorls from Winchester suggest that whereas those of bone and stone fall largely within a narrow range of weights, the less common lead ones are spread over a wider weight range, and more evenly than Nos 803–4 on their own suggest (M Woodland in Biddle 1990, 217, table h).

The marked sparsity of decorated medieval whorls of lead from London extends to more recently excavated sites in the city, and also to the established Museum of London collections (this may be widely true of sites in major towns), though reported casual finds from the London area include a limited number of them (Brian Spencer pers comm – they are also present at a slightly earlier date in the city). Along with plain lead whorls, they seem to be much more widely known in the period considered here in the north of England and Wales (of 44 published whorls from Meols in Cheshire, 34 were of lead – Hume 1863, 151–9 – though there the only decorative ones are the additional nos 1 and 8 in pl 15, see also Lewis 1987c, 278–9, fig 4); several decorated ones have been reported from parts of Yorkshire (e.g., Haldenby 1990, 59; *idem* 1992, 34, 36; cf. Lee Burgess/Nick Griffiths and Jim Halliday pers comm). A number of markedly crude, and asymmetrical, pierced conical lead objects of similar size to Nos 803–4 have been omitted as they are thought not to be whorls (cf. Biddle 1990, 1128, nos 4343–4, fig 368).

803 BWB83 6003 (318) 11 Fig 203
Plano-convex; d 29mm; h 16mm; 77.5gms; worn.
804 SWA81 2218 (2114) 12 Fig 203
Plano-subconvex; d 24mm; h 9mm; 38.5gms; worn.

Bone

805 WAT78 52 (2053) 9 Fig 203
Plano-convex; d 41mm; h 17mm; trimmed; 16.5gms.

Possibly residual as the deposit produced some Roman finds.

Bone whorls are encountered more frequently in earlier deposits in London, though see Margeson 1993, 184–5, nos 1436–40 for some from Norwich which are apparently from the period covered by this present volume.

Unidentified (?resin-like material)

806 BC72 4333 (88) 11 Fig 203
Fragment, biconvex; heavily encrusted; original material almost entirely replaced by mineral products; d *c.*25mm; h *c.*19mm.

This object has been examined by staff of the Museum of London Conservation Department and of the Ancient Monuments Laboratory, but the original material is so degraded that no identification seems possible.

LEAD SEALS FOR CLOTH

Although these objects were in the first instance used as part of a system of quality control in the textile industry (Endrei & Egan 1982; Egan 1989a; *idem* 1992), they must have been as familiar at the market stalls to purchasers of textiles for domestic use as they were to other buyers. Concentrations of cloth seals, particularly in foreshores and other deposits near running water, may be indicators of a dyeing establishment in the area (cf. Egan 1991a), but those listed below all appear to be single finds or from reclamation dumps. They are published here as they may well be domestic refuse.

Only examples on which the original provenance is indicated are included. All are two-disc seals (with single rivets unless stated otherwise).

// = next disc.

London

(Seals with the head of St Paul (the City's patron))

The sealing of English cloths with *lead* was apparently first specified in 1380 in London

(Sharpe 1907, 145–6), though some kind of marking was probably long established by that date.

807 BWB83 Acc No 1939 (Context 351) Ceramic Phase 11 Fig 204
Incomplete; one disc survives; d 14mm; two rivets:

> Bearded, balding head facing, surrounded by halo // (missing disc, incomplete stamp on rivets) lines at right angles to each other

A similar seal was found in Kongsgården, Oslo, in Norway (Oldsaksamling collection, Oslo, acc no C32439d).

808–810 SWA81 975 and 3323 (both 2112) and 4448 (2106) 12 Fig 204
Three seals with stamps from the same dies: ds 27mm (No 809 has stamps in reverse order to other two); the description of the stamps combines elements from each seal:

> crown, +SIGILLVM PAИИORVM around // bearded, balding head facing, upright sword to side, CIVITATIS LOИDOИIAL around (roman lettering)

The legend means 'seal of cloths of London'; the sword is that from the arms of the City.
Compare Egan 1994, 39–40, 170, fig 19, no 57.

811 SWA81 4690 (2106) 12 (possibly intrusive?) Fig 204
Incomplete and worn; one disc survives; d 26mm; Hero Granger Taylor comments: textile imprint (slightly distorted by rivet) of *c*.10×8 threads per 10mm, apparently a fairly coarse tabby; probably wool:

> bearded, balding head facing, in double, six-arched tressure, with (S'VLNAGII PANNORVM) IN CIVITAT(E LONDON) around (Lombardic lettering)

The other stamp can be restored from several parallels found in London (e.g., MoL acc no 84.107/5 – see Fig 204; Egan 1994, 40, 170, fig 19, nos 58–60) as a crown in a six-arched tressure, with S'SVBSIDII:PANNORVM:IN:CIVITATE:LONDON around. Seals with similar stamps probably continued in use into the early 16th century. The present example seems remarkably early in view of the admittedly slender dating indications for similar finds; it may perhaps be intrusive. The legends ('seal of alnage/subsidy of cloths in the city of London') refer to the alnage system of quality control for the textile industry, instituted to examine saleable cloths and to levy on behalf of the king a tax (subsidy) of a few pence on each piece. The textiles which were judged to be satisfactory were marked individually with one of these seals of good quality before they could legally be sold. An account detailing the London procedures survives from 1439 (Johnson 1914, 216–20).

Continental imports

812 SWA81 Acc No 380 (Context 966) Ceramic Phase 11 Fig 204
Ds 15mm (the legends can partly be restored from parallels, e.g., MoL acc nos 87.219/4 and 88.87/3):

> crozier, S.L(EOD..) around // shield with three pales, crozier above, (...O BE)RTH(VL..) around (Lombardic lettering)

The arms are the former ones of the city of Malines (Mechelen) in modern Belgium, and the legend EPS.LEODI . . . and crozier refer to the bishop-prince of Liège, whose authority was acknowledged by Malines from 1305 onwards, while FLO.BERTHVL refers to one of the most important lords in the Malines area, Florent (Floris) Berthoult, who lived from 1275 or before to 1331+ (the author is grateful to Stephane Vandenberghe of the Busleyden Museum and H Installé, archivist of Malines, for help with interpreting the legend). The seal must have been residual in its late 14th-century context, unless the stamps remained in use for some time after the death of Florent Berthoult.

Malines was one of Brabant's centres of production of fine woollens in the Middle Ages (Munro 1983, 29, 39–40; Van Uytven 1983, 170–1). More late medieval seals from here than from any other single location on the Continent have been recorded in England (London and Yorkshire finds), e.g., Egan 1994, 112, 194, fig 43, no 325. There is apparently no local seal of comparably early date in Malines itself (Stephane Vandenberghe pers comm).

In 1319 a dispute between London merchants and the commune of Malines began to be resolved at the London Guildhall by placing cloths belonging to the commune in the custody of a third party. The detailed list of these textiles includes some of Genoese origin, but the others may well include Malines products brought by Malines traders to London (Riley 1868, 130–1). Another cloth, definitely

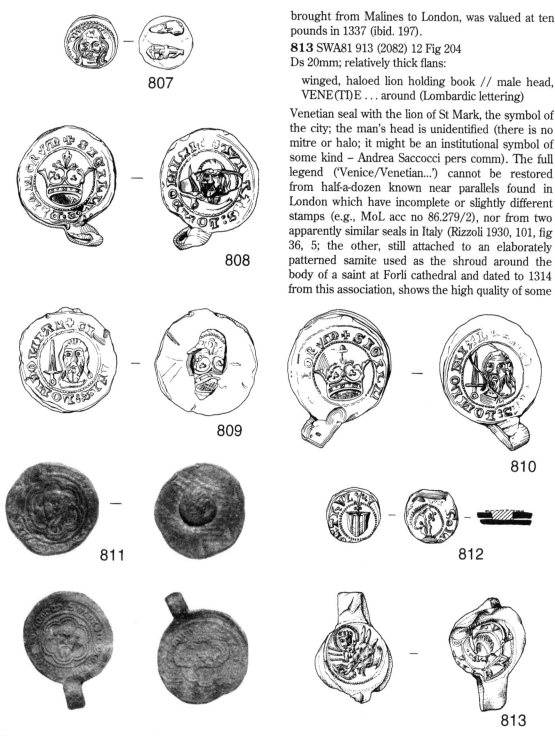

brought from Malines to London, was valued at ten pounds in 1337 (ibid. 197).

813 SWA81 913 (2082) 12 Fig 204
Ds 20mm; relatively thick flans:

> winged, haloed lion holding book // male head, VENE(TI)E ... around (Lombardic lettering)

Venetian seal with the lion of St Mark, the symbol of the city; the man's head is unidentified (there is no mitre or halo; it might be an institutional symbol of some kind – Andrea Saccocci pers comm). The full legend ('Venice/Venetian...') cannot be restored from half-a-dozen known near parallels found in London which have incomplete or slightly different stamps (e.g., MoL acc no 86.279/2), nor from two apparently similar seals in Italy (Rizzoli 1930, 101, fig 36, 5; the other, still attached to an elaborately patterned samite used as the shroud around the body of a saint at Forlí cathedral and dated to 1314 from this association, shows the high quality of some

Fig 204   Seals for cloths (1:1) with parallel for No 811 lower left (private collection)

Fig 205 Thimbler drilling pits, from the German Mendelschen Hausbuch

of the Venetian fabrics marked in this way – Cuoghi Costantini 1992; it also suggests that the design for the stamps may have been current for at least a century; the last reference was kindly provided by Lisa Monnas).

In the early 15th century a range of silk, cotton and woollen textiles was woven in Venice. The city was particularly well known for the production of silks, though thick seals of the present kind seem unsuitable for thin textiles, which they might easily have torn (from the 16th century, silks woven at Lyons in France had much smaller seals of a single-disc form – Sabatier 1908, esp 12–14, and there is a Venetian seal apparently of a similar form in a French collection – ibid. 146–7, no 57). Seals like No 813 may have been for heavy silk fabrics, or for the woollens and fustians (mixed cotton and linen textiles) produced in Venice through much of the medieval period. Another possibility, outside the domestic sphere, is for Venetian sailcloths (Mazzaoui 1981, 64, 101, 103, 108, 113–14). Customs records of Venetian textiles imported into England at the time in question only mention silks (Helen Bradley pers comm; cf. Cobb 1995, 3, 5, detailing textiles brought to London by a Venetian galley in 1420/21, though not all of these were necessarily woven in Venice). It seems likely from the numbers of similar seals now recorded that the present one was for a fabric exported in some quantity to London.

The above seven seals provide an indication of the precise origins of some of the textiles available in late medieval London; this can be compared with the range of excavated fragments of surviving fabrics (Crowfoot et al. 1992) and with historical sources. The five London seals, probably all for woollen cloths, and one each for a Low Countries woollen and an Italian textile, are also representative of the more common range of finds of comparable date in this category from other London sites not included in this survey. They may therefore be taken to typify the wider picture emerging from late medieval cloth seals of known origins that have been found in London (though several other Continental towns can now be added from finds recovered more recently).

Small flans (d *c.*15mm) are characteristic of late 14th-century seals, as are the two rivets of No 807, though all the recorded Malines seals of that date (like most later ones more generally) have a single rivet. The strip to connect both discs, as in Nos 808–11, seems to have come in early in the 15th century for English seals.

THIMBLES

Copper alloy

No medieval thimble indisputably dating from before the 14th century has been found in England (cf. Holmes nd, 1; 1985, 17–19, 22) and No 814 below is among the earliest firmly dated examples known in this country. All those listed below are of stamped and hammered sheeting or cast copper alloy. Pits ('holes'/'indentations') were punched or drilled (see Fig 205). Both light duty (Nos 814–25) and heavier duty (Nos 829–31) thimbles are represented. The lightest complete example (No 824) now weighs *c.*1.25gms and the heaviest (No 830) 10.50gms. The notches on Nos 829–31 may have been from some device to hold the thimble firmly during lathe turning or the adding of the pits.

The series is notable for the early sheet-ring examples (Nos 814–19), which have previously not been dated to earlier than the mid-15th century (Holmes nd, 2); No 814 is from a context from the mid-14th century at the latest. (The author is grateful to Edwin Holmes for discussion and suggestions about the thimbles described below.)

The diameter given is that at the base in each instance.

Soldered sheet rings ('sewing rings')

(Separate caps are not known until the post-medieval period.)

All have vertical rows of pits, and engraved lines at the top and base (single unless otherwise stated).

814 BWB83 Acc No 4541 (Context 285) Ceramic Phase 9 Fig 206
Incomplete; h 15mm; d uncertain; drilled pits.
815 BWB83 3482 (153) 11 Fig 206
Incomplete; h 16mm; d uncertain; drilled pits.

816 BWB83 3728 (338) 11 Fig 206
Distorted; h 14mm; d *c*.15mm; drilled pits; double engraved lines at top and base.
817 BWB83 3981 (401) 11
Distorted; h 10.5mm; d estd *c*.16mm; punched pits.
818 BWB83 318 (204) 11 Fig 206
Incomplete and distorted; h 13mm; d uncertain; punched pits.
819 BWB83 1135 (370) 11
Distorted; h 15mm; d *c*.17mm; irregular rows of drilled pits; solder traced (MLC).
820 BWB83 5274 (326) 12 Fig 206
Distorted; h 13mm; d *c*.14mm; irregular rows of punched pits.

Domed with central hole

(Stamped sheet metal, as shown by folding at base)

821 BC72 Acc No 4637 (Context 250) Ceramic Phase 10 Fig 206
H 11mm; d 14mm; drilled pits in concentric circles on top around central hole, and in vertical rows on sides; engraved line around base; two opposed notches on base.
822 BWB83 1509 (108) 10
Distorted; h 14mm; d estd *c*.18mm; two engraved lines around base; drilled pits in concentric rings at top and vertical rows on sides.
823 TL74 2382 (1955) 11 (*c*. 1360+)
Distorted; h 12mm; d *c*.15mm; engraved line around base; drilled pits perhaps added in four groups on dome, with vertical rows on sides; several pits now pierce the sheeting.
824 BWB83 1260 (110) 11 Fig 206
H 12mm; d 15.5mm; as No 822; drilled pits of slightly differing sizes; several pits now pierce the sheeting.
825 BC72 2804 (89) 11
Very corroded; h 17mm; d *c*.17mm.

Domed with no central hole

(Made from sheet metal, as shown by folding at the base)

826 BWB83 5939 (310) 12 Fig 206
Distorted; h 18mm; d *c*.19mm; the pits, unevenly punched in a spiral, are very faintly registered towards the base (virtually non-existent on one side).

The effectiveness of this thimble's pits is somewhat doubtful.

Domed, (?)stamped or possibly cast

(No central hole and no definite folding at the base is evident. These may, however, belong with the preceding category.)

827 SWA81 2102 (994) 11
H 17mm; d *c*.17mm; drilled pits in spiral; two engraved lines around base; several pits now pierce the sheeting.
828 BWB83 2313 (286) 11
Fragment; h 13mm; d *c*.17mm; drilled pits (some now pierce the metal).

Domed, cast and turned

(No central hole)

829 SWA81 973 (2112) 12
H 15mm; d 17mm; plain area on dome; drilled pits in spiral, with separate short row at base; notch on base.
830 SWA81 1996 (2107) 12 Fig 206
H 21mm; d 20mm; drilled pits in continuous spiral; engraved/turned line around base; four notches in base.
831 SWA81 3281 (2112) 12 Fig 206
H 20mm; d 20mm; drilled pits in continuous spiral, with short additional filler row of seven holes at one point at base (see Fig); engraved/turned line around base; notch in base; several pits now pierce the metal.

NEEDLES

Examples of basic, simple types in both copper alloy and iron are included below. More elaborate forms that had specialised, non-domestic purposes are omitted (as are examples of bone, which for the period under consideration are extremely crude and of uncertain purpose).

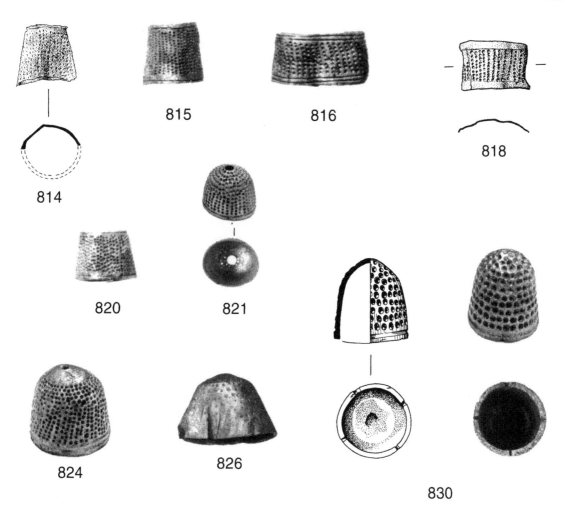

Fig 206   Thimbles (1:1); No 831 (2:1)

The finest of the iron needles, Nos 876–8, from deposits attributed to the late 12th to mid-13th centuries, are also the earliest. They may have been for embroidery; if so, they are among the first published needles of such early date to be associated with this activity (cf. Staniland 1991, 31–2; see Margeson 1993, 186–7, nos 1454–5 for examples excavated at Norwich). It is possible that some of the copper-alloy needles were used for sewing leather (cf. M Rhodes in Milne & Milne 1982, 88). Drilled eye holes appear to have been most common in the late 12th century, with a few perhaps up to two centuries

831

later. Numbers 845 and 867, both attributed to the late 14th century, have punched eyes which were subsequently drilled.

For needle cases see Egan & Pritchard 1991 (384–6, nos 1780–4 – needle No 884 was found in case no 1784) and Crowfoot et al. 1992 (151, fig 123).

Only whole examples up to 100mm long are included here. Longer examples of both copper alloy and iron are common in deposits where metalwork is both prolific and well preserved, but they were probably used for purposes other than day-to-day domestic sewing and embroidery. (The needles from the CUS73 site published by Henig – 1974, 193, 195, nos 84–92 – were not located for this present catalogue.)

No	Site	Acc No	Context	Ceramic phase	Fig	Length (mm)	Eye	Diameter of shaft (mm)	Point
Copper alloy									
832	BIG82	2833	4761	6		65	D	1.95×1.45	R/T
833	BIG82	2880	3918	6		67	D	1.83	R
834	BIG82	2733	4368	6	207	68	D	1.80	R
835	BIG82	3048	5560	6		69	D	1.85	R
836	BIG82	3046	4766	6		76	D	1.85	R
837	BIG82	2692	4030	6		83	D	2.45	R
838	BIG82	3240	6279	6		67	P	1.75	R
839	BIG82	2888	4064	6		70	P	2.10	R
840	BWB83	2105	290	9		81	P	1.45	T
841	SWA81	1244	2147	9	207	90	P	1.85	R
842	BWB83	2184	108	10		55	P	1.85	R
843	BWB83	6045	108	10		68	P	1.60	T
844	BWB83	2716	329	11		40	D	2.10	R
845	BC72	2382	78	11		60	P and D	1.55	T
846	BWB83	4213	401	11		64	P	1.50	T
847	BWB83	2715	329	11		65	P	1.60	T
848	BC72	2534B	79	11		66	P	1.75	R
849	TL74	741	415	11		67	D	2.05	R
850	BWB83	1366	149	11		67	P	1.50	R
851	BC72	2763	83	11		67	P	1.90	T
852	BWB83	1701	282	11		68	P	1.40	T
853	BC72	3814	89	11		68	P	1.65	R
854	BWB83	5035	370	11		68	P	1.70	T
855	TL74	2146	1956	11		70	P	1.80	R
856	BWB83	2149	126	11		70	P	1.30	T
857	BC72	2534A	79	11		72	P	1.75	R
858	BC72	2535A	79	11		73	P	1.32	T
859	BWB83	2068	142	11		76	P	2.10	T
860	BC72	2393	83	11		76	P	1.55	T
861	TL74	2145	1956	11		76	P	1.70	R
862	TL74	2191	1992	11		79	P	2.05	T
863	TL74	2237A	416	11		81	P	1.90	T
864	BC72	2535B	79	11		84	P	2.05	T
865	BC72	4147	88	11		84	P	1.65	T
866	BWB83	640	117	11		86	P	2.05	T
867	BC72	1760	55	11	207	90	P and D	1.90	T
868	BWB83	2067	142	11		90	P	2.20	T
869	BWB83	6035	305	11		97	P	1.70	T
870	TL74	1108	274	12		75	P	1.70	T

Eye: P = punched; D = drilled   **Point**: R = round section; T = triangular section (filed)

No	Site	Acc No	Context	Ceramic phase	Fig	Length (mm)	Eye	Diameter of shaft (mm)	Point
Copper alloy									
871	TL74	2677	368	12		77	P	1.80	T
872	SWA81	3532	2108	12		83	P	1.10	(?)R
873	BWB83	5989	314	12		84	P	1.75	T
874	TL74	1062	1264	12		86	P	1.80	T
875	TL74	2678	368	12		88	P	1.60	R
Iron									
876	SWA81	4107	3015	6	207	47	P	1.00	R
877	BIG82	3740	3150	7		79	P	1.50	T
878	SH74	135	386	8		57	P	1.65	T
879	BC72	4653	250	10		83	P	1.95×1.80	T
880	BC72	4654	250	10		119	P	2.00	T
881	BWB83	376	399	11		35	P	1.65×1.50	?T
882	BWB83	2941	291	11		74	P	2.20	T
883	BC72	2533	79	11		76	P	2.50	?R
884	BWB83	348	147	11		76	P	1.85	R
885	BC72	2394A	83	11		82	P	1.85	T
886	BWB83	3306	367	11		88	P	1.85×1.70	T
887	BC72	3815	89	11		94	P	2.65×2.50	T
888	BC72	2394B	83	11		100	P	2.20	T

Eye: P = punched; D = drilled   **Point:** R = round section; T = triangular section (filed)

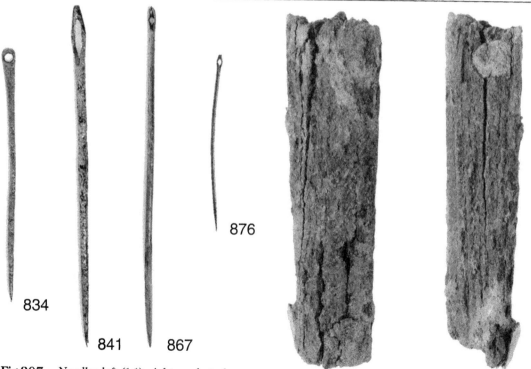

834

841 867

876

889

Fig 207   Needles left (1:1); right, packet of needles with imprint of textile wrapping (2:1)

889 BWB83 Acc No 3834 (Context 146) Ceramic Phase 11 Fig 207
Rusted mass of 20+ needles l 48mm (some possibly shorter); (?) eyes not immediately evident among the rust (including on X-ray plate); imprint from a textile wrapping on the surface of the mass. Hero Granger Taylor comments that the imprint is of a tabby weave with c.12–13 threads per 10mm in both systems, probably wool. Possibly unfinished.

THREAD REELS

Wood

890 SWA81 Acc No 1342 (Context 2209) Ceramic Phase 6 Fig 208
Incomplete; surviving l 113mm; broken off at both ends; turned; group of eight grooves in middle,

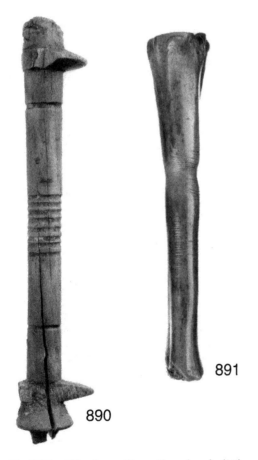

891

890

Fig 208   Wooden and bone thread reels (1:1)

flanked by two further apart, all between discus-shaped flanges; flaring (?)finial at one end.

Bone

891 BC72 Acc No 2261 (Context 83) Ceramic Phase 11 Fig 208
Caprovid metapodial; l 94mm; trimmed at distal end; shaft highly polished and worn from sustained use, with grooves especially towards middle.

Articles for record-keeping and reading/writing

LEAD STYLI

Presumably in the main for use with waxed tablets (see No 912), though lead was used for writing on parchment and paper, and probably also by architects/builders on stone (D Brown in Biddle 1990, 735–8, 743–6; cf. nos 2290–2316). The wedge-shaped ends could be used for erasure in wax. (An alternative suggestion that items of this kind in lead might be masonry wedges – Woods 1992, 358 – seems difficult to sustain in view of the absence of deep abrasions or mortar on such finds and the lack of function in such a context for the fine points.)

892 BIG82 Acc No 5131 (Context 4178) Ceramic Phase 6 Fig 209
Rough, square-section rod; l 53mm; tip broken off and wedge at other end.

893 BIG82 2857 (3803) 6 Fig 209
As preceding item, but with pointed tip; l 78mm.

894 BIG82 2950 (3682) 7
Corroded and bent; l c.87mm; narrows to constriction near middle.

895 SWA81 2417 (2279) 7
Tapered rod, now bent; l c.85mm.

896 TL74 1442 (2416) 9 Fig 209
Rod l 121mm; pointed tip and flattened end. There are transverse incisions and shallower marks around the shaft, and traces of wood were found along it, possibly from some kind of sheath or cover.

897 BC72 4679 (250) 10
L 75mm; pointed at one end, wedge-shaped at the other, with irregular, spiralling grooves near the former.

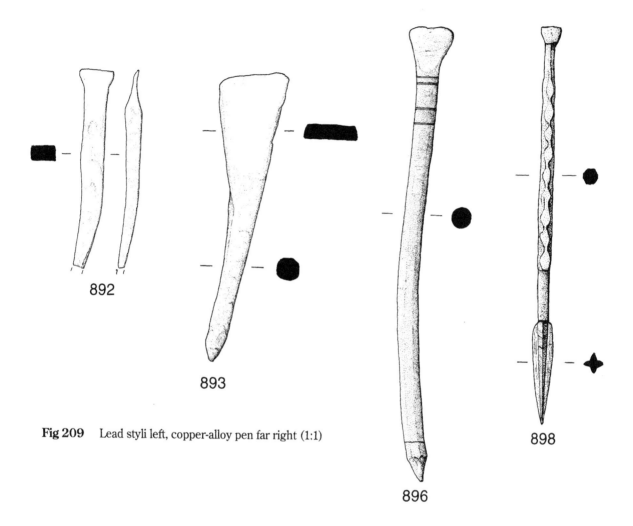

Fig 209   Lead styli left, copper-alloy pen far right (1:1)

COPPER-ALLOY PEN

898 BIG82 Acc No 903 (Context 896) (?)Residual in post-medieval context, or perhaps a post-medieval object Fig 209

Cast rod; slightly bent; l *c.*105mm; knobbed shaft with four lengthways rows of facets forming each of the narrower parts; roughly hemispherical top; four-sided, lanceolate end with a bevelled groove filed along each side to form the point.

Presumably for writing on parchment or paper. A fair amount of ink could have been held in the grooves.

Identical pens found in London include ones that have been published as medieval (Cook 1958b, where a 13th-century date is tentatively suggested;

N Ramsay in Alexander & Binski 1987, 383, no 422, where further, similar examples are mentioned; Finlay 1990, 167, pl 271; plainer pens of this general kind include MoL acc nos 86.109/17 and 87.128/18).

The faceted shaft of the present example is perhaps comparable with some cutlery handles of various materials from the 16th century; if this is a valid comparison, the post-medieval context of No 898 would be a reliable indication of its date.

The two 'bronze pins' with crowned heads published by Ward Perkins (1940, 288, pl 83) may be another kind of stylus for waxed tablets rather than ecclesiastical dress pins as originally suggested.

BONE STYLI

(Text revised for publication from a preliminary draft by I Riddler)

It is probable that these neatly turned items are writing implements for use with waxed tablets (N L Ramsay in Alexander & Binski 1987, 382–3, nos 420–1, and Arthur MacGregor pers comm, revising an earlier interpretation that they were used to mark horizontal lines in manuscripts to act as writing guides – cf. D Brown in Biddle 1990, 733–5; MacGregor 1985a, 125). The revised interpretation is supported by the occurrence of such implements in surviving late medieval writing sets, e.g., from Hamburg in Germany; this set also includes waxed tablets (Hanse 2 1989, 202, no 12.3). The use of these objects as styli would explain their frequent occurrence in scholastic and ecclesiastical establishments (e.g., Egan 1989b, 231–2, nos 22–7, fig 66; J Geddes in

Hare 1985, 149–51, fig 45, nos 6–20; Woodfield 1981, 103, fig 10, no 4).

These items were also formerly identified as being of Roman date (e.g., Guildhall Museum Catalogue 1908, 43). Some from Whitby in Yorkshire, which were long accepted as Anglo-Saxon, are likely to have come from later medieval levels (MacGregor 1985a, 124). The 13 stratified examples listed below confirm a late medieval date for these objects, underlined by further examples from 13th- and 14th-century contexts at Southampton, King's Lynn, Hull and Oxford (ibid; Platt & Coleman Smith 1975, nos 1928, 1936–7; Clarke & Carter 1977, fig 143.9; Durham 1977, fig 38.15). They may well have continued into the post-medieval period, as examples from 16th-century contexts are recorded from London and elsewhere (e.g., Woodfield 1981, 103, fig 10, no 4).

The points of Nos 904 and 905 (the latter is rather blunt) have been roughly cut in the bone, presumably following breakage of the shafts and the loss of original iron tips.

No	Site	Acc No	Context	Ceramic phase	Fig	Length (mm)	Diameter of shaft (mm)	Point	Comments
899	CUS73	265	I,12	9		42+	6	missing	shaft incomplete
900	CUS73	256	I,12	9		61	5	missing	
901	CUS73	269	III,10	9	210	78	6	(?)iron	
902	TL74	1482	353	10		54+	7	iron	knop missing
903	TL74	156	309	10	210	65	6	missing	
904	BC72	2799	118	10–11	210	85	9	bone	point recarved
905	TL74	584	414	11	210	54	8	bone	point recarved
906	BWB83	2676	334	11	210	72	7	iron	
907	TL74	155	291	11		74+	8	iron	knop missing
908	TL74	790	414	11	210	83	5.5	missing	
909	TL74	162	306	11	210	86	7.5	missing	
910	TL74	2649	10	10–12		65	5.5	missing	
911	SWA81	802	2108	12	210	91	9	(?)iron	

Numbers 899–901 have been published (Henig 1974, 197–8, nos 216 and 218–19, fig 197; nos 214–15 and 217 were not located for the present catalogue).

IVORY WRITING TABLET

912 BC72 Acc No 3 (Context 23) Residual in post-medieval context Fig 211 and Col Pl 1B
(Object mislaid; described from photographs and other records) Incomplete panel, 60mm× (estd) 36mm complete; the bas-relief representation of Christ crucified, flanked on the left by the Virgin, who looks away from her son and downwards, is

rather roughly executed. The scene is set below a pointed arch with spandrels, ending in an angled corbel on the surviving side, and surmounted by trefoils and a central crocket – all within a plain, straight border. The other face has two recessed areas, the deeper being at the top, and both are crudely scratched with cross-hatching and areas of more concentrated, deeper lines.

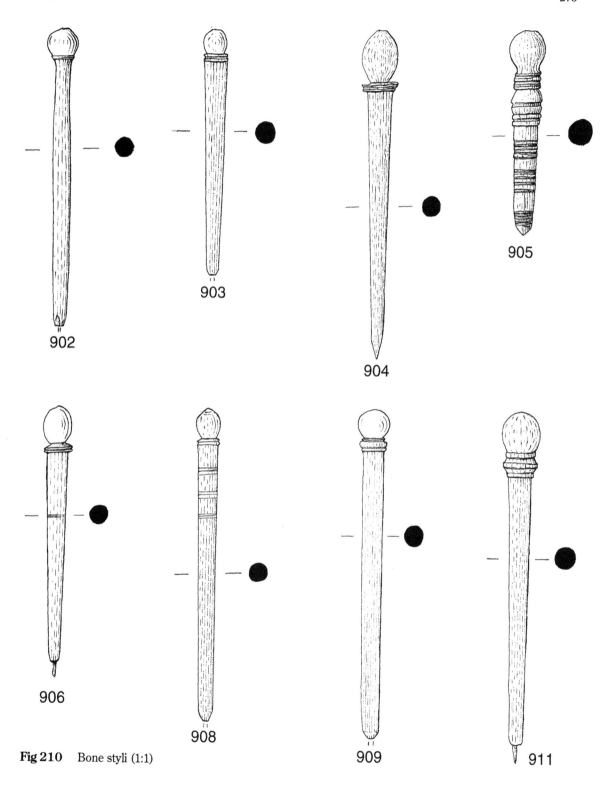

Fig 210   Bone styli (1:1)

The recess for the wax is unusual in being bipartite. The carving, which is of relatively poor quality (despite the exotic material), is from either a French or an English workshop and can be attributed to the middle of the 14th century.

This kind of item might be found in a moderately affluent milieu. Thanks are due to Paul Williamson of the Victoria and Albert Museum for his comments on the tablet and the style of its carving.

Compare N Ramsay in Alexander & Binski (1987, 384–5, no 428) for another writing tablet carved with a romantic scene; Ward Perkins (1940, 292, pl 89, no 1) for a further London find, attributed to a French workshop of the 14th century.

PERSONAL SEALS

Several personal seal matrices, of both lead/tin and copper alloy found at the sites included in this survey have already been published (Cherry 1982b; Spencer 1984). Names on the matrices include those of several men and one woman (Matilda Islebel, see Fig 211 bottom left – TL74 acc no 2357 from a context attributed to ceramic phase 11; Cherry 1982b, no 19, pl 18). Walter of Reigate's tin matrix (Spencer 1984, 378–9, no 2 – SWA81 acc no 446 from context 2018, attributed to ceramic phase 9, see Fig 211 bottom right) is a reminder that London was a great draw for people in the medieval period, whether they visited on business or to settle more permanently. This matrix was cancelled by a series of cuts at the edge and by gouging through the centre before it was discarded.

WOODEN TALLYSTICKS

Surviving tallysticks (Latin *talea*, a stake) for recording commercial transactions were discussed in detail by Jenkinson (1911, 1925; see also Dalton 1924, 233–5 and Guildhall Museum Catalogue 1908, 162, nos 123–5, pl 96, no 7). They were usually made from a strip of hazel wood split lengthways into two unequal parts, with corresponding notches cut transversely across both parts while they were still joined. The two parts were then divided by an oblique cut. The larger part (the *stock*), with its undivided base, was in effect a counterfoil to be

912

Fig 211 Ivory writing tablet and personal seals, TL74 acc no 2357 and SWA81 acc no 446 (the latter two, not in catalogue, are reversed for legibility (all 1:1)

retained by one party to a transaction, and the smaller part (the *leaf* or *foil*) was taken by the other party. When payment of a debt was made, or in case of query, both parts could be reunited to check that the notches indicating the sum of money concerned did indeed correspond. The size of the cuts for indicating sums of money according to Exchequer conventions was as follows: a 20–pound notch was the thickness of a little finger; one pound, the thickness of a ripe grain of barley; one shilling, a smaller notch; and one penny, a single cut without removing any wood (Jenkinson 1911, 373; *idem* 1925, 296, 329). Tallysticks were used by the Exchequer until the 19th century.

The earliest of the tallies listed below, No 913, is of the standard ('public') form. Six such tallies of alder were excavated in a late 13th-century pit at Southampton (Platt & Coleman Smith 1975, 229, 231–2, pl 117, nos 1647–52). The four examples (below) from the BC72 site, from two contexts of the same phase, may well have come from a single establishment and, although only a small group, they are of particular interest because of their diversity. They comprise both the standard form (No 913) that is well represented in the Public Record Office collection, and others which are probably private records and which exhibit traits that are more difficult to parallel (cf. Jenkinson 1911, pl 51, fig 2 lower four; *idem* 1925, 329–32; ibid. 320–1 details some differences between 'public' and 'private' tallies). The present tallies of the latter kind may not all be of the familiar divided form; they could have been used by one person simply to keep count of goods in store or to keep track of some aspect of work in progress. Number 916 below appears particularly rough-and-ready, retaining much of the appearance of the original twig. Jenkinson observes that 'the form of private tallies varies indefinitely with circumstances' (1911, 380), and that 'their use was … fairly universal in the 13th and 14th centuries' (1925, 313–14). None of those listed here has been definitely identified as hazel (see No 913), though poplar/willow and a fruit wood are represented; none shows any sign of writing in ink, even when examined under ultraviolet light. The author is grateful to David Crook of the Public Record Office for his helpful advice on these objects. An object from the CUS73 site, published as a possible tally (Henig 1974, 200–1, no 248, fig 42) was not located for the present catalogue.

The British Museum also holds tallies of various kinds, including one with bark; some are believed to have been used by woodcutters and one, from the end of the 19th century, by a French baker (BM, MLA acc nos 88,10–14,5; 1936,12–13,1; '1896' – Dora Thornton kindly helped with these items).

The group of deposits at the BC72 site in which the tallies below were found have already been (very tentatively) discussed in relation to the nearby Royal Wardrobe (see Dating and context of the finds in this volume and Egan & Pritchard 1991, 3). Tallies were certainly used by the Wardrobe (Jenkinson 1925, 304–5) as

well as by other institutions. The present four items might be taken to strengthen the possibility of a connection, without making one certain. Many of the 'private' tallies surviving in the PRO collection indicate not sums of money but amounts of various goods (grain etc.) supplied officially for the king by private individuals, the payer taking the stock and the receiver the foil (ibid. 314–15). The great difficulty with such tallies is the uncertainty as to what material(s) in what denomination(s) or standard(s) are indicated (ibid. 316–17, 319–20; a cut, as for a penny, often indicated a bushel, etc.).

913 MLK76 Acc No 327 (Context 3061) Ceramic Phase 8 Fig 212
(?)Alder/hazel (*?Alnus* sp/*Corylus avellana*); broken off at one, probably both, ends; surviving l 53mm; 13×7mm; rectangular in section; 9+ medium notches on one side and 3 small notches on the other, then 4+ cuts after a gap.

Part of a stock or foil; (?)nine pounds+ / four shillings+ and three pence.

914 BC72 2808 (150) 11 Fig 212
(?)Oak (*?Quercus* sp); broken off at one end; roughly trimmed; rectangular in section; surviving l 390mm; 14×5mm; slightly angled at surviving original end; series of notches – 10 small, 11 medium, 1 large, 10 medium, 1 large, 10 medium, 1 large, 7+ medium (broken off here).

This is a very long tally by medieval standards (?perhaps the longest example known from the period), though an 18th-century example reaches the prodigious length of 8ft 6in (Jenkinson 1925, 307). The cyclical repetition of notches of two different sizes cannot readily be paralleled or interpreted.

915 BC72 3115 (88) 11 Fig 212
Wood unidentifiable; incomplete; surviving l 62mm; 19×3.5mm; nine or ten surviving small notches; cut off obliquely at one end.

Presumably a foil.

916 BC72 3221 (88) 11 Fig 212
Wood unidentifiable; incomplete; surviving l 102mm; 12×6mm; sub-rectangular section; 17 surviving small notches; cut off obliquely at one end; bark survives on one side.

The extent of the survival of the bark seems to be unparalleled, though several of the sticks in the PRO collection retain small slivers at the corners.

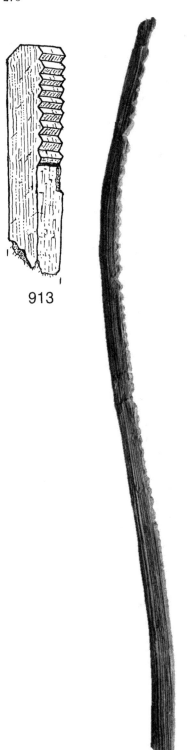

913

914

915

916

917

Fig 212   Wooden
tallysticks Nos 913,
915–17 (1:1), 914 (1:2)

917 BC72 3428 (88) 11 Fig 212
(?)Poplar/willow (?*Populus/Salix*); incomplete; surviving l 71mm; 6×5.5mm; rectangular section;
medium notches and transverse cuts on opposed
sides: one small notch, three cuts, one small notch /
one small notch, (?)14 cuts, one small notch, 15+
cuts (damaged section – broken off here).

The cuts might usually indicate pence and the
small notches shillings, though the repetition of the
two forms and the large number of cuts together
mean this interpretation is difficult to sustain (at
least as an indicator of a single sum).

Willow is mentioned for tallies in contemporary
records, though no example was known to Jenkinson
(1911, 373).

SPECTACLES

918 TL74 Acc No 2216 (Context 274) Ceramic
Phase 12 Fig 213
The almost complete, hinged, two-piece cattle-bone
frame of a pair of spectacles has already been fully
published (Rhodes 1982).

This is probably one of the most pertinent items of excavated evidence for literacy in late medieval London, though spectacles could have been used for other kinds of close work.

See Stevenson 1995 for a close parallel, also from London. Two further, fragmentary London finds of bone, from deposits of later date (VAL88 acc nos 4199 and 4777), are from a site which also produced a piece of waste bone that may be from the production of similar frames (acc no 6576; same (?)late 16th/early 17th-century context as the former). Fragments from other, similar frames have been found at the monastic site of Battle Abbey, Sussex (J Geddes in Hare 1985, 151–2, fig 46, no 27) and at Chester Dominican Friary (Lloyd Morgan 1990, 177–8, fig 127, no 5). Of nine medieval spectacle frame fragments from England listed by Stevenson, five are from London and the others are from the sites of religious establishments (1995, 321). A further fragment with delicate openwork decoration probably based on window tracery (from the site of Merton Priory in Surrey – MPY88 acc no 4354 – see Fig 213) may indicate the origin of the decorative piercings which characterise the arms of the most complete London finds. Glass from early spectacles so far seems to have remained elusive or unidentified among excavated material in England.

MacGregor has published customs references to imports of thousands of ivory spectacles to London in the late 14th century and of ones of unspecified material in the early 15th century (1989, 123–4).

See Hanse 2 1989, 107, no 6.7 for spectacle frames of copper-alloy wire found in London and attributed to the 15th century.

BOOK CLASPS

Copper alloy

The following seven items can be identified as clasps from books by comparison with examples surviving on a German girdle book of 1454 (Fig 214 left; New York Public Library collection; a leather object, d *c*.50mm and similar to the finial on this book, was found at the BC72 site in a context ascribed to ceramic phase 11 – acc no 3621).

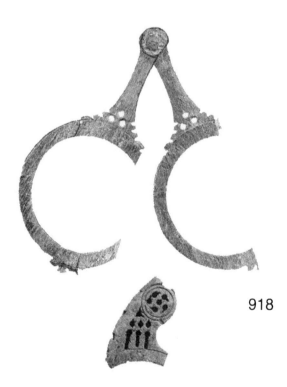

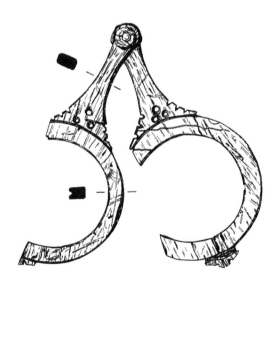

918

Fig 213 Bone spectacles frame and below fragment from MPY88 site, acc no 4354 (1:1)

These have previously been published as nos 720–6 in Egan & Pritchard, where this function was anticipated (1991, 154–5, fig 10; cf. Henig 1974, 191, nos 9–11, fig 54). Descriptions are by Frances Pritchard.

Length and width are for both parts together, with internal diameter of loop hole at end given in brackets; all are cast. This small group of clasps from late 14th- and early 15th-century deposits are composed of a hinged, double-sided plate to which a strap was riveted and a cast loop. The loop has a central hole and the reverse is flat; it terminates in a small loop 2–2.5mm in diameter, which is sometimes in the form of an animal head, with the hole at right angles to the rest of the clasp (for the AML analyses, see Egan & Pritchard 1991, 387ff).

919 BWB83 Acc No 4606 (Context 279) Ceramic Phase 11 Fig 214
Brass (AML); tapering; concave attachment edge; two rivets; loop with a flat back and central hole; 32× (max) 8mm (2.5mm).
(Egan & Pritchard 1991, no 720)

920 BC72 4859 (25) 11 Fig 214
Incomplete and corroded; gunmetal (AML); engraved cabling defined by linear border along sides; hinged part ends in a stylised animal head, which is broken off at the loop; two rivets; 39+× 9mm; on leather strap.
(Egan & Pritchard 1991, no 721)

921 SWA81 2027 (2106/2107) 12 Fig 214
Gunmetal (AML); engraved linear border on plate; single rivet; 29×10mm (2mm).
(Egan & Pritchard 1991, no 722)

922 BWB83 113 (265) 12 Fig 214
Brass (AML); concave attachment edge; two rivets; loop has two notches on terminal; 33×20mm (2mm); on silk tablet-woven strap.
(Egan & Pritchard 1991, no 723)

923 SWA81 1202 (2100) 12
Bronze (AML); concave attachment edge; single rivet; loop similar to that on No 919; 34×10mm (2mm).
(Egan & Pritchard 1991, no 724)

924 BC72 731 (15) Unphased
Corroded; similar to preceding item; 33×(max)10mm (2mm).
(Egan & Pritchard 1991, no 725)

925 BWB83 41 (12) Unphased Fig 214
Gunmetal (AML); similar to No 919; 36 × (max) 13mm (2.5mm); on leather strap.
(Egan & Pritchard 1991, no 726)

Survivals on books show that these late medieval clasps had corresponding strap-and-pin mounts on the covers, each consisting of a rod (see Fig 214 bottom), which was fitted through the clasp's central hole. Each rod or pin was set in a hole through the book cover and held in place by a small, lozenge-shaped rove of copper-alloy sheeting, which was kept fixed by having its corners bent slightly down into the wood (obscured by leather cover in Fig 214 left, see drawing lower right, showing only wood). Such pins survive with clasps on several books in the British Library (e.g., a 12th-century copy of the *Parables of Solomon* from Fountains Abbey, Add MS 62130, and a late 15th-century *Life of St Gilbert of Sempringham*, Add MS 36704; this information was kindly provided by Michelle Brown). None of these very simple pins has so far been identified among London assemblages (re-assessment of unidentified items could well produce some). Two published items from elsewhere may well be excavated examples (Egan 1991, 91–2, no sf 175, fig 32: M Henig in Sherlock & Woods 1988, 181, 183, no 15, fig 55). Both are from religious sites where clasps like Nos 919–25 were found, and both have what may be interpreted as an appropriate area of wear on one side of the shafts (the latter parallel was discovered in the same deposit as two such clasps). Two further possible examples, perhaps later in date, from a school are published by Woodfield (1981, 95–6, fig 6, nos 84–5).

The loops on the end tabs of the clasps could originally have had cords etc. attached to provide purchase during opening and closing. The animal heads of No 920 and parallels from contexts of similar date (e.g., Egan 1991b, 89–1,

Fig 214   Left, girdle book with clasps pinned (New York Public Library collection; not to scale); right, book clasps (1:1) and, below, corresponding pin set through book cover and held by sheet rove (not in catalogue, not to scale)

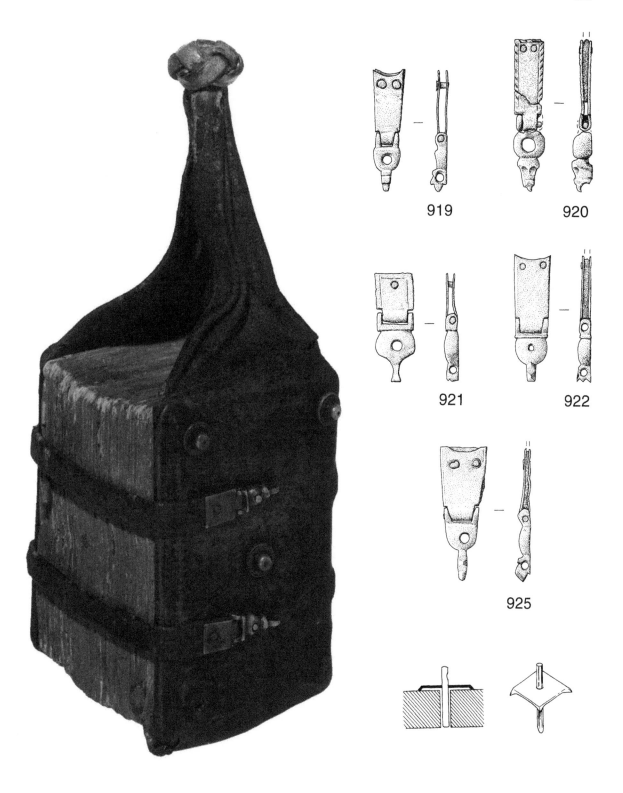

919

920

921

922

925

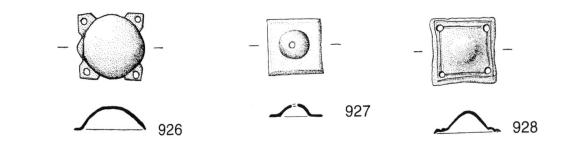

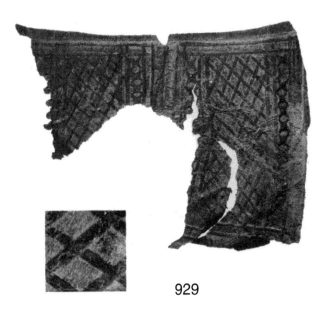

929

Fig 215   (?)Book mounts (1:1) and leather cover
(1:2; detail of tooling leather enlarged)

decorated) leather book covers from being
abraded by contact with flat surfaces (cf. Fig
214 left).

926 BWB83 Acc No 2725 (Context 328) Ceramic
Phase 11 Fig 215
17×18mm; brass (AML); circular boss with four flat
projecting, angled tabs, each with a hole for a missing rivet.
    (Egan & Pritchard 1991, no 905)
927 BWB83 3667 (359) 12 Fig 215
Probably cast; brass (AML); rectangular; 15×14mm;
bevelled at edges; hole for single missing rivet.
    (Egan & Pritchard 1991, no 1061)
    The bevelled edges of this item, which would
make it flush with the surface to which it was
attached, would have made it a particularly suitable
mount for a book, but its single, central rivet is
perhaps less appropriate.
928 BWB83 3996 (202) 12 Fig 215
Rectangular; 17×18mm; engraved double perimeter
line; holes for four missing rivets.
    (Egan & Pritchard 1991, no 1062)
    A similar item was found at Castle Acre in Norfolk
(A R Goodall 1982, 238–9, no 41, fig 44).

See also iron chain No 79, Fig 40, for a possible
library book guard (cf. similar examples surviving attached to the covers of books in the
British Library, e.g., Add MS 44055, an early
15th-century German volume with wooden
covers, probably of oak; information kindly
provided by Michelle Brown).

fig 31) are a late occurrence of this motif (it
seems unlikely that all the clasps are significantly older than the majority of other items
with which they have been found). Comparable
clasps found in northern France (Fingerlin
1971, 464, no 521, fig 240) and in the Netherlands (Boymans-van Beuningen Museum, Rotterdam, acc nos F6554–62) indicate that they
also had a Continental distribution.

PROBABLE BOOK MOUNTS

Copper alloy
These can be tentatively identified by the relatively robust, convex, round centres, which
would have served to keep the (sometimes

LEATHER COVER

(Perhaps from a pouch rather than a book)

929 BC72 3496 (250) 10 Fig 215
Incomplete; (?)deer leather (G Edwards); *c*.165×*c*.115mm, implying a cover when folded originally of approx 80×125mm (shrinkage not taken into account); mitred corners; the edges (which were originally folded back) are less worn than the surface of the main part; (?)rubbed straight-line decoration of oblique cross-hatching defined by borders of double lines, with rows of stamped saltire crosses, each with a central cross in a frame of four concave sides and further double lines; the decoration appears darker than the field and may have been intentionally coloured, perhaps by singeing. Phillipa Marks of the British Library observes that the lines are rather heavy and thick and do not look as if they were produced by tools of the kinds associated with surviving bookbinding decorations.

Possibly a binding for a devotional aid of some kind (e.g., image of a saint) or a comb holder etc. The use of deer leather at this date was not common.

Articles for leisure

TOYS

(Miniature objects for children's play)

These can be very difficult to identify with certainty (Weber 1981, 91–2). Parts of elaborate, decorative metal items can easily be confused with the present category (for example, see miniature sword No 469 – Fig 136, and the human figures on lead candlestick No 366, Fig 102). Some miniature items from the medieval period are beginning to be published as toys by archaeological researchers on the Continent (e.g., S Schutte in Wittstock 1982, 202–10 with references; *idem* in Hanse 1 1989, 441–2, and ibid. 2, 557–63). The identification of the following items as toys, rather than (in the case of No 932) as ecclesiastical objects, becomes more convincing when they are seen as part of a continuing tradition of a range of lead/tin miniatures from at least the early 14th to the 17th century. By the mid-1600s an extensive variety of such items (known to contemporaries

as 'trifles') leaves no doubt that they are indeed children's playthings (Egan 1985, 1996; Haraucourt nd, 70; Verster 1958, pls 101–2; Dufour et al. 1979, 243–5, nos 216–22; Groeneweg in Bos et al. 1987, 71–3; Vandenberghe 1988, 191). Definite association with dolls' houses goes back only to the earliest known examples of these in the 16th century.

The miniature chalk house (Frontispiece – CKL88 site acc no 8, from a (?)late medieval deposit) is presumably a toy. It has scratches on the roof, which suggest thatch, and a few traces of red pigment elsewhere. The only parallel traced so far is a more accomplished, (?)late 12th-century limestone carving, just under 50mm high, found in Saint Denis, France (Meyer 1979, unpaginated; there tentatively identified as a toy).

There seems little prospect of readily locating contemporary references to toy miniatures (as opposed to gaming items) among written sources for London (Hanawalt 1993, for example, does not mention any).

Lead/tin

930 BWB83 Acc No 1298 (Context 124) Ceramic Phase 9 Fig 216
Flattened and distorted, hollow male head of tin (MLC), open at both ends and with two rod-like attachments at the sides; h 39mm, estd original d of neck 12mm; hair is represented on the back of the head by a lattice; an apparent circlet (or other open form of headgear, probably not a crown) with a ridge protruding above a cross-hatched band has three spikes (?locks of hair) now hanging down across it both in front and at the back – these and other upward-pointing spikes at the sides now curve inwards at the top above an internal, (?)horizontal flange (obscured by distortion). The rods at the sides may originally have looped back to the head to form grotesquely exaggerated ears. The staring eyes and spiky (?)hair, too, seem to have more than a hint of caricature. The disproportionately long neck suggests this may have been a finger puppet of a size suitable for children (for the diameter, cf. finger rings nos 1642–3 in Egan & Pritchard 1991, 334). Also published in Egan 1996 (fig 7).

Several broadly comparable medieval lead/tin heads and busts are known from London, e.g., Museum of London Annual Report 1986, 3 – MoL acc no 84.240/4. One has an integral flat base,

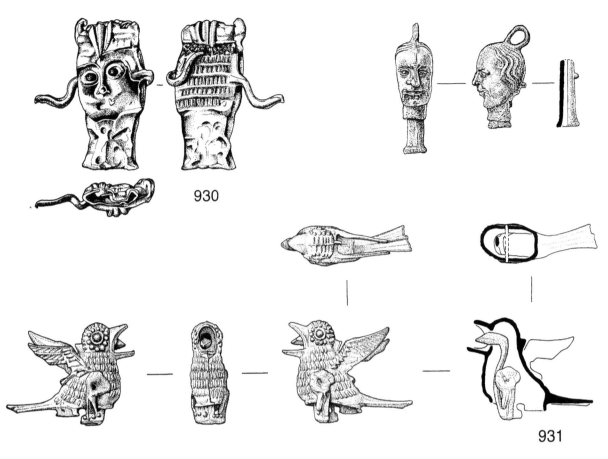

930

931

Fig 216 Toys; top right MoL acc no 80.70/11;
bottom right private collection (all 1:1)

showing that it was intended to be freestanding; it
may be a pilgrim souvenir (Spencer forthcoming, no
255; see also ibid. no 326e). Another, possibly of later
date, has the neck with a second internal tube,
probably to allow it to be extended and pushed back
(MoL acc no 80.70/11, see Fig 216 top right – this
one is stylistically similar to a group of whistles with
human heads, see Spencer 1990, 92, figs 191–2, nos
147–8). By no means all of these items were children's toys.

931 BWB83 136 (285) 9 Fig 216 and Col Pl 4B
Hollow figure of a bird; tin (MLC); h 26mm, l 34mm;
the wings are outstretched behind; body plumage is
indicated by rows of crescents; both eyes are surrounded by a circle of dots; cast in a five-part mould;

932

a lead-tin (MLC) stand (?incomplete) with beading along the top of the base has a pair of support struts terminating in a ring on each side; in the middle, inside the body, is a third, longer rod, the top of which comes out through the open mouth to terminate in a point, representing the tongue.

The body would originally have rocked on a missing horizontal rod set through the side rings, making the tongue (top of long rod) go in and out of the mouth as the tail was pushed; the two support struts have been soldered in a fixed position, presumably following damage or loss of the horizontal pivot.

This remarkable object, originally with moving parts, is a revelation of the early ingenuity of mass produced children's toys in medieval London (Egan 1985/6, 46, fig 7; idem. 1988, 1, fig 2 and 1996 fig 11; Orme 1995, 57, pl 2).

932 BWB83 5809 (292) 11 Fig 216
Miniature jug of tin (MLC); corroded and distorted; surviving h 37mm; form is closest to those of 'large rounded' type among full-sized ceramic jugs, but the body is slightly oval in horizontal section; body has vertical, ladder-like motifs surmounted with a band, which has oblique hatching on one side and transverse hatching on the other; on the neck is a band of opposed, obliquely hatched triangles (the upper part of the design is not clear); the rim is probably missing and the lozenge-section handle is probably distorted; there is cross-hatching on the base; a seam from the join between the two parts of the mould is prominent on the lower half of the vessel.

A better preserved example, h 38mm, also found in London (private collection; published in Egan 1988, 1, fig 3 and idem. 1996, fig 12 lower right; Orme 1995, 59, pl 3 right; Hornsby et al. 1989, 55, no 19) has been reshaped subsequent to discovery and, despite its less squat profile, may well be from the same mould (cf. the bases in Fig 216).

The zoned decoration of transversely hatched vertical lines on the body, with triangles or chevrons at the neck reflects that on several full-sized ceramic jugs, including some in London ware fabric (cf. Pearce et al. 1985, 55, fig 13, no 15 for the shape, 73, fig 31, nos 83–5 and 77, fig 35, no 116 for the decoration; there are also comparable traits in some ceramic vessels traded from Rouen in France). This might be taken to support a hypothesis that the miniature jugs are London – or perhaps French – products. Other miniature lead/tin jugs, from different moulds but also with transversely hatched verti-

cal lines, have been found in London (private collection). More than a score of broadly comparable miniature medieval vessels, some with decoration derived from metalwork, are now known here (e.g., Guildhall Museum Catalogue 1908, 305, no 74; pl 93, no 2, more clearly illustrated in King 1973, 5 right). A similar vessel to the Guildhall one was excavated from a context probably of mid-14th-century date at York Minster (Margaret Hanson pers comm), and part of a stone mould for somewhat cruder miniature vessels, attributed to the 15th century, has been excavated in Hereford (Shoesmith 1985, 17, 19–20, figs 12.1, 14).

A number of further miniature vessels of this general kind are known abroad. The closest example is from Reimerswaal in the Netherlands (van Beuningen collection); there are other examples of the same general category from Voorst near Zwolle (Verlinde 1983, 43–4, fig 16), others from elsewhere in the Netherlands (Verster 1958, 102, 104) and unpublished examples from Utrecht and Amsterdam, also in the van Beuningen collection. Two of them attributed to France are now in Cologne (Haedeke 1976, 57, no 11, mistakenly described as an ampulla, and 74, no 70A, which has been closed with wax stamped with an illegible episcopal seal as a form of reliquary container; however since several ordinary drinking glasses have been used in the same way, there is no need to see this as the primary function of miniature metal jugs, cf. Baumgartner & Krueger 1988, 202, no 180; 339–40, nos 405–7; 375–6, no 463, etc.). Another miniature jug of this general category was excavated at Saint Denis near Paris (Meyer & Wyss 1985, 95, fig 68). The overwhelming majority of the comparanda, including all the London examples, come from non-ecclesiastical contexts.

MUSICAL INSTRUMENTS
Angela Wardle

Medieval illustrations show a great variety of musical instruments, which were played both professionally and at a more popular level. Iconographical evidence, with its considerable stylisation, should be treated with caution, but the variety of musical practice is also attested in contemporary accounts such as that of the minstrel of *Les deux Bordeors ribaus* who, besides singing, played the fiddle, bagpipe, flute, harp, chifonie, giga, psaltery and rote (Bachmann 1969, 119).

Instruments of various classes and status are represented among the finds from London's waterfront sites, the most remarkable without doubt being the trumpet from Billingsgate (Lawson & Egan 1988). Strings are represented by the pegs used for tuning a variety of instruments; wind by bone pipes and by musically simple but technologically advanced metal whistles. No wooden pipes have survived. Popular music making is also illustrated by the ceramic figure of a bagpiper from the lid of a lobed cup in Coarse Border ware dating from the 15th century. The bagpipe, which has an ancient origin, was widely enjoyed in medieval society. Several percussion instruments were important in medieval music making, but of these, the Jew's harp, an ubiquitous and ancient folk instrument (whose classification as an instrument of percussion is sometimes questioned), is the only form to have survived.

Bells have not been included in this volume, although their musical characteristics are not in doubt (Lawson in Biddle 1990, 711). The considerable variety of bells attached to medieval dress have been discussed elsewhere (Egan & Pritchard 1991, 336–41, nos 1644–92) and the few remaining small-scale examples are likely to be animal or harness bells, pilgrim souvenirs or priests' ritual items.

Jews' harps

The jew's harp, or trump, is an ancient folk instrument with a wide geographical distribution. It is indigenous to South-East Asia, and was certainly introduced to Europe by the time of the Crusades. Evidence for an earlier introduction (Baines 1983, 1000) appears to be unsubstantiated (G Lawson in Biddle 1990, 724). In its simplest form the instrument was made in one piece, from such materials as bamboo or bone, and consisted of a flexible tongue or lamella held within a frame.

The European jew's harp, familiar today, is made of metal, usually iron, and the tongue is a separate component hammered into a rabbet in the thickest part of the frame. At its other end the tongue is bent into a prong, but this

rarely survives in archaeological contexts. In play, the instrument is held in one hand and the frame is lightly supported between the player's teeth, while the metal tongue is plucked with the fingers of the other hand. The mouth cavity acts as a resonator and the pitch is modified by the position of the lips, tongue and cheeks. There have been various attempts to explain the origin of the name and the suggestion that it is a corruption of 'jaws harp', reflecting the method of playing, has not been proved (Wright 1980, 645).

There are three basic forms among the excavated examples from London. The first has a flattened head (Nos 933–6), the second, a small rounded one (SUN86 acc no 1609, see Fig 217 bottom), and the rounded head of the third type, found only in post-medieval contexts, is larger and wider. Most examples are in a poor state of preservation and only Nos 933 and 935 retain part of the tongue, which projects beyond the head in the former. Most, however, show the rabbet on the head for attachment of the tongue, and the arms of the better preserved examples have a characteristic diamond-shaped section. The three types are paralleled on the Continent, as exemplified by instruments from Paris (Saint Denis) and Montsegur in France from 13th- and 14th-century contexts (Homo 1984, 14) and several groups from various sites in Sweden (Rydbeck 1968, 252–60). Although the form is known in medieval deposits, similar examples, dated by context to the 17th century, were excavated in the Louvre courtyard in Paris (Homo 1986, 29, nos 403 and 630).

Iron

FLATTENED HEAD

933 CUS73 Acc No 30 (Context III,10) Ceramic Phase 9 Fig 217
L 66mm; w of head 18mm; well-formed head, slightly rounded, with flat, tapering tongue welded to it, the upper end projecting beyond; arms have a lozenge cross-section.
(Published by Henig 1974, 193, fig 39; 195, no 83)
934 BC72 4123 (250) 10 Fig 217
L 55mm; w of head 17mm; narrow, flattened head with filed rabbet for attachment of the tongue; arms have lozenge cross-section.

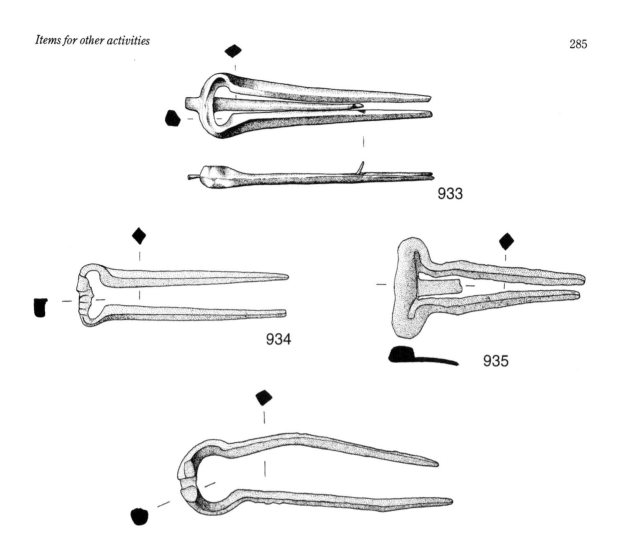

Fig 217   Jews' harps, bottom SUN86 acc no 1609 (1:1)

935 BWB83 3782 (149) 11 Fig 217
L 53mm; w of head 26mm; the flat tongue is partially preserved on the head.

936 BWB83 5257 (354) 11
L 53mm; w of head 25mm; identical to No 935 but the tongue is lost.

ROUNDED HEAD

937 TL74 Acc No 1513 (Context 1877) Ceramic Phase 9
L 66mm; w of head 21mm (dimensions from X-ray); small, rounded head with rabbet for tongue.
    Similar to SUN86 acc no 1609 (Fig 217 bottom).

938 BC72 812 (5128) Unphased
L 62mm; w of head 20mm (dimensions from X-ray plate); similar to preceding example; faint trace of tongue visible on X-ray.

Stringed instruments

TUNING PEGS OF BONE

Tuning pegs from a variety of medieval stringed instruments are increasingly recognised among excavated finds from sites in Britain. The typology devised by G Lawson is used here (in Hare 1985, 153; in Biddle 1990, 711).
    Six bone tuning pegs were recovered from the waterfront excavations, all in contexts

dating from the mid-14th to the mid-15th centuries. Five pegs, between 50 and 60mm in length, have a cylindrical shaft with a squared end; the other, narrower, end is perforated with a circular hole through which the string was attached (Lawson's type A). The remaining example is shorter (45mm), with the perforation in the squared end (type B). Pegs were turned with a wrench or key, and the damage to the squared end caused by such an implement, as noted on the pegs from Battle Abbey (*Hare* 1985, 153), can be clearly seen on No 943. The peg has been reduced in width at the end and heavily scored across its section. No tuning keys have yet been identified from London excavations (keys Nos 747–8 above, of copper alloy, are too large for the pegs described in this section). The string holes are neatly drilled and vary from 1.5 to 2.5mm in diameter. Several pegs show rasp lines; others show signs of usage superimposed on these marks – but none are with certainty caused by string wear.

As Lawson has pointed out (in Hare 1985, 154), despite the increased recognition of such pegs, the instruments on which they were used remain uncertain (a possible wooden peg found together with the tail piece of a stringed instrument in Winchester is the only association among excavated finds so far suggested (Lawson in Biddle 1990, 711–18)). Pegs perforated at the narrow end may have been used for instruments such as harps, lyres, lutes and fiddles, all of which had an open frame allowing access to both ends of the peg. The general arrangement of pegs on such instruments can be seen on many medieval illustrations, and methods of string fastening are summarised by Remnant (1986, 20–1, table 2, pls 6, 34, 149). There is a general similarity of length among four of the examples from the TL74 site – all of this type, which might indicate that they came from similar instruments, perhaps the rebec/ fiddle or related forms, for which their size is consistent.

Pegs with a string hole in the head were clearly intended for instruments with a closed box-like form, such as the psaltery, a member of the zither family. Examples of this plucked instrument, made in wood, came from 11th- and 14th-century contexts at Novgorod in

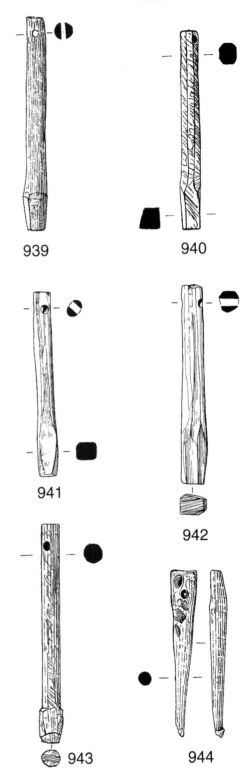

939   940

941   942

943   944

Russia (Kolchin 1989, 140–1, 386, pl 141) and the type is familiar in medieval art. Number 944 below can be compared with a group of eight bone psaltery pegs from St Aldates, Oxford, where two pegs of type A were also found (Durham 1977, 164–5). The small diameter of its hole might indicate the use of a metal string (the possible identification of copper-alloy wire found at the TL74 site as strings for a musical instrument is entirely speculative (M Rhodes in Milne & Milne 1982, 91)).

PERFORATION AT NARROW END
(Lawson's type A)

939 BC72 Acc No 4428 (Context 150) Ceramic Phase 11 Fig 218
L 59mm; d of perforation 2.5mm; the coarsely filed shank tapers gently from shoulder to tip (7–5mm); sharp cuts and file marks visible on the roughly squared end.

940 TL74 118 (306) 11 Fig 218
L 54mm; d of perforation 1.5mm; the gently tapering shank (6–4mm) is roughly cut and not completely smoothed, retaining angles and visible rasp marks; similar marks can also be seen on the squared head (w 4mm) which is sharply cut.

941 TL74 2224 (416) 11 Fig 218
L 50mm; d of shank 4mm; d of perforation 2mm; tapering shank with squared head, highly polished, with no obvious wear marks.

942 TL74 2212 (416) 11 Fig 218
L 53mm; d of shank 4mm; d of perforation 2mm; straight shank with perforation, fairly roughly fashioned, expands to a squared head which is highly polished.

943 TL74 1123 (274) 12 Fig 218
L 59mm; d of shank 5mm; d of perforation 2.5mm; shank tapering slightly to the perforated end (5–4mm) on which can be seen rasp marks and scratches, possibly caused by use; the squared end has a marked shoulder and the wear pattern on the end clearly indicates the use of a socketed tuning key.

Fig 218   Bone tuning pegs (1:1)

PERFORATION IN SQUARED END
(Lawson's type B)

944 TL74 434 (453) 12 Fig 218
L 45mm; w of head 8mm; d of perforation 2–1.5mm; perforated expanded head and tapering shank (7.5–3mm), damaged at the tip; gouge marks on the upper surface, the side from which the hole has been drilled.

Wind instruments
PIPES OF BONE
(Bone identifications by Barbara West)

Simple pipes and whistles belonging to a folk tradition that goes back to prehistoric times have been found on many sites in Britain and Europe (Megaw 1960, 6–13; *idem* in Biddle 1990, 718; Rimmer 1981, 234–7). They can be made from animal or bird bone and have a varying number of finger holes, though commonly three – as on an example from Southampton found in a context dated to *c*.1300 (J Megaw in Platt & Coleman Smith 1975, 252–3). Number 945, from an early 13th-century context, is very similar in construction, although its range differs; while No 946, also fashioned from a goose ulna, is a simple block-and-duct whistle without finger holes. The sound was created when the player's breath, directed through a narrow duct formed by blocking the upper end of the pipe, struck the sharp edge of a hole cut in the tube. The perishable blocks, made of wood, are, as always, lost. These pipes can be compared with another instrument from London, of 11th-century date (Pritchard 1991, no 243), which is made from the ulna of an unusually large bird, possibly a crane (B West pers comm). It retains traces of a finger hole at the distal end and may have had up to three holes. The other pipe illustrated here (Fig 219 top) was found in an unphased deposit at the TEX88 site (acc no 1243) and is a more elaborate instrument, made from an ovicaprid tibia, with four finger holes and a thumb hole on which a wider range of notes could be produced. It could have been played with the fingers of one hand; the thumb hole falling

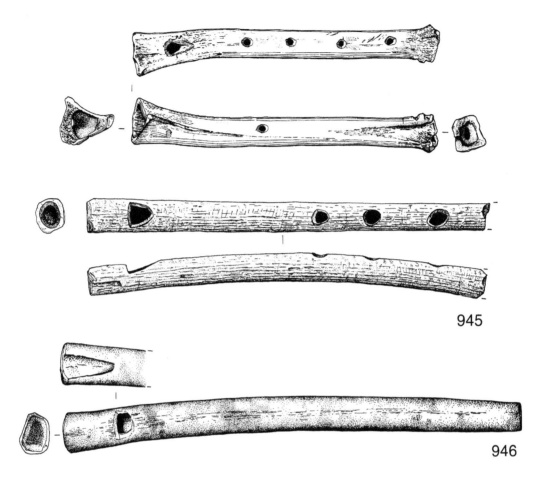

Fig 219   Bone flutes, top TEX88 acc no 1243 (1:1)

naturally under the left thumb, thus perhaps leaving the other hand free to beat a drum. Many excavated pipes, such as those found in the Netherlands (Rimmer 1981, 235), can be played single handed, although the traditional tabor pipe had only two finger holes and a thumb hole on which, by the use of harmonics, it was possible to produce a complete scale.

945 WAT78 Acc No 244 (Context 4084) Ceramic Phase 7 Fig 219
L 109mm; d at upper end 9×7mm; d at lower end 8×7mm; block-and-duct flute made from a goose ulna with a natural curve. The three finger holes, which have an average diameter of 3mm, have been cut with a knife and, unlike in the Southampton example, are spaced irregularly; the distance between the centres of the upper and central hole is 15mm and between the central and lower hole, 17.5mm. The voicing lip on the anterior surface, 16mm from the proximal end, is neatly finished. Experimental blowing carried out in 1980 (S Foot, unpublished DUA archive report) without any additional mouthpiece produced five clear notes: g', a', c", e", f" – a lower range than that produced by Megaw on the Southampton pipe (in Platt & Coleman Smith 1975, 273).

946 NFW74 175 (75) Unphased Fig 219
L 125mm; d at upper end 10×8mm; d at lower end 7×8mm; simple pipe or whistle made from a goose ulna, with a blow hole 14mm from the proximal end; no finger holes.

WHISTLES

Other wind instruments belong more to the category of novelties or toys rather than musical instruments for serious performance. The waterfront sites produced several fragments of a distinctive type of whistle in the form of a bird, complete examples of which have been found in the Low Countries (G Groeneweg in Bos et al. 1987, 74, no 602; Verster 1958, pl 103). The illustrated example in the form of a cockerel is very similar (see Fig 220 top right). The whistle mechanism and the blow pipe were attached to the lower part of the bird's finely detailed body and a trace of the tube can be seen. Ceramic whistles are also represented in the excavated material and in the MoL established collections.

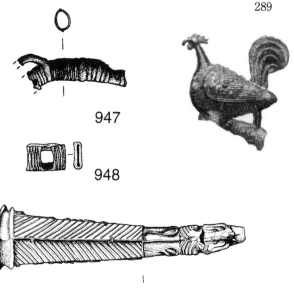

947

948

Lead/tin

947 SWA81 Acc No 662 (Context 2061) Ceramic Phase 9 Fig 220
Surviving l 22mm; d 4mm; fragment of blow pipe from a whistle; continuous ribbing around the circumference.

948 BWB83 1426 (355) 11 Fig 220
Fragment; rectangular plate 9.5×7mm with ribbed decoration and roughly shaped square hole.
From mouthpiece.

949 SWA81 2996 (2101) 12
Fragment of pipe; surviving l 29mm; d 5mm; as No 947.

950 BWB83 4710 (247) Unphased
Fragment as No 948; 11×9mm; distorted.

951 TL74 2544 (Unstratified) Fig 220
L 69mm; the tapering hexagonal tube has a square blow hole and terminates in an animal head, with the exit hole between its teeth; the inscription, which covers two opposite faces, reads (Lombardic characters, with the two underlined letters transposed) AVE MAR / IA:GRACA:PL.

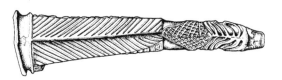

951

Fig 220 Whistles, top right private collection (drawing 1:1, photograph reduced)

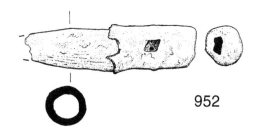

952

Ceramic

952 SWA81 Acc No 3741 (Context 994) Ceramic
Phase 11 Fig 220

L 46m; blow pipe from a ceramic whistle in Kingston-
type ware, the lower part unglazed for insertion into
the body of the vessel.

Compare a miniature ceramic jug with whistle
spout, MoL acc no 80.93/9 (Pearce & Vince 1988,
128, fig 83, no 210).

OBJECTS USED FOR GAMES

(Not exclusively for children)

The text for bone and wooden items below was
revised for publication from a preliminary draft
(including identification of the chess pieces) by
I Riddler.

Dice of bone

The two dice listed are from late medieval
contexts. They are of cubic form, with values
indicated by ring-and-dot motifs. It is likely that
they were produced from solid bone (*compacta*)
although the specific bone used cannot be
determined. Their method of manufacture follows the procedures outlined by Ulbricht (1984,
39–40): rods of bone of square cross-section
were sawn from the raw material and cut into
cubes; the edges were then smoothed, numeri-
cal values were added, and the dice were
polished. Evidence for the manufacture of
medieval dice has come from Göttingen in
Germany (Hanse 2 1989, 311–12, no 14.130),
and there is a piece of possible waste from a
pre-12th-century context at Winchester (D
Brown in Biddle 1990, 261–2, 694, fig 56, no
352).

Medieval dice can sometimes be dis-
tinguished from Roman ones on the basis of
the arrangement of the values on their faces
(Ulbricht 1984, 59, note 26; D Brown in Biddle
1990, 692–4, 699). The two dice listed below
use a system in which opposite sides add up to
seven (Roman examples are invariably of this
kind, e.g., Crummy 1983, 96–7), but on some
medieval ones the opposite sides add up to

various totals. This latter arrangement, known
at Lund in Sweden for example (Persson in
Mårtensson 1976, 379–80, fig 329), appears to
have been widespread in north-west Europe in
the medieval period (MacGregor 1985a, 131–2).

Geoff Egan writes:

There are in fact sixteen distinct arrangements
possible for the numbers on 'standard' dice (i.e.,
those with 1–6 on which the numbers on the
opposite sides total seven) depending on the relative face positions and the orientations of the twos,
threes and sixes – the numbers which are, ideally,
symmetrical only in two rather than four planes
(Potter 1992, 89–91; cf. Egan forthcoming c). No
953 below is Potter's first type, while No 954 is his
13th type. It is too early to try to draw any
conclusion about the prevalence of any of these
particular types during the medieval period as
there are relatively few dice of this date available
to consider by this system; for the moment it may
be worth noting that of 13 dice published from
Winchester, eight of which are standard ones,
there are two of each of types 1 and 13, though
none of these appears to correspond in date with
the period considered here (D Brown in Biddle
1990, 693, 700 – a similar classification is used
there, type A (cf. standard) and B, where 1 and 2,
3 and 4, and 5 and 6 are opposite). Figure 221
includes sketches of the three determining faces
on the dice listed below in their distinctive configurations. The author is grateful to Eddie Potter for
drawing his novel and definitive categorisation for
standard dice to his attention.

Medieval dice are occasionally found together
in some numbers. Although no groups of dice
have been recovered from the recent excavations,
a (?16th-century) container from London holding
24 false ones (18 weighted internally with mer-
cury, three of them with only high numbers, each
appearing twice, and three with only low ones)
has been published (Spencer 1985; Hanse 2 1989,
108, no 6.8).

Some indication of the variety of dice games
current in the medieval period is provided by
Murray (1952, 113–57).

953 TL74 Acc No 2215 (Context 1644) Ceramic
Phase 11 Fig 221

c.3.5×3.5×3.5mm; neat cube; double ring-and-dot
numerals; Potter type 1.

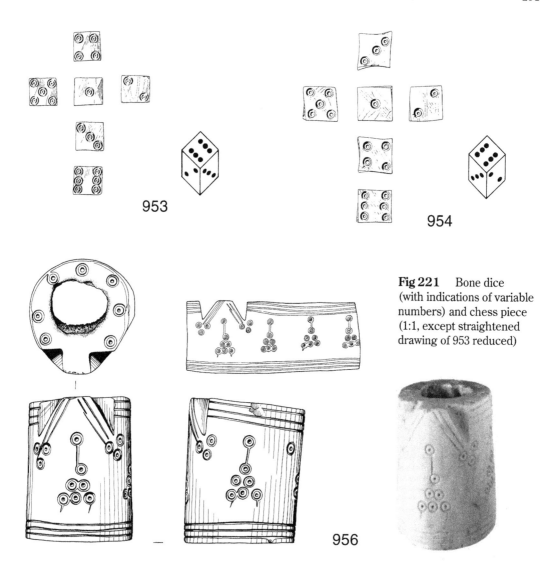

Fig 221 Bone dice (with indications of variable numbers) and chess piece (1:1, except straightened drawing of 953 reduced)

954 TL74 2708 (275) 12 Fig 221
*c.*4×4.5×5mm; slightly irregular cube; single ring-and-dot numerals; Potter type 13.

Chess pieces

The seven chess pieces listed below include three kings, two bishops, a rook and two pawns. All are non-figurative versions, or virtually so, made from bone, antler and wood. The occasional use elsewhere of jet as an alternative presumably stems from a desire to differentiate pieces by colour (MacGregor 1985a, 137). Bishop No 958 retains traces of red paint, also observed on a pawn found at Ludgershall Castle (Wiltshire) (ibid.). It has been suggested that some of the pieces from Witchampton (Dorset) had been deliberately fire-blackened, but this is thought unlikely – ibid. 67–70; see, however, wooden counters Nos 962–4 below. Generally wooden medieval chess pieces seem to be comparatively rare among finds in England, though this may be a factor of survival.

The king pieces include hollow bone cylinder No 956, which originally held an inserted head in the manner of other chess pieces from London and elsewhere (MacGregor 1985a, 138–9, fig 73d, with references to others). A smaller and simpler variant is represented by wooden piece No 955.

Bone and antler pieces are often composite, sometimes including wedges or cylinders inserted into the hollow bone centre or into the cancellous tissue in antler. Rook No 959 originally had four such wedges; three of these remain (see Fig 222). The wedges on the upper part allowed the engraved line pattern on the sides to be continued over the top, and a similar intention is seen with pawn No 960. A bone rook with a plugged centre (MoL acc no 4866) is illustrated by MacGregor (1985a, fig 73b; Kluge Pinsker 1991, 143–6, details eight chess pieces found in London).

Wooden bishops Nos 957–8 are simple, schematic pieces with two projections pointing forwards from a rounded apex. Both are undecorated, differentiating them from bone pieces of comparable form. Bone examples have previously been found in London (Dryden 1882, 421–2, nos 5, 6), and undecorated bishops of wood are known from Bergen (Hanse 2 1989, 146, no 8.8).

The seven pieces listed below come from contexts of 13th- and 14th-century date. This includes some attributed to a slightly later period than the 11th- to 13th-century dating suggested for similar pieces by MacGregor (1985a, 137–9).

The game of chess itself is attested in western historical sources from the late 10th century onwards, and references to it proliferate from the 12th century (Murray 1913, 394–495). The dating of medieval chess pieces in England, particularly those from the recent London excavations, reinforces the information from documents.

KINGS

955 BIG82 Acc No 2891 (Context 4342) Ceramic Phase 7
Wood; *Buxus sempervirens* (box); fragmentary piece; w 29mm; h 34mm; rounded-oval section; a slender, cylindrical projection extends from the top surface; a notch on the front, formed by two diagonal lines, allows the piece to be identified as a king.

956 SH74 363 (Unstratified) Fig 221
W 30mm; h 39mm; polished, hollow bone cylinder; possibly made from a horse metatarsus; the front face is notched to form a *mahout* (elephant driver) and identifies the piece as a king; cancellous tissue visible on the inner surface and traces of a foramen (but no medial line); ring-and-dot motifs engraved with framing lines are double about the mahout and triple about the top and bottom circumferences; some of the ring-and-dot motifs are linked by short lines.

BISHOPS

957 BIG82 Acc No 2288 (Context 2278) Ceramic Phase 8 Fig 222
Wood; *Buxus sempervirens* (box); d 25mm; h 33mm; identifiable as a bishop from the rounded apex with twin projections; cylindrical form with circular cross-section, narrowing towards the apex.

958 TL74 2588 (2467) 9
Wood; *Acer campestre* (field maple) or possibly *Pomoideae* sp. (pomaceous fruitwood); h 39m; d 26mm; abraded piece with rounded apex and twin projections; traces of red paint.

See also No 961.

ROOK

959 TL74 Acc No 2361 (Context 2666) Ceramic Phase 11 Fig 222
Antler; w 41mm; h 39mm; flattish cross-section; cut from the crown area of a fallow or red deer antler; of a characteristic rook form, with a curved V-notch cut into the upper surface and a perforation below the central point; the front and back panels are decorated by ring-and-dot motifs conjoined in four three-armed motifs with double rings and dots at their centres; two further double rings and dots extend below the central perforation; engraved triple framing lines surround this pattern (which is the same on both sides of the piece) and continue across the wedges over the top surface; a further, vertical engraved triple band adorns each short side; cancellous tissue remains but was plugged on the upper surface and base by four wedges of solid antler tissue, three of which survive.

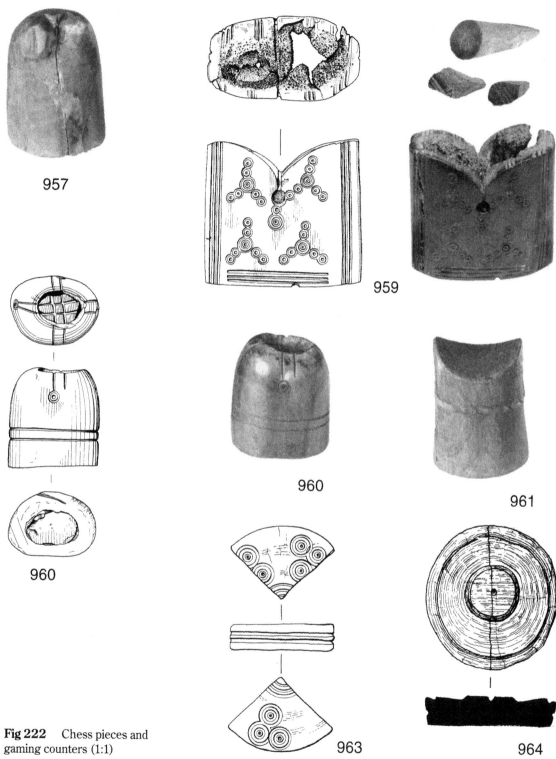

957

960

960

959

960

961

Fig 222 Chess pieces and gaming counters (1:1)

963

964

PAWNS

960 SWA81 Acc No 1338 (Context 2145) Ceramic Phase 9 Fig 222

Bone cylinder with rounded apex; w 25mm; h 25mm; hollow, with a cross-section suggesting that it was produced from a cattle metacarpus; plugged by a solid bone cylinder, with engraved double lines crossing and continuing onto the sides and ending in single ring-and-dot motifs; horizontal, paired engraved lines around the cylinder towards the base.

961 CUS73 157 (I,12) 9 Fig 222

Wood; *Taxus baccata* (yew); d 27mm; h 33mm; lathe-turned cylinder with flat base and bifacially concave, diagonally cut apex; horizontal, raised medial band with diagonal incisions, suggesting a cord pattern; a doubled variant of this motif extends vertically from the band on both sides, separated in one instance by a plain, raised band.

(Published by Henig – 1974, 199–200, no 243, fig 42 – 'probably a bishop'.)

Gaming counters

No counter of stone, bone or ceramic has been recognised in any deposit of appropriate date from the sites considered here, though bone examples are known from slightly earlier, and adapted ceramic sherds appear somewhat later (e.g., Pritchard 1991, 205–7, nos 238–43; Pearce 1984, 118–19, nos 101–7).

Wood
(Wood identifications are by Nigel Nayling)

These three counters all have black staining, and could be from sets in which the white pieces were of bone or even ivory, as opposed to pale wood. Only No 963 has decoration on both faces; the reason for this elaboration is unknown.

962 TL74 Acc No 233 (Context 414) Ceramic Phase 11

Wood unidentifiable (NN); turned; d 30mm; groove near perimeter; reserved, slightly concave central circle; groove around edge; trace of black staining; scratched on base.

963 SWA81 1707 (1031) 11 Fig 222

(?)Boxwood (?*Buxus* sp; NN); fragment; turned; d *c.*36mm; central dot with three concentric rings, and groups of three dots with two concentric rings, on each face; two grooves around edge; trace of black staining.

964 BC72 2811 (88/1) 11 Fig 222

(?)Pomaeceous fruitwood (?*Pomoideae* sp; NN); as No 962 (but no scratches); d 37mm.

Skates of bone

The late 12th-century account by Fitzstephen of skating on the marsh at London using animal bones (*ossa, tibias scilicit animalium*) is one of the major medieval documentary sources for the activity (Kingsford 1971, 2, 228). The iron ferrules on the poles used to propel the skaters forwards, which he also mentions (ibid.), have yet to be identified among archaeological material. The use of bone skates survived in London until the late 18th century (MacGregor 1976, 66). A full account of excavated skates is provided by MacGregor, who has also looked at the evidence of their wear patterns (1975; 1976; 1985a, 141–4). Stratified examples from London were briefly described by West (1982).

Bone skates (Fig 223) could be manufactured comparatively easily from horse or cattle metapodia or radii. Numbers 965–6 are fashioned from horse metapodia. After some use, the surface became narrow and flattened with wear. Holes were occasionally drilled to enable the feet to be fastened to the skate by cords, though none of the listed skates has this provision. In these, the weight of the body and the roughening of the posterior face for additional grip would have facilitated movement, particularly over very smooth ice (Ulbricht 1984, 61).

Skates Nos 965–6 are fashioned from the bones of mature horses with fused epiphyses. They may be compared with the size domains of 200–20mm established for skates found at Lund in Sweden (M Cinthio in Mårtensson 1976, 385). Number 965 is extremely short and comes from a young animal smaller than the average Shetland pony.

The London finds from deposits of appropriate date for this present study seem few, particularly when compared with the numbers retrieved at York, Schleswig (Germany), Lund

Fig 223 Bone skates from various London sites (reduced)

(Sweden), and elsewhere (MacGregor 1976, 65; Ulbricht 1984, 60; M Cinthio in Mårtensson 1976, 383–5). However, larger numbers of skates have been found in London in somewhat earlier deposits (Pritchard 1991, 208–9, 266, nos 253–9).

The skates listed here may have been used on any of the frozen waterways within or outside the city.

965 GPO75 Acc No 3671 (Context 540) Ceramic Phase 6
L 174mm; small horse metatarsus; proximal end is trimmed slightly on anterior face; distal end is shaped to an upswept point around the central condyle; anterior face has a series of knife marks, clustering towards the proximal end (not smoothed).
(West 1982, no 7)

966 WAT78 1030 (2526) 9
Fragment of distal end; surviving l 75mm; modified horse metacarpal; asymmetrically pointed; anterior face is smoothed but only slightly modified from the natural surface.
(West 1982, no 5)

967 WAT78 1190 (2526) 9
L 159mm; cattle metacarpal; flat, pointed distal end; proximal end slightly narrowed; no wear.
Apparently unused.
(West 1982, no 6)

Balls of leather

968 BC72 Acc No 3481 (Context 251) Ceramic Phase 10 Fig 224
Incomplete; ?sheep/goat leather (G Edwards); roughly circular piece; d *c*.60mm; stitch holes around perimeter.
Two such circles and a strip would have made up a ball – Fig 224 top right – which would have been stuffed with moss etc. (cf. J H Thornton in Biddle 1990, 707–8, nos 2246–7, fig 198 for two earlier examples).

969 BC72 3414 (150) 11 Fig 224
Incomplete and distorted; present dimensions *c*.42×*c*.34mm; (?)cattle leather (G Edwards); three surviving pieces, each a quarter sphere or somewhat less, from the original four; core of tightly packed moss survives.

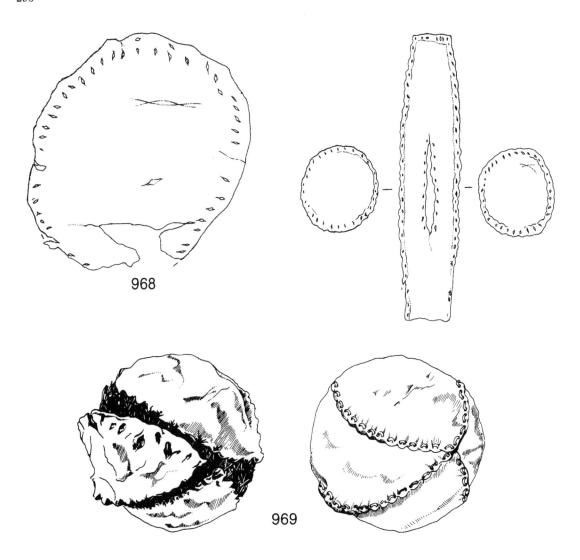

Fig 224   Leather balls (top left and below 1:1; top right after Biddle 1990, not to scale)

ARTICLE FOR A DOMESTIC PET

Chain swivel

Copper alloy

970 BWB83 Acc No 3600 (Context 391) Ceramic Phase 11 Fig 225

Cast oval link with round section, 144mm, and swivel attached to another link of different form having a central, circular collar at one end; the swivel is made from a cast rod, which tapers to a terminal knop, and beyond a rabbet to fit the collared link it is turned back on itself so that the end fits into a bent, circular, rectangular-section collar; total l of surviving parts 97mm; there is wear at the point of swivelling, and the collared link is bent from strain.

Probably from a lead for a pet. While the form might be appropriate for a chain for suspending a cooking pot over the fire (cf. No 499), the use of copper alloy rather than iron seems more appropriate to a domestic animal, such as a large dog.

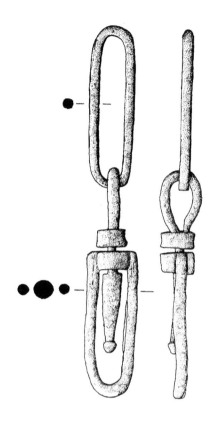

970

Fig 225   Chain swivel, (?)for a pet (1:1)

Articles relating to religion and beliefs

STAND FOR A RELIGIOUS FIGURINE

Lead/tin

971 BWB83 Acc No 603 (Context 401) Ceramic Phase 11 Fig 226

Pewter (AML, Table 8); found twisted; four-footed support stand; 78×58mm; h 43mm; the trilobed feet are on short legs that taper towards the flat top, which has an edge rabbet, and a cross-hatched triangle at each corner, two with round holes and two with damaged ones, and there is a slot in the plain, central area; the sides have openwork vine-scroll motifs, including trilobed leaves and bunches

of grapes on sinuous stems, with beading along the upper and lower borders and cross-hatching at the ends; there is a blob of excess metal on top at one corner; probably from a six-part mould.

The item missing from the top of this decorative stand may have been a figure of a Virgin/Virgin and Child, or of a saint. The plain, central octagonal area of the stand may provide a hint as to the figure's basal shape, and the five holes would have held it in place. Despite its relatively crude execution, the design on the side panels is strikingly effective.

Compare a free-standing, seated figurine of the Virgin (h 86mm) found in Salisbury, for a rare survival of a lead/tin devotional representation in the round, of the general character that may be appropriate for the present stand (B Spencer in Alexander & Binski 1987, 224, no 85; *idem* 1990, 24–5, 73, fig 40, no 35). A 13th-century Limoges enamelled copper-alloy Virgin and Child on a stand (270×130mm, see Fig 226) provides a closely comparable form in more expensive materials (Mickenberg et al. 1985, 165–7, no 48), and the seated Virgin with Child figurines published by Hildburgh (1955) include a range of broadly similar copper-alloy enamelled images with and without stands. The cheaper metal of No 971 may have been appropriate for a devout household.

JET BOWL

972 TL74 Acc No 2746 (Context 368) Ceramic Phase 12 Fig 227

Base/side fragment of turned and polished bowl; d at surviving top 139mm; d at base 60mm; h 30mm+; worn on foot-ring.

No parallel is known (indeed, no other medieval vessel of jet has been traced, though there are less highly polished shale bowls from the Roman period). With the exception of the shallow concavity and central spur (chuck) mark in the foot-ring, and allowing for a slight increase in thickness at various points to make this easily shattered material less liable to breakage, the form is similar to that of contemporary wooden bowls (e.g., No 589). Carole Morris suggests that the present vessel was probably turned by someone used to producing wooden ones, despite the minor differences on the base.

Investigation of a sample from the bowl using a Carbon/Hydrogen/Nitrogen micro-combustion analyser at the Department of Mineralogy (British

971

Fig 226   Stand for religious figurine (1:1) and, right, Limoges enamelled figure of Virgin and Child on stand (reduced)

Museum, Natural History) and kindly carried out by Garry Jones, produced a result that fits well with the known content of jet (carbon 75.9, hydrogen 6.9 and nitrogen 1.9 by weight).

Presumably the vessel is made from jet obtained in the Whitby area of Yorkshire, though jet from northern Spain was also used in the medieval period (Qualmann 1991, 71). The use of this material for such an item is remarkable. It is likely that jet was only exceptionally available in lumps of this size (some pieces on display in shops in Whitby in 1993

and claimed to be the largest known might just about have produced a bowl of similar dimensions, if the missing top portion did not make it much taller). That the bowl was traded over a considerable distance may imply that, despite its everyday form, it was regarded as an item that was special in some way. It was almost certainly a very expensive item.

Some of the supposed powers of jet are mentioned in 15th-century English lapidaries, for example: in powder form it was used to clean the teeth; when burned it apparently drove away serpents; it allegedly alleviated gout; 'undoth and voideth witchecraft and shames'; furnished a test for virginity; eased problems with dysmenorrhaea; and 'if a woman travails of a child, and drinks of the water that it has lain in three days and three nights, soon shall she be

Pritchard 1991, 310. The complete absence of the original rim could possibly be the result of rough removal of a mount, perhaps of precious metal, set around the lip, but this is pure speculation.

BENT TOKENS

A number of folded, late 13th–14th-century lead/tin tokens of the kind intended for use as small change have been found at the waterfront sites among large numbers of undamaged examples. The deliberate distortion of these coin-like objects may relate to beliefs in sacrificial practices originating in the remote past, perhaps being intended in the medieval period to bring good luck for a journey or other enterprise (Merrifield 1987, 109–11, where it is suggested that these items represent some kind of continuing water cult deposition). All the tokens examined were found in reclamation

delivered' (Evans & Serjeantson 1933, 32, citing the *London Lapidary of King Philip*; ibid. 90–1, 130, citing the related *Peterborough Lapidary* and the *Sloane Lapidary*). Liquid drunk from a vessel made of jet may well have been credited with the same virtue for helping ease childbirth as water in which jet had been placed for the required period; this seems (to a modern commentator at least) the most plausible of the possible uses for this item. A background of the beliefs outlined would account for the manufacture and long-distance trade of an otherwise improbable object: it can be seen as a very valuable piece of medical equipment for treating women in accordance with folk tradition. For the likely association of red coral items excavated at waterfront sites with beliefs about childbirth and babies, see Egan &

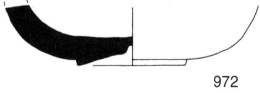

972

Fig 227 Jet vessel (1:2)

dumps rather than foreshore deposits, which means that a direct connection between the River Thames and the discarding is uncertain; they may have been thrown away or lost some distance from the waterfront. Most of the bent tokens (at least seven examples) are from the SWA81 site, the great majority being from Group 74 deposits attributed to the late 13th century. There appears to be only one bent example from any other phase among the assemblages considered (BWB83 acc no 994, from a layer attributed to ceramic phase 11). None of the large number of tokens thought to be from ceramic phases 11 and 12 from the TL74 (S E Rigold in Milne & Milne 1982, 102–6, nos 60–110) and SWA81 sites has been treated in this way. Many of the later issues of the series have smaller flans than those illustrated, perhaps making bending slightly more difficult, but it would by no means have been impossible. Overall, the evidence so far for the practice is focused on the late 13th century, and it could arguably be attributed to less than a handful of individuals. The purpose, if there was one, remains obscure. A selection of bent tokens from the SWA81 site is illustrated in Fig 228.

Fig 228   Bent tokens from SWA81 site (2:1)

Weighing apparatus

GEOFF EGAN

Weights

The complicated documentary history of weights for the period concerned has been investigated by Zupko (1977) and Connor (1987), while Biggs (1992, 1995) provides useful summaries of the main varieties excavated. Hall & Nicholas (1929) give contemporary tables etc. of weight systems and equivalents. The excavated medieval weights from Winchester have recently been considered in detail against the documented background (Biddle 1990, 1908–25). As the present work goes to press, a complete reappraisal of documentary and some of the artefact evidence (Simpson & Connor 1996; Connor & Simpson forthcoming) is providing a new analysis within a broad north-European context. Especial use has been made in that work of the commentary on merchant trading by the Italian representative of the banking house of Bardi, Francesco Pegolotti, who was the manager of the London branch in 1317–21 and of others elsewhere in Europe during his career. What follows tries to take account of some of the very recent re-interpretations; at the same time, it is felt that since so much basic information in this most complex subject is being altered, reference should be made to the framework broadly accepted up to now (enshrined in Connor 1987) – at least until a wider readership has had a chance to assimilate and consider over a longer period the sometimes radical implications. The range of possible standards can be bewildering to all but those at the forefront of research, and debate on key points is unlikely to be over. To quote Allen Simpson, it just is a very involved subject (pers comm).

The objects listed below in this category are all pan (lay) weights, or items of similar form; that is, if they have indeed been correctly identified, they were for setting in the pans of scales rather than for suspension/attachment directly from the arms of steelyards (steelyard weights, like weights for fishing nets and lines would probably all have had holes for suspension/attachment – see Cherry 1991a, 47; Steane & Foreman 1988, 153–6, 162–5, figs 9, 10, 15; 1991, 94–8, figs 12.5, 12.8). It is remarkable that none of the armorial copper-alloy steelyard suspension weights, of the kind from London published by Ward Perkins (1940, 171–4, pl 38) were found at the sites included in this survey (No 1032 of lead and its parallel seem to have one of the shields of arms commonly found on the steelyard series – the holes in these lead weights may possibly mean that they too were for suspension).

Attribution of many of the items listed below to any of the main postulated medieval systems (mercantile, avoirdupois, troy and perhaps to Tower and apothecaries' standards – see Table 14) can be difficult for a number of reasons. English troy and the apothecaries' systems are identical at one ounce and upwards, while for the mercantile system at 16 ounces to the pound and the Tower system the ounce and its divisions are identical. Interpretation at this stage of investigations inevitably comes down to a consideration of the degree of deviation from a suggested standard, sometimes along with a value judgement of the likelihood that the particular form was indeed intended to be used as a weight in the first place. Many of the objects listed would probably not have been considered 'household' items by the users; they are included here in order to present together all the information about this difficult and broad category of objects.

It would be unfair to use the apparent inaccuracy of many of the catalogue items to condemn, from a modern standpoint, weighing practice in the Middle Ages as a pretty comprehensive shambles (though this was the temptation prior to trying the recently reappraised standards). Overall, the close correspondence

Table 14: Systems of weights suggested to have been in use in England in the Middle Ages

Figures are given in **grams**. To convert to grains multiply gram figures by 15.4323.
(The table is adapted from Biddle 1990, 911, with supplements – including several from Allen Simpson. The figures given as standards do not represent a single point of view; instead they seek to include the most plausible suggestions put forward over recent years.)

	Mercantile systems		Avoirdupois systems		Tower system (mint use ?etc.)	English troy system	Apothecaries' system
	1lb=15oz of 29.2gm	1lb=16oz of 29.2gm both from pre-1300	1lb=15oz of 28.4gm from ?pre-1280	1lb=16oz of 28.4gm from pre-1300	1lb=12oz of 29.2gm from 1250 or earlier	1lb=12oz of 31.1gm 1350s/70s+	1lb=12oz of 31.1gm, as English troy ?c.1400+
1lb	437.4	466.6	425.3	453.6	349.9 (240 pence)	373.2 (French system 367/gms)	373.2
2/3lb					1 mark=233.3 (160 pence)	248.8 (=1 mark)	
1/2lb	218.7	233.3	212.6	226.8	175.0	186.6	
1/3lb					1 noble=116.6 (80 pence)	124.4 (=½ mark)	
1/4lb	109.4	116.6	106.3	113.4	87.5	93.3	
1/6lb					58.3	62.2 (=¼ mark)	
1/8lb	54.6	58.3	53.2	56.7	43.7	46.6	
1/12lb					29.2 (20 pence)	31.1 (=20 pennyweight) (French system 30.6gms)	31.1
1/15lb	[29.2]	[31.1]	[28.4]	[30.2]			
1/16lb	(27.3)	29.2	(26.6)	28.4			
				dram 1.77 (¹⁄₁₆oz)	penny coin 1.46	12 pennyweight 18.70	1 drachm 3.89
					halfpenny coin .73	4 pennyweight 6.23	1 scruple 1.29
						2 pennyweight 3.11	
						1 pennyweight 1.56	
						half pennyweight .78	

Note: The weight of the penny coin (troy pennyweights etc. above are unrelated to coins) was changed during the period considered: from the Norman Conquest to the mid-14th century the full sterling penny weighed 32 grains of wheat (dry, in the midst of the ear'), the equivalent of 22.5 grains of barley (though in practice the weights of newly minted pennies of this date might be anything between 18 and 24 grains – Feavearyear 1963, 8–10); in 1351 the standard was officially altered to 18 grains of barley, and in 1412 to 12 grains.

Avoirdupois weights are thought to have come into use in the 13th century (probably between 1280 and 1300 according to Connor 1987, 129; Allen Simpson notes an English husbandry reference of c.1280 to wool-weighing with a 16oz standard – pers comm) and Biggs regards the English troy system as starting between 1351 and the late 1370s under the influence of goldsmiths, correspondence with earlier systems being fortuitous (1995, 14).

The problems of the number of ounces in a pound, and of which standard a pound referred to in documentary sources actually respects, is highly complex (see Simpson & Connor 1996 and Connor & Simpson forthcoming for the most recent view). The 16oz mercantile pound was in use from the 13th century, but before that the pound was made up of 15oz (claims that a 16oz mercantile pound of 497.7 grams was in use for a period in the 14th and 15th centuries seem to result from relatively recent confusion of documentary evidence – Connor 1987, 128). A London pound of 12 ounces is mentioned some time prior to 1327. Norman Biggs (pers comm) suggests that there was a 'Roman-tradition' system of ounces, or *ore*, of *c.*27gms still in usage in the early part of the period covered (this might arguably correspond with Simpson's sixteenth usage of a mercantile 15-ounce pound), and that the avoirdupois pound was re-divided from 15 into 16 ounces as late as *c.*1380 under the influence of the Grocers' Guild (which had an obvious concern for the regulation of weights for expensive spices etc. and was checking the accuracy of those in use in London by 1386 – see Nightingale 1995, 202–3). Connor identifies pounds used in England of 15 and 16 ounces, but both, Simpson believes (pers comm), were always divided into 16 parts for everyday weighing – i.e., any surviving weights will be based on binary divisions rather than fifteenths (but see Biddle 1990, 912–13, nos 3188, 3194, 3194A for items there identified as possible one-third pound weights). The apothecaries' system appears to have been particularly chaotic until the post-medieval period.

Other possible standards of ounces of *c.*24.4gms and – based on study of mainly slightly earlier weights found in Dublin – *c.*26.6gms (cf. Biggs's *ore* again?), have been suggested for the period just preceding that covered here (cited by Kruse 1992, 86; cf. Wallace 1988); these might be considered for potential residual items or late usage.

Simpson & Connor have found further complexity with evidence for the use in medieval England of some Continental standards, relating to usage in the places particular goods were traded from: e.g., a Paris pound of 489.9gms, a Bruges pound (14oz) of 435.5gms, a Florentine grosso of 452.5gms – and the pound of 471.0gms used in London for spices was that of Antwerp, the port from which this commodity entered England (Simpson & Connor 1996, 1989–95).

of a significant number of the catalogue items with suggested standards is surely more striking. Limitations on production technology meant that contemporary hardware was simply unable to sustain standards acceptable today, and items which are other than very accurate for defined standards may have had some different function (it can nevertheless be difficult to resist wishing things were just a little more closely definable).

The author is grateful to Professor Norman Biggs (London School of Economics), Professor R D Connor (University of Manitoba, Canada) and to Allen Simpson (National Museums of Scotland, Edinburgh) for many useful suggestions in this still developing field of study. There are discernible clusters among the listed finds around the (?)26.5, 54, 110, 220 and 440gm marks (and in these Allen Simpson sees support for the 15-ounce mercantile pound standard using binary divisions – see below). Figure 229 gives an indication of the listed weights that can potentially be identified with standards that have been suggested. Overall, Simpson's various proposals have the merit (presuming the results are not misleading) that almost a quarter more of the entire total of the items listed below are now provisionally identifiable (see Table 15) than was achieved using the standards as previously defined by researchers. (The recent work appears to give a new perspective particularly on the listed conical/pyramidal weights, Nos 1033–8, none of which was previously given an identification, but for which four of the six now have tentative attributions to standards.) There are, on the other hand, now more standards to consider, and the additional possibilities inevitably give more scope for identifications. For this author, the most difficult notion in Simpson's views is the key one that while contemporary documents mention 15-ounce mercantile and avoirdupois pounds, these pounds were regularly (invariably?) divided into sixteen parts in everyday usage, and that excavated objects, the weights, will reflect only binary divisions of the pounds (pers comm). Binary divisions are those used for calculations and attributions in this present chapter, and the results do seem to lend support to this view. Cup weight No 976, which must surely represent some particu-

Table 15: Weights of catalogued items
Listed in order of increasing heaviness (unstratified items are not included)

Catalogue no	Ceramic phase	Shape	Weight (gms)	Catalogue no	Ceramic phase	Shape	Weight (gms)
Copper alloy				*Lead*			
977	9	R	2.45	1033✓✓−/✓+	7	C	29.5
978	11	S	2.45	990✓✓−/✓+/−	10	R	30.0
973	6	R	5.25	1036	11	C	39.5
979	11	S	7.35	1000	11	R	43.5
974	6	R	[12+]	1018(?)✓✓/✓+	9	S	47.5
976✓✓−	7	R (cup)	13.5	1001	11	R	49.0
975	6	R	[14.5+]	1002✓−	11	R	51.0
				1010 ✓−	12	R	51.0
Lead				987✓✓+	9	R	53.5
1023✓✓+	12	S	1.72	1037✓✓+	11	C	53.5
1024	12	S	2.46	1011✓✓−/+	12	R	54.0
995	11	R	3.65	988✓✓−	9	R	54.5
1029✓−	11	H	3.80	1003✓+	11	R	64.5
982✓✓−	7	R	4.35	993(?)✓+	10	R	72.0
1027✓✓+	8	H	4.40	989	6–9	R	74.0
980 [✓✓+]	6	R	4.68	1038✓✓+	11	C	94.0
1025	12	S	5.40	1012	12	R	98.5
1034	11	C	5.85	984	7	R	101.0
1022✓✓+/✓−	(?)11	S	6.75	1004✓✓+	11	R	109.5
1026✓−/+	xf(?)12	S	6.95	1019✓✓/✓−	9	S	111.5
1009(?)✓✓−	12	R	7.00	1005✓✓/✓+	11	R	118.5
985	8	R	8.00	981	6	R	196.0
1028✓✓+	8	H	8.80	1013	12	R	[<201.5]
1031	11	Sh	12.5	1020✓✓−	9	S	208.5
1035✓−	11	C	13.0	1006✓✓−/✓+	11	R	218.5
986✓✓−	9	R	14.0	1014✓✓+/✓−/+	12	R	219.5
983	7	R	16.0	1007✓✓−	11	R	226.0
996	11	R	20.0	1015(?)✓−	12	R	266.0
991	10	R	21.0	994✓+	10–11	R	390.5
992	10	R	22.5	1008✓−	11	R	440.5
997✓−	11	R	26.0	1017✓✓+/✓−	7	R	441.5
1032✓✓−	11	Sh	26.5	1021(?)✓✓−	9	S	541.5
998✓✓+	11	R	27.0				
999✓✓+	11	R	28.5				

C=conical/pyramidal
R=round (including semicircular and ovoid)
S=square/rectangular
H=hide-shaped
S=shield-shaped
[ ]=measured weight does not accurately reflect that intended
✓✓=*probable* correspondence with a standard (i.e., +/− <2%)

✓=*possible* correspondence with a standard
   (i.e., +/− 2 to 5%)
+=heavy for standard suggested
−=light for standard suggested

Measured weights for listed items over 10gms are correct to nearest 0.5gm (0.1gm for those between 10 and 5gms, and 0.01gm for those of 5gms or less).

lar standard, becomes identifiable using binary divisions, for example. Some of the listed weights respect specified standards very precisely indeed – 17 of the 66 catalogue items are within 1% of a suggested weight without further qualifications (such as apparent anachronisms). Numbers 1019 and 1028 have seemingly been slightly adjusted, the former by adding metal, the latter by removing it; both adaptations imply a concern for high-precision weigh-

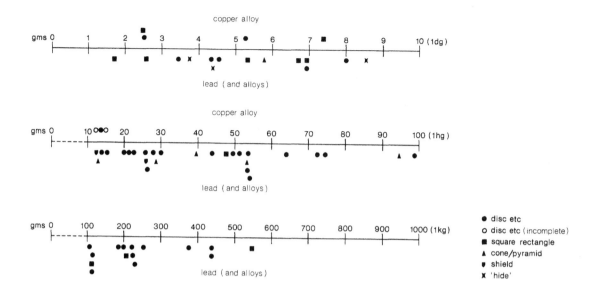

Fig 229 Distribution of weights of catalogued items

ing. The susceptibility of lead to abrasion from long-term use, and of both lead and copper alloys to corrosion during burial, may not present a major difficulty with the exceptionally well-preserved objects discussed here, few of which appear to have sustained a significant degree of wear (instances in which such factors are considered significant are indicated by the use of square brackets around the measured weights – Nos 974–5, 1013). Together with the advantage to the seller in many kinds of everyday transaction if the weights were deliberately short, wear could mean there is a tendency for some items to be rather lighter than the appropriate standards. As it turns out, 24 catalogue items for which standards have been suggested appear to be a little light, while 23 appear to be slightly heavy (some of these objects are light for one suggested standard and heavy for another). A marginally heavy weight would, in theory, benefit a trader buying goods, though it is unlikely that sellers would have failed to insist on checks, using their own or other trusted weights to avoid being put at a disadvantage.

London was a centre for weighing standards from before the Norman Conquest (see Stenton 1934, 11, for 'the weight of the hustings of

London' used for silver cups, in a document from the late 10th century). The Assize of Weights and Measures (date uncertain, 'before the reign of Edward III' – i.e., pre-1327) mentions the 'London pound' of 12 ounces, but 'the pound of pence, spices, confections ... [and] electuaries [medicines] consists of twenty shillings', while 'the pound of all other things weighs twenty five shillings' (Statutes of the Realm 1, 204–5), while Connor cites a 13th-century mention of a London pound of 15 ounces (1987, 126; see Sharpe 1905, 300 for a London reference from 1372 to 'the Guildhall weight, viz 15 ounces to the pound', for groceries, spices, drugs etc.). The implications of these and other early texts are further analysed by Simpson & Connor 1996 and Connor & Simpson forthcoming. Statute 14 Ed III st 1 c12 (1340) reiterated legislation from 1297 and additionally prohibited selling by the bushel, gallon or ell, unless the measure was marked with 'the king's iron' (i.e., stamp or brand), as in an earlier pronouncement of uncertain date (??51 Henry III or perhaps 13 Edward I, i.e., 1266 or 1285 – see Statutes of the Realm 1, 203). This tradition of officially marking measures, probably of wood in these particular instances, is reflected in some of the metal items catalogued below (see on marking the equipment for weighing coins and on coin weights issued by the authorities).

Although a degree of imprecision might be expected of weights made in a period lacking the extremely accurate weighing devices available today, serious deviation would have been limited by the attempts of the authorities to maintain contemporary standards by official marking (from at least 1357 under the authority of Statute 31 Ed III st 1 c2 for avoirdupois weights, which were checked and stamped at the Guildhall, and from the early 1370s for troy weights, which came under the control of the Goldsmiths' Company – Reddaway 1975, 33, 56).

The easiest way today of obtaining a basic identification of some of the likely standards for excavated items is by means of a fairly simple set of scales with the main units of measurement then in use marked, taking the pointer as an approximate indicator. Very accurate scientific apparatus (like the Sartorius electronic precision toploader balance used in measuring the actual weights given below against each catalogue item) is less immediately helpful for this purpose.

There are very few cases among the items listed below of repeated standard forms to help identify any recognisable series, and even where typological similarity is beyond question (e.g., Nos 974–5 with 985–6, Nos 1023–4 and Nos 1036–7, the last pair having been found together) there is no clear relationship in terms of the measured weights (in the instances of Nos 1036–7 and of 1032 and its parallel, their apparently similar size would have added further confusion to this; such indications as there are suggest that particular forms of weight were not restricted to any single system – that is, similar-looking items will not necessarily prove to belong to a single series). A surviving late medieval set of nest weights from London furnishes a rational series, though it almost certainly just post-dates the period considered in this volume (see on No 976). Individual medieval weights do not necessarily conform to a measure that is immediately apparent to latter-day researchers, partly because of the diversity of weight systems now understood to have been in use at trade centres like London

at this period (cf. Simpson & Connor, 1996). A rare survival of an official lead weight, from Yorkshire, dated to the late 13th/early 14th century, has been claimed to represent a 6¼lb avoirdupois standard (i.e., 1 clove, used for weighing wool – Connor 1987, 136–7, fig 29), though it may alternatively relate to a Venetian bullion standard of 12 marks (Allen Simpson pers comm). Some of the items listed which are among the most certain in terms of their precise measures are of markedly crude form (e.g., Nos 987, 999, 1006). Conversely, it is quite possible that even some of the neatest forms among the catalogue items are simply ingots. The standard(s) represented by the relatively few items dated to prior to c.1250 are debatable (the mercantile/goods 15-ounce pound and English troy systems give close correspondence with Nos 976, 980 and 1017 – the troy system may not have been introduced as early as this, though – while No 1033 has more than one likely correspondence with other systems, none of which seems entirely satisfactory at such an early date). The most likely everyday standards for the excavated weights from later deposits (the various mercantile and avoirdupois systems) are presumed to have been used mainly for measuring comestibles such as bread and salt as well as other goods; the mercantile system was eventually not used for spices or bullion, the latter being catered for by the troy system. These three systems, mercantile, avoirdupois and troy, all appear to be prominently represented among the interpreted finds. Numbers 976, 988, 990, 1004–6, 1011, 1014, 1017, 1019, (?)1021, 1022–3, 1033 and 1035 may represent the mercantile goods weight of the internal English markets, while Nos 986–7, 997–9, 1002, 1005–8, 1010–11, 1014, 1017, 1019–20, 1022, 1026, 1032, 1035 and 1037 may represent the avoirdupois system. The troy systems (E=English, F=French) may be represented by Nos (?)980 (E), 990 (F or E), 994 (E), 1003 (E), (?)1009 (E), (?)1015 (E), 1018 (E or F), 1033 (F) and 1038 (E). The Tower-standard pound of 12 ounces has one item potentially identified, No 1033, though it could equally plausibly relate to the mercantile 16-ounce pound system (Connor believes the Tower system was probably used only by the Mint authorities to check newly

produced coins at the Tower of London – 1987,
125–6; the Tower ounce was also the Cologne
standard, as well as the definition ounce for the
English 15- and 16-ounce mercantile pound).
Similarly, only one catalogue item is provisionally identified below for the apothecaries'
system, which was probably introduced around
the turn of the 15th century (No 1029, a small,
'hide'-shaped weight attributed to ceramic
phase 11), though others could be identified as
above with the English troy system, which was
identical at one ounce and upwards. Numbers
982, (?)993, and 1027–8 could relate to the
weight of coins.

More of the listed items were found in land
reclamation rubbish dumps than from foreshore deposits, so the waterfront findspots
cannot be claimed necessarily to indicate trading at the river's edge rather than elsewhere in
the city. It is impossible to say, for instance,
whether any of the large number of weights
recovered in the Billingsgate area relate to the
salt market there (Bridbury 1955, 139) or to
other specific commerce in the riverside local-
ity, like selling fish and shellfish; alternatively
they may derive from the wider trade in the
city.

The lead discs (Nos 980–1016) are very
diverse, ranging from 3.65 to 440.5gms. The
likely identifications for the cones/pyramids
(1033–8) imply that, contrary to previous suggestions, these were indeed used during the
medieval period for precise weighing. Each of
the copper-alloy and the 'hide'-shaped lead
items (Nos 973–9 and 1027–30) weighs less
than half a modern ounce. Only one catalogued
item, No 1021, weighs (approximately) as much
as a pound and a quarter by any of the systems
considered.

With the above uncertainties, and with at
least three main systems of weighing current
by the end of the medieval period, it can be
easy to fall into the snare of trying to define
some items by allowing too great a tolerance
from the standards, or by trying to identify
them as improbable measures or fractions (see
following No 975 and on Nos 1009, 1015, 1021).
No 980 has one of the most precise matches
with a specified standard among the catalogued
items, but its early context appears to pre-date
the use of the particular system. The nest of

weights described under No 976 seem each to
be within 6.5% of the intended standard (the
lightness of the majority may largely be
explained by over cleaning subsequent to
recovery) and a series of six standard weights
for the city of Winchester from the time of
Edward III have all been said to be well within
2% of the precise measures, even if they are all
very slightly light (Connor 1987, 129; their lead
adjustment plugs may have been altered in
1558 to make them conform with a new standard and so they can reveal nothing precise
about the medieval standard – Allen Simpson
pers comm). If one were to suppose a deviation
in weights greater than, say, 10% – which would
have had serious implications for profit margins
etc. – the chances are that an alternative standard equally close and equally plausible could
be identified (some researchers regard a 2%
deviation as the maximum likely to have been
at all widespread among honest dealers).

In the listing and discussion below, an object is
taken *'probably'* to be a weight of a specified
measure if it falls within a tolerance of 2% (one
fiftieth) or less of the suggested standard, and
'possibly' of the specified measure if the tolerance
lies between 2% and 5% (one twentieth) of the
standard (the deviations from suggested standards are given to the nearest 0.1%) and 'almost
precise' additionally indicates matches with less
than 1% deviation. Possibilities involving greater
variance than one-twentieth of standard are indicated by *'perhaps'*.

This approach brings a measure of objectivity
into the broader framework of uncertainties.
Bearing in mind the above reservations, items
having less than 2% deviation are in most cases
taken to be intended for the weight suggested.
Only one of the seven catalogued copper-alloy
weights has been identified using these conventions, but 39 of the 57 stratified lead ones
have a standard suggested – with varying
degrees of confidence – see Table 15 (a couple
of these seem implausible for the reasons
stated in the catalogue entries); several of these
items have two or more suggested identifications relating to different standards. There may
well be more scope for identifying some of the
smaller items as fractions of ounces than is
indicated in the catalogue; but for the present

it remains uncertain which fractions are most likely to have been used (would troy and Tower ounces at twelve to the pound themselves be divided by twelve or sixteen, for example? – see following No 979). It is quite possible, with so many standards to consider, that some of the correspondences indicated are purely fortuitous, and this may even be true of some of the most exact matches (e.g., No 980). A few items, which seem from their appearance surely to have been weights of some kind, are left without suggested identifications (e.g., No 1024). With 40 items potentially having identifications, 24 appear slightly light and 23 slightly heavy (several have more than one possibility) – of these, 17 have almost exact correspondences (i.e., within 1% of suggested standard) and Nos 1004 and 1006 are only about 0.09% heavy (less than 1/1000th). As mentioned above, assuming true weights in the first place, a tendency towards lightness due to wear is perhaps to be expected with lead items, though this would be difficult to differentiate from deliberately light weights to favour the seller of goods.

Figure 229 suggests some groupings among the present London finds, which may become clearer and allow further inferences to be drawn in future, as information from other weights, including ones from elsewhere, is added. It is hoped that future publications of probable and possible weights will always include the weight as measured for each item (in a readily accessible standard such as grams).

The stamps from official checking, the cast or scratched privy marks signifying the owners, and the integral decoration (even where it is rather crude, as on No 1032) on some of the items below can in most cases be taken to indicate that they are indeed weights. The Judgement of the Pillory (?Statute 51 Hen III, i.e., 1266) mentions 'pounds, a half pounds and other little weights [material unspecified] wherewith the bread of the town or of the Court is measured', requiring that 'on every measure weight ... the name of the owner [should be] distinctly written'. Though this may indicate a temporary administrative expedient while all weights in use for bread were themselves being measured against the standards (Statutes of the Realm 1, 201), from around this time the

practice of adding personal names may gradually have become more widely equated with fair dealing. None of the excavated weights has a clear owner's name (No 1011 could possibly have an illegible one) but privy marks, as on Nos 990, 997 and 1015, might perhaps in due course have been considered an acceptable substitute. Crown stamps, as on Nos 1007 and 1014, have only recently been recognised. They suggest governmental regulation (cf. the Statutes of 1340 and earlier mentioned above, which made provision especially for wooden measures, and also Statute 20 Ed I, 4 of 1292, whereby weights for coins should be delivered to the warden of the exchange for marking with the king's stamp – Mayhew 1975, 395). The variance in weight from the suggested standards for these two items is very slight indeed for the former and just over 3% for the latter if they were for an avoirdupois system (another, unprovenanced disc-shaped, (?)one-pound avoirdupois weight of *c*.456gms in a private collection has a similar stamp; cf. also Biggs 1992, 44).

Few of the weights listed here are small enough to have been used with the scale pans or with the parts of balances catalogued at the end of this section, most of which may have been for weighing precious items, perhaps spices, and for checking coins. Balance fork No 1056 is from a very small version (no large balances or even identified parts of them were recovered at the sites included in this survey).

Even though, according to documentary sources, coin weights produced by those working in the Mint were available in the 13th and 14th centuries (e.g., a 'penny poise' from 1205), of the listed items only three – No 982 attributed to the early 13th century and Nos 1027–8 attributed to the 13th/early 14th centuries – emerge from detailed analysis as probably suitable for testing coins in small numbers, and none from the (?)official series that is certainly this early has been identified from wider enquiries (cf. Withers & Withers 1994, 6–8; Biggs 1990, 69–75 – e.g., pl 14.6 for a possible rectangular lead example with a king's head, found in London and probably from the 14th century). Lead and copper-alloy coin weights with appropriate issue-specific designs (as on those produced respectively from the mid-14th

Fig 230 Copper-alloy weights (1:1)

and early 15th centuries – cf. Biggs 1990, pls 14.7–9, 15; Withers & Withers 1994, 8–10) are absent from the excavated assemblages. The coin weights marked with the king's stamp referred to above from the Statute of 1292 may have been for bulk measurements rather than for individual coins. Balances similar in form to No 1059 below, which did not require separate weights, would also have been used. The main need for weights for individual coins would have come from 1344 when the first regular English gold issues began, though French gold (current from 1255) might have warranted an earlier, more limited use. Further, unofficial, weights for this purpose may perhaps survive unrecognised among the great numbers of amorphous pieces of copper alloy and lead found at most waterfront sites and widely elsewhere. See Egan & Pritchard for the apparent use of a coin pennyweight standard for precious metal dress accessories (1991, 255, no 1337).

Copper alloy

These all weigh less than the modern ½oz. An unidentified standard of (?)2.45gms may perhaps be represented by Nos 977–9 (see also No 1024 of lead), apart from which only one of the seven items listed here has a likely identification – No 976 for the mercantile 15-ounce pound system. More investigation of usage of fractions of ounces could furnish further potential identifications here.

973 SWA81 Acc No 1612 (Context 2176) Ceramic Phase 6
Disc; d 18mm; th 2mm; 5.25gms; worn.

974 BWB83 3036 (173) 6
Corroded; copper-alloy sheeting around iron core; round, bifacially bevelled with flat ends; d 16mm; stamped at each end with three circles in beaded border [12.0gms+].

975 SWA81 1389 (2188) 6 Fig 230
As preceding item, but d 18mm [14.5gms+].

The two preceding weights are clearly related typologically, though it is difficult, particularly in view of the damage, which involves weight loss, to suggest a common unit of measurement.

A larger, complete weight of this form (d 23mm; 51gms) was found in VHA89 spoil (reference no V590). Compare also Mårtensson 1976, 191, fig 134, for three similar examples excavated at Lund in Sweden and dated to the 11th and 12th centuries. The form is well known in earlier, Viking period, contexts elsewhere in England and on the Continent (cf.

Biggs's 'barrel-shaped weight for the Saxon-Viking ora, 10th–11th century' – 1992, 14; Biggs regards these as bullion weights). Kruse cites a suggested standard of *c*.24.4gms for weights of this form (1992, 86) – Nos 974–5 might respectively be seen as a half and (??)seven-twelfths of such a standard, but there are too many uncertainties to get very far towards a satisfactory explanation with this line of thought. It is possible that Nos 974–5 are residual in the deposits in which they were found, but Nos 985–6 of this form in lead are from even later contexts.

976 SWA81 2556 (2252) 7 Fig 230
Circular, tapered cup weight; d 22mm; th 7mm; 13.5gms; series of circle-and-dot motifs around top.

Presumably from a set of nested weights.

Probably a half of one-sixteenth of a mercantile pound of 15 ounces (*c*.1.0% light). Compare Oakley 1979, 257–8, fig 111, no 93, dated to the mid-13th/14th centuries, wt given as 15.5gms; Biddle 1990, nos 3197–9, 916–22, fig 282, dating from the 15th/16th centuries, wts 6.7, 14.1 and 12.2gms; Biggs 1992, 15 and *idem* 1995, 13, 15–16, where the French troy-ounce standard of 30.6gms for some of these items is suggested. Biggs publishes similar items as bullion weights.

A set of six lead/tin weights of similar form in the British Museum and apparently found in the area of Aldersgate in London appears to be a near complete, late medieval survival. Their measured weights are 7.30, 13.29, 27.25, 54.24, 113.75 and 129.39gms – the largest of these may have gone together with the lid to make a specific weight in the series (acc no 1868, 8-5, 26). The lid, recorded as having the arms of England and a border of roses and stars or suns (taken to indicate the reign of Edward IV), cannot now be traced (information kindly provided by Beverley Nenk). The measured weights clearly indicate a binary series, though they appear (?after abrasive cleaning) to vary between *c*.0.2% heavy and at the other extreme *c*.6.5% light for avoirdupois weights at 16 ounces to the pound – which is presumably the system represented.

977 BWB83 2357 (290) 9
Crude disc; d 12.5mm; th 3mm; 2.45gms.
See on No 979.

978 BWB83 5095 (359) 11
Flat, squarish block; 12×12mm; th 2.5mm; 2.45gms.
See next item.

979 BWB83 3672 (359) 11 Fig 230
Similar to preceding item; 18×15mm; th 3.5mm; bevelled sides; filed on larger face; three drilled blind holes in smaller face; 7.35gms.

Compare Nos 993 and 1027–8, all of lead, for the holes, which presumably indicate a specification, though the measured weights of the latter two are not easy to relate to that of the present example. Biggs illustrates comparable squarish items, which he describes as bullion (i.e., goldsmiths') weights (1992, 15).

The last three items clearly relate to a standard (being precisely 1:1:3 by weight, the three holes in No 979 perhaps underlining this) but the significance is unclear as none of the usual English systems relates obviously to 2.45gms. R D Connor has suggested this could perhaps represent a twelfth French troy ounce at 2.55gms (for which it would be *c*.3.9% light) and that No 1024 (one of two similar items with a fleur-de-lis motif) may respect the same system (pers comm).

Lead

For this easily shaped metal, only weights of relatively simple forms suitable for use with balances are listed. A number of elongated weights, probably used for a variety of purposes, are omitted (e.g., tall pyramidal, tall conoid etc., some pierced or with iron rods through – cf. V Jones in Biddle 1990, 304–6, figs 71a, 71b for a variety of lead plumb bobs). The omitted items include several rolled-sheet cylinders thought to be sinkers for fishing nets. A lentoid, triangular-section weight with a hole at one end, and weighing 100.5gms (BWB83 acc no 1361, from a deposit attributed to ceramic phase 11, see Fig 231) is one of the most clearly defined and widely found of these forms, which may also be for nets, or a form of plumb bob or sounding lead for use on ships. The will from 1477 of a London (tallow) chandler listed 900 lead weights 'great and small' among his effects (many of which related to the manufacture of candles) along with scales, balances and beams (Schofield 1995, 164, no 27); it is not clear what form these weights took or which standards were represented.

The privy marks on Nos 990, 997 and 1015 (?and 998) probably indicated the owners, while

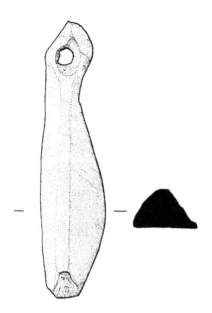

Fig 231   Pendent weight, probably for industrial use (1:1; not in catalogue)

the stamped crowns on Nos 1007 and 1014 presumably relate to official checks for accuracy.

DISCS AND RELATED ROUND FORMS

(Plain discs unless otherwise stated)

980 BIG82 Acc No 2846 (Context 4178) Ceramic Phase 6
Slightly oval; max d 19mm; th *c*.1mm; 4.68gms; pared around edge.
   Almost precise (despite the rough appearance) for English troy three-pennyweight at 4.67gms, though apparently too early in date for this system to be a probable identification.
   See No 1009.

981 SWA81 1195 (1354) 6 Fig 232
D 43mm; th 13mm; 196.0gms.

982 SWA81 2467 (2257) 7 Fig 232
Crude; d 17mm; th 1.5mm; apparently filed on both faces; 4.35gms.
   Probably a weight for three sterling pennies (almost precise at *c*.0.7% light).

983 BIG82 3799 (3204) 7 Fig 232
Crude; made by hammering a bent slug; d *c*.17mm; th *c*.8mm; 16.0gms.
   Compare No 989.

984 SWA81 2528 (2254) 7
Crude and irregular; d *c*.50mm; th 9mm; hammered along edges; 101.0gms.

985 BIG82 2521 (2591) ?8 Fig 232
Bifacially bevelled with flat ends; d 12mm; th 7mm; 8.00gms; abraded.

986 BWB83 5418 (285) 9
Bifacially bevelled with flat ends; d 17mm; h 10mm; 14gms; abraded.
   Probably a half avoirdupois ounce at 16 ounces to the pound (*c*.1.4% light).

The two preceding items are comparable in form with copper-alloy weights Nos 974–5.

987 SWA81 2917 (2061) 9 Fig 232
Irregular, plano-convex form; d 38mm; th 6mm; 53.5gms; random scratches on top, roughly scratched grid and other lines on base; worn.
   Probably an eighth avoirdupois pound of 15 ounces (almost precise at *c*.0.6% heavy).

988 BWB83 4103 (269) 9 Fig 233
D 18mm; th 13mm; relief cross and linear border on top; 54.5gms; worn.
   Probably an eighth mercantile pound of 15 ounces (almost precise at *c*.0.2% light).

989 BWB83 5286 (217) 6–9
Crude; made by hammering a bent slug; d *c*.28mm; th 17mm; 74.0gms; worn.
   Compare No 983.

990 BWB83 1381 (108) 10 Fig 233
D 35mm; th 2mm; six raised, slightly irregular, radiating lines, with pellets between; reverse has neatly scratched privy mark; 30.0gms; worn.
   Probably one French troy ounce (*c*.2.0% light), or *possibly* one mercantile ounce at 16 to the pound or one Tower ounce (*c*.2.7% heavy for both) or one English troy ounce (*c*.3.5% light).

991 BWB83 1386 (108) 10
Crude disc; d *c*.37mm; th 2mm; scratched (?)cross on one face, and roughly tooled, off-central cross of lines made up of repeatedly punched V marks on the other; 21.0gms; abraded.

992 BWB83 1354 (108) 10
Crude; d *c*.37mm; th 2mm; scratched lines on both faces; 22.5gms.

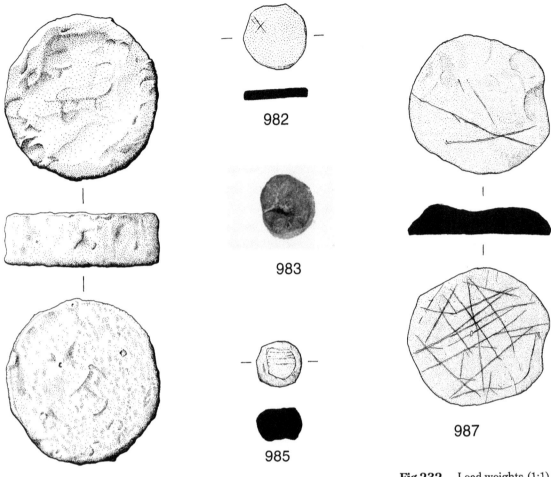

982

983

987

985

981

Fig 232   Lead weights (1:1)

If there was any close relationship between the three preceding items, which are all from the same foreshore deposit, this would emphasise the complexity and inexactness of medieval weighing practices. The point remains speculative.

993 BC72 3056 (250) 10 Fig 233
D 39mm; th 8mm; on top, central knop (flattened) and two opposed fleurs-de-lis with trilobed motifs at the sides (almost forming seeded fleurs-de-lis); on base, scratched double cross with transverse lines at ends of arms (abraded) and four drilled holes; 72.0gms; worn.

See on No 979 for the holes.

Possibly a coin weight for forty-eight pennies or four shillings (*c*.2.7% heavy).

For the decoration compare Biddle 1990, 910, 918–19, fig 280, nos 3188 and 3194, respectively from a 14th-century context and unphased (although both are there attributed on stylistic grounds to the late Saxon period, it seems likely that they are later – cf. Kruse 1992, 84). Both are roughly twice the weight of No 993. The 14th-century context for this London example seems appropriate, and the same dating may well be applied to the parallels.

What may be a five shillingweight of lead with an ornate cross motif, thought to be for post-1279 coins, has been published (Biggs 1990, 70, pl 14,3; Withers & Withers 1994, 6). The motif is completely unrelated to that on the present item and its Winchester parallels. A four-shilling standard would be unusual, as Biggs observes that bulk coin was usually weighed in five-shilling batches.

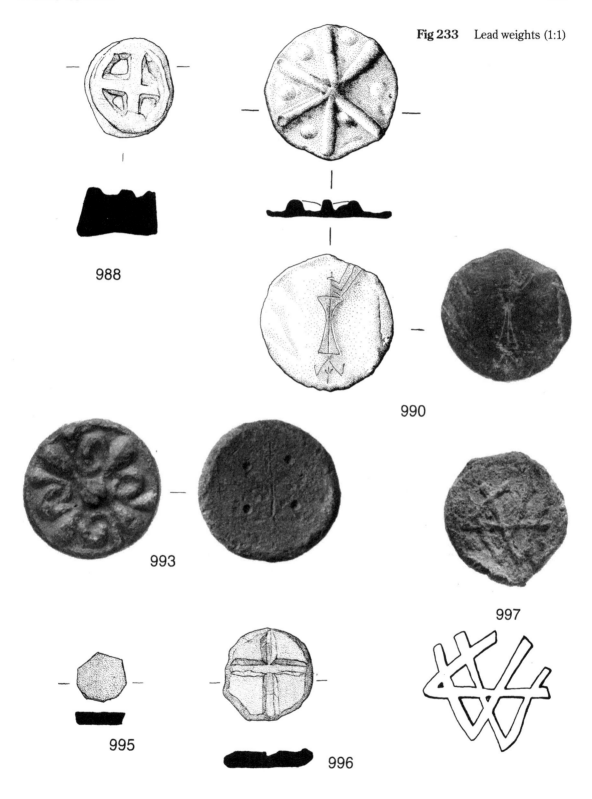

Fig 233   Lead weights (1:1)

988

990

993

997

995

996

994 BC72 4529 (119) 10–11
Plano-convex; very crude; d *c*.73mm; 390.5gms; the unevenness of the convex side suggests this may be simply a rough ingot.
Possibly one English troy pound (*c*.4.6% heavy).

995 BWB83 5373 (303) 11 Fig 233
Irregularly cut (sub-polygonal); d 14mm; th 2.5mm; 3.65gms.

996 BWB83 2688 (330) 11 Fig 233
D 25mm; th 4mm; (?)filed cross on top; 20.0gms: worn.

997 BWB83 5468 (361) 11 Fig 233
D 29mm; th 5mm; integrally cast privy mark on top (orientation uncertain); 26gms; worn.
Possibly a sixteenth avoirdupois pound of 15 ounces (*c*.2.3% light).

998 BC72 2860 (150) 11
Plano-convex; very crude; d 33mm; th 10mm; integrally cast, five-pointed star with circle on top; 27.0gms.
Probably a sixteenth avoirdupois pound of 15 ounces (*c*.1.5% heavy).

999 BWB83 2744 (329) 11
Crude; d 34mm; th 4mm; 28.5gms; worn.
Probably one avoirdupois ounce at 16 to the pound (almost precise at *c*.0.4% heavy).

1000 BC72 2387 (88) 11
Irregular; d 33mm; th 5mm; two flattish opposed sides; hammered around rest of perimeter and on one face, three parallel cuts on the other face; 43.5gms; worn.

The cut lines on this and No 1002 could in each case indicate a standard, though they do not appear to relate to that suggested for the latter.

1001 SWA81 1755 (2032) 11 Fig 234
D 37mm; th 5.50mm; random scratches on both faces; 49.0gms; worn.

1002 BWB83 5334 (310) 11 Fig 234
Half a disc; d 51mm; th 5mm; three transverse lines cut on straight edge; 51.0gms.
Possibly an eighth avoirdupois pound of 15 ounces (*c*.4.1% light).
See on No 1000.

1003 SWA81 394 (966) 11
Crude; d 41mm; average th 5mm; 64.5gms; edge very abraded.
Possibly two English troy ounces (*c*.3.7% heavy).

1004 BC72 2446 (79) 11
Plano-convex; d 49mm; th 8mm; edge thickened by (?)hammering at perimeter; scratched circular lines on top; 109.5gms.
Probably a quarter mercantile pound of 15 ounces (very precise at *c*.0.09% heavy).

1005 BWB83 7057 (136) 11
Half disc; d 67mm; th 6mm; 118.5gms; worn.
Probably a quarter mercantile pound of 16 ounces (*c*.1.6% heavy), or *possibly* a quarter avoirdupois pound of 16 ounces (*c*.4.5% heavy).

1006 BWB83 1378 (117) 11
Crude; d 45mm; th 14mm; 218.5gms; various knock marks on both faces and edge; worn.
Probably a half mercantile pound of 15 ounces (very precise at *c*.0.09% light), or *possibly* a half avoirdupois pound of 15 ounces (*c*.2.8% heavy).

1007 BWB83 2048 (308) 11 Fig 234
Crude; plano-convex; d *c*.55mm; th 11mm; stamped incuse crown on base; 226.0gms; worn.
Probably a half avoirdupois pound of 16 ounces (almost precise at *c*.0.4% light).
Compare stamp on No 1014.

1008 BWB83 3637 (292) 11 Fig 235
Crude; bevelled edge; d 68mm; th 12mm; eight integrally cast lines radiating from central knop, with pellets between; 440.5gms; abraded.
Possibly one avoirdupois pound of 16 ounces (*c*.2.9% light).

1009 BWB83 5826 (314) 12 Fig 235
Circular/shallow conoid with six facets; d 18mm; th 5mm; 7.00gms; probably cast in the back of a sexfoil copper-alloy sheeting mount for a strap.
Almost precise for four and a half English troy pennyweight: 7.01 for 7.02gms (*c*.0.1% light). (Also published as no 1299 in Egan & Pritchard 1991, 242–3, fig 155.) Perhaps the coincidence in weight is fortuitous rather than a pointer to *probable* identification – this item could alternatively be a patron (master form) used in making clay moulds for casting strap mounts similar to the common sheet ones. See No 980.

1010 SWA81 1939 (2082) 12 Fig 235
Irregular disc; d 31mm; th 6mm; edges roughly hammered over towards middle on both faces; 51gms.
Possibly an eighth avoirdupois pound of 15 ounces (*c*.4.1% light).

1011 SWA81 2050 (2106) 12 Fig 235
Abraded; d 36mm; th 6mm; crude design of cross

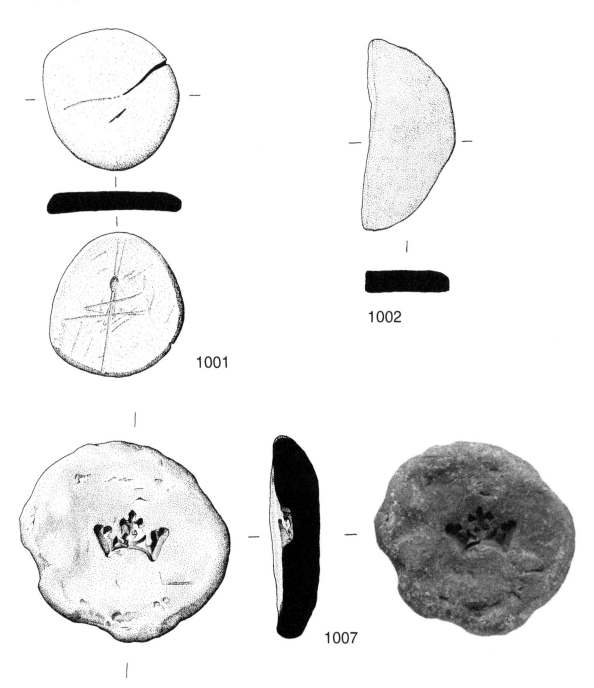

Fig 234 Lead weights (1:1)

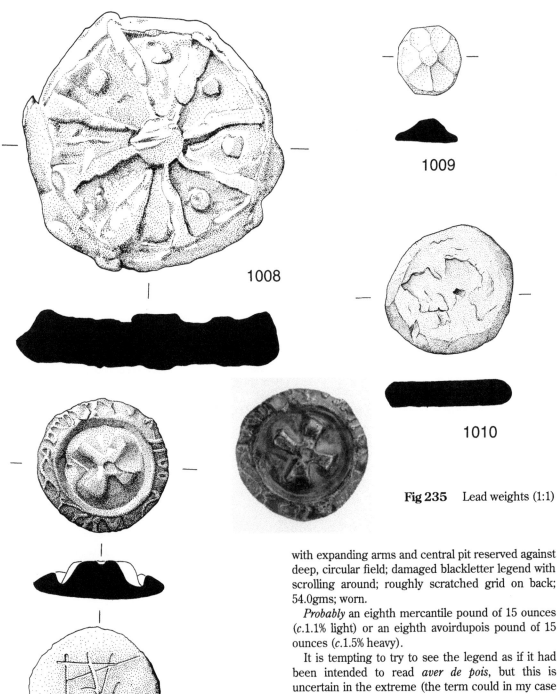

1008

1009

1010

1011

Fig 235   Lead weights (1:1)

with expanding arms and central pit reserved against deep, circular field; damaged blackletter legend with scrolling around; roughly scratched grid on back; 54.0gms; worn.

Probably an eighth mercantile pound of 15 ounces (*c*.1.1% light) or an eighth avoirdupois pound of 15 ounces (*c*.1.5% heavy).

It is tempting to try to see the legend as if it had been intended to read *aver de pois*, but this is uncertain in the extreme (the term could in my case refer to any system for merchandise other than spices and bullion in the 15th century, not necessarily the one now known exclusively as 'avoirdupois' – Allen Simpson pers comm); alternatively, it could perhaps be the owner's name (see discussion at the

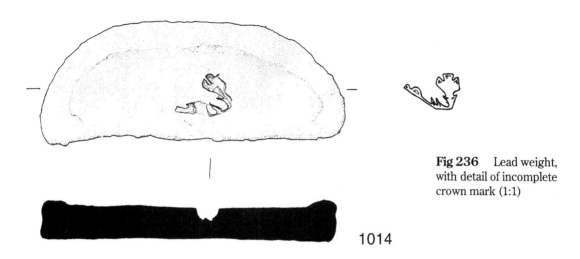

Fig 236 Lead weight, with detail of incomplete crown mark (1:1)

1014

start of this section) or a pious legend. An example in better condition is needed before even a single character can be confirmed.

1012 SWA82 3324 (2112) 12
D 43mm; th 7mm; 98.5gms; worn.

1013 SWA81 2196 (2006) 12
Similar form to preceding item; d 50mm; th *c*.13mm; coated with mortar [201.5gms uncleaned].

1014 BWB83 4714 (309) 12 Fig 236
Rough segment of disc; d *c*.84mm; th 12mm; incompletely stamped incuse crown; 219.5gms; worn.

Three half-pound standards each seem likely candidates; *probably* a half mercantile pound of 15 ounces (almost precise at *c*.0.4% heavy), or *possibly* a half avoirdupois pound of 16 ounces (*c*.3.2% light) or a half avoirdupois pound of 15 ounces (*c*.3.2% heavy).

Compare stamp on No 1007 (which has a probable avoirdupois identification).

1015 SWA81 2158 (2114) 12 Fig 237
D 64mm; th 10mm; integrally cast privy mark with (?)legend to sides; reverse has rough grid, (?)punched or integrally cast, and series of punched rectangles and crosses; 266.0gms; very abraded, so that the cast devices cannot fully be made out.

Possibly a three-quarter English troy pound (*c*.5.0% light), though the standard seems an awkward one.

Similar punched crosses appear on an irregular-shaped weight that is pierced for attachment (BWB83 acc no 5335, not included in the present catalogue, from a context attributed to ceramic phase 12).

1016 SWA81 3557 (Unstratified)
Rough; hemispherical; d *c*.18mm; th 11mm; 17.0gms.

OVOID

1017 SWA81 Acc No 2529 (Context 2254) Ceramic Phase 7
Rough, ovoid block; 49×39mm; th 24mm; 441.5gms; worn.

Probably one mercantile pound of 15 ounces (almost precise at *c*.0.9% heavy), or *possibly* one avoirdupois pound of 16 ounces (*c*.2.7% light).

RECTANGULAR/SQUARE

1018 BWB83 Acc No 5408 (Context 285) Ceramic Phase 9
Roughly square, plano-convex; 29×27mm; th 8mm; 47.5gms; worn.

(?)*Probably* an eighth English troy ounce (*c*.1.9% heavy), or *possibly* an eighth French troy ounce (*c*.3.5% heavy), though eighths would be awkward divisions for systems based on 12-ounce pounds.

1019 SWA81 1053 (2140) 9 Fig 238
Rectangle with rounded corners; two separately applied, or flattened, irregular pads; 92×41mm; th 8mm; 111.5gms.

The two irregular pieces may have been added to make up a specific weight (as was sometimes done with official standards – Connor 1987, 129).

Probably a quarter avoirdupois pound of 16 ounces (*c*.1.7% light), or *possibly* a quarter mercantile pound of 16 ounces (*c*.4.4% light).

1020 SWA81 3078 (2025) 9
Irregular, rounded rectangle; *c*.50×*c*.43mm; th *c*.14mm; 208.5gms; worn.

Probably a half avoirdupois pound of 15 ounces (*c*.1.9% light).

1021 BWB83 4929 (269) 9 Fig 238
55×53mm; th 18mm; top has integrally cast (??bird) motif; 541.5gms; worn.

(?)*Probably* one and a quarter mercantile pounds at 15 ounces to the pound (*c*.1.0% light) – the standard is an awkward one.

Compare a weight of similar size and shape, found in spoil deriving from the TEX88 site, with the crude motif of a deer (private collection). The present item is not from the same mould but could be related.

1022 BWB83 5217 (122) ?11 Fig 238
22×20mm; three-towered, crenellated castle (conventional heraldic representation) in relatively high relief; 6.75gms.

Probably a quarter avoirdupois ounce at 15 ounces to the pound (*c*.1.5% heavy), or *possibly* a quarter mercantile ounce at 16 ounces to the pound (*c*.3.7% light). This item seems an unusual form for a weight.

1023 SWA81 2884 (2106) 12 Fig 238
17×8.5mm; th 1mm; demi fleur-de-lis; 1.72gms.

Probably a sixteenth of one sixteenth of a mercantile pound of 15 ounces (almost precise at *c*.0.6% heavy).

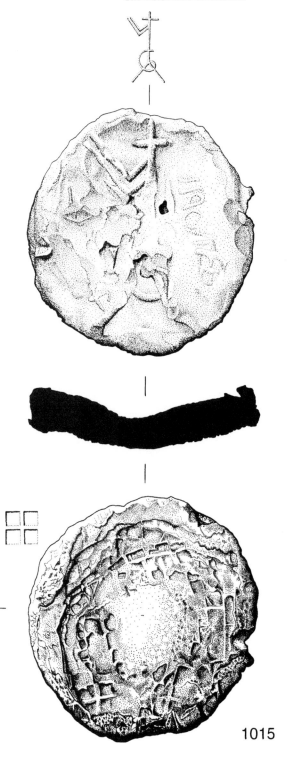

1015

Fig 237   Lead weight (1:1)

Fig 238   Lead weights (1:1)

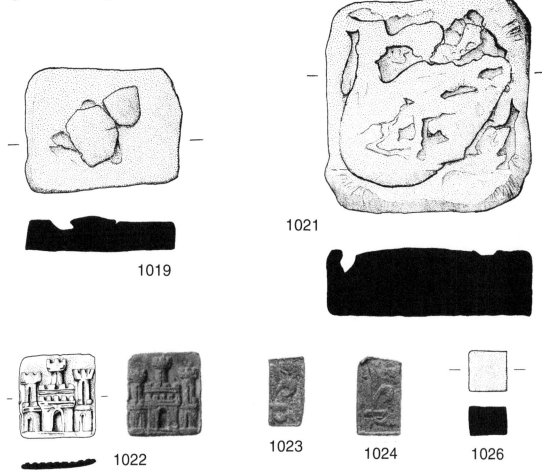

1021

1019

1022

1023

1024

1026

Compare the following item from the same series of dumped deposits, and cf. Biggs (1992, 15) for a rectangular copper-alloy weight with a fleur-de-lis – described as a bullion weight.

1024 SWA81 2583 (2117) 12 Fig 238
18×10mm; th 1mm; demi fleur-de-lis (slightly offset from the edge, showing that the horizontal line continues over to the absent half – i.e., it was not a larger weight with a complete fleur-de-lis, which has been cut in two); 2.46gms.

See preceding item; also on copper-alloy weights Nos 977–9.

1025 SWA81 2941 (2109) 12
11×10mm; th 5mm; 5.40gms; ?cut horizontally through middle; worn.

1026 SWA81 2931 (2108) 12 Fig 238
10×10mm; th 6mm; 6.95gms.

Possibly a quarter avoirdupois ounce at 16 ounces to the pound (*c.*2.1% light) or a quarter of a mercantile sixteenth pound at 15 ounces to the pound (*c.*2.2% heavy).

'HIDE'-SHAPED

(Four concave sides)

The first two items clearly respect a system, in view of their exact 1:2 relationship and the presence respectively of three and six holes.

A coin pennyweight of 1.46gms seems the most likely standard.

Holes presumably indicating specifications are also known on the faces of earlier rectangular weights. Compare No 993, and also No 979 of copper alloy, which appears to relate to a different system.

1027 BIG82 Acc No 2440 (Context 3176) Ceramic Phase 8 Fig 239
16×15mm; th 2mm; three drilled, blind holes on both faces; 4.40gms.
Probably a coin three-pennyweight (almost precise at *c*.0.5% heavy).

1028 SWA81 575 (2055) 9 Fig 239
14×13mm; th 5mm; edges pared; six irregularly placed blind holes on both faces; 8.80gms.
Probably a coin six-pennyweight (almost precise at *c*.0.5% heavy).

1029 BWB83 4014 (292) 11 Fig 239
13×12mm; th 2mm; 3.80gms; abraded.
Possibly one apothecaries' drachm (*c*.2.6% light). If the identification is correct, this is one of the earliest weights known for a system that was probably introduced around the turn of the 15th century.

1030 SWA81 3950 (Unstratified)
21×18mm; th 3mm; 12.0gms.

SHIELD-SHAPED

A shield-shaped, decorated lead weight that has been identified as 6¼lb avoirdupois (1 clove) attributed to the reign of Edward I is in the Science Museum collection (Connor 1987, 136–7, fig 29; Allen Simpson finds this identification difficult to accept, pers comm). Of the two following items only No 1032 can be reasonably identified as a weight, but its parallel introduces an unresolved difficulty as to the standard represented.

1031 BWB83 Acc No 3606 (Context 368) Ceramic Phase 11 Fig 239
30×26mm; max th 7mm; (?)heraldic arms in relief: cross with arms having tripartite ends (?cf. cross fleury), pellets (?roundels/bezants) in first, second and third quarters, raised field in fourth; 12.5gms.
The raised field may indicate a different heraldic tincture from the remainder.

1032 BWB83 3262 (207) 11 Fig 239
Rough, triangular/shield shape; 27×22mm; th 7mm; bevelled sides with transverse hatching, crude lion rampant on top, its head missing because of a rectangular hole in the casting; 26.5gms.
Probably a sixteenth avoirdupois ounce at 16 ounces to the pound (almost precise at *c*.0.4% light).

A crowned lion rampant, in a border bezanty are the arms of the 13th-century earls of Cornwall (Richard and Edmund, who held the title from 1225 to 1300), and have been identified with those on some copper-alloy steelyard weights presumed to be of late 13th-century date (see Cherry 1991a for a recent discussion of these, with bibliography). The significance of the use of these arms in this context is conjectured to be that the weights were somehow regulated by the authority of the earl, on behalf of the monarch (in 1325 weights used in the tin industry in Cornwall – the smallest being four pounds – were brought to London for adjustment; these were at that time believed to have been in use since the time of Earl Richard – Sharpe 1903, 203–4; there could be some trace of a connection between these earls and the weights in all this). The use of billets or straight lines/rectangles rather than roundels (bezants) in the border is a consistent feature of the arms on weights (floor tiles with arms identified as those of the earls have border roundels, though only one of these appears to have the lion crowned (see, e.g., Eames 1980, nos 1524, 1526–7 for illustrations) but there are billets on one of two harness pendants with the arms given the same attribution, while the other has roundels – J Cherry in Alexander & Binski 1987, 258, nos 159, 157). No alternative identification for the minor variations has been proposed, and they may well not be of significance. Further finds of weights of similar form to the present one have an obliquely hatched border (Biggs 1992, 43, where a date of *c*.1380–90 is suggested).

Conclusive evidence to explain why the above earls' arms should appear on *London* weights has yet to be found, and the late 14th-century dating for No 1032 may mean that any connection is even less clear (could the Black Prince have used the old arms when he was created Earl of Cornwall in 1337? – there seems to be absolutely no other hint that he might have done so – John Goodall pers comm). Closely dated steelyard weights might go some way to resolving the difficulty. At present the arms need not be considered a specific reference so much as an intended suggestion of some remote

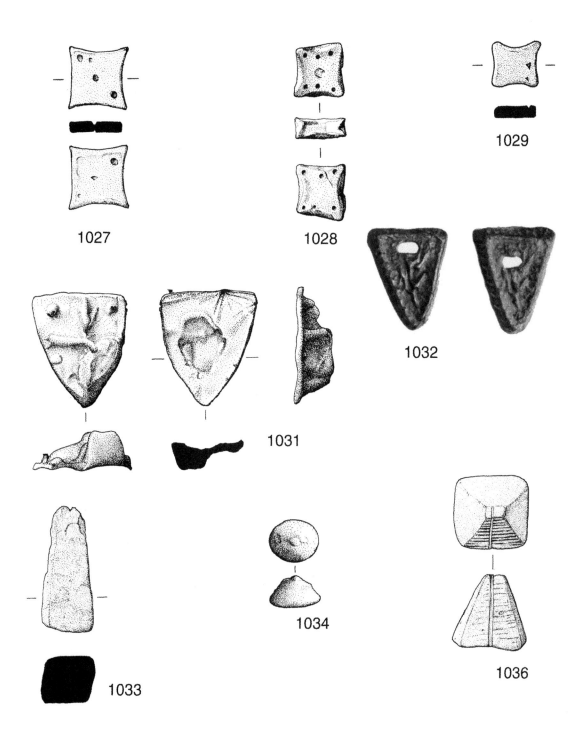

Fig 239   Lead weights, middle right VHA89 site acc no 244 (all 1:1)

authority's approval of the weights on which they appear.

A very similar sized, but thicker, item to No 1032 was excavated at the VHA89 site (acc no 244, weight 31.5 gms – see Fig 239). These two clearly related objects do not obviously respect any single standard weighing system; indeed, their similar size would have made differentiation during use somewhat difficult. Two different systems appear to be represented. The most likely identification for the cited parallel is *probably* one English troy ounce (for which it is *c.*1.3% heavy – it would be almost 12% heavy for one avoirdupois ounce at 16 ounces to the pound. Further London finds imply that the form was quite common; two similar items were found in spoil deriving from the Billingsgate site (Biggs illustrates two more with rabbeted, diagonally hatched borders; 1992, 43; cf. Simpson & Connor 1996, 1995, fig 3, apparently a London find, with the arms *three lions passant*).

The holes in these weights (piercing has had the same disastrous effect on all the lions) may be compared with those in much later, far larger examples of this form in copper alloy, used for weighing wool; there the holes are interpreted as being for a strap (which some retain) to hold pairs of weights, perhaps when travelling by horse, with one slung on each side of the animal's back (Dent 1927, 31). The holes in the present small items may have been for storage on a bar or strap etc., though their slight bulk and weight should not have presented any particular problem in transportation.

CONICAL/PYRAMIDAL

Four out of six of these items have likely suggested standards, implying that these forms were regularly used for precise weighing in the Middle Ages.

1033 SWA81 Acc No 2439 (Context 2266) Ceramic Phase 7 Fig 239
Tall, pyramidal form; 14×11mm; h 34mm; 29.5gms; worn.
Probably one ounce, either mercantile system at 16 ounces to the pound or Tower (almost precise at *c.*1.0% heavy for both), or *possibly* one French troy ounce (*c.*3.6% light).

1034 BWB83 5476 (361) 11 Fig 239
Slightly oval cone; 12.5×10.5; th 7mm; 5.85gms.

1035 BWB83 4641 (299) 11
Rough cone; d 16mm; h 13mm; 13.0gms; worn.
Possibly a half of one sixteenth avoirdupois pound of 15 ounces (*c.*2.3% light) or a half of one-sixteenth mercantile pound of 15 ounces (*c.*4.4% light).

1036 BWB83 3747 (334) 11 Fig 239
Pyramidal; 20×20mm; h 20mm; parallel marks and vertical scratched line on one face; 39.5gms; worn.
Compare with next item.

1037 BWB83 3744 (334) 11
Pyramidal; 24×21mm; h 24mm; 53.5gms; worn; similar to preceding item and from the same deposit.
Probably an eighth avoirdupois pound of 15 ounces (almost precise at *c.*0.6% heavy).

1038 BWB83 1489 (354) 11
Crude, round-topped cone; d *c.*40mm; h 23mm; 94.0gms; (may possibly have a central hole).
Probably a quarter English troy pound (ie., three ounces – almost precise at *c.*0.8% heavy).

Items of other, less regular, forms that could perhaps be weights, but which seem unlikely both from their shape and measured weight to have represented any standard, have been omitted.

Balances

See Fig 240 (top) for a reconstructed balance and Fig 142 for a folding instrument found in its box.

These may have been used primarily for accurate weighing of precious items (coins, jewels – as depicted in late medieval paintings – or of expensive spices and medicines).

SCALE PANS

All are of sheet *copper alloy*, with three holes for suspension from the beam by strings. Numbers 1039, 1044–5 and 1049–50 bear stamped marks attesting that the accuracy of their weight had been officially tested (the numismatic connection for the stamps on Nos 1039, 1044 and 1050 probably indicates that such precision instruments were produced by those who worked for mints and that the accuracy of each instrument was reliable for testing specie). The weighing

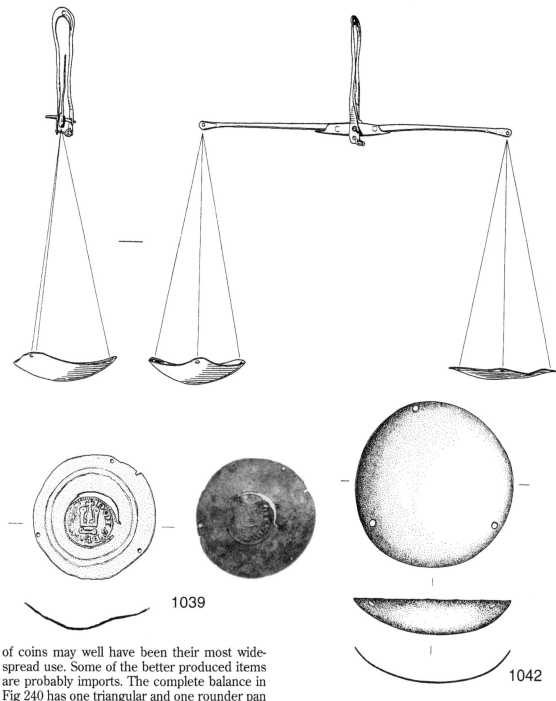

1039

1042

of coins may well have been their most wide-spread use. Some of the better produced items are probably imports. The complete balance in Fig 240 has one triangular and one rounder pan (any significance for the different shapes is unknown; this instrument probably dates to the late 15th century).

Fig 240 Balance (drawing HBMC(E), not to scale) and balance pans (1:1)

Circular

(All are concave)

1039 BWB83 Acc No 2119 (Context 290) Ceramic Phase 9 Fig 240
D 33m; two concentric, engraved grooves around a circular stamp d 13mm with stylised representation of a castle, POIS:DE:(T)O. ... around (Lombardic lettering, E reversed) with beaded border.

The legend may be restored from a more complete example as POIS DE TOR DEN – i.e., *pois de Tournai denier* (Dieudonné 1925, 92, no 15 and pl I no 40).

This stamp 'weight of denier [penny] Tournois' has the conventional representation of a city (*chastel turnois*), taken originally from the coins of the Abbey of Tours in France, and later widely adopted as a motif on the silver currency of many other towns across Europe (Grierson 1980, 148–50, no 675A; Mayhew 1988, 34–5, no 57).

1040 BWB83 4471 (256) 11
Incomplete and corroded; d *c.*33m.

1041 BWB83 4196 (401) 11
Distorted; d *c.*43mm.

Cf. next item from same deposit – ?perhaps originally part of the same instrument.

1042 BWB83 4194 (401) 11 Fig 240
D 44mm.

See previous item from same deposit.

1043 BWB83 4068 (305) 11
Corroded; d 48mm; central turning mark.

Triangular

(All are flat)

1044 BC72 Acc No 2863 (Context 150) Ceramic Phase 11 Fig 241
All sides l 44mm; incomplete stamp of king wearing long robe, (?)holding upright sword, and seated on an elaborate throne, all in beaded border.

The stamp is similar to the design for the French gold *écu de la chaise* coin of *c.*1350 onwards; this design is also known on coin weights (Dieudonné 1925, 87, no 5, pl 1, nos 10, 15).

1045 BWB83 3479 (117) 11 Fig 241
One corner broken off; sides l *c.*46mm; engraved line near perimeter; sub-rectangular stamp with lion rampant.

1046 BWB83 5991 (314) 12 Fig 241
Sides l 39–41mm; crudely engraved zigzag around perimeter.

1047 SWA81 2879 (2106) 12 Fig 241
Sides l 31–4mm; paired lines of punched rectangles around perimeter.

1048 SWA81 2043 (2101) 12
Sides l 32–4mm.

Sub-hexagonal

(Both are flat)

1049 TL74 Acc No 512 (Context 414) Ceramic Phase 11 Fig 241
W 34mm; nick in middle of each side; small, expanded-armed cross stamp.

1050 BWB83 3627 (395) 11 Fig 241
Alternate right-angled and oblique corners; w 34mm; two compass-engraved, concentric circles; stamp of shield with three fleurs-de-lis.

A shield with three fleurs-de-lis appears on French gold écu coins from 1385 onwards (cf. the device on weights for these coins – Biggs 1990, 75, pl 15, 43–9).

ARMS

Copper alloy

Rigid

1051 SWA81 Acc No 3662 (Context 3015) Ceramic Phase 6 Fig 242
137mm; round section; pointer l 50mm soldered in slot in thicker, central part; wire rings survive in holes at each end.

1052 BIG82 2947 (5511) 7 Fig 243
Slightly distorted; l *c.*228mm; wire ring survives in hole at one end; pointer l 34mm set in slot in thicker, central part of arms is (?)integrally riveted, vertically, at base.

1053 SWA81 2093 (2020) 9
Incomplete; surviving l 183mm (originally *c.*230mm); flanges on each side next to surviving pierced end,

Fig 241   Balance pans (1:1)

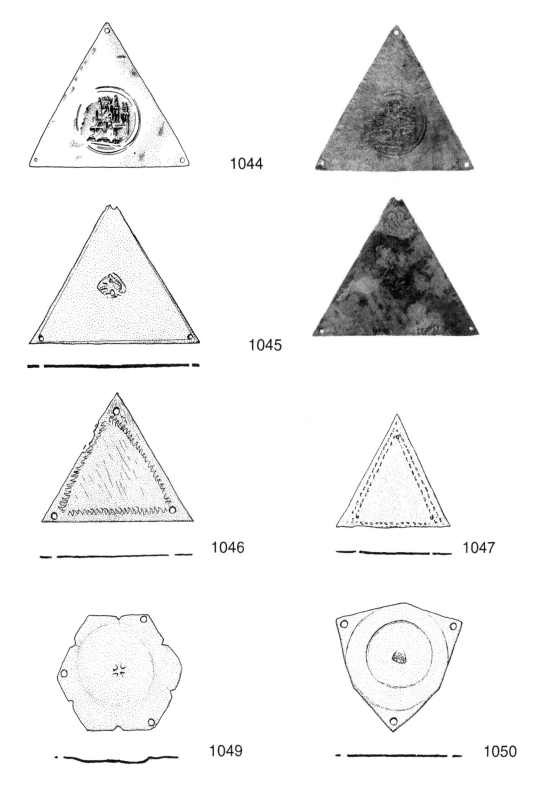

1044

1045

1046

1047

1049

1050

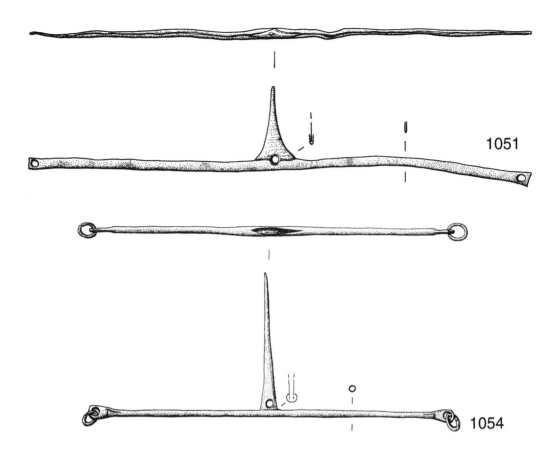

Fig 242   Balance arms (1:1)

which retains a wire ring; slot and horizontal rivet hole for missing pointer.

1054 BWB83 1867 (5) Unphased Fig 242
L 106mm; hammered (?)sheeting, with separate pointer l 46mm soldered into fold.

Folding

(Compare Fig 142)

1055 BWB83 17 (204) 11 Fig 243
Small piece broken off at one end; l with arms extended 114mm; h of horizontally riveted pointer 41mm.

FORKS
('stirrups')

Paired arms with tab (or hole for one) in arch at top, and riveted pivot at base to hold pointer.

Copper alloy

1056 BWB83 Acc No 4212 (Context 401) Ceramic Phase 11 Fig 244
Incomplete; l 34mm; broken at hole at top.
   A very flimsy example.

1057 BWB83 639 (117) 11 Fig 244
Incomplete; l 49mm; arch is hammered rod; wire-rod pivot.

Iron

1058 BC72 2768 (83) 11 Fig 244
Slightly distorted; l 91mm; indicator to match against pointer; hole for suspension at right angle to lost pivot.

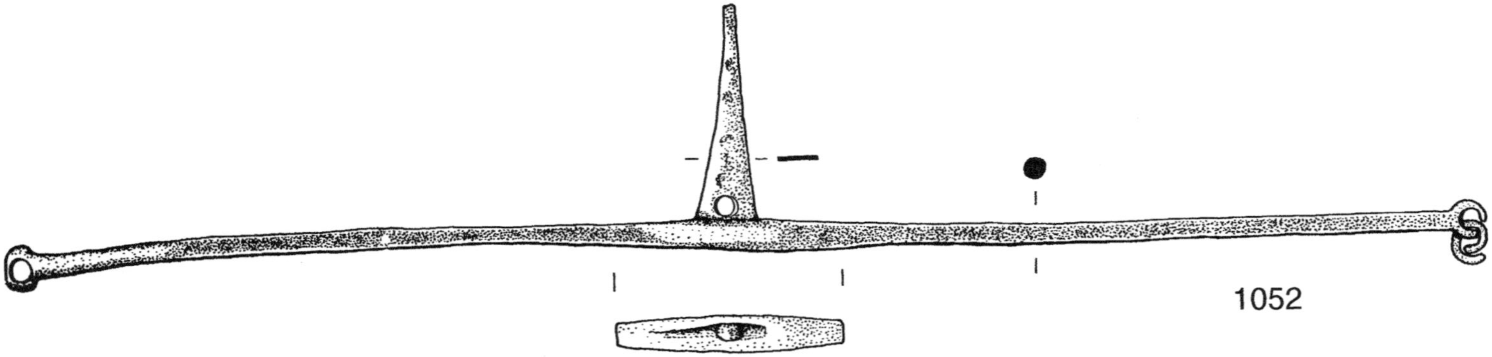

Fig 243 Rigid and folding balance arms (1:1)

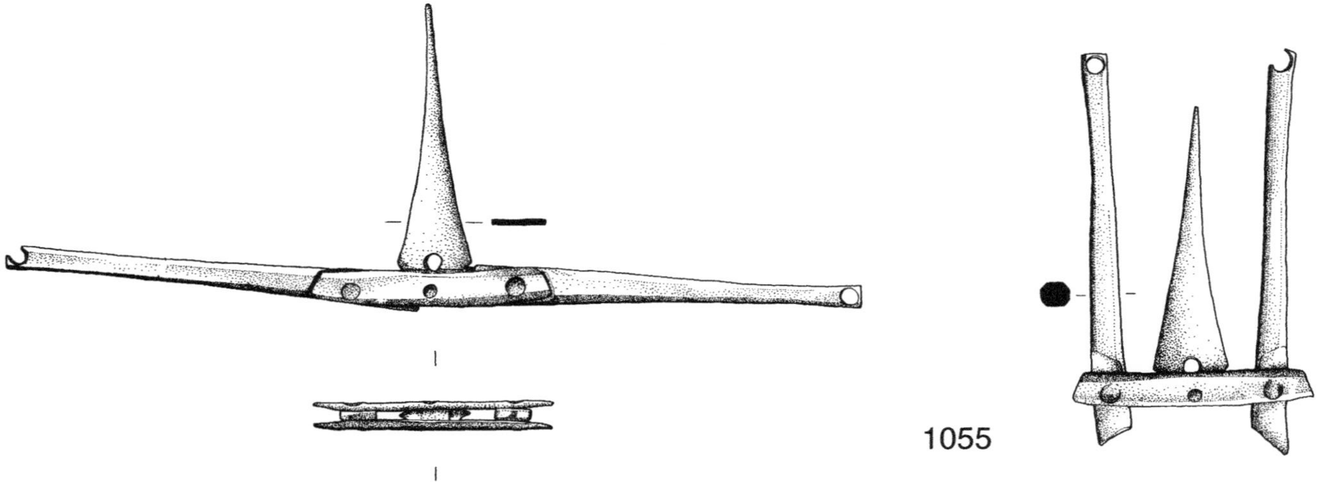

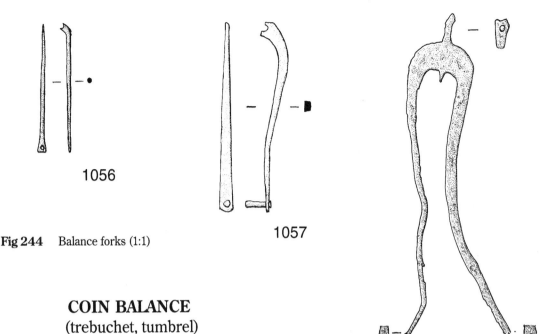

1056

1057

Fig 244   Balance forks (1:1)

1058

COIN BALANCE
(trebuchet, tumbrel)

Lead-tin

1059 BWB83 Acc No 2222 (Context 131) Ceramic
Phase 11 Fig 245
Incomplete; pewter (MLC); both parts broken off at
both ends; the upright narrows at each end near
breaks; surviving l 17mm; iron pivot is visible on one
side only; arm, surviving l 33mm, has central trough
for upright to fold flat and expands at one end with
rabbet (presumably down to missing tray); the other
end of the arm has been pared away on both sides
with a sharp instrument and is also distorted (the
identification of the upright and the arms depends
largely on the interpretation of the paring of the
surviving, heavier, part).

Several coin balances, of a variety of materials
(not including pewter), have recently been published
(Mayhew 1975; MacGregor 1985a, 128–9, 1985b;
Biggs 1990, 70–1, pl 14.4–5; Rogers 1993). Pewter
would seem to be an inherently perilous material to
use for a precision instrument of this kind (intended
to be in equilibrium only for unclipped coins of full,
specified weight), though the parallels cited include
examples of bone. A complete example from London
of copper alloy with a spike for fixture at the base
(upright h 82mm, l of arms 65mm) shows how the
present one would have worked, with the weight of
the arm balancing that of the tray plus appropriate
coin – Fig 245 right (MoL acc no 87.51/4).

The paring away of the weighted counterbalance
in the present example was presumably a way of
adapting the instrument to be in equilibrium for
short-weight coins, almost certainly with the intent
to deceive (metal has been removed mainly from the
underneath and one side of the arm, and this adaptation would not be easy to see if the balance was
used with that side turned away from a second
party). Mayhew (1975) refers to documented
instances in the medieval period of persons weighing
coins somehow doing this deceitfully, though practised misplacement of a coin on the tray in some
balances could produce an inaccurate equilibrium
relative to the standard. Statute 20 Ed I, 4 of 1212,
recognising the existence of false balances, required
the warden of the exchange to mark accurate ones
presented for examination with the king's stamp –
none of the known coin balances from the medieval
period appears to have any mark. The bending and
comprehensive breakage of the present instrument
suggests that the deceit was noticed there and steps
were taken to ensure that it could never be used
again.

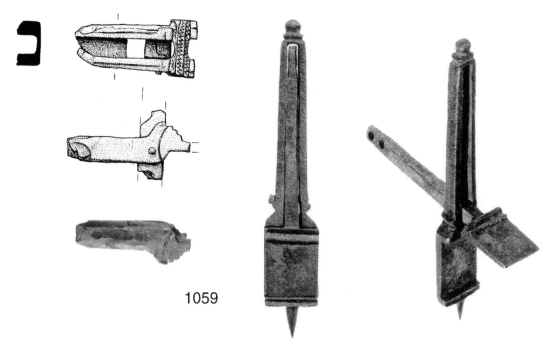

1059

Fig 245 Broken balance for coins, and, right, parallel (MoL acc no 87.51/4; all 1:1)

Bibliography

ADDYMAN, P J & PRIESTLEY, J, 1977 'Baile Hill, York: a report on the Institute's excavations', in *Antiq J* **134**, 115–56

AKERMAN, J Y, 1857 'On the distaff and the spindle, as the insignia of the female sex in former times', in *Archaeologia* **37.1**, 83–101

ALEXANDER, J & BINSKI, P (eds), 1987 *Age of Chivalry: Art in Plantagenet England 1200–1400*, Royal Academy of Arts, London

ALLAN, J P, 1984 *Medieval and Post-Medieval Finds from Exeter 1971–1980*, Exeter

ANON, 1928 'Padlocks from the City', in *Antiq J* **8**, 524–6

ARMITAGE, K, PEARCE, J E & VINCE, A G, 1981 'Early medieval roof tiles from London', in *Antiq J* **61.2**, 359–62

ARMITAGE, P L, 1982 'Studies on the remains of domestic livestock from Roman, medieval and early modern London: objectives and methods', in HALL, R A & KENWARD, H K, *Environmental Archaeology in the Urban Context* (*CBA Res Report* **43**), 94–106

ARMSTRONG, P & AYERS, B, 1987 *Excavations in High Street and Blackfriargate* (*E Riding Archaeol* **8** / *Hull Old Town Rep* **5**)

— TOMLINSON, D & EVANS, D H, 1991 *Excavations at Lurk Lane, Beverley, 1979–82* (*Sheffield Excavation Report* **1**), University of Sheffield

AUSTIN, D, 1989 *The deserted medieval village of Thrislington, County Durham, Excavations 1973–1974* (*Soc Med Arch Monograph* **12**)

BAART, J M, KROOK, W, LAGERWEIJ, A B et al., 1977 *Opgravingen in Amsterdam*, Amsterdam

BACHMANN, W 1969 *The Origins of Bowing* (trans Deane, N), London

BAINES, A, 1983 'Jew's Harp', in ARNOLD, D (ed), *A New Oxford Companion to Music*, Oxford, 1000

BAKER, E, 1981 'The medieval travelling candlestick from Grove Priory, Bedfordshire', in *Antiq J* **61.2**, 336–8

BAKER, O, 1921 *Black Jacks and Leather Bottels*, London

BANGS, C, 1995 *The Lear Collection: A Study of Copper Alloy Socket Candlesticks AD200–1700*, Easton, Pennsylvania (USA)

BAUMGARTNER, E, 1987 *Glas des Späten Mittelalters: die Sammlung Karl Armendt* (exhibition catalogue), Kunstmuseum, Dusseldorf (Germany)

— & KRUEGER, I, 1988 *Phoenix aus Sand und Asche: Glas des Mittelalters*, Munich (Germany)

BAYLEY, J, 1987 'Viking glassworking: the evidence from York', in *Annales du 10e Congrès de l'Association Internationale pour l'Histoire du Verre*, Amsterdam, 245–54

— 1992 *Non ferrous metalworking from Coppergate* (*The Archaeology of York* **17/7**), York Archaeological Trust/CBA, London

BELL, W G, 1938 *A Short History of the Worshipful Company of Tylers and Bricklayers of the City of London*, London

BETTS, I M, 1985 *Milk Street: Medieval Building Material* (unpublished archive report), Museum of London

— 1986 *Seal House: Roman and Medieval Building Material* (unpublished archive report), Museum of London

— 1991 *Billingsgate Fish Market Car Park, Lower Thames Street* (unpublished archive report), Museum of London

BEZBORODOV, M A, 1957 'A chemical and technological study of ancient Russian glasses and refractories', in *Journal of Glass Technology* **41**, 168–84

BIDDLE, M (ed), 1990 *Object and Economy in Medieval Winchester; Artefacts from Medieval Winchester* (*Winchester Stud* **7.2**, two vols), Oxford

BIGGS, N, 1990 'Coin weights in England – up to 1588', in *Brit Numis J* **60**, 65–79

— 1992 *English Weights: An Illustrated Survey*, Egham

— 1995 *Bullion Weights: An Outline Catalogue*, Egham

BIMSON, M & FREESTONE, I, 1985 '"Rouge Clair" and other late 14th-century enamels on the Royal Gold Cup of the kings of France and England', in PHILIPPE J (ed), *Annales du 9e Congrès de l'Association Internationale pour l'Histoire du Verre*, Liège (Belgium), 209–22

BINSKI, P, 1986 *The Painted Chamber at Westminster*, London

BÍRÓ, T M, 1987a 'Bone carvings from Brigetio in the collection of the Hungarian National Museum', in *Acta Archaeologica Academiae Scientiarum Hungaricae* **39**, Budapest (Hungary), 153–92

— 1987b 'Gorsium bone carvings', in *Alba Regia* **23**, (Hungary), 25–63

BLAIR, C & BLAIR, J, 1991 'Copper alloys', in BLAIR, J & RAMSAY, N, *English Medieval Industries*, London, 81–106

BLAIR, J & RAMSAY, N, 1991 *English Medieval Industries*, London

BOS, H, GROENEWEG, G, VAN HAM, W et al., 1987 *Schatten uit de Schelde* (exhibition catalogue), Markiezenhof Museum, Bergen op Zoom (Netherlands)

BRIDBURY, A R, 1955 *England and the Salt Trade in the Later Middle Ages*, Oxford

BRIGHAM, T, 1992 'Reused house timbers from the Billingsgate site', in MILNE, G, *Timber Buildings Techniques in London c.900–1400* (*London & Middlesex Archaeol Soc Spec Pap* **15**), 86–105

BRILL, R H & HOFFMAN, C A, 1987 'Some glass beads excavated on San Salvador Island in the Bahamas', in *Annales du 10e Congrès de l'Association Internationale pour l'Histoire du Verre*, Amsterdam, 373–9

BROWNSWORD, R & CIUFFINI, T, 1988 'Three late medieval latten candlesticks from Bedford', in *Bedfordshire Archaeol* **18**, 113–21

— & PITT, E E H, 1983 'A note on some medieval pewter spoon alloys', in *Hist Metall* **17.2**, 119

— & — 1984 'X-Ray fluorescence analysis of English 13th–16th century pewter flatware', in *Archaeometry* **26.2**, 237–44

— & — 1985 'Some examples of medieval domestic pewter flatware', in *Medieval Archaeol* **29**, 152–5

CABLE, M & SMEDLEY, J W, 1987 'Liquidus temperatures and melting characteristics of some early container glasses', in *Glass Technol* **28.2**, 94–8

CAL WILLS: SHARPE, R (ed), *Calendar of Wills Proved Enrolled in the Court of Husting, London*, 1889, **1** *1258–1358*, 1890; **2** *1358–1688*

CAMERON, H K, 1974 'Technical aspects of medieval monumental brasses', in *Archaeol J* **131**, 215–36

CASPALL, F, 1987 *Making Fire and Light in the Home pre-1820*, Woodbridge

CELORIA, F, 1974 'Tools and artifacts of London type or pattern', in *London Studies* **1**, 15–37

CHAMBERS, R W & DAUNT, M (eds), 1931 *A Book of London English, 1384–1425*, London

CHARLESTON, R J, 1960 'Lead in glass', in *Archaeometry* **3**, 1–4

— 1984 *English Glass and the Glass Used in England c.400–1940*, London

— 1991 'Vessel glass', in BLAIR, J & RAMSAY, N (eds), *English Medieval Industries*, London, 236–64

CHERRY, J, 1980 'Medieval metal finds from Lübeck', in *Lübecker Schriften zur Archäologie und Kulturgeschichte* **3**, Bonn (Germany), 175–8

— 1982a 'The Talbot casket and related late medieval leather caskets', in *Archaeologia* **107**, 131–40

— 1982b 'Seal matrices', in SPENCER, B, 'Pilgrim souvenirs from the medieval waterfront excavations at Trig Lane, London, 1974–76' (*Trans London & Middlesex Archaeol Soc* **33**), 304–23

— 1985 *Some Ecclesiastical and Monastic Finds* (*Finds Research Group 700–1700 Datasheet* **2**), Coventry

— 1987 'Cauldrons and skillets: metal and pottery in cooking', in VYNER, B & WRATHMELL, C (eds), *Studies in Medieval and Later Pottery in Wales: Essays Presented to John Lewis*, Cardiff, 145–60

— 1991a 'Steelyard weights', in SAUNDERS, P & E (eds), *Salisbury and South Wiltshire Museum Medieval Catalogue* **1**, Salisbury and South Wiltshire Museum, 47–9

— 1991b 'Leather', in BLAIR, J & RAMSAY, N (eds), *English Medieval Industries*, London, 295–318

— 1991c 'Pottery and tile', in BLAIR, J and RAMSAY, N (eds), *English Medieval Industries*, London, 189–209

CHRISTIE'S, 1993 *Oak, Country Furniture and*

Early Works of Art, Including a Collection of Medieval and Later Antiquities, 3/10/93 (sale catalogue), Christie's South Kensington, London

CHRISTY, M, 1926 *The Bryant and May Museum of Fire-making Appliances, Catalogue of the Exhibits*, London

CLARK, J, 1983 'Medieval enamelled glasses from London', in *Medieval Archaeol* **27**, 152–6

— 1986 'Medieval glass', in BLACKMORE, L & SCHWAB, I, 'From the Templars to the tenement: a medieval and post-medieval site at 18 Shore Road, E9', in *Trans London & Middlesex Archaeol Soc* **37**, 180–1

— 1988 'Some medieval smiths' marks', in *Tools & Trades* **5**, 11–22

— (ed), 1995 *Medieval Finds from Excavations in London: 5 The Medieval Horse and its Equipment*, London

CLARKE, H & CARTER, A (eds), 1977 *Excavations in King's Lynn 1963–1970 (Soc Medieval Archaeol Monogr Ser* **7**)

CLARKE, T H, 1974 'Lattimo – a group of Venetian glass enamelled on opaque white ground', in *Journal of Glass Studies* **16**, Corning (USA), 25–56

CLAY, P, 1981 'The small finds', in MELLOR, J E & PEARCE, T, *The Austin Friars, Leicester* (*CBA Res Report* **35**), 130–45

CLIFFORD SMITH, H, 1923 *Catalogue of English Furniture and Early Woodwork: 1 Gothic and Tudor* (Victoria and Albert Museum), London

COBB, H S, 1990 *The Overseas Trade of London: Exchequer Customs Accounts 1480–1* (*London Rec Soc* **27**)

— 1995 'Textile imports in the 15th century: the evidence of the customs accounts', in *Costume* **29**, 1–11

COLVIN, H (ed), 1971 *Building Accounts of King Henry III*, Oxford

CONNOR, R D, 1987 *The Weights and Measures of England*, London

— & SIMPSON, A, forthcoming *The Weights and Measures of Scotland*

CONSITT, F, 1933 *The London Weavers' Company: 1 From the 12th to the Close of the 16th Century*, Oxford

COOK, J M, 1958a 'A fragment of early medieval glass from London', in *Medieval Archaeol* **2**, 173–7

— 1958b 'An early medieval pen from the City of London', in *Medieval Archaeol* **2**, 177–8

COOK, N C, 1967 'Medieval glass from the City of London' (exhibit at Ballots 3), in *Antiq J* **47.2**, 287

COWGILL, J, DE NEERGAARD, N & GRIFFITHS, N, 1987 *Medieval Finds from Excavations in London: 1 Knives and Scabbards*, London

CRABBE, P J, 1971 'Låse og Nøgler', in HELLMUTH ANDERSEN, H, CRABBE, P J & MADSEN, H J, *Århus Søndervold* (*Jysk Arkæologisk Selskabs Skrifter* **9**), Copenhagen (Denmark), 183–95

CRAMP, R, 1970 'Decorated window glass and millefiori from Monkwearmouth', in *Antiq J* **50.2**, 329–30

CROSSLEY, D W & ABERG, F A, 1972 'Sixteenth century glass making in Yorkshire: excavations at furnaces at Hutton and Rosedale, North Riding 1968–71', in *Post-Medieval Archaeol* **6**, 107–59

CROWFOOT, E, PRITCHARD, F & STANILAND, K, 1992 *Medieval Finds from Excavations in London: 4 Textiles and Clothing*, London

CROWLEY, N, 1992 *The Priory Hospital of St Mary Spitalfields* (unpublished archive report), Museum of London

CRUMMY, N, 1983 *Colchester Archaeological Report 2: The Roman Small Finds in Colchester 1971–9*, Colchester

CUMING, H S, 1856 'A history of keys', in *Brit Archaeol Ass* **12**, 117–29

CUNLIFFE, B, 1964 *Winchester Excavations 1949–1960* **1**, Winchester

CUOGHI COSTANTINI, M, 1992 'Le Linceul du Bienheureux Giacomo Salamoni', in *Bull de Liaison du Centre International d'Etude des Textiles Anciens* **70**, 111–15

CURLE, A O, 1927 'Fourteenth- to 18th-century candlesticks', in *Proc Soc Antiq Scot* **60** (5th ser **12**), 183–214

CURTEIS, A & MORRIS, C, forthcoming, report on excavations at Perth High Street

D'ALLEMAGNE, H R, 1968 *Decorative Antique Ironwork* (Dover edn), New York

DALTON, O M, 1922 'On two medieval bronze bowls in the British Museum', in *Archaeologia* **72**, 133–60

— 1924 *A Guide to the Medieval Antiquities and Objects of Later Date*, British Museum, London

DARLINGTON, I (ed), 1967 *London Consistory Court Wills 1492–1547 (London Rec Soc 3)*

DEGNAN, S & SEELEY, D, 1988 'Medieval and later floor tiles in Lambeth Palace Chapel', in *London Archaeol* **6.1**, 11–18

DENEUX, H, 1929 'A 13th-century mould for making calm lead', in *J Brit Soc Master Glass Painters* **3.2**, 81–4

DENT, H C, 1927 *Old English Bronze Wool Weights*, Norwich

DIEUDONNÉ, A, 1925 *Manuel des Poids Monétaires*, Paris

DODWELL, C R (ed and trans), 1986 *Theophilus, the Various Arts (Oxford Medieval Texts series)*, Oxford

DORIGATO, A, 1986 *Murano Glass Museum* (trans Langley, M), Milan (Italy)

DRACK, W, 1997 'Die Römische Wasser Armaturen und Mittelalterlichen Zapf Hahnen aus der Schweiz und dem Fürstentum Leichtenstein', *Mitteilungen der Antiquarischen Gesellschaft in Zürich* **64** (Switzerland)

DRIJBER, T, WOLTERS, W J, MEISCHKE, I R et al., 1980 *Thuis in de Late Middeleeuwen, Het Nederlands Burgerinteieur 1400–1535* (exhibition catalogue), Overijssels Provincial Museum, Zwolle (Netherlands)

DRURY, P J, 1982 'The bronze binding strip from Saffron Walden', in BASSETT, S R, *Saffron Walden: Excavations and Research 1972–80 (CBA Res Report 45)*, 86–7

DRYDEN, H E L, 1882, 'Proceedings at meetings of the Institute,' in *Archaeol J* **39**, 421–2

DUFOUR, I, DUBBE, B, VAN DEUN, J et al., 1979 *Keur van Tin uit de Havensteden Amsterdam, Antwerp en Rotterdam*, Amsterdam

DUNCAN, H B & MOORHOUSE, S A, 1987 'The small finds', in MOORHOUSE, S and WRATHMELL, S, *Kirkstall Abbey: 1, The 1950–64 Excavations: A Reassessment* (Yorkshire Archaeology 1), 120–48

DUNNING, G C, 1937 'A 14th-century well at the Bank of England', in *Antiq J* **17**, 414–18

— 1961 'Medieval chimney pots', in JOPE, E M (ed), *Studies in Building History*, London, 78–93

— 1976 'Attached ventilator finial', in KETTERINGHAM, L L (ed), *Alsted: Excavation of a 13th–14th-Century Sub Manor House with its Iron Works in Netherne Wood, Merstham, Surrey (Surrey Arch. Soc. Research 2)*, 51–5

DURHAM, B, 1977 'Archaeological investigations in St Aldates, Oxford', in *Oxoniensia* **42**, 83–205

DYER, C, 1989 *Standards of Living in the Later Middle Ages: Social Change in England c.1200–1520*, Cambridge

EAMES, E, 1980 *Catalogue of Medieval Lead Glazed Earthenware Tiles in the Department of Medieval and Later British Antiquities*, British Museum, London

EAMES, P, 1977 *Medieval Furniture in England, France and the Netherlands from the 12th to the 15th Centuries (Furniture Hist Soc Journal 13)*

EGAN, G, 1985/6 'Finds recovery on riverside sites in London', in *Popular Archaeol* **6.14**, 42–50

— 1988 *Base Metal Toys (Finds Research Group 700–1700 Datasheet 10)*, Oxford

— 1989a 'Leaden seals for textiles: some archaeological evidence relating to textiles and trade', in *Costume* **23**, 39–53

— 1989b 'Lead and lead alloy objects', in HASSALL, T G, HALPIN, C E & MELLOR, M, 'Excavations in St Ebbe's, Oxford, 1967–76 1: Late Saxon and medieval domestic occupation, tenements and the medieval Greyfriars', in *Oxoniensia* **54**, 227

— 1991a 'Industry and economics on the medieval London waterfront', in GOOD, G L, JONES, R H & PONSFORD, M W (eds), *Waterfront Archaeology (CBA Res Report 74)*, 9–18

— 1991b 'Clasps for books', in HODDER, M A (ed), *Excavations at Sandwell Priory and Hall 1982–88 (S Staffordshire Archaeol & Hist Soc Trans 31)*, 90–1

— 1992 (first edn 1985) *Leaden Cloth Seals (Finds Research Group 700–1700 Datasheet 3)*, Coventry

— 1994 *Lead Cloth Seals and Related Items in the British Museum (Brit Mus Occas Pap 93)*, London

— 1996 *Playthings from the Past* (exhibition catalogue), London

— forthcoming a, report on finds in THOMAS, C, SLOANE, B & PHILLPOTTS, C, *Excavations at the Priory and Hospital of St Mary Spital, London, 1935–91*

— forthcoming b, report on lead items in SAUNDERS, P (ed), *Salisbury and South Wiltshire Museum Medieval Catalogue* 3

— forthcoming c, *Dice (Finds Research Group 700–1700 Datasheet* series)

— HANNA, S D & KNIGHT, B, 1986 'Marks on milled window leads', in *Post-Medieval Archaeol* 20, 303–9

— & PRITCHARD, F, 1991 *Medieval Finds from Excavations in London: 3 Dress Accessories*, London

ENDREI, W & EGAN, G, 1982 'The sealing of cloth in Europe, with special reference to the English evidence', in *Textile Hist* 13.1, 47–74

EVANS, D H & TOMLINSON, D G, 1992 *Excavations at 33–35 Eastgate, Beverley, 1983–86 (Sheffield Excavation Report* 3), University of Sheffield

EVANS, J & SERJEANTSON, M S, 1933 *English Medieval Lapidaries (Early English Text Soc* 190), Oxford

FAIRBROTHER, J R, ARCHIBALD, M M, CRADDOCK, P T et al., 1990 *Faccombe Netherton, Excavations of a Saxon and Medieval Manorial Complex (Brit Mus Occas Pap* 74, two vols)

FEAVEARYEAR, A, 1963 *The Pound Sterling: A History of English Money* (2nd edn), Oxford

FEILD, R, 1984 *Irons in the Fire: A History of Cooking Equipment*, Marlborough

FINGERLIN, I, 1971 *Gürtel des Hohen und Späten Mittelalters*, (*Kunstwissenshaftliche Studien* 46), Munich (Germany)

FINLAY, M, 1990 *Western Writing Implements in the Age of the Quill Pen*, Carlisle

FORD, B, 1987 'Wooden objects', in HOLDSWORTH, P (ed), *Excavations in the Medieval Burgh of Perth 1979–81 (Soc Antiq Scot Monogr* 5), 141–7

FOY, D, 1985 'Essai de typologie des verres médiévaux d'après les fouilles Provençales et Languedociennes', in *Journal of Glass Studies* 27, Corning (USA), 18–71

— 1988 *Le Verre Médiéval et son Artisanat en France Méditerranéenne*, Paris

— & SENNEQUIER, G, 1989 *A Travers le Verre*, Rouen (France)

FREESTONE, I C, 1991 'Looking into glass', in BOWMAN, S (ed), *Science and the Past*, London, 37–56

— BIMSON, M & BUCKTON, D, 1990 'Compositional categories of Byzantine glass tesserae', in *Annales du 11e Congrès de l'Association Internationale pour l'Histoire du Verre* (held 1988), Amsterdam, 271–9

GAIMSTER, D R M, MARGESON, S & HURLEY, M, 1990 'Medieval Britain and Ireland in 1989', in *Medieval Archaeol* 34, 162–252

— & VERHAEGHE, F, 1992 'Handles with face masks: a cross channel type of late medieval highly decorated basin', in GAIMSTER, D R M & REDKNAP, M (eds), *Everyday and Exotic Pottery from Europe c.650–1900*, Oxford, 301–23

GEDDES, J, 1991 'Iron', in BLAIR, J & RAMSAY, N, *English Medieval Industries*, London, 167–88

GOODALL, A R, 1977 'Objects of copper alloy', in BARTON, K J & HOLDEN, E W, 'Excavations at Bramber Castle, Sussex 1966–7', in *Archaeol J* 134, 11–79

— 1981 'The medieval bronzesmith and his products', in CROSSLEY, D W (ed), *Medieval Industry (CBA Res Report* 40), 63–71

— 1982 'Objects of copper alloy', in COAD, J G & STREETEN, A D F, 'Excavations at Castle Acre, Norfolk 1972–77', in *Archaeol J* 139, 235–40

— 1987 'Medieval copper alloy', in BERESFORD, G, *Goltho: The Development of an Early Medieval Manor c.850–1150 (HBMC(E) Arch Report* 4), 173–6

— 1989 'Copper alloy objects', in HASSALL, T G, HALPIN, C E & MELLOR, M, 'Excavations in St Ebbe's, Oxford, 1967–76: 1 Late Saxon and Medieval domestic occupation, tenements and the Medieval Greyfriars', in *Oxoniensia* 54, 223–6

GOODALL, I H, 1981 'The medieval blacksmith and his products', in CROSSLEY, D W (ed), *Medieval Industry (CBA Res Report* 40), 51–62

— 1989 'Iron objects', in HASSALL, T G, HALPIN, C E & MELLOR, M, 'Excavations in St Ebbe's, Oxford 1967–76: 1 Late Saxon and Medieval domestic occupation, tenements and the Medieval Greyfriars', in *Oxoniensia* 54, 227–31

GOSLING, K, 1989 'The runic material from Tønsberg', in *Universitets Oldsaksamling Årbok 1986/88*, Oslo (Norway), 175–87

GREEN, L & HART, F, 1987 'Colour and chemical composition in ancient glass: an examination of some Roman and Wealden glass by means of ultraviolet visible infra-red spectrometry and electron microprobe analysis', in *J Archaeol Sci* **14.3**, 271–82

GREW, F & DE NEERGAARD, M, 1988 *Medieval Finds from Excavations in London: 2 Shoes and Pattens*

GRIERSON, P, 1980 'Western Christendom 700–1450', in JESSOP PRICE, M (ed), *Coins: An Illustrated Survey 650 BC to the Present Day*, London, 142–77

GRUPE, G, 1984 *Das Neue Bild des Altes Göttingen*, Göttingen (Germany)

GUILDHALL MUSEUM CATALOGUE, 1908: *Catalogue of the Collection of London Antiquities in The Guildhall Museum*, London (the 1905 edition is differently paginated)

HAEDEKE, H U, 1976 *Zinn (Katalog des Kunstgewerbemuseums* **3**), Cologne (Germany)

HALDENBY, D, 1990 'An Anglian site on the Yorkshire Wolds', in *Yorkshire Archaeol J* **62**, 51–63

— 1992 'An Anglian site on the Yorkshire Wolds (continued)', in *Yorkshire Archaeol J* **64**, 25–39

HALL, H & NICHOLAS, F J, 1929 'Select tracts and table books relating to English weights and measures, 1100–1742', in *Camden Miscellany* **15**, 1–68

HALL, R, 1984 *The Excavations at York: The Viking Dig*, London

HANAWALT, B, 1993 *Growing up in Medieval London*, Oxford

HANSE 1989: ARNOLD, K, ARNOLD, U, ANGERMANN, H et al., *Die Hanse, Lebenswirklichkeit und Mythos* (exhibition catalogue, two vols), Hamburg (Germany)

HARAUCOURT, E, nd *Medieval Manners Illustrated at the Cluny Museum*, Paris

HARDEN, D B, 1956 'Glass and glazes', in SINGER, C, HOLMYARD, E J, HALL, A R and WILLIAMS, T I (eds), *A History of Technology* **2**: *The Mediterranean Civilization and the Middle Ages*, Oxford, 311–46

— 1961 'Domestic window glass: Roman, Saxon and medieval', in JOPE, E M (ed), *Studies in Building History*, London, 39–63

— 1968 'Medieval glass in the west', in *Proceedings of 8th International Congress on Glass*, Liège (Belgium), 97–111,

— 1972 'Ancient glass **3**: Post Roman', in *Archaeol J* **128**, 78–117

— 1975 'Table glass in the Middle Ages', in RENAUD, J G N (ed), *Rotterdam Papers* **2**, 35–45

— 1977 'Glass', in CUNLIFFE, B (ed), *Excavations at Portchester Castle: 3 Medieval, the Old Bailey and its Defences (Research Ctee of the Soc Antiquaries Report* **34**), 210–11

— 1978 'Anglo Saxon and later medieval glass in Britain: some recent developments', in *Medieval Archaeol* **21**, 1–24

HARE, J N (ed), 1985 *Battle Abbey: The Eastern Range and the Excavations of 1978–80 (HBMC(E) Arch Report* **2**)

HARRISON, E R, 1928 *Harrison of Ightam*, Oxford

HATCHER, J & BARKER, T C, 1974 *A History of British Pewter*, London

HEMP, W J, 1918/19 'Exhibit at ballots', in *Proc Soc Antiq* (2nd ser) **31**, 214–16

HENDERSON, J, forthcoming, 'Chemical analysis of window glass', in *Further Excavations at Beverley Dominican Priory, Beverley 1986–89*

HENIG, M, 1974 'Small finds', in TATTON BROWN, T, 'Excavations at the Custom House site, City of London 1973', in *Trans London & Middlesex Archaeol Soc* **25**, 186–201

— 1975 'Medieval finds', in TATTON BROWN, T, 'Excavations at the Custom House site, City of London 1973 **2**', *Trans London & Middlesex Archaeol Soc* **26**, 152–4

HENKES, H E, 1994 *Glass without Gloss (Rotterdam Papers* **9**), The Hague (Netherlands)

HERTEIG, A E, 1969 *Kongers Havn og Handels Sete*, Oslo (Norway)

HILDBURGH, W L, 1955 'Medieval copper champlevé enamelled images of the Virgin and Child', in *Archaeologia* **96**, 115–58

HODGES, H, 1976 *Artifacts: An Introduction to Early Technology*, Harmondsworth

HOLMES, E F, 1985 *A History of Thimbles*, London

— nd *Sewing Thimbles (Finds Research Group 700–1700 Datasheet* **9**), Oxford

HOMER, R F, 1985, 'The medieval pewterers of

London c.1190–1457', in *Trans London & Middlesex Archaeol Soc* **36**, 137–63

— 1991 'Tin, lead and pewter', in BLAIR, J & RAMSAY, N (eds), *English Medieval Industries*, London, 57–80

HOMO, C, 1984 'Trois guimbardes', in *Music-Archaeol Bulletin* **2**, 14–15

— 1986 'Les Guimbardes des Fouilles de la Cour Napoléon au Louvre', in *Music-Archaeol Bulletin* **6**, 28–32

HORNE FUGLESANG, S, 1991 'Spoons', in SCHIA, E & MOLAUG, P (eds), *De Arkeologiske Utgravninger i Gamlebyen, Oslo* **8**, *Dagligliv-ets Gjenstander* **2**, Oslo (Norway), 223–50

HORNSBY, P R G, WEINSTEIN, R & HOMER, R F, 1989 *Pewter: A Celebration of the Craft 1200–1700*, Museum of London

HUME, A, 1863 *Ancient Meols: Some Account of the Antiquities Found near Dove Point on the Sea Coast of Cheshire*, London

HURST, D, 1992 'Lead', in WOODIWISS, S, *Iron Age and Roman Salt Production and the Medieval Town of Droitwich* (*CBA Res Report* **81**), 170

ISINGS, C & WIJNMAN, H F, 1977 'Medieval glass from Utrecht', in *Journal of Glass Studies* **19**, Corning (USA), 77–83

JAMES, T B & ROBINSON, A M, 1988 *Clarendon Palace* (*Research Cttee Soc Antiq London Report* **45**), London

JENKINSON, H, 1911 'Exchequer tallies', in *Archaeologia* **62.2**, 367–80

— 1925 'Medieval tallies, public and private', in *Archaeologia* **74**, 289–351

JENNING, C, 1974 *Early Chests in Wood and Iron* (*Public Record Office Museum Pamphlet* **7**), London

JOHNSON, A H, 1914 *The History of the Worshipful Company of the Drapers of London* **1**, Oxford

JONES, P E (ed), 1954 *Calendar of Plea and Memoranda Rolls, 1437–57*, Cambridge

JOPE, E M, & DUNNING, G C, 1954 'The use of blue slate for roofing in medieval England', in *Antiq J* **34**, 209–17

— & THRELFALL, R I, 1959 'The 12th century castle at Ascot Doilly, Oxfordshire: its history and excavation', in *Antiq J* **39**, 219–73

KAHSNITZ, R & BRANDL, R, 1984 *Aus dem Wirtshaus zum Wilden Mann: Finde aus dem Mittelalterlichen Nürnberg* (exhibition catalogue), National Museum, Nuremberg (Germany)

KEENE, D J, 1990 'Shops and shopping in medieval London', in GRANT, L (ed), *Medieval Art, Architecture and Archaeology in London* (*British Archaeol Ass Conference Trans* **10** for 1984), 29–46

— & HARDING, V, 1987 *Historical Gazetteer of London before the Great Fire: 1 Cheapside* (University of London Inst of Historical Research), Cambridge (fiche publication)

KENYON, G H, 1967 *The Glass Industry of the Weald*, Leicester University

KING, D, 1963 *Opus Anglicanum*, London

KING, E, 1973 *Toys and Dolls for Collectors*, London

KINGSFORD, C L, 1920 'Historical notes on medieval London houses', in *London Topogr Rec* **12**, 1–66

— (ed), 1971 *John Stow, A Survey of London* (two vols), Oxford (reprint of 1908 edn)

KLUGE PINSKER, A, 1991, *Schach und Trictrac* (*Römisch Germanisches Zentralmuseum Monograph* **30**), Sigmaringen (Germany)

KOLCHIN, B A, 1989 *Wooden Artefacts from Medieval Novgorod* (*BAR Int Ser* **495**, two vols), Oxford

KRUSE, S, 1992 'Late Saxon balances and weights from England', in *Medieval Archaeol* **37**, 67–95

LAMM, C J, 1929 *Mittelalterliche Gläser und Steinschnittarbeiten aus dem Nähen Osten* **1** & **2**, Berlin

LAWSON, G & EGAN, G, 1988 'Medieval trumpet from the City of London', in *Galpin Soc* **61**, 63–6

LEACH, P, 1984 *The Archaeology of Taunton* (*Western Archaeol Trust Excav Monogr* **8**)

LEWIS, J M, 1978 *Medieval Pottery and Metalware in Wales*, Cardiff

— 1984 'A medieval brass mortar from south Wales and its affinities', in *Antiq J* **64.2**, 326–36

— 1987a *Bronze Aquamaniles and Ewers* (*Finds Research Group Datasheet 700–1700* **7**), Oxford

— 1987b 'Roof tiles: some observations and

questions' (6th Gerald Dunning Memorial Lecture), in *Medieval Ceram* **11**, 3–14

— 1987c 'A collection of medieval artefacts found near Holywell, Clwyd', in *Bull Board Celtic Stud* **34**, 270–86

— BROWNSWORD, R & PITT, E E H, 1987 'Medieval "bronze" tripod ewers from Wales', in *Medieval Archaeol* **31**, 80–93

LIEBGOTT, N K, 1973 *Lys – Lamper, Stager og Kroner fra Middelalder og Renaessance*, National Museum, Copenhagen (Denmark)

LIGHTBOWN, R W, 1978 *Secular Goldsmiths' Work in Medieval France: A History* (*Research Cttee of Soc Antiq London Report* **36**)

LLOYD, N, 1925 (1975 reprint) *History of the English House*, London

LLOYD MORGAN, G, 1990 'Organic artefacts', in Ward, S, *Excavations at Chester: The Lesser Medieval Religious Houses, Sites Investigated 1964–1983* (*Grosvenor Museum Archaeol Excav and Survey Report* **6**), 177–8, Chester City Council

THE LUTTRELL PSALTER, 1932 (introduction by MILLAR, E G), London

MCCARTHY, M R & BROOKS, C M, 1988 *Medieval Pottery in Britain AD 900–1600*, Leicester

MACGREGOR, A, 1975 'Problems in the interpretation of microscopic wear patterns: the evidence from bone skates', in *J of Archaeol Sci* **2**, 385–90

— 1976 'Bone skates: a review of the evidence', in *Archaeol J* **133**, 57–74

— 1982 *The Anglo Scandinavian Finds from Lloyds Bank, Pavement and other Sites* (*The Archaeology of York* **17.3**), London

— (ed) 1983 *Tradescants' Rarities, Essays on the Foundation of the Ashmolean Museum 1683, with a Catalogue of the Surviving Early Collections*, Oxford

— 1985a *Bone, Antler, Ivory and Horn: The Technology of Skeletal Materials since the Roman Period*, London

— 1985b 'Coin balances in the Ashmolean Museum', in *Antiq J* **65.2**, 439–43

— 1989 'Bone, antler and horn industries in the urban context', in SERJEANTSON, D & WALDRON, T, *Diet and Crafts in Towns* (*BAR* **199**), 107–28

MCLEES, C, 1990 *Games People Played* (*Fortiden i Trondheims Bygrunn: Folkebibliotekstomten* **24**), Riksantikvaren, Trondheim (Norway)

MANDEL, G, 1992 *Clefs*, Ars Mundi (French edn)

MANNING, W H, 1985 *Catalogue of Romano British Iron Tools: Fittings and Weapons in the British Museum*, London

MARGESON, S (ed), 1993 *Norwich Households: The Medieval and Post Medieval Finds from Norwich Survey Excavations 1971–78* (*E Anglian Archaeol Report* **58**)

MÅRTENSSON, A W (ed), 1976 *Uppgrävt Förflutet för PK Banken in Lund* (*Archaeologica Lundensia* **7**), Lund (Sweden)

— & WAHLÖO, C, 1970 *Lundafynd, en Bilderbok* (*Archaeologica Lundensia* **4**), Lund (Sweden)

MAYHEW, N, 1975 'A tumbrel at the Ashmolean Museum', in *Antiq J* **55.2**, 394–6 & pl 81

— 1988 *Coinage in France*, London

MAZZAOUI, M F, 1981 *The Italian Cotton Trade in the Later Middle Ages, 1100–1600*, Cambridge

MEGAW, J V S, 1960 'Penny whistles and prehistory', in *Antiquity* **34**, 6–13

MELLOR, J E & PEARCE, T, 1981 *The Austin Friary, Leicester* (*CBA Res Report* **35**)

MENDE, U, 1981 *Die Türzieher des Mittelalters* (*Bronzegeräte des Mittelalters* **2**), Berlin

MERRIFIELD, M P, 1967 *Original Treatises on the Arts of Painting*, New York

MERRIFIELD, R, 1987 *The Archaeology of Ritual and Magic*, London

MEYER, O, 1979 *Archéologie Urbaine à Saint Denis*, Saint Denis (France)

— & WYSS, A, 1985 *Saint Denis, Récherches Urbaines 1983–1985*, Saint Denis (France)

MICHAELIS, R F, 1978 *Old Domestic Basemetal Candlesticks from the 13th to 19th Century*, Woodbridge

MICKENBERG, D, CALDWELL, S, SZABO, G et al., 1985 *Songs of Glory, Medieval Art from 900–1500* (exhibition catalogue), Oklahoma Museum of Art (USA)

MICKLETHWAITE, J T, 1892 'A filtering cistern of the 14th century at Westminster Abbey', in *Archaeologia* **53.1**, 161–70

MILNE, G, 1991 'Waterfront archaeology and vernacular architecture: a London study', in GOOD, G L, JONES, R H & PONSFORD, M W (eds), *Papers from the Third International*

Waterfront Conference (CBA Res Report **74**), 116–20

— & MILNE C, 1982 *Medieval Waterfront Development at Trig Lane* (London & Middlesex Archaeol Soc Spec Pap **5**)

MONK, E, 1974 *Keys: Their History and Collection*, Princes Risborough

MOORHOUSE, S, 1978 'Documentary evidence for the uses of medieval pottery: an interim statement', in *Medieval Ceram* **2**, 3–21

— 1981 'The medieval pottery industry and its markets', in CROSSLEY, D W (ed), *Medieval Industry*, 96–125

— 1987 *The Medieval Kitchen and its Equipment* (synopsis of paper presented to a joint meeting of the Finds Research Group and the Medieval Pottery Research Group at Leeds)

MORGAN, N J, 1982 *Early Gothic Manuscripts: 1 1190–1250*, Oxford

MORRIS, C A, forthcoming *Wood and Woodworking in York* (*The Archaeology of York* **17**)

MULDOON, S & BROWNSWORD, R, nd (c.1987?) *Pewter Spoons and Other Related Material of the 14th–17th Centuries in the Collection of the Herbert Art Gallery and Museum*, Coventry

MULLER, W & BOCHYNEK, G, 1989 'Possibilities of approximate dating of medieval glasses using their chemical composition', in *Proceedings of the 15th International Congress of Glass*, Leningrad (Russia), 47–52

MUNRO, J H, 1983 'The medieval scarlet and the economics of sartorial splendour', in HARTE, N & PONTING, K (eds), *Cloth and Clothing in Medieval Europe* (*Pasold Studies in Textile History* 2), London, 13–70

MURDOCH, T, CLARK, J, ELLMERS, C et al., 1991 *Treasures and Trinkets: Jewellery in London from Pre-Roman Times to the 1930s*, London

MURRAY, H J R, 1913 *A History of Chess*, Oxford

— 1952 *A History of Board Games Other than Chess*, Oxford

MUSEUM OF LONDON, 1986 *The Museum of London Annual Report 1984–1985*, London

MUSTY, A E S, nd *A Study of the Spring Padlocks (Barrel Locks) in Salisbury Museum, with Reference to Other Examples of this Lock Type* (unpublished typescript)

MUSTY, J, ALGAR, D J & EWENCE, P F, 1969 'The medieval pottery kilns at Laverstock, near Salisbury, Wiltshire', in *Archaeologia* **102**, 83–150

NATIONAL MUSEUM OF IRELAND, 1973 *Viking and Medieval Dublin: National Museum Excavations, 1962–63* (exhibition catalogue), Dublin

NENK, B, MARGESON, S & HURLEY, M, 1992 'Medieval Britain and Ireland in 1991', in *Medieval Archaeol* **36**, 184–308

NEUGEBAUER, W, 1975 'Arbeiten der Böttcher und Dreschler aus den Mittelalterlichen Bodenfunden der Hansestadt Lübeck', in RENAUD, J G N (ed), *Rotterdam Papers* **2**, Rotterdam (Netherlands), 117–37

NICKEL, E, 1964 *Der 'Alte Markt' in Magdeburg*, Berlin

NIGHTINGALE, P, 1995 *A Medieval Mercantile Community: The Grocers' Company and the Politics and Trade of London 1000–1485*, London

NÖEL HUME, A, 1974 *Archaeology and the Colonial Gardener* (*Colonial Williamsburg Archaeological Series* **7**), Colonial Williamsburg Foundation, Virginia (USA)

NÖEL HUME, I, 1957 'Medieval bottles from London', in *Connoisseur* **150**, 104–8

OAKLEY, G E, 1979 'The copper alloy objects', in WILLIAMS, J H (ed), *St Peter's Street, Northampton, Excavations 1973–1976*, Northampton, 248–64

ODDY, W A, LANEICE, S & STRATFORD, N, 1986 *Romanesque Metalwork: Copper Alloys and their Decoration*, London

ORME, N 1995 'The culture of children in medieval England', in *Past and Present* **148**, 48–88

PEARCE, J E, 1984 'Ceramic counters', in THOMPSON, A, GREW, F & SCHOFIELD, J, 'Excavations at Aldgate, 1974', in *Post-Medieval Archaeol* **18**, 1–148

— & VINCE, A, 1988 *A Dated Type Series of London Medieval Pottery: 4 Surrey Whitewares* (London & Middlesex Archaeol Soc Spec Pap **10**)

—, — & JENNER, M A, 1985 *A Dated Type Series of Medieval Pottery: 2 London Type Ware* (London & Middlesex Archaeol Soc Spec Pap **6**)

—, — & WHITE, R, 1982 *A Dated Type Series of London Medieval Pottery: 1 Mill Green Ware*, in *Trans London & Middlesex Archaeol Soc* **33**, 266–98

PINDER WILSON, R, 1991 'The Islamic lands and China', in TAIT, H (ed), *Five Thousand Years of Glass*, London, 112–43

PITT RIVERS (Lieut General), 1883 *On the Development of Primitive Locks and Keys*, London

PLATT, C, 1975 'The excavations 1966–1969', in PLATT, C & COLEMAN SMITH, R, *Excavations in Medieval Southampton 1953–1969: 1 The Excavation Reports*, 232–330

— & COLEMAN SMITH, R, 1975 *Excavations in Medieval Southampton 1953–1969: 2 The Finds*, Leicester

POTTER, E C, 1992 'On being interested in the extreme', in *Journal of the Royal Society of New South Wales* **125** (Australia), 79–91

PRITCHARD, F A, 1982 *Swan Lane Medieval Building Material* (unpublished archive report), Museum of London

— 1991 'The small finds', in VINCE, A G (ed), *Aspects of Saxo Norman London: 2 Finds and Environmental Evidence* (*London & Middlesex Archaeol Soc Spec Pap* **12**)

QUALMANN, K E, 1991 'A medieval jet cross from the latrine pit', in SCOBIE, G D, ZANT, J M & WHINNEY, R, *The Brooks, Winchester: A Preliminary Report on the Excavations, 1987–88*, (*Winchester Museums Service Archaeology Report* **1**), 52, fig 43, 69–71

REDDAWAY, T F, 1975 *The Early History of the Goldsmiths' Company 1327–1509*, London

REMNANT, M, 1986 *English Bowed Instruments from Anglo Saxon to Tudor Times*, Oxford

RHODES, M, 1982a 'A pair of 15th-century spectacle frames from the City of London', in *Antiq J* **62.1**, 57–73

— 1982b 'A discussion of the significance of the waterfront dumps and their contexts', in MILNE & MILNE, 84–92

RIGOLD, S E, 1978 'A medieval coin balance from Roche Abbey, Yorkshire', in *Antiq J* **58**, 371–4

RILEY, H T (ed), 1868 *Memorials of London Life in the 13th, 14th and 15th Centuries*, London

RIMMER, J, 1981 'An archaeo-organological survey of the Netherlands', in *World Archaeology* **12.3**, 233–45

RIZZOLI, L, 1930 *L'Universita dell' Arte della Lana in Padova*, Padua (Italy)

ROACH SMITH, C, 1842 'Ancient copper bowls found in Lothbury', Appendix in *Archaeologia* **29**, 367–8

— 1854 *Catalogue of the Museum of London Antiquities*, London

ROBINS, F W, 1939 *The Story of the Lamp (and the Candle)*, Oxford

ROGERS, D J, 1993 *Tumbrels (Finds Research Group 700–1700 Datasheet* **16**)

ROOKSBY, H P, 1962 'Opacifiers in opal glasses through the ages', in *Journal General Electric Company* **29.1**, 20–6

ROWLAND, D, 1994 (Sept) 'Price guide', in *The Searcher* **109**, 28

RUEMPOL, A P E & VAN DONGEN, A G A, 1991 *Pre-industrial Utensils 1150–1800*, Rotterdam (Netherlands)

RYDBECK, M, 1968 'Maultommeln in Funden aus dem Schwedischen Mitteltalter', in BLOMQUIST, R, *Res Mediaevales* (*Archaeologica Lundensia* **3**), Lund (Sweden), 252–60

SABATIER, A 1908, 'Étude Revisionelle des Scéaux de Plomb Fiscaux et Commerçiaux', in *Bulletin de la Société des Sciences et Arts du Beaujolais* **9,** Villefranche (France), 5–30, 111–47

SABINE, E L, 1937 'City cleaning in medieval London', in *Speculum* **12.1**, 19–43

SALZMAN, L F 1926 *Medieval English Life*, Oxford

— 1952 *Building in England down to 1540*, Oxford (2nd edn 1967)

SAMUEL, M, 1989 'The 15th-century garner at Leadenhall, London', in *Antiq J* **69.1**, 119–53

SAUNDERS, A D, 1980 'Lydford Castle, Devon', in *Medieval Archaeol* **24**, 123–86

SCHIETZEL, K, 1970 *Das Archäologische Fund Material der Ausgrabung Haithabu 1963–64: 1* Neumünster (Germany)

SCHOFIELD, J, 1984 *The Buildings of London from the Conquest to the Great Fire of London*, London

— 1991 'The construction of medieval and Tudor houses in London', *Construct Hist* **7**, 3–28

— 1995, *Medieval London Houses*, Yale, New Haven (USA)

— ALLEN, P & TAYLOR, C, 1990 'Medieval buildings and property development in the area of Cheapside', in *Trans London & Middlesex Archaeol Soc* **41**, 39–237

— & DYSON, T, in preparation *Medieval Waterfront Tenements*

SEYMOUR LINDSAY, J, 1970 (revised edn) *Iron and Brass Implements of the English House*, London

SHARPE, R R (ed), 1899 *Calendar of Letter Books of the City of London: Letterbook A*, London

— 1903 *Calendar of Letter Books of the City of London: Letterbook E*, London

— 1905 *Calendar of Letter Books of the City of London: Letterbook G*, London

— 1907 *Calendar of Letter Books of the City of London: Letterbook H*, London

SHEPHERD, J, in preparation, note on finds of glass ring flasks

SHERLOCK, D & WOODS, H, 1988 *St Augustine's Abbey: Report on Excavations, 1969–1978 (Kent Archaeol Soc Monogr Ser* **4**), Maidstone

SHOESMITH, R, 1985 *Hereford City Excavations: 3 The Finds (CBA Res Report* **56**)

SHORTT, H, 1973 *Salisbury Heritage: Illustrations from the Museum Collection*, Salisbury and South Wiltshire Museum

SIMPSON, A & CONNOR, R D, 1996 'Weighing in the early 14th century' **1**, in *Equilibrium* **1**, 1987–98, **2** in **2**, 2015–24

SMITH, T P, 1985 *The Medieval Brickmaking Industry in England 1400–1450 (BAR* **138**)

SPENCER, B, 1984 'Medieval seal dies recently found at London', in *Antiq J* **64.2**, 376–82

— 1985 'Fifteenth-century collar of SS and a hoard of false dice and their container from the Museum of London', in *Antiq J* **65.2**, 449–53

— 1990 *Pilgrim Souvenirs and Secular Badges (Medieval Catalogue* **2**), Salisbury and South Wiltshire Museum

— forthcoming *Medieval Finds from Excavations in London: 7 Pilgrim Souvenirs and Secular Badges*, London

STANILAND, K, 1991 *Embroiderers (Medieval Craftsmen* series), London

STANLEY STONE, A C, 1925 *The Worshipful Company of Turners of London: Its Origin and History*, London

STATUTES OF THE REALM **1**, 1810, Records Commission, London

STEANE, J M & FOREMAN M, 1988 'Medieval fishing tackle', in ASTON, M (ed), *Medieval Fish, Fisheries and Fishponds in England (BAR* **182**), 137–86

— & —, 1991 'The archaeology of medieval fishing tackle', in GOOD, G L, JONES, R H & PONSFORD, M W (eds), *Waterfront Archaeology (CBA Res Report* **74**), 88–104

STENTON, F M, 1934 *Norman London (Historical Association Leaflet* **93–4**), London (rev edn)

STEVENSON, J, 1995 'A new type of late medieval spectacle frame from the City of London', in *London Archaeologist* **7.12**, 321–7

STONE, L M, 1974 *Fort Michilimackinac 1715–1781 (Michigan State University Museum Anthropological Series* **2**), Mackinac Island State Park Commission, Michigan (USA)

TAIT, H, 1979 *The Golden Age of Venetian Glass*, British Museum, London

— 1991 'Europe from the Middle Ages to the Industrial Revolution', in TAIT, H (ed), *Five Thousand Years of Glass*, British Museum, London, 144–87

TATTON BROWN, T 1974 'Excavations at the Custom House site, City of London 1973', in *Trans London & Middlesex Archaeol Soc* **25**, 117–219

TEGNÉR, G, 1984 'Ett Tennlock från Kalmar', in KARLSSON, L, LAGERLÖF, E, LINDGREN, M et al., (eds), *Den Ljusa Medeltiden (Statens Historiska Museet, Stockholm, Studies* **4**), Uddevalla (Sweden), 289–300

THEUERKAUFF LIEDERWALD, A E, 1988 *Mittelalterliche Bronze und Messinggefasse, Eimer – Kannen – Lavabokessel (Bronzegeräte des Mittelalters* **4**), Berlin

THOMAS, A H (ed), 1929 *Calendar of Plea and Memoranda Rolls Preserved among the Archives of the Corporation of the City of London at the Guildhall, 1364–1381*, Cambridge

— 1932 *Calendar of Plea and Memoranda Rolls, 1381–1412*, Cambridge

— 1943 *Calendar of Plea and Memoranda Rolls, 1413–37*, Cambridge

THOMPSON, M W, 1967 *Novgorod the Great*, London

THORNTON, P, 1978 *Seventeenth-Century Interior Decoration in England, France and Holland*, Yale, New Haven (USA)

THRUPP, S, 1933 *A Short History of the Worshipful Company of Bakers of London*, London

TRACY, C, 1988 *English Medieval Furniture and Woodwork*, London

TREUE, W, GOLDMANN, K, KELLERMAN, R et al., (eds), 1965 *Das Hausbuch der Mendelschen Zwolfbrüderstiftung zu Nürnberg* (two vols), Munich (Germany)

TURNER, W E S & ROOKSBY, H P, 1959 'A study of the opalizing agents in ancient glasses throughout three thousand four hundred years', in *Glastechnische Berichte* **32.8**, 17–28

TYLECOTE, R, 1986 *The Prehistory of Metallurgy in the British Isles*, London

TYSON, R, 1996 *Medieval High Lead Glass Table Vessels* (*Finds Research Group 700–1700 Datasheet* **21**), Oxford

— & CLARK, J, 1994 *Bibliography of Medieval Glass Vessels from British Sites AD1200–1500*, London

UITZE, E, 1990 *Women in the Medieval Town* (trans Marnie, S), London

ULBRICHT, I, 1984 *Die Verarbeitung von Knochen, Geweih und Horn im Mittelalterlichen Schleswig* (*Ausgrabungen in Schleswig* 3), Neumünster (Germany)

ULLRICH, R G, 1989 'Halbedelsteine und Glasfunde', in VON MÜLLER, A & VON MÜLLER MUCI, K (eds), *Ausgrabungen, Funde und Naturwissenschaftliche Untersuchungen auf dem Burgwall in Berlin Spandau* (*Berliner Beiträge zur Vor und Frühgeschichte*, NS **6**), Berlin, 57–99

UNWIN, G, 1962 'London tradesmen and their creditors', in UNWIN, G (ed), *Finance and Trade under Edward III*, London (reprint of 1918 edn), 19–34

VANDENBERGHE, S, 1988 'Metalen Voorwergen uit Recent Archeologisch Onderzoek te Brugge', in DE WITTE, H (ed), *Brugge Onder Zocht*, Bruges (Belgium), 160–91

VAN UYTVEN, R, 1983 'Cloth in medieval literature of western Europe', in HARTE, N B & PONTING, K G (eds), *Cloth and Clothing in Medieval Europe* (*Pasold Studies in Textile History* **2**), 151–83

VAUDOUR, C, 1980 *Clefs et Serrures dès Origines au Commençement de la Renaissance* (*Catalogue du Musée le Secq des Tourenelles* **2**), Rouen (France)

VEALE, E M, 1969 'Craftsmen and the economy of London in the fourteenth century', in HOLLAENDER, A E J & KELLAWAY, W (eds), *Studies in London History*, London, 133–51

VERHAEGHE, F, 1991 'An aquamanile and some thoughts on ceramic competition with metal quality goods in the Middle Ages', in LEWIS, E (ed), *Custom and Ceramics: Essays Presented to Kenneth Barton*, Wickham, 25–61

VERITÁ, M, 1985 'L'invenzione del cristallo Muranese: una verifica analitica delle fonti storiche', in *Rivista della Stazione Sperimentale del Vetro* **1**, (Italy), 17–29

VERLINDE, A D, 1983 'Het Kasteel Voorst', *Rijkdienst voor het Oudheidkundig Bodemonderzoek*, offprint **220** (Netherlands)

VERSTER, A J G, 1958 *Old European Pewter*, London

VINCE, A G, 1985 'The Saxon and medieval pottery of London: a review', in *Medieval Archaeol* **29**, 25–93

— 1991 'Early medieval London: Refining the chronology', in *London Archaeologist* **6**, 263–71

VON FALKE, O & MEYER, E, 1935 (1983 reprint), *Romanische Leuchter und Gefässe – Giessgefässe der Gotik* (*Bronzegeräte des Mittelalters* **1**), Berlin

VOSE, R H, 1980 *Glass*, London

WALLACE, P F, 1988 'Coins and weights' in WALLACE, P & O'FLOINN, R, *Dublin 1000: Discovery and Excavation in Dublin, 1842–1981*, National Museum of Ireland, Dublin, 24

WARD PERKINS, J B, 1939 'A medieval spoon in the Guildhall Museum, London', in *Antiq J* **19**, 313–16

— 1940 *London Museum Medieval Catalogue*, London

WEAVER, L, 1909 *English Leadwork: Its Art and History*, London

WEBER, B, 1981 'Leker Eller – ?', *Viking* **24**, Oslo (Norway), 81–92

WEBSTER, L E & CHERRY, J, 1973 'Medieval Britain in 1972', in *Medieval Archaeol* **17**, 138–88

WEDEPOHL, K H, KRUEGER, I & HARTMANN, G, 1995 'Medieval lead glass from northwestern Europe', in *Journal of Glass Studies* **37**, Corning (USA), 65–82

WEITZMANN FIEDLER, J, 1981 *Romanische Gravierte Bronzeschalen*, Berlin

WELLS, C, 1988 'An early medieval case of death in childbirth', in WHITE, W, *The Cemetery of St Nicholas Shambles* (*London & Middlesex Archaeol Soc Spec Pap* **9**), 71–3

WENZEL, M, 1984 'Thirteenth-century Islamic enamelled glass found in medieval Abingdon', in *Oxford J Archaeol* **3.3**, 1–21

WEST, B, 1982 'Bone skates: a review of the evidence', in *Trans London & Middlesex Archaeol Soc* **33**, 303

WHEELER, R E M, 1946 *London in Roman Times* (*London Museum Catalogue* **3**), London

WIBERG, C, 1977 'Horn og Benmaterialet fra Mindets Tomt', in HØEG, H J, LIDÉN, H E & LIESTØL, A et al., (eds), *Feltet Mindets Tomt* (*De Arkeologiske Utgravninger i Gamlebyen, Oslo* **1**), Oslo (Norway)

WILLAN, T S (ed), 1962 *A Tudor Book of Rates*, Manchester

WILLIAMS, V, 1987 in ROGERSON, A & WILLIAMS, P, 'The late 11th-century church of St Peter, Guestwick', in *Three Norman Churches in Norfolk* (*E Anglian Archaeol Report* **32**), 67–80

WINBOLT, S E, 1933 *Wealden Glass, the Surrey-Sussex Glass Industry, 1261–1615*, Hove

WITHERS, P & WITHERS, B R, 1994 *British Coin Weights*, Llanfyllin

WITTSTOCK, J (ed), 1982 *Aus dem Alltag der Mittelalterlichen Stadt* (Focke Museum, Bremen, Hefte **62**), Bremen (Germany)

WOOD, M, 1965 *The English Medieval House*, London

WOODFIELD, C, 1981 'Finds from the Free Grammar School at the Whitefriars, Coventry, *c*.1545–*c*.1557/8', in *Post-Medieval Archaeol* **15**, 81–159

WOODS, H, 1982 'Excavations at Eltham Palace, 1975–79', in *Trans London & Middlesex Archaeol Soc* **33**, 214–65

— 1992 review of EGAN 1991b, in *Medieval Archaeol* **26**, 358

WRIGHT, J, 1980 'Jew's Harp', in SADIE, S (ed), *The New Grove Dictionary of Music and Musicians* **9**, 645

WRIGHT, S M, 1987 'Much Park Street, Coventry: the development of a medieval street, excavations 1970–74' (*Trans Birmingham, Warwickshire Archaeol Soc* **92** for 1982)

YOUNGS, S M, CLARK, J & BARRY, T B, 1983 'Medieval Britain and Ireland in 1982', in *Medieval Archaeol* **27**, 161–229

ZARNECKI, G, HOLT, J & HOLLAND, T (eds), 1984 *English Romanesque Art 1066–1200* (Hayward Gallery exhibition catalogue), London

ZECCHIN, L, 1987 *Vetro e Vetrai de Murano* **1**; 1989 vol **2**, Venice (Italy)

ZUPKO, R E, 1977 *British Weights and Measures*, Wisconsin (USA)

Supplementary Bibliography

EGAN, G 1998, 'Medieval opaque white glass from London', in *Journal of Glass Studies* **40**, 182–5

EGAN, G 2000, 'Butcher, baker, spoon-and-candlestick maker? Some highly decorated medieval leadwares in Northern Europe', in D Kicken, A M Koldeweij & J R ter Molen, *Lost and Found: Essays for H J E van Beuningen* (*Rotterdam Papers* **11**), Rotterdam, 102–15

EGAN, G 2005, *Material Culture from London in an Age of Transition: Tudor and Stuart Period Finds c1450-c1700 from Excavations at Riverside Sites in Southwark* (*MOLAS Monograph* **19**), Museum of London, London

EGAN, G 2007, 'Later medieval non ferrous metalwork', in D Griffiths, R Philpott & G Egan (eds.), *Meols: The Archaeology of the North Wirral Coast, Discoveries and Observations in the 19th and 20th Centuries, with a Catalogue of Collections* (*Oxford University School of Archaeology Monograph* **68**), Institute of Archaeology, University of Oxford, Oxford 165–84

GUILDHALL MUSEUM CATALOGUE 1908: *Catalogue of London Antiquities in the Guildhall Museum*, Library Committee of the Corporation of the City of London, London

MACGREGOR, A, MAINMAN, A J, & ROGERS, N S H 1999, *Craft, Industry and Everyday Life: Bone, Antler, Ivory and Horn from Anglo Scandinavian and Medieval York* (*The Archaeology of York* **17.12**), Council for British Archaeology, York

MORRIS, C A 2000, *Craft, Industry and Everyday Life: Wood and Woodworking in Anglo Scandinavian and Medieval York* (*The Archaeology of York* **17.13**), Council for British Archaeology, York

OTTAWAY, P & ROGERS, N 2002, *Craft, Industry and Everyday Life in Medieval York* (*The Archaeology of York* **17.15**), Council for British Archaeology, York

TYSON, R 2000, *Medieval Glass Vessels Found in England c AD 1200–1500* (*CBA Research Report* **121**), Council for British Archaeology, York

WOOD, R 2005, *The Wooden Bowl*, Stobart Davies, Ammanford